LEFTY

LEFTY

AN AMERICAN ODYSSEY

—

VERNONA GOMEZ

and

LAWRENCE GOLDSTONE

BALLANTINE BOOKS

NEW YORK

Published in the United States by Ballantine Books,
an imprint of The Random House Publishing Group,
a division of Random House, Inc., New York.

BALLANTINE and colophon are registered
trademarks of Random House, Inc.

LIBRARAY OF CONGRESS CATALOGING-IN-PUBLICATION DATA

Gomez, Vernona.
Lefty : an American odyssey /
Vernona Gomez and Lawrence Goldstone.
p. cm.
Includes index.
ISBN 978-0-345-52648-9
eBook ISBN 978-0-345-52650-2
1. Gomez, Vernon, 1908–1989.   2. Baseball players—
United States—Biography.   3. Pitchers (Baseball)—
United States—Biography.
I. Goldstone, Lawrence. II. Title.
GV865.G59A3 2012
796.357092—dc23 [B]   2012004000

Printed in the United States of America on acid-free paper

www.ballantinebooks.com

9 8 7 6 5 4 3 2 1

FIRST EDITION

*Title page photograph of Lefty Gomez in 1937
copyright © Bettman/Corbis*

*Part title photograph on pages 1, 93, and 283
from the Associated Press*

*Photograph on page 376 copyright © 2011
by Vernon Lefty Gomez LLC. All rights reserved*

Book design by Barbara M. Bachman

For June and Lefty's grandchildren:

John, Andrew, Scott, Vernona Elizabeth,

Jennifer, Serena, and Tiffany

**Memo from
VERNON "LEFTY" GOMEZ**

Wilson®

When a guy gets to be my age, he probably has read a book. I've read a few, and now I'm going to write one.

Each year, my daughter Vernona designs my Christmas card. Now, I find out she even knows how to spell, so Vernona and I will write the book together.

I want folks to know about all the wonderful people I've known in and out of baseball.

And I'll tell some stories. I've told so many, so many ways I figure it's time for Vernona to get it kind of right.

We'll need your help. Vernona will be in touch with you and record your comments. I, of course, will make sure you tell the truth by telling my version.

PREFACE

___

PENNING HIS BIOGRAPHY WOULD NEVER HAVE OCCURRED TO LEFTY. When asked, he would reply, "Why would I write a book about my life? I lived it." But in the 1950s, the literary seed was planted due to a chance encounter with two icons of the publishing world, Bennett Cerf, the co-founder of Random House, and James Michener, one of Cerf's baseball-loving authors.

While a mystery guest on the television show *What's My Line?* Lefty met Cerf, one of the show's panelists. He asked Lefty for his autograph as a surprise gift for one of his authors, James Michener. Upon receiving the autograph, Michener rang Lefty up, and a lifelong friendship began. Listening to Lefty's tales, Michener would often chuckle and say, "The old West. The roaring East. Baseball. Broadway. That life of yours is the dream of every American boy."

In 1978, Lefty was on location for the filming of *Centennial,* Michener's runaway bestseller about the American West, to say hello to Jim and the actors on the set. As Lefty explained: "Jim autographed a copy of his book to me, which is a treasure in my library. 'To Lefty Gomez, from a writer who has always loved baseball and who often saw you pitch. Aloha, Jim Michener.'

"Then Jim surprised me by saying, 'Lefty. Let's write your life story.' But it was never to be, only for the fact that I couldn't find the time to sit down with Jim and do that endless chatting that is so necessary for a book to come about. One day my daughter Vernona said, 'Okay, Dad, I'm not

Michener, but we bump into each other a lot. Let's write that life of yours.' And that's how this book came to be."

Sixty years after Lefty first shook hands with Bennett Cerf on the set of *What's My Line?* the seed planted by Michener blossomed in a New York conference room when Ballantine Books, a Random House affiliate, met with me and offered to publish *Lefty: An American Odyssey*. It has been a delight working on this project with them.

CONTENTS

_____

PREFACE *ix*

PROLOGUE *xv*

PART I

"AMERICA'S PASTIME
FOR BAREFOOT BOYS"

_____

PART 2

"WHAT DO YOU THINK OF
MY BOY VERNON NOW?"

PART 3

"WHEN I MARRIED LEFTY,
I MARRIED BASEBALL"

PROLOGUE

O N SATURDAY, AUGUST 4, 1962, 30,000 FANS CROWDED INTO CANDLE-stick Park in San Francisco to see the Giants defeat the Pittsburgh Pirates 6–5. The Giants were new to the city, one of two major league franchises from New York that had arrived in California in 1958, a century after professional baseball began. The Brooklyn Dodgers had also moved to the West Coast, settling in Los Angeles, 400 miles to the south.

Large crowds were uncommon at Candlestick, an uncomfortable, hastily designed stadium known for violent, swirling winds. During the All-Star Game the year before, Stu Miller had been blown off the pitcher's mound by a powerful gust and charged with a balk. Although the Giants would go on to win the 1962 National League pennant and then lose to the New York Yankees four games to three in a thrilling World Series, the team would average only 19,000 paying spectators per game. The reason 30,000 people had come out on this day was to see not the players of the present but those of the past. The Giants had chosen August 4 to stage their first-ever Old-Timers' Game. To evoke the nostalgia crucial to the success of such an event, the three-inning contest would pit the old New York Giants against veterans of the San Francisco Seals of the Pacific Coast League.

The Giants might have been storied in New York, but the Seals were the legends in San Francisco. Minor league baseball had grown with the city since 1903, through earthquake, depression, and wars, filling a series of intimate, rickety ballparks, and was a part of both the city's heritage and its fabric. For California boys growing up in the 1920s and 1930s, the majors were as removed from their lives as if on another continent. With only sixteen big league teams, the farthest west 1,500 miles away in St. Louis, with no air travel or live broadcast media, the closest Depression-era Bay Area fans could come to the majors was through newspaper accounts or radio re-creations read by local sportswriters off telegraph wires. And such was the quality of Pacific Coast League baseball that some players preferred remaining where they were to going east to play in the majors.

The Seals themselves had been the most successful franchise in minor league history, and not all San Franciscans had been pleased to see the team fold after the 1957 season to make way for the New Yorkers. In its fifty-four-year history, the Seals had finished first in a highly competitive league on twelve occasions, all while sending a steady stream of star players to the majors. Six Seals alumni had been voted into the Hall of Fame, more than some major league franchises.

Which is why, on August 4, 1962, desperate to fill some seats, the new San Francisco Giants chose to celebrate the team that it had displaced.

The Seals' starting outfield was a big reason the Candlestick stands were full. For the first time in their storied careers, the three DiMaggio brothers would play together: Dom in left, Vince in right, and, in center, the great Joe, "The Yankee Clipper," perhaps the most complete player ever to don a uniform. The Seals' starting pitcher would be another Hall of Famer and a local legend in his own right: Joe's old Yankee roommate, Vernon "Lefty" Gomez.

Joe DiMaggio, notoriously taciturn, was all smiles that day, posing for photographs flanked by Dom and Vince, bantering with the other players and—astoundingly—the assembled members of the press. But unbeknownst to those fans, reporters, fellow players, or his brothers, the source of Joe DiMaggio's elation had nothing to do with the game or even the opportunity to play alongside Dom and Vince. Only two people in the stadium knew the truth: Lefty Gomez and Lefty's wife, the former Broadway musical comedy star June O'Dea.

Lefty had roomed with Joe from 1936, when Joe first broke in, until 1942, Lefty's last year with the Yankees. Although Lefty was six years Joe's senior, they shared common roots. Both had grown up poor in

Northern California of immigrant stock—Joe's father, Giuseppe, was a first-generation fisherman; Lefty's father, Francisco, known to everyone as Coyote, was a second-generation cowboy. But where Joe was dour and almost painfully shy, Lefty was gregarious, at ease with people, and known for a stunning wit. When Joe got to the majors in 1936 at age twenty-two, Lefty took the young man under his wing and became not only Joe's closest friend but also his most intimate confidant. Perhaps his only confidant. In fact, what was not widely known was that, despite the pictures in the newspapers of the three smiling brothers, Joe didn't speak much to either Vince or Dom.

But Joe told everything to Lefty.

As the aging ballplayers milled about, pulling on uniforms that now bulged more in the waist than in the shoulders, Joe sought Lefty out.

"There's always a lot of noise in the locker room of an Old-Timers' Game," Lefty said. "Joe and I were sitting on the bench with the players around us, slapping each other on the back, happy to be together again. I hadn't seen him for about three months. We both had tough traveling schedules, and to catch up I told him that after the game June and I were driving to L.A. to see Bing and Lou Russell. Joe knew Bing from '36, when he and Buddy were down at St. Pete making a pilot out of me." Bing and Lou Russell were the actor Kurt Russell's father and mother. Buddy, Bing's father, was a famous stunt pilot who had taught Lefty to fly.

" 'For how long in Thousand Oaks?' Joe asked.

" 'I dunno. Till Bing throws us out.'

" 'Lefty, Marilyn and I are getting remarried Wednesday. I want you and June there. Spend some time together.'

"Joe was smiling a thousand watts, happier than he'd been for a long time. He still carried the torch. Crazy about her. Now he was saying whatever Marilyn wanted to do, even if it meant the movies, was okay as long as they were together."

The two couples had history. "Back in the fifties, when Joe and Marilyn were first married, June and I had gotten together with them over dinner at the Plaza and out at the ballparks. Marilyn and June talked showbiz. Joe and I talked baseball. Or let's say, I talked and Joe listened. June thought Marilyn had so much acting talent and charisma that she'd be a natural on Broadway. Marilyn wanted to know all about the legends June had worked for, like Gershwin and George M. Cohan. So it was a good mix. We had fun."

In the game, Lefty pitched the first inning for the Seals, giving up a hit but no runs. Joe played all three innings without a hit. The other players razzed him about taking the collar, but Joe clearly had other things on his mind. Lefty and June stayed overnight in San Francisco, then left the next morning.

"Driving to L.A., the news came over the radio that Marilyn had been found dead in her Brentwood home. An accidental overdose or suicide. June and I were stunned. How could it be suicide when Marilyn was getting married on Wednesday? And what about her talk of doing stage work in New York? We couldn't believe that her death was a suicide and don't to this day. I pulled into the nearest restaurant and called Joe.

" 'What do you want me to do, Joe?' I said.

" 'Come and talk to me, Lefty, I want to talk,' Joe told me.

"Joe had flown first thing to L.A. and was at the Miramar Motel making the arrangements for the funeral. Marilyn's sister was flying in from the East Coast. Together they decided on a private service at Westwood. No celebrities, no fanfare. About twenty-five people, counting her relatives and people working around her career like agents and accountants, and Lee Strasberg doing the eulogy.

"Joe said, 'No personalities. If one comes, they'll all come. And I don't want to see the bastards. If it wasn't for them, she'd still be here.'

"When we got to L.A., I went over to the Miramar and spoke with Joe for about two hours. June and I didn't attend the funeral. Joe wanted it private, and it was important to us to do what he wanted. For the next eight to twelve months I called him about twice a week from wherever I was just to say hello."

Lefty paused.

"That's what roomies are for."

LEFTY GOMEZ IS BOTH one of the best-known and one of the least-known stars in baseball history.

To the public and press, he was "El Goofo," a unique combination of high-velocity fastball, affable eccentricity, and irreverent wit; a free spirit and natural clown who was so relaxed on the mound that he paused during a World Series game to watch an airplane fly over the Polo Grounds. He was famous for a series of one-liners, such as "I'd rather be lucky than good," or "The secret of my success is clean living and a fast outfield." As anyone who read the newspapers knew, here was a bon vivant, a man who loved the nightlife; he was on New York's best-dressed list and was married to a Broadway star. He played the saxophone well enough to sit in with the Jack Teagarden and Eddy Duchin bands and was sufficiently adept at stunt flying that he was specifically forbidden in his Yankee contract to attempt loop-the-loops.

To the public, Lefty cruised through life, eliciting smiles and affectionate shakes of the head, well-placed in a boys' game, someone to be amused by, certainly, but to be taken no more seriously than he seemed to take life.

His friends and teammates, however, knew a far different person. And a more complex one. Lefty Gomez was widely considered the glue of the Yankee clubhouse throughout the 1930s and perhaps the most ferocious competitor on the team. Losses ate at him. His commitment to the Yankees was without equal. His manager, Joe McCarthy, once asked him to leave a hospital bed to pitch. Lefty did. He pitched hurt so often that he was forced to retire when he was only thirty-three. On the day he was told his mother had died of uterine cancer, he refused to beg off his scheduled start, went out and pitched a three-hit shutout, then sat weeping in the locker room after the game.

To his teammates, he wasn't even Lefty. Yankee teammates used that moniker when talking to the press, because that was how the public knew him, but inside the locker room he was Vernon. With the more serious name came a more serious role. Teammates confided in him and asked his advice. Not by accident was Lefty assigned to be Joe DiMaggio's roommate when the most celebrated rookie in Yankee history joined the team in 1936. And it was Lefty who consoled Lou Gehrig in the dugout after the seemingly indestructible first baseman removed himself from the lineup on May 2, 1939, after 2,130 consecutive games.

There was actually very little that was goofy about Vernon Gomez. His one-liners, while noteworthy, were only a scant reflection of deep insight and wry humor about both baseball and life, every bit the equal of Damon Runyon's or Ring Lardner's. He read voraciously, spoke knowledgeably of world events, and had almost total recall.

Although he certainly ran with a sophisticated crowd in New York, he never really ceased being the small-town boy. Each off-season he drove home to spend the winter with family and to play baseball with the local kids. And five years before dapper Lefty Gomez made the best-dressed list, seventeen-year-old Vernon had left home to play semipro baseball with only one pair of pants to his name.

When his career was done, cut short after only thirteen seasons, he embarked on a new vocation with Wilson Sporting Goods, less glamorous but far more profound. Logging 100,000 miles a year, Lefty touched thousands of lives, speaking not only of his love of baseball but of the importance of honesty, integrity, and effort.

And then there is a brilliant record on the mound. Lefty pitched for the Yankees from 1930 to 1942, amassing a lifetime record of 189–102; he won 20 games four times, led the American League in strikeouts three times, three times in shutouts, and twice in earned run average. His World Series record is among the greatest ever. He started seven games, winning six and losing none with an earned run average of 2.86. Lefty was the starting and winning pitcher in the first All-Star game. He pitched in four more All-Star games, winning two and losing once, although the only run scored while he was on the mound came in on an error. He was elected to the Hall of Fame only in 1972 because the sportswriters who do the voting were deceived by the plethora of self-deprecating remarks for which Lefty was famous.

But Lefty's persona wasn't a contrivance, invented by agents, publicists, and media consultants. Lefty was simply himself.

PART **1**

"AMERICA'S PASTIME

FOR BAREFOOT BOYS"

I.

THE COWBOY'S SON

V ERNON GOMEZ WAS BORN ON NOVEMBER 26, 1908, AT HIS FAMILY'S homestead in Rodeo, California, on the south coast of San Pablo Bay, northeast of San Francisco. "Five hundred people if you counted the cows," he would say. "Rodeo was a town with two local trains, one comin' and one goin'. Down by the depot, there was a haystack close to the train tracks. If we rode the express, we jumped into it as the train passed through."

Although he was later referred to in the New York press as "the lanky Castilian" or "the singular senõr," Lefty's heritage was in many ways more quintessentially American than that of any newspaperman who wrote about him. Lefty's paternal grandfather had sunk roots in California pastureland courtesy of that most American of events, the Civil War. While California might not have been the scene of epic battles between blue and gray, throughout the war the navies of both sides did engage in an ongoing series of skirmishes just off the Pacific coast. Confederate raiders prowled the San Francisco coastline trying to disrupt the flow of commerce, while Union warships tried to head them off and keep the sea-lanes open.

The stakes for a port far removed from Antietam and Gettysburg were surprisingly high. By the early 1860s, San Francisco had been transformed from the sleepy mission settlement of the 1830s into America's most prominent boomtown, swelled to bursting by the throngs who had come west either to search for gold or to reap the immense profits engendered by those who did. Shipments of wheat, constantly in demand in Europe, or kerosene, a new fuel for illumination derived from petroleum, left by the hour in the holds of clipper ships to begin the torturous journey around the Horn, their crews often supplemented by sailors who had chosen the wrong drinking companions along the Barbary Coast. A steady stream of whaling vessels sailed for the Bering Sea.

With the explosion of enterprise, trading vessels from the Americas, Europe, and the Pacific flocked to San Francisco. The captain of one of those vessels, a Spaniard named Juan Gomez, arrived in 1862, his ship laden with fine leather goods to satisfy the appetites of the West's nouveau riche. After selling his cargo, he loaded his ship with wheat for the return trip. Just after he embarked, Juan Gomez's ship was shot out from under him, torched to the waterline by a Confederate privateer. Juan was rescued but his cargo was lost.

Juan did not sail again. Instead, he sent for his Portuguese wife, Rita, to join him in California with their seven-year-old son, Juan Enrique. Rita arrived to find that her husband had turned in his compass and sextant to try his hand at growing wheat and raising horses on a 150-acre ranch in El Sobrante in the Pinole Valley. Rita and Juan enrolled their son in a local school, then set to pioneering. In late 1863, the couple had a second son, Francisco, who was christened in the San Bautista mission, a native-born American. Francisco would not be sent to school but would remain home to help on the ranch. An illiterate son, it was then believed, would be less likely to up and leave for another profession, and so only the eldest received a formal education. Francisco grew up with a keen intelligence and prodigious memory, but completely unlettered. By early adulthood, he was fluent in three languages, Spanish, Portuguese, and English, though he was unable to sign his name in any of them. But he had learned roping from the Mexican vaqueros who worked the ranches and earned the moniker "Coyote" as a slick predator with a lasso in his hand.

Coyote had not been made to toil his life away in a wheat field. He dreamed, as did many boys in the 1870s, of driving longhorns up the Great Western Trail from Bandera, Texas, to the railhead at Dodge City, Kansas. In 1879, only fifteen years old, Coyote did just that. He drifted east to Nevada, then Texas, ranch to ranch, breaking horses. Then for ten years he rode with the cowboys from Oklahoma to Montana, enduring dust, stampedes, broiling days and frigid nights, long hours in the saddle, and the constant threat of attack from hostile tribes. By his mid-twenties,

Coyote had grown into a hardened trail hand, expert at reading tracks and understanding the instincts of the cattle and horses, a master at throwing loops, branding calves, breaking horses, running the fall roundup, and moving cattle to market.

But the open range was disappearing. Cowboys were sometimes forced to avoid shotgun-wielding homesteaders none too keen to watch thousands of cattle tromp across their fields. Barbed-wire fences increasingly blocked the path of the herds. In 1890, Coyote learned that his father had died of a heart attack. He returned home to help his two younger brothers, Carlos and Manuel, run the El Sobrante ranch. He would never ride the trail again.

But the homecoming did have its advantages.

One of Coyote's responsibilities was to bring the cash crops to the grain warehouses on the Pinole waterfront. Wheat, barley, and oats from the Pinole Valley were then shipped to Port Costa, where the European ships were docked.

The Gomez farm sold to the area's most prominent broker, Bernardo Fernandez. In 1892, Fernandez hired a new bookkeeper. Her name was Lizzie Herring, a recent arrival from San Francisco. There, Lizzie had performed similar duties for the postmaster general, B. F. McKinley, whose brother William would that year be elected governor of Ohio and, four years afterward, president of the United States.

Lizzie was a sixth-generation American of Welsh-Irish descent; her grandparents had struck out decades earlier in search of winter sun, free land, and an escape from Bleeding Kansas, where Lizzie's great-uncle Franklin had been murdered with a Bowie knife for opposing slavery. In Independence, Missouri, her grandfather John B. P. Williams had purchased a Conestoga wagon and then set out in 1857 on the Oregon Trail with his wife, Lucinda, a son, and three daughters. The family crossed the Rockies at Fort Hall in Idaho, took a cutoff to the Humboldt River in northern Nevada, and finally made their way through a pass in the Sierra Nevada range to Old Shasta in California.

Each of John B. P.'s daughters married a pioneer; one of them, Mary Jane, wed a logger named Elias Herring. Lizzie was born in 1870 in Bodega Township, near the Russian River, in redwood country. Five years later, her parents were dead. Lizzie was raised by an aunt and sent to school; as an adult, she journeyed south to San Francisco. Another aunt moved north, settling in Oregon, then journeyed farther still, not stopping until her family reached the salmon fisheries in Homer, Alaska, where they started a cannery.

Lizzie described what happened one fall afternoon at the Fernandez warehouse. "I was sitting behind the counter on a stool, my head bent over a bookkeeping ledger as I tallied up the bales of hay and sacks of wheat that the ranchers had brought in from the valley. I heard the staccato of high-heeled boots on the wooden floor. I looked up at the cowboy and met a pair of pale blue eyes under a battered broad-brimmed hat. He pulled off the hat and held it in his hand.

" 'Coyote's the name. Four hundred bushels of wheat, two hundred hay.' Having said that, he stood waiting for his cash. I handed him the money, then asked him to sign his name to the receipt.

"He gave me a slow grin. 'I spell it with an X.' He made his mark on the paper, laid the receipt on the counter, said, 'Thank you, ma'am,' then turned on his heel and walked out the door. Within minutes, he was back inside. 'Miss Lizzie, ain't it?' When I said yes, he smiled again.

" 'Seein' as how I'm goin' to the square, would you want to be goin' with me to the Saturday dance?'

" 'I'd like that fine, Coyote.' "

Coyote Gomez, the hard-bitten, taciturn cowboy, married Lizzie Herring, the shy young bookkeeper, in August 1893. For Coyote, Lizzie, who read English novels purely for enjoyment, represented a sophistication he had never before encountered. After their marriage, the couple moved to the El Sobrante ranch that Coyote was now running for his mother. But Rita had a tyrannical streak and thought Lizzie "soft," not the pioneer woman her son should have married. When Lizzie became pregnant, Rita refused to even discuss hiring a midwife to help with the delivery. Childbirth was "women's work," Rita insisted; a midwife was an affectation. Lizzie would give birth alone, as Rita had seven times before her.

In rural California in 1894 a mother-in-law could make such a demand stick, especially a mother-in-law in whose home you were living. So in solitude Lizzie delivered her child, a son, whom she and Coyote named

Earl. Lizzie cut and knotted the umbilical cord herself, then tended to the newborn without help, as Rita had done. The next year another son was born, Milfred, named, as had been Earl, for a character in one of Lizzie's favorite English novels. Lizzie birthed Milfred alone as well.

A third child, Albert, was born on Christmas Eve, 1896, while Coyote was in Nevada selling horses at a saddle stock auction. Albert was a month premature and there were immediate problems. The baby had entered the birth canal feetfirst, and midway through the delivery his arms and head became trapped. After the baby was out, Lizzie began to bleed profusely. She feared she might faint from loss of blood. She yelled for help, but Rita either couldn't hear or wouldn't respond. Lizzie flailed about for something she could use to tie off the umbilical cord. All that was available was a white bib lying on the table, which Milfred had worn when Lizzie fed him breakfast that morning. She ripped off the strings, used them to tie off the cord, then stanched her own bleeding.

Days later, Albert grew ill. On New Year's Eve, 1896, he went into convulsions and died. Rita had refused to call a doctor. Albert, it was later determined, had contracted an infection from the contaminated bib strings. Lizzie had carried her child for nine months, and now he was dead by her own hand. She never ceased blaming herself for Albert's death, but she also knew full well that if a doctor or midwife had been present, the boy would have lived.

Coyote returned home from Nevada shortly after New Year's, in time, he thought, for his baby's arrival. Lizzie met him at the door. She told him his son had already been born and was already buried. Then she issued an ultimatum. "Never again. It's your mother or me. I'm leaving." Coyote walked to the barn, hitched the horses to the spring wagon, then left with his wife, two boys, and meager savings. They stopped at Rodeo, a dusty backwater about three miles up the coast where land was cheap. Coyote and Lizzie placed a small down payment on a $450 plot of land and set to building a house. Rita remained in Pinole on her 150 acres of ranchland, stubborn and uncompromising. In 1906, the state of California appropriated all but fifteen acres of her land under eminent domain to make way for the San Pablo Dam Reservoir. Rita fought the order in court, but the state prevailed. Once the "American bandits" had taken her land, Rita vowed never again to speak another word of English, nor allow it to be spoken in her home. She kept that vow until the day she died.

Coyote and Lizzie had four more children in the next six years: Lloyd, Irene, Cecil, and Gladys. A doctor helped with each delivery. Then, on November 26, 1908, the last of their children was born. They named him Vernon Louis.

2.

"AN ABERRANT DEVIATION
IN THE
EVOLUTIONARY PROCESS"

VERNON GOMEZ SPENT HIS BOYHOOD IN THE ODD SHADOW WORLD OF the homesteader—devoid of luxury, but never wanting for the necessities. "We weren't poor," he noted. "We just didn't have any money."

Coyote had finally finished the two-story Gomez house six years after it was begun. Upstairs were five bedrooms for the kids, and downstairs a country kitchen, a dining room, a parlor, Lizzie and Coyote's bedroom, and a bathroom on the back porch with a commode and tub. "We had coal-oil lamps and gas jets," Lefty recalled. "There was no electricity until 1924. No telephone, no inside plumbing, and a windlass pumping spring water from a well in the backyard."

While the kitchen was always warm from the coal stove, the rest of the house was not. "Our bedrooms were freezing. Contrary to what science tells us, the heat from the coal stove did not sneak up the back stairs through the grates in the kitchen ceiling. Heat was only a memory as I stripped down to my underwear upstairs. Germs entering my bedroom were instantly freeze-dried."

Cackling chickens wandered the Gomez property, a vegetable garden was cultivated, and fruit trees were plucked. For linens and crockery, there was the once-a-week visit of Charlie Wong, a peddler from San Francisco, who arrived with a wicker basket hanging from each end of a bamboo pole he balanced across his shoulders. For anything else, there was mail order or the occasional trip across the bay.

The kitchen was the heart of the house, Lizzie its soul. She prepared jams and jellies, canned fruits and vegetables, and served meals made from scratch. She grew all the vegetables in the backyard kitchen gardens; baked her own bread, pies, and cakes; put up berry preserves; and sewed the wardrobes for the nine people in the Gomez family right down to the single-breasted suits Coyote and the five boys wore for Sunday best.

Lizzie Gomez also concocted herbal medicines, knitted and crocheted sweaters and hats, and quilted goose down comforters. "Clothes were scrubbed by hand and hung on lines outside to dry," said Lefty. "Ironing was by flatirons heated on the wood-burning stove. Floors were scrubbed on her hands and knees and the throw rugs in the parlor were taken outside and whacked with a metal carpet beater to get the dust out." Irene and Gladys helped out, but Lizzie nonetheless worked every day, morning until night.

"My first thought of my mother always goes to her love of flowers," Lefty remembered. "Her vegetable gardens were bordered by rows and rows of colorful roses, irises, and hollyhocks that brought beauty into our drab surroundings. I hoed a row and then Lizzie sprinkled the seeds from the flowering plants that had bloomed the year before. I can still picture her walking through the geranium-covered trellis and onto the back porch, her arms laden with flowers. As she stood in the kitchen putting the blooms into a blue-tinted jar Lizzie would say, 'Love rounds out the sharpness of life.' "

At Christmas, Lizzie and Coyote sent invitations to all their relatives within traveling distance. They thought it important that at least once a year the family be together. The tree was set up in the parlor, trimmed with aromatic garlands made of the fruit of eucalyptus trees strung together with cotton thread. Coyote placed slender white candles in black tinplate holders attached to the branches. "Every night, Gladys and I took turns walking round the evergreen with a long taper in hand, lighting the candles from top to bottom. The burning white candles glittered like stars in a rain puddle, and to me it was a magical tree."

What made Lizzie's achievements all the more striking was that they were done with a husband absent six days a week. Soon after Vernon was born, Coyote was hired as ranch manager for Rodeo's lone mogul, Sebastian J. Claeys, called "SJ" or "Cattleman." Claeys was a butcher from Michigan who had come to Rodeo in early 1907, got married in April of that year, purchased the local meat market, then proceeded to buy up a good bit of Rodeo's surrounding property. Within a decade, he was the richest man in the area.

Rodeo was isolated, but SJ wasn't. Claeys's Market held the town's only telephone, and SJ owned its first automobile. When Rodeo built a new school in 1913, four rooms for eight grades, with a bell in a cupola on top for calling the children to class, "S. J. Claeys" topped the list of trustees carved into the stone marker outside the front door. When Rodeo entered a float boasting of Rodeo's cattle in the Panama-Pacific International Exposition in San Francisco in 1915, Claeys financed the construction and his son Linus rode in the front seat.

SJ had his pick of employees and for running a ranch Coyote was the best there was. It was fortunate that Coyote had learned self-reliance on the trail, because being Claeys's foreman took temperament as well as skill. Laconic and self-contained, Coyote lived during the week on Claeys's thousand-acre ranch in Franklin Canyon, in a wooden shack with no running water and only cowhands for company. He returned home only on weekends and sometimes not even then, arriving after sundown Saturday night and leaving before sunup on Monday. His pay was $100 per month.

During the week Coyote's sons headed out to Franklin Canyon on horseback and became hired hands on Claeys's ranch. They worked the spring and fall roundups, branding the calves and herding the cattle to the Oakland slaughterhouses with Claeys's sons, Reder and Linus. During the harvest season, they mowed the hay, baled it, and sowed for the following year. Vernon was riding almost as soon as he could walk and spent his early boyhood on the fence trail with his dad, checking on grass, waterholes, and cattle.

Most boys in town were raised with guns in their hands, hunting wild game in the hills or out in the willows bordering the creek near Claeys's ranch. There were few poor shots in Rodeo. "As a boy of eight, my brother Earl, who was twenty-one at the time, taught me to hunt rabbits, ducks, pheasants, and quails with a .22 rifle. As I grew older I graduated to a 12-

gauge shotgun. I had good eye-hand coordination and I didn't get excited sighting on game. That's my nature and I was a good shot. Even as a youngster, I could spot a deer or a wild turkey hidden in the brush before Earl. Hunting small game was a way of bringing meat to the table."

At one point, Lizzie purchased fifteen dairy cows, which she grazed in the pastures alongside San Pablo Bay, rimmed by the tracks of the Southern Pacific Railroad.

"Ma ran the pint-sized Gomez Dairy with old-fashioned family teamwork," Lefty said. "I rolled out of bed and into the barn at 4:00 a.m. to help milk the cows, then carry the buckets of milk back to the house with Cecil and Lloyd. On my way back from school, I cut across the pasture, driving the fifteen cows to our milking barn . . . a towheaded eight-year-old running barefoot over the grass. As the cows ran through the pond, my collie, Jack, jumped in and paddled across while I dawdled at the water's edge, hand-fishing, until a call of 'Vernon' put me on my way again."

As the youngest, he was also in charge of slinging cow dung out of the box stalls. "The only reason I made good in baseball," he noted later, "was because I didn't want to go back to that dairy farm. It's not all Chanel No. 5 out there." Irene and Gladys bottled the milk in the kitchen, then hitched up the wagon to old Maude, the Gomez dray horse. The younger children took turns delivering the milk that their mother had sold to the neighbors, five cents a bottle, a label reading "Gomez Dairy" affixed to the side.

"Old Maude worked the dairy route like a machine," Lefty said. "She ground to a halt the very instant Gladys and Irene bounded out of the wagon and ran down the path to a customer's house. As soon as they left the milk bottles on the back porch, she revved up her engine and moved on down the road. Gladys and Irene ran back, taking a flying leap onto the wagon, and Maude pulled them to the next stop.

"Sometimes my sisters saw a girlfriend at the back door and they lingered a bit too long for the old horse. She had no patience with talkative kids. Maude allowed them just so much time from doorstep to wagon. Then she pulled the wagon around in a wide circle and plodded back to the barn. Gladys and Irene ran down the road, pigtails flying. 'Stop! We'll be late for school!' But Maude never stopped plodding homewards. No second chances from her."

Vernon got no allowance. Even at five or six, if he wanted money for ice- cream cones or candy, he had to earn it. "Rodeo awakened to a pack of wolves howling down the moon. I ran all around town, turning off the streetlights. Every corner had a glass globe atop a wooden pole. At the bottom was a white ceramic knob. I twisted the knob off at sunrise and on again at sunset. Mr. Downer, who owned the power company, put me on the payroll. Ten cents a day."

Not every task was so benign. One day, he was helping out at the ranch with his brother Cecil.

"Cecil was like a mustang, never broke. He was part of the land. Tall, blond, and spare, his jingling spurs accounted for most of his weight. By fifteen he was bringing home trophies and prize money as a rodeo competitor in saddle bronc, roping, and bull-riding. Cecil became a rancher like Pa and he had little patience with crybabies working a ranch. 'I'm running a cattle outfit,' he'd say, 'not a kindergarten.'

"That day, a couple of heifers had wandered off into the hills . . . one to drop a calf, the other to die. 'Swallowed nuts and bolts,' Cecil told me. Trouble comes in batches. Another steer had slipped in the boggy bottom of the Rodeo Creek. He was stuck fast with split shins. The coyotes were circling. Cecil had to go tend to something else. Back in the tack room, he told me to 'buckle on the six-iron with five beans in the wheel,' then go creekside. 'Steer's past fixin'. He's sufferin' bad. Put him down, Vernon, before the coyotes do.'

"Thinkin' about those miserable eyes lookin' up at me, suddenly I didn't feel so good. I moaned and doubled over. 'I'm gonna vomit.' Cecil was having none of it. 'Chrissakes, Vernon, you're nine years old. What are you, a goddamn baby?' He walked past me out of the barn, then turned back. 'If you got any quit in you, don't hit the saddle.'

"I stood in the doorway, watching Cecil ride out until he was just a speck on a faraway hill. 'He thinks I'm yellow,' I thought, and the thought pained. I brushed away the tears with the back of my hand and picked up the Colt. Then I swung into the saddle and rode out to Rodeo Creek."

But being the youngest of the seven Gomez kids wasn't all mending fences and killing injured cows. Four years younger than his nearest sibling, Gladys, Vernon was indulged by everyone except Coyote, and Coyote was only around one day a week. While he was certainly expected to pull his weight, Vernon also got to run off to swim, play baseball, or just hang out with his friends.

"I swam probably every day in San Pablo Bay, year-round, skinny-dipping down at the beach. At low tide, I undressed in a sandstone cave by the water's edge and left my overalls on the rock ledges that protruded from the walls. I swam for miles up and down the coastline, long-distance conditioning. I loved the rhythm of swimming all my life."

Often at night Vernon swam with his friends in settings that might have been lifted from early twentieth-century sketches such as Booth Tarkington's *Penrod*. "Frequently we built a campfire on the beach and threw potatoes on the fire, watching them pop and explode in the flickering firelight onshore as we splashed in the water." But Penrod was hardly angelic, and neither was Vernon.

"When we heard a freight train approaching along the shoreline, we ran out of the water, dripping wet. The train had to slow down to crawl around the bend at Lone Point. I grabbed hold of the rail on the ladder on the side of a boxcar and climbed up. In the spring and early summer, the open-topped boxcars were loaded with grapes, peaches, and melons, and in autumn the harvest trains carried sugar beets." Vernon was always designated to jump on the moving trains because he was the most agile. When he got to the top, he reached between the slats of the crates piled up inside and tossed out peaches, bunches of grapes, or whatever fruit was in season. Then, before the train gained too much speed, he jumped off to share the booty.

Vernon's partner in crime was often Reder Claeys. "We were all hellions," Reder recalled. "On warm summer nights, I knocked on the Gomezes' back door and asked his mother if Vernon was home. Most times, I could tell he was home if his collie, Jack, was in the yard. Jack followed Vernon around like he was tied to him. Vernon organized the kids into groups of three. Two guys stood lookout while Vernon went over the fence to grab a watermelon out of a vegetable patch. Vernon was very springy on his feet. At Halloween, he took the gate off the schoolyard fence and ran it up the flagpole in the town center."

"Vernon could size up a situation quicker than most," one of his grammar school teachers observed. "When he wanted a vacation from school, he put skunks under the schoolhouse."

School personnel won their share of skirmishes, however. Anastasia Dean, the grammar school principal, also taught penmanship. "Her eyes were as cold as a gray sky on a bleak February morning," Lefty later remembered. "She began class by telling us how much she pitied the students who failed the writing drills. I was the only left-hander in her class, the only left-hander in a lifetime of teaching penmanship. Miss Dean didn't approve of my hooked writing, said I was 'an aberrant deviation in the evolutionary process.' So there I was, a dead end on the road of humanity. She cracked my knuckles till they bled, and I switched. When fans ask me for my autograph I sign Lefty Gomez with my right hand and they look at it like it's a forgery. I can thank Miss Dean for that. She whacked every bit of left-handedness out of me except the way I pitch, play golf, and think."

Rodeo's Independence Day celebration in 1917 was in honor of all the local boys who had signed up to fight in Europe, Milfred and Lloyd Gomez among them. Earl had been rejected because of a withered arm, injured when he fell off a roof on a construction job, and Cecil was too young. The town hosted a barbecue—steer donated by S. J. Claeys— fireworks at the beach, and, of course, a parade. Invited to march was a forty-piece navy band from the nearby base, conducted by a young officer named Paul Whiteman. The highlight of their program was a rousing, jazzed-up rendition of George M. Cohan's hit song "Over There."

Eight-year-old Vernon Gomez was transfixed. "Right then and there, I told Earl that I wanted to play sax and have my own band. I even had the name picked out. The Syncopats. 'A sax?' Earl asked me. 'Costs around $26, Vernon.'" Lefty was thunderstruck. "Where can I get that kind of dough?" he moaned to Earl. "By the time I do, jazz will be gone." The following November, Earl had a surprise. "Happy birthday, squirt," he said, and presented his brother with a tenor sax.

Of course, owning a musical instrument was only the first step. Vernon asked Coyote when he could start lessons at Del Turco's Music Studio in

Crockett, a five-mile walk up the road, a dollar an hour, eight lessons a month.

Coyote's response was terse: "You play. You pay."

Eight dollars a month was a heady sum for a kid who generally earned only dimes turning on streetlights. An increase of that magnitude would involve not only more rigorous employment but also forgoing the ice-cream cones and candy on which his earnings were generally spent.

His first attempt to raise the money was hiring himself out to the local spring water company, owned of course by S. J. Claeys, but he was fired his first day when two customers caught him tromping barefoot through the spring. His next job was at Claeys's Meat Market, plucking chickens. "Ninety chickens a month, plucked clean of feathers at ten cents a chicken. It would have netted me nine dollars, but Pa believed in tithing, giving away 10 percent of your earnings to St. Patrick's Church, which meant I paid a penny on every chicken I plucked."

But ninety chickens equaled eight dollars for lessons and a couple of five-cent ice-cream cones a month. Each afternoon Lefty was escorted into the back room by the cleaver-wielding butcher. "*Whack!* Off came the chicken's head, the feathered body tossed onto the floor next to the table where I sat waiting to pluck it clean. Life taken by force. But its headless body with the blood oozing out did not drop down dead right away. Yuck! The feet skittered across the floor, the claws scratching their way through the sawdust. Feathers in my hair, down my shirt, up my nose."

But Lefty wanted to play sax, so he stayed at the job for two years. And no one had to admonish him to practice. "Any kid who plucks feathers off ninety chickens a month to pay for sax lessons," he would say, "is self-motivated."

He played constantly. "In and out of rooms, up and down stairs, I blew my lungs out on my sax, a long line of jazz-tinged notes with emotional conviction, thinking myself a slick cat, in the blues vernacular. Ma brought me back to reality. 'Vernon,' she shouted, 'take that *noise* to the cow pasture!' " Vernon did precisely that. Neighbors remember him tootling away as he drove the cows home after school.

And, true to his word, Vernon Gomez started the Syncopats, six pre-teens blowing hot jazz. They practiced in various members' houses until the adults couldn't take it anymore, then moved on to a new venue.

TWO YEARS EARLIER, Vernon had discovered another lifelong passion when Coyote and Lizzie took the ferry across the bay to the same 1915 Panama-Pacific International Exposition in which S.J. Claeys entered his cattle float.

Commonly referred to as the San Francisco World's Fair, the exposition occupied 635 acres and was filled with enough modern marvels to leave even the most sophisticated adult goggle-eyed. For Vernon Gomez, who lived without plumbing or electricity and had rarely even seen an automobile, it was like walking through a portal to another world.

At the east end of the grounds was "The Zone," sixty-five acres filled with rides, games, food from around the world, concessions, performers, and exhibits, including replicas of Yellowstone Park, the Grand Canyon—to scale, of course—and a five-acre working model of the Panama Canal. The actual Liberty Bell was on display, on loan from Philadelphia, and the news of the day was churned out automatically on an immense Underwood typewriter. States, counties, and industrial firms exhibited their wares and their wonders. There was a "Street of Fun," hula dancers, midgets, a railway, a submarine ride, and a compartment on a swing arm that sent those inside swinging to and fro over the grounds.

At the Palace of Transportation, the Ford Motor company had set up an assembly line that turned out a car every ten minutes for three hours every afternoon except Sunday. More than four thousand cars were produced during the fair's ten months. A wood and steel building called the Palace of Machinery was more than three hundred yards long, one hundred yards wide, and forty yards high. The entire complement of U.S. Army and Navy personnel could have stood at attention under its roof. Mabel Normand and Roscoe "Fatty" Arbuckle, two major stars of the silent screen, were filmed touring the fair by the Keystone Film Company.

The effect of the fair on its visitors was electric, literally as well as figuratively. The General Electric Illuminating Engineering Laboratory put on perhaps the greatest display of lighting ever seen. William D'Arcy Ryan, the director, who eight years earlier had lit Niagara Falls to a brilliance of 1.115 billion candles, outdid himself in San Francisco. One historian later wrote, "When he presented his plans before the architects, designers, and color artists who were involved in preparation for the Exposition, his proposals seemed so fantastic that there was scarcely a detail which was not opposed." The centerpiece of Ryan's plan was a forty-three-story "Tower of Jewels," which was decorated with more than 100,000 pieces of polished stained glass, called "novogems," imported from Vienna, strung on wires, and each backed by a tiny mirror. Twenty colored spotlights, hidden from spectators' view, illuminated the tower each night. Edwin Markham, a local poet, announced after seeing the General Electric display, "I have tonight seen the greatest revelation of beauty that was ever seen on the earth."

But outdoing even the tower was the air show. At a time when many Americans could still not understand what held an airplane aloft—or believed it could actually be done—for fifty cents a fair visitor could ride in a biplane, sitting behind the propeller while the pilot soared, dipped, and banked over the Pacific Ocean. For those who remained anchored to the earth, the Panama-Pacific had engaged the services of the world's greatest stunt flyer, "The Genius of Aviation," "The Man Who Owns the Sky," Lincoln Beachey.

Beachey, born right in San Francisco, was only twenty-eight but had already flown loop-the-loops for President Woodrow Wilson, skimmed Niagara Falls in a biplane, performed a corkscrew twist directly over a crowd of 20,000 spectators, and won a race with a train. His signature stunt was the "dip of death," a vertical dive from 5,000 feet with the plane's engines turned off and his arms stretched out to the side. Beachey pulled out of the dive at the last possible instant by tugging the stick with his knees and then glided to a safe landing. There had been accidents as well. Beachey had crashed often and on one occasion had flown too close to the roof of a hangar, sweeping four people off and killing a twenty-year-old woman. He had once quit flying, "disgusted with the public's morbid expectation of spectacular accidents," only to return weeks later to attempt even more dangerous stunts.

At the San Francisco World's Fair, Beachey planned a spectacular display of aerobatics for the home folks, including a run through the Palace of Machinery, the world's first indoor flight. After watching Beachey's incredible performance on February 15, Vernon immediately asked his parents to allow him to take flying lessons, a request ridiculous on grounds of both practicality and cost. But his decision on that day to become a pilot turned out to be as irrevocable as his decision to play the sax or his determination almost from the moment he picked up a baseball to become a pitcher. Vernon Gomez seemed to be one of those rare children who knew his mind, even at six, and he set out on a lifetime quest from which he would never look back and never regret.

On March 14, Vernon returned to the fair, this time escorted by Earl. That day, Lincoln Beachey was to try a feat of aerobatics never before attempted. Rather than the biplane in which he customarily flew, Beachey had designed an aluminum monoplane, then fitted it with an engine powerful enough to set up a dive from 3,000 feet. A crowd of 50,000 had gathered to see Beachey attempt in this new machine stunts that he had previously only performed in a biplane.

Beachey made two flights that day. In the first he "electrified the crowd with a series of aerial somersaults," then landed before attempting the perpendicular drop. That would be a finale all its own.

Soon afterward, Beachey took to the air once more, circling up into the sky above San Francisco Bay. To prepare the crowd for the grand climax, he looped-the-loop and even flew upside down. Then, at 3,000 feet, he switched off the power. The monoplane hurtled toward the water in a vertical drop. Nearing the surface of the bay, Beachey pulled back on the stick. Instead of sending the plane into a glide, the increased air pressure from the change in trajectory ripped the aluminum wings from the body. The fuselage turned over and over, crashing into the bay. As thousands of spectators rushed to the waterfront, launches from the battleship *Oregon* sped to the site. Sailors threw grappling hooks into the water in an attempt to grab the sunken plane. Minutes later divers from the ship arrived and plunged into the water. Joseph Maerz, one of the most experienced divers in the navy, succeeded in attaching a line to the plane's tail in forty feet of water. The fuselage was hauled up; Beachey was dead, still strapped in his seat. Examination proved that he had drowned. The crash had merely broken his leg. If Beachey could have freed himself from the cockpit, he could have floated to the surface and survived.

Six-year-old Vernon watched the accident with the same horror that gripped the other spectators. "What really brought the tears to my eyes was the fact that Beachey was one of our own, a San Francisco boy who had taken to the sky. I never forgot that day at the fairgrounds."

But he also never lost his love of flying. Coyote later said something to him about keeping his feet on the ground, but Vernon wasn't dissuaded by the danger. He might, in fact, have been drawn to it. Coyote had pioneered in his way; Vernon would pioneer in his.

"When Uncle Vernon pitched for the town team, I was in kindergarten," recalled his niece, Vivien Sadler, "and he put me on the handlebars of his bike, told me to hang on for dear life, and off we'd go, bouncing over the potholes. But he didn't talk endless baseball. Uncle Vernon read every newspaper he could get his hands on. When the Frisco papers and the *New York Times* were thrown off the train, Vernon was grabbing copies and diving into articles, especially ones about aviation. Vernon was going to be a ballplayer and an aviator all at the same time. This was before Lindbergh's flight to Paris. He was going to get his pilot's license and fly one of those puddle-jumpers when he grew up. And that was just what he did."

Vernon came home from his visits to the fair with a far grander ambition than simply to become an aviator. He had discovered there was a bigger, more fascinating world outside Rodeo, filled with adventure, and he intended to experience it.

3

"PICK A SPOT, MAKE A DIAMOND"

———

WHILE FLYING AND MUSIC BECAME VERNON GOMEZ'S PASSIONS, BASE-ball would be his life.

"No car, no phone, no money . . . and if the battery ran down in the radio, no news," Lefty observed. "The kids played the one game in town. Baseball. America's pastime for barefoot boys."

"Vernon had a burning desire to be a big league pitcher, even in grammar school," his friend Harry Lakeman recalled. "Just one of those things you're born with. He stood across the street pitching to the center of a tire he had hung on a rope in front of the Gomezes' buggy shed. Hour after hour, day after day, he practiced his location. His fastball exploded right through the center of the tire, boring a hole in the buggy shed door. His brothers gave him hell for that."

There was no organized baseball for young boys in those days, so they made do. "We all started out playing sandlot," said Lefty. "Get a ball, a bat, a couple of kids . . . girls and boys gathered all over Rodeo to choose up sides." The lack of regulation and the absence of adults allowed Vernon to immerse himself in baseball for the sheer joy of it. "Sandlot ball was a bunch of kids working out a relationship amongst themselves. No one coached us from the sidelines. If a player whiffed at the plate, his parents didn't care, and the family mutt still wagged his tail. The player bounced back through his own desire to excel."

The players made the rules. "With twenty kids in the lineup, the games weren't limited to nine innings. We played till we went home or someone called for you and you had to go home. You forgot about lunch, sometimes even dinner. Two kids from down the road, Ditty Shearer and her brother Tokus, played outfield until way after sundown. Most nights, their mother was out on the foul lines waving a wooden spoon over her head. 'Come home for supper or I'll hang your guts on the clothesline.' "

Little concern was given to equipment or facilities. "Pick a spot, make a diamond. We walked down into the raw land in bib overalls, a hoe in one hand, a rake in the other. If there were rocks to cart away, someone ran home for a wheelbarrow. Empty land, open spaces. Home run territory. No floor-to-ceiling windows to break. The town was a big backyard to play in . . . a nice setup for growin'-up kids."

Anyone who wanted to play could. No one was cut out and no one was better than anyone else. "Fair play was a given. Try being a wise guy. You were pounded by your own teammates. They broke from the bench like the zing of a slingshot."

As with the chores at home, everyone pitched in. "Once we cut the dust from the infield with a bucket of spring water, home plate was somebody's mother's roasting pan turned upside down. We got rid of the cow plop, unless of course it was stiff and dry, hardened by the sun. Then we used the cow patties for bases." On the few occasions there was no dry cow manure to be had, the kids snuck off with their parents' burlap sacks.

The games did feature one means of establishing hierarchy. "We always had one ball and one bat. The kid who owned the ball played any position he wanted. The kid who owned the bat played any position except the one chosen by the kid who owned the ball."

Balls received special treatment. "If the ball was brand-new, we covered it with black tape. We knocked the tape off the ball seven or eight times, until it was worn-out. Then we still had the original horsehide cover. It's a wonder anyone had an arm left after throwing that heavy ball all day. A home run meant the ball was lost. The game was stopped while both sides ran out and found it."

Vernon always wanted to be a pitcher. His skill at keeping the hitters from parking the ball where no one could find it made him a natural for the position. When a hitter with power was hunched over the home plate roasting pan, "even my own teammates yelled, 'Gomez, strike him out.' "

Gloves were a luxury. Some lucky kids had them, but most wrapped strips of leather around their fingers and across their palms. Some, like Vernon, played bare-handed.

He finally got his first glove not from his parents but from a resident old-timer named Norman Kuhn, a first baseman who had knocked around the minors, never getting any higher than a brief stint in the Pacific Coast League. Retired and with time on his hands, Kuhn took to watching the kids scuffle at sandlot ball. He picked out Vernon, even at this early age, as a player with potential. But he noticed the boy's palms were raw and bleeding from stopping line drives. Kuhn brought his own glove to the sandlot and tossed it to the kid. It was a first baseman's mitt, a prized remembrance of the glory days of Kuhn's youth. "You should've seen the smile on Gomez that day," recalled Taft Prairo, a childhood friend. "Now he had a glove. It was the wrong type for pitching, but it was that or no glove at all."

The commitment of a lifetime had begun. "To play baseball hour after hour, day after day. Thousands and thousands of innings. That's all we cared about. Then, as we became teenagers, the boys graduated from sandlot to the town team. The thousands of innings became the regulation nine."

Lefty's siblings realized the passion their kid brother felt for the game and helped where they could. "My brother Lloyd loved baseball and had a good glove as a catcher. He said my fastball was my ticket to the Seals and he was going to help me make the team. When I was ten and he was twenty, he set up daily practice sessions. After our chores were done, we walked out into the pasture behind Pa's milking barn and I pitched to Lloyd crouched down in the tall grass." Lloyd could be hard as well. One day, during a sandlot game Lloyd was catching, Vernon got hit in the ribs by a pitch. He went down and began to cry. Lloyd yelled to stop crying and get back in the game. Vernon was later found to have two cracked ribs.*

---

* Lloyd's toughness had been steeped in war. He had recently returned from France, where he had been a motorcycle messenger and had taken to racing his Excelsior bike through the town, "weaving in and out of the Model As on their way to the Rodeo–Vallejo ferry docked at the pier," as Lefty described it. Once, just as the ferry pulled away from the dock, "Lloyd and his Excelsior flew through the air, landing with a thud on the boat, scaring the passengers out of a year's growth."

The other Gomez siblings helped out as well. "My brothers didn't play baseball. They never had the luxury of spare time, something I was born to as baby of the family. In school and out, they held down regular jobs in addition to buckarooing at Claeys's and farming the Gomez land. When drought turned our crops to dust or flooding caused rot, they challenged the elements once more. Always once more. And it goes without saying, Ma and Pa worked till they couldn't stand up, every single day. So sure, I had chores to do, but my brothers and sisters were always around to lend me a hand, and once my chores were done, I could run off to the sandlot."

The one member of the family who did not take to Vernon's infatuation with baseball was his father. Coyote had been denied an education and it stung him every minute of his life. Lefty never forgot watching him, seated at the kitchen table, the gas lamps casting shadows on the grammar-school primer open in front of him while Lizzie laboriously tried to teach him to read. Coyote implored for his children to do better, and Vernon was to go to college and become an electrical engineer.

What was more, for a man who toiled as long and hard as Coyote did, playing a kid's game wasn't an honest day's work. He didn't talk about baseball and didn't want to hear about it on the days when he was home from Franklin Canyon.

One Saturday night, when Lefty was about twelve, Coyote was sitting in on a poker game at the saloon. Lefty was there watching and recounted the incident. " '*Eee*-yah,' a cowpoke shouted, tossing a whiskey down. 'That kid of yours torches the plate. Vernon oughta go for a Seals tryout.' Suddenly, across the table, there's an icy stare from pale blue eyes on a face sun-blazed as saddle leather. Coyote Gomez, the original curmudgeon when it came to baseball."

Coyote's antipathy was not without justification. Most professional baseball players traveled from town to town, staying in hotels and cutting a swath through both the local liquor supply and the women. Impeccably behaved Christy Mathewson of the Giants was referred to as "The Christian Gentleman," as if that distinction was unique among his fellows.

Jack McDonald, who began with the San Francisco *Call-Bulletin* in 1926 and wrote about Bay Area sports for forty years, saw many situations like this one arise between parents and children. "Many of the parents were first-generation immigrants and wanted their sons to pursue a career through education. College was the ideal, but at least high school and then a trade where a boy could make a steady income. Baseball wasn't considered a wise career choice—one blaze of glory on the eastern diamonds and then to return home a broken-down bum. Ballplayers were looked on as roughnecks, a hard-bitten crew. Many of the ballplayers had contributed to this reputation. Not all, but many."

Lefty's Yankee teammate and close friend Frank Crosetti related an incident that occurred when he and Lefty were with the Seals that epitomized what kids were up against in trying to convince their parents that baseball was an upstanding way to make a living.

"We were staying at the old Imperial Hotel in Portland. I was in a room with Lefty and Jerry Donovan on the second floor that had a little balcony that looked out over the street below. So we're in the lobby, getting ready to go to the ballpark, when one of the veterans says to me, 'What room are you in?' It was that rowdy bunch . . . Dick Moudy, Ollie Mitchell, and Junk Walters. 'I think we're in room 200,' I say. Then Junk asks me, 'Can we use your room?'

" 'I'm only a kid of seventeen, and I don't know what to do, so I gave him the key. Then Moudy asks me, 'Do you have a pair of tweezers?' I didn't even know what a pair of tweezers was in those days. After a while, Lefty, Jerry, and I say to one another, 'Let's go and see what they're doing in *our room.*' There were six players in there and I see one of them is holding a nickel with a tweezers and another is heating it up with a cigarette lighter. Lefty, Jerry, and I are watching them wide-eyed. We don't know what they're up to. Then the guy holding the nickel goes out onto the balcony and I'm right behind him, lookin' to see what's gonna happen. He drops the hot nickel and it goes *plink, plink, plink* on the sidewalk below. I'm leaning over the balcony and I see someone come by, pick the nickel up and boy, he dropped it like a hot potato.

"I thought, 'Oh my God!' I was that kind of a kid. I'd die if trouble came and something happened to me. Then I look across the street and see a policeman and he's looking *right at us.* I run back inside and say, 'Lefty. Jerry. We better get the hell out of here.' After the game, we're back in the lobby and I hear the manager, Nick Williams, and he's *mad*, talkin' to Junk Walters. 'You better get yourself an extra shirt, Junk, because you'll probably have to stay in jail six months.' We soon found out that after we left, they dropped some more hot nickels down on the sidewalk, and one hit a woman on top of her head. She went to pick it off and burned her fingers. She ran and got an attorney. So the players have to pay the attorney fees and buy the woman a new hat. Fifteen bucks. A few days go by. Then the veterans corner Lefty, Jerry, and me. One of them asks, 'Were you in that room at any time we was there?' 'Yeah,' I said, 'we were there.' 'Well, if you was there, give us six dollars.' We're rookies and have no say. So for the few minutes Lefty, Jerry, and I were in our own room, we had to cough up six dollars and we had nothing to do with it."

As the years went by, the more immersed Vernon became in the game, the more resistant Coyote became to his becoming a ballplayer. Coyote was pure gristle, but his son matched him. It would be a source of pain to them both, but neither would back down. Coyote seemed to have forgotten that chasing a dream was something he had done himself, and that his father had been no more pleased about it than he was about Vernon.

4.

"I'D GO ANYWHERE TO PITCH"

FOR LEFTY, THE NEXT STEP UP FROM PICKUP GAMES WAS THE RODEO town team. He began in 1922, when he was thirteen.

"Sandlotters wore sneakers," Lefty later said, "but there were no sneakers on the town team. We were big-time. We wore the traditional baseball shoe . . . kangaroo calfskin tops with steel spikes on the sole. Mine were special-order, size thirteen."

Special-order shoes meant special-order money—which he gave to Al Erle, the area's only sporting goods salesman. "For the love of kangaroo spikes and nine bucks in the hole," Lefty said, "I hired out to the Union Oil refinery. My job was to clean the ponds around the crude oil stills. I sloshed around in the stuff, pushing a stringy mop, for thirty-eight cents an hour. The soles of my work shoes fell off and the leather toes curled up like Egyptian slippers. Three days later, I grabbed my spike money and split. How many ballplayers can run the bases without feet?"*

And the Rodeo team would be properly clothed. When he heard the boys couldn't afford uniforms, S. J. Claeys bailed them out by advancing the money—and he purchased them, of course, from Al Erle. The uniforms were pinstripe flannels with RODEO across the front. But SJ hadn't gained his station in life through charity; the team had to pay him back. They organized a benefit at the town hall at which they raffled off a slew of donated items, fifty cents a ticket—quilts, aprons, afghans, elderberry

---

* Many years later, when Erle was well into his eighties, he attended a San Francisco Giants dinner at which Lefty was the keynote speaker. As soon as Lefty saw Al, he called to him. "You remember me?" Erle asked incredulously. "Hell, yes," Lefty said. "You charged me double for my first pair of steel spikes because I had such big feet." "Yup," Erle chuckled, "that's me."

jam, baked beans, and sweet breads—with entertainment provided by that famous local band, the Syncopats.

"We opened up with 'Barnyard Blues,'" said Lefty. "Town hall was filled with the honks, squeaks, and earsplitting blast of our brass section. The band's signature was the fact that we finished a song together. There were a helluva lot of clunkers in between."

Town teams and industrial league teams were the backbone of baseball in the early 1920s, where virtually every young player got started on the road to the minor leagues and, they all hoped, eventually the majors. And the towns supported the teams with the sort of passion currently reserved for high-school football in places such as Texas. "Men got into heated discussions down at the barbershops," Lefty recalled. "All the thrilling moments of last Sunday's game were recounted . . . the shoestring catches, the stolen bases, the last strikeout with the winning run on third. Baseball tapped into the kids' spirits and the spirit of the towns."

Moral support, however, was all the players got from townsfolk. "Rodeo's fabulous nine pulled their flannels on at home. Then we walked the railroad tracks to the town ball fields . . . past cornfields and grazing cows and clapboard houses with shady porches. You had to love the game to hike so far to play nine innings."

In the ad hoc world of town team baseball, Vernon, since he was possessed of a first baseman's glove, was initially assigned to play first base and Pokey Grisham, originally slated for first, was put on the mound. Vernon raised a squawk but was told by Taft Prairo, the shortstop, "This here is the Rodeo town team, and we play it like the big leagues."

But big league pitchers could actually get batters out and Pokey Grisham could not. Rodeo's fabulous nine lost one game after another. Lefty seethed. "He jumped out of the cradle wantin' to win," Taft Prairo observed. Vernon got so mad one day that he ran to the mound and grabbed the ball, only to be shunted back to first by Prairo.

As the losing streak lengthened, the seeds of rebellion were sown. "The team's buzzing around my head like a swarm of angry hornets," said Prairo. "They told me to hell with the big leagues, to put Gomez on the hill. I wasn't dumb . . . I could see my days at short were numbered. 'Gomez,' I yelled, tossin' him the ball, 'stick to pitchin'.' We won after that."

While the fortunes of the local team occupied much of the conversation, another topic, alcohol, was always close to the lips of Rodeo's adult community.

Prohibition came to Rodeo in a big way. The West Coast was crawling with both federal agents and bootleggers, and sleepy bay towns such as Rodeo became favored stopovers for smugglers on the run. "The action took place down on the bay," Lefty recounted. "Canadian ships stood three miles offshore, carrying a cargo of liquor packed in boxes pasted with shoe advertisements. Rodeo's thirteen saloon keepers unloaded the 'shoes' onto the beach, then hauled them up the steep bluffs to town. If the men dropped a box, they wept."

Rodeo and other small towns on the bay were often a better market for the bootleggers than San Francisco, where enforcement tended to be more robust. Not that Rodeo was immune to some hot pursuit. "With the feds hot on their trail, the bootleggers hid out where nothing earth-shattering happened," Lefty recounted. "In Rodeo, they cooled their heels and their passions at the local bordello. Karen's Kalico Kittens danced round the cathouse in rhinestone-studded satins and served Jackass Brandy to the love-hungry crowd—160-proof alcohol sweetened with apricot nectar. A half dozen jolts and you got a free snake. That's when the floozies raked in the dough.

"Occasionally a bootlegger arrested by the feds turned stoolie and fingered our little community. Getting wind of the sting, Rodeo barmen stashed the rotgut under the floorboards of Mrs. Woods's ice-cream parlor. Cowboys rode the brass rails at saloons, sipping sarsaparilla."

To supplement the imports, many families made their own. "Pa's foot juice was red wine, no bouquet, no vintage. During the crush, my sister Gladys and I jumped on grapes in a dank, windowless shack." But purple feet could be dangerous. "When the feds came to town, they frisked and cuffed anyone who looked suspicious. Those days, Gladys and I made ourselves scarce down by the old swimming hole. We were wine-purple clear up to our belly buttons."

The gangsters occasionally ventured out into the town. "I made the mistake of running home and telling Ma I saw a gun-twirling thug at Cardoza's barbershop," Lefty lamented. "A week later, she sat me down on a kitchen stool, put a bowl upside down over my mop, and with blunt shears hacked whatever lay between the rim and my ears." He further observed, "It doesn't pay to pass the time of day with your ma."

The profits from the Gomez dairy were kept in a sugar bowl. The kitchen account turned out to be safer than a deposit at the local bank. On September 26, 1929, members of the notorious Fleagle gang shot their way into the Rodeo branch of the Bank of Pinole and forced the manager to open the vault. The gang's ruthless ways had stunned the nation, and they had been pictured on wanted posters. The Fleagles grabbed the gold bullion and money bags containing the Union Oil payroll, $27,000, and stuffed the bank's customers inside the vault. The sound of shotgun blasts brought the town's one constable, Arthur "Jerry" MacDonald, rushing to the scene. MacDonald managed to hit one of the bandits with a shotgun blast to the chest before being gunned down himself. The wounded outlaw, later identified as Jake Fleagle himself, fled to a waiting car, "leaving a trail of blood." After MacDonald's body had been removed, a number of Rodeo's residents stood in the street outside the bank, gawking at the bullet holes in the window. "Of course, the Fleagle gang got away and the successful robbery was played up in the newspapers," Lefty observed. "And even though Rodeo mourned the death of their constable . . . and Jerry was a good ol' constable . . . the town was delighted to make the front pages."

ALTHOUGH HE SOLD SPORTING GOODS to put bread on the table, Al Erle's passion was semipro baseball. Employing the telephone, pencil and paper, and an exhaustive list of contacts, he booked thirty to thirty-five games in the Bay Area each weekend for teams such as Orange Crush, Motion Pictures, Wurlitzer Music, Mechanics Bank, and Piggly Wiggly. Half of the sixty or seventy teams involved would be traveling, of course, some as much as three hundred miles. Keeping the scheduling straight was almost a full-time job, and Erle already had one of those.

Elemental baseball fan that he was, Erle was always on the lookout for new talent. The minute he saw Vernon Gomez pitch for the Rodeo town team as a fourteen-year-old eighth grader, Erle asked him if he was interested in the semipro circuit. Vernon would venture up and down the California coast for the next three years, from Monterey to Eureka and inland from Fresno to Mount Shasta. "I'd go anywhere to pitch."

On these weekend journeys, Vernon generally had an unlikely companion, his older sister Gladys, who went along for an unlikely reason. "Gladys was an outstanding ballplayer. Incredible talent. She was passionate about baseball and her ability humbled me. Five feet two, petite and wiry, she ran like the wind and pitched to the corners of the plate. Her fastball knocked the glove right out of my hand. She wanted desperately to be a ballplayer and it broke her heart she couldn't get to the big leagues. Ornery as a hog on ice, Gladys beat me royally whatever the sport. At track, she exploded toward the finish line, broke the tape, turned, gave me a thumbs-up, and grinned. I was 'worm' or 'squirt' and she punctuated her remarks by tweaking my nose. How much can a kid brother take?"

If the game was on a Sunday, the two Gomez siblings finished milking the cows and running the dairy route by 6:00 a.m., then found their own transportation to whatever ballpark was scheduled that day. "I didn't even ask Dad," Lefty noted. "I already knew his answer. Besides, who's gonna ride hundreds of miles in a horse and buggy so his kid could pitch nine innings? Even our horse said no."

Occasionally they hitched a ride, but generally they had to catch the bus. "Most times Gladys and I stood on the corner, our eyes peeled for the once-a-day bus that roared through town. There were no traffic lights to stop it. To flag the bus down, we ran out into the middle of the road, windmilling our arms and screaming, 'Stop!' The driver saw we were desperate and slammed on the brakes."

The bus rides would dissuade all but the fervently committed. "We rattled down dirt roads, stopping at every one-horse junction. Our backsides were tattooed from jouncing around on the iron springs popping through the torn leather seats." Vernon tried to do his schoolwork on the journey, which presented some unique difficulties. "I pulled out something like Chaucer's Old English. I focused in on the print and the bus hit a pothole. I fell on the floor cross-eyed."

Long trips to towns such as Eureka, three hundred miles from Rodeo, or weekenders, where Lefty pitched a game on Saturday and another on Sunday, irritated Coyote all the more.

"My brothers covered my chores at the dairy. They doubled their own workload, a fact duly noted by Pa. He was less than pleased that his youngest son and daughter were traipsing around the countryside playing baseball. 'Meanwhile,' he grumbled, 'the family business is going to hell.' I think Pa suspected that baseball was fun."

But industrial league semipro was the perfect place for a kid with major league aspirations to gain experience. It was highly competitive, with players on the rosters who had played minor league or even major league ball. And they had knowledge as well as ability.

Lefty was in demand from the first. "Erle said the managers were burning up the telephone wires, clamoring for my services after my reputation as a flamethrower made the rounds. Pretty heady stuff for a pipsqueak like me, 125 pounds and built like six o'clock. I went out to the faraway diamonds with fire in my eyes, a greenhorn who thought he could stand on the hill and stare the hitters down."

Gladys insisted on warming Lefty up before games. "Take or leave it," she told Al Erle. Then she egged her brother on. " 'Burn 'em in,' she'd whisper in my ear. 'There might be a scout at the game.' " Talented as he was, at fourteen Lefty wasn't always up to facing former major leaguers. "The hitters laughed at my arrogance. They slammed me hard, knocking me out of the box on my fanny. But sometimes they didn't. When a pitch mowed them down, damn, it felt good. The game within a game. I loved it."

There were other advantages. "Traveling the semipro circuit with Gladys was great. It was our first time away from home. We discovered a bigger world than the one we knew in Rodeo, a world beyond hayfields and riding the range. My sidekick and I peered into windows, poked into shops, talked to the locals passing by. Sometimes their opinions agreed with ours, most times they differed. It opened our eyes wider."

Semipro status implies pay, although the Gomez siblings never saw any actual money. "If I pitched and won, the team treated Gladys and me to a feed at the local diner. If I lost, it was a boot in the pants. That's the way they worked it. I was there to gain experience, not make a living."

Semipro baseball attracted not only players who could not make the major leagues but those who were not allowed in the major leagues. When he was fifteen, Vernon Gomez was booked by Al Erle to pitch both ends of a doubleheader. The opposing pitcher would also pitch both games. The other pitcher's name was Leroy Paige, but even at this point, in what probably was his twenties, Paige had acquired a soaring reputation and the nickname "Satchel."

Gomez, generally as self-possessed as they come, was awestruck. Before the first game, he stood on the sidelines, chatting with a pitcher already thought to be the equal of any in the game. At one point Lefty asked him what he was getting for a win.

"Satch poked me in the ribs. 'Share of the gate,' he said. 'What are you getting?' I told him a pair of Guaranty dress shoes. Satchel looked down at my size thirteen feet and he broke into a sly grin. 'Either way, kid, a win is gonna cost them leather.' "

In the first game, Paige ambled out to the mound as if someone had just woken him up from a nap. "Then he reared back with his high leg kick and blazed a pitch that seemed to come out of his foot. The hitters complained they couldn't see the fire, only the ashes left on the plate. Satch had promised the crowd he'd strike out the first nine men he faced. And he did. Satch could wipe you out on charisma alone."

Gomez didn't do so badly either. He was so excited to pitch against the great Satchel Paige that the catcher couldn't hold on to his fastballs. Lefty's team won the second game, and not because his team scored a lot of runs.* But Lefty had received a lesson in pitching that day—getting batters out was as much art as power. "Satch could beat you in so many ways. Overhand, sidearm, submarine. Then there was his 'hesitation pitch' that hung in midair."

Once he understood that pitching was a craft, Lefty soaked up all he could from men who had played the game for longer than he had. Al Erle remembered that "he listened to the veterans and tailor-made their advice to suit his style. I saw it happening when I sat on the bench. He'd watch a

---

* In the end, Lefty never got paid for the win. He said later, "It crossed my mind to call up the Guaranty Shoe Company and tell them they owed me a pair of shoes for a game I pitched fifty years ago, but I knew I wouldn't get past the switchboard."

veteran and the next thing you know, he'd be asking, 'Can you teach me what you're throwing out there? How do you throw that pitch?' Everyone knew he was major league material. They all talked about it. High-kick delivery. Whiplash arm. The players were unfailingly generous to Gomez, because he was smart enough to know his limits and ask the experts for help. And he was a nice kid."

Underneath the easygoing demeanor, however, Lefty was a fierce competitor. "He was shy away from the ballpark," Erle added, "but on the field aggressive as all get-out."

"If I got beat, it killed me," Lefty said. "Anytime, anywhere, if I lost, it ripped me to shreds. I let the team down. Myself down. But I didn't run home and wail about it. I learned early on not to use a loss as an excuse to argue with the people I loved. I kept it inside. The loss kicked my ass to go out and win the next one. I didn't have to look outside my family to know you played tough."

5.

"ABOUT AS SKINNY AS YOU CAN GET
AND STILL BE LIVING"

———

THE ROAD FROM EAST BAY SEMIPRO TO THE MAJOR LEAGUES WENT through the Pacific Coast League, and the best team in the PCL was the Seals. But to get to the Seals, Lefty had to break through a wall almost as formidable as Coyote: the team's chief scout and eventual manager, Richard Lloyd Williams, known to everyone as "Nick."

Nick Williams was one of baseball's many great characters of whom almost no one has ever heard. He was the kind of guy who shows up in old movies played by stock-character grouches like William Frawley. He came to scout for the Seals after a stint as manager of the Moose Jaw Robin Hoods in the Western Canada League, where he finished third behind the Calgary Bronchos and the Edmonton Eskimos. A poor kid himself, a graduate of both the San Francisco sandlots and the University of California, Williams had been half of a "reversed battery" with Orval Overall, who would win fifteen games for the Cubs in the 1908 season, plus two in the World's Series.* Overall would pitch and Williams would catch, then the roles would reverse for the following game. Williams never made the majors, his playing career limited to seven years as a pitcher, catcher, and first baseman in the Pacific Coast League, mostly with the Seals. His last year on the field was 1910.

But Williams was a lifer. He umpired for a season when he could no longer play. He managed in the B leagues at Portland, left for a stint in the army in World War I, returned to the B leagues in Spokane, then moved to

———

* The Cubs, of course, have not won a World Series since.

Moose Jaw in 1920. After two years in the wilds of western Canada, Williams returned to San Francisco at age forty-one to scout. He was named manager in 1926, then fired in 1931 after a pennant-winning season for "unsatisfactory personal habits," likely involving fighting and alcohol.

As the man responsible for ensuring that the Seals would have an ongoing flow of quality ballplayers, Williams was crusty, no-nonsense, knowledgeable, and stubborn as a stuck door. He knew what it took to make it in the game, or at least was convinced he did. But Williams equated weight with stamina. Overall had stood six foot two and weighed 225 pounds; Gomez was the same height and a hundred pounds less. "Vernon was about as skinny as you can get and still be living," said Tom Keena, one of Lefty's buddies. There was no way Nick Williams was to be convinced that a kid that insubstantial could stand up to the rigors of the Seals' two-hundred-game season.

But Lefty was determined to play for the team. After facing down his father, Vernon Gomez was not going to be dissuaded by Nick Williams. A battle of wills began between the crusty old pro and the kid of fourteen.

The first skirmish came at the end of the Seals' 1923 season, when the team held its annual tryouts. Nick would choose about seventy-five players he considered prospects, generally ages sixteen to eighteen, then have them report to spring training the following year. About fifteen of those were then signed to contracts and sent off to the lower minors to develop their skills. Some went on to stardom while others languished in virtual exile until their dreams of major league ball were scorched out of them.*

The tryouts were held on Saturday mornings in Recreation Park in the Mission Delores district, where the Seals played their home games. The stadium was actually Recreation Park II, the first having been destroyed in the earthquake. Nonetheless, locals called the new facility "Old Rec," and a wreck it was, constructed in 1907 largely of warped lumber that creaked in the San Francisco wind and seemed perpetually on the verge of collapse. The grandstand contained an eight-row, ground-level section enclosed by rusted chicken wire called the "Booze Cage," a vestige of

---

* Nick Williams would die at age sixty on June 2, 1941, the same day as Lou Gehrig. The headline of his obituary is visible on the newspaper read by Elisha Cook Jr., playing Wilmer the gunsel in the hotel lobby scene of *The Maltese Falcon*.

pre-Prohibition days when the forty-cent admission included either a slug of whiskey, two bottles of beer, or a ham and cheese sandwich. Most patrons chose the whiskey. After passage of the Eighteenth Amendment, hip flasks replaced the shot and patrons often shared the contents with players so inclined. The men who chose to sit in the Booze Cage—women were not allowed—sat on raised, pew-like benches and mixed their baseball with profanity, fistfights, and vomit. Only fifteen feet separated the boozers from the foul lines, thus providing an intimacy between spectator and player that encouraged not only shared whiskey but insults, needling, and left hooks.

In addition to the Booze Cage, Old Rec sported its very own "Gamblers' Section" in the upper grandstand beyond first base. Gambling was illegal, of course, but the local coppers turned a blind eye to the proceedings. Sometimes they participated in them. Those placing wagers used hand signals, not unlike floor traders on the New York Stock Exchange, and were careful to never openly exchange money.

Lefty was already attracting raves for his speed and control, so Milfred decided to see if his kid brother really had the goods. "He was too young to be a full-fledged prospect," Milfred said, "but I wanted to know if we should give any credence to people who were saying he was big league material."

There were no bridges in those days, so getting to Recreation Park meant a ferry ride across the bay. Getting to the ferry, in turn, involved a train ride to Oakland on the local. "Then," Lefty said, "you walked over the railroad tracks to the Mole, the Southern Pacific Ferry pier where the ferry was docked. The ferry captain left port when he felt like it. More than likely, just as you arrived, the boat pulled away from the pier without you, and over the ever-widening gap of churning water, a passenger yelled, 'Hey, bonehead! Why don't you swim the bay?' After flipping the bird to Mr. Nice Guy, you waited for the ferry's return. After you actually boarded the boat, in twenty minutes you were in at the Ferry Building in San Francisco, walking down Market Street."

Not surprisingly, the Gomez brothers didn't arrive at Recreation Park until the tryouts were already under way. When Milfred and Lefty walked up the ramp to the field, they saw "more kid ballplayers than blades of grass." Pitchers warmed up in the bullpen and were then waved to the mound one by one by a glowering Nick Williams, standing like an inquisitor on the first-base line. The kids threw until Williams told them to go, some after only a few pitches.

Milfred left his brother in the bullpen and waited in the stands. When Williams finally called Lefty to the mound, Nick craned his neck forward. Lefty owned only the first baseman's mitt, so he had bummed a fielder's glove off a right-hander and wore it backward, with his pinky in the thumb. Williams asked him about it, and Lefty told him, "I don't own a left-hander's glove, but it doesn't take away from the fun." Nick Williams actually laughed and told Lefty to throw a few. He was still chuckling to himself when Lefty went into his windup.

The fun stopped when Lefty threw his first pitch. "The catcher's mitt popped and so did Nick's eyes," Milfred said. "When Vernon had thrown some more, Nick called me down from the stands. 'He's got the arm all right,' Nick said. 'No doubt about it. But he looks sickly. He's gotta fatten up or forget the Seals.' "

But Williams was not about to let a high-powered fastball get too far away. He told Lefty he could report to the Seals training camp at Monterey for a couple of weeks in the spring if he could get permission from his school principal. And Lefty had to have a regulation glove by then. The Seals didn't supply equipment to kids trying out.

Milfred had his answer: his brother could pitch. Of Lefty's two immediate obstacles, the glove was to prove more formidable than the principal. Raising the money to buy it meant a trip back to Union Oil. "There was always work to be had at the refineries in the summer. Their market exploded when Americans went mad for Henry Ford's Tin Lizzie. Everybody wanted a set of wheels. By the end of the twenties, twenty-three million cars were roaring across the land. Every one of them needed gasoline, lube oil, and roads paved with asphalt or tar."

Lefty and a few of his buddies, all of whom needed money for something, got hired on at the refinery in Oleum for work on the yard gang. There is no grimmer form of employment in the oil business, as Lefty soon discovered. "The stills were filled with crude oil that was 'burned'— refined—and then the lids on top of the stills were opened to the outside air to cool the oil down. When it dropped to a certain temperature, the oil was drained out of the stills into the waiting trucks and ships. During the cooling process, some of the impurities—sludge—dried hard and stuck to the walls of the stills. Before they could be filled again, the sludge had to be cleaned out.

"On the side of the still, near the bottom, was a covered manhole. We took off the cover and crawled on our hands and knees into the stinking darkness. It was so hot inside it took your breath away. Scalding. We sat on stacks of sawdust with wooden shoes so our feet wouldn't burn, nose to nose with nauseating fumes, while we knocked the sludge off the walls with a chipping hammer and scraped the scale around the rivets. We each had a rake, a horizontal one-foot wooden board on the end of a pole. When the sludge fell on the floor we raked it to one side of the still and dumped it or wedged it out of the manhole into the yard. Then we pulled a sack of sand in through the manhole and sprinkled it on the floor of the tank to soak up the rest of the liquid. If you fell down, you were sliding around in grease."

The workday was eight hours and the crew couldn't come out for air until they had been in the still for four. Then a twenty-minute lunch, eating a sandwich brought from home, and back into the tank to finish the shift.

"We had constant headaches, our eyes were bloodshot. There seemed to be no ventilation except for the little bit of air and daylight coming in through the lid on top of the still and the manhole opening at the bottom. We thought every moment was our last."

Lefty's co-worker Jim Lakeman remembered a day that had truly threatened to be their last. "Once we got knocked silly from the fumes. They had to drag us out. They laid us on the hillside and gave us milk to drink. But the foreman was an old son of a gun. Just before, he was standing *outside*, yelling at us *inside*, 'Keep movin' the damn sludge.' "

"In those early years of the petroleum industry," Lefty said, "no one was aware of the health hazards. We were lucky we didn't burn our lungs out. Cancer? My friends and I didn't know what cancer meant. But we did know what $4.25 a day meant."

To Vernon Gomez, age fourteen, it meant a new, top-of-the-line, left-hander's Bill Doak signature glove.* "Without Union Oil, I wouldn't have had the glove I so desperately needed and I owe them a barrel of thanks. But good grief! What a job."

Even at Union Oil, baseball wasn't far away. "The company fielded a team in the Twilight Refinery League with Shell, Standard, and Associated. You had to work in the refinery to take the field with the company team. After chipping sludge all day, my friends and I figured that meant we worked for Union Oil so we went to the team manager to sign up.

" 'You gotta be brass, a big shot, a graduate of Stanford or Berkeley,' he told us. 'You gotta work for the company.'

" 'Whaddaya mean, work?' we said. 'We do work here! Scrapin' sludge.'

" 'Work means president, a VP, or a manager. You're nuthin' but screwbeanies . . . a bunch of Humpty-Dumpties. Scram.' "

The manager could not have known that he had just turned away not only the best baseball player the town would ever produce but also the O'Leary brothers, who had a little pull of their own.

"Somehow the press got wind of the confrontation. It may have taken place at the O'Leary home that night when Sean and Mike, my soon-to-be shortstop and second baseman, sat down to a corned beef dinner. As my double play combination passed the mustard, they also passed the news to their two older brothers, who happened to be reporters."

The yard gangs at Standard, Shell, and Associated Oil, it turned out, were none too keen at having their compatriots at Union Oil being described as not working for the company. They all got together and decided to start their own league—called, of course, the Screwbeanies.

"The Screwbeanies were big news. Sportscasters announced the

---

* William Leopold "Spittin' Bill" Doak, his moniker acquired for his favored method of achieving break on the ball, spent sixteen years in the majors. He was one of seventeen pitchers grandfathered when spitters were outlawed in 1920. Doak would have faded into oblivion with a lifetime record of 169–157 if not for his idea, also in 1920, of changing the design of the standard fielder's glove. Rather than simply providing protection from hard-hit ground balls and line drives, Doak suggested to the Rawlings Company that a web be laced between the first finger and thumb to create a natural pocket to catch the ball. The idea caught on instantly, and within two years the Bill Doak glove had become standard equipment in the majors and minors. Spittin' Bill himself hung on in the majors for nine more years, then retired to Florida to live off the proceeds of his invention.

standings of the Twilight League and the Screwbeanie League to listeners tuning in on crystal radio sets. A local druggist gave a baseball to every kid in the league. A haberdasher promised a trophy to the first-place winner. The plight of the Screwbeanies had grabbed the heartstrings of the community.

"As the long, hot summer wore on, the Union Oil team began its spiral toward last place. In the final days, the team slid into the gloom of the cellar with an 8–12 record. And who won the Screwbeanie League championship? We did. The Union Oil Humpty-Dumpties. Fifteen wins against five losses. Sure, we were labor. But on the diamond, our first-place finish beat the brass pants off the Union Oil diploma guys, and they knew it."

WITH A LARGELY SUCCESSFUL Seals tryout and the Screwbeanie League championship under his belt, Lefty was more determined than ever to pursue his dream. But Crockett High School didn't have a baseball team, so Lefty refused to go. When Coyote demanded that he attend, Lefty countered that he would go to Richmond High School, a train ride away to the west. Coyote refused but Lizzie sent Milfred to Richmond to secure permission. Richmond High was only too glad to have both Gomez and his fastball. Reder and Linus Claeys would also be on the train, to attend St. Mary's High School, but Lefty was otherwise striking out on his own.

At Richmond, he quickly made an impression. "Baseball was his profession, even in high school," said Richmond classmate George Gordon. "He was totally focused on the game. He always had his glove and his ball with him, even in the classroom. If he had a ten-minute wait for his train, he would ask anyone who had a mitt to catch him. A skinny kid firing bullets. Burned right through their gloves.

"Lefty feared nothing, but he wasn't one of those tough-talking guys. He had a soft personality. Got what he wanted through dogged determination, but still he was kind and gentle with people."

Although quiet, Lefty was an excellent student, always curious. One of his teachers noticed that he was the only one in her class who read the daily newspapers. When she threw open a question for discussion, Lefty spoke of the famine in China, the jazz coming out of Chicago, or the labor disputes between the San Francisco longshoremen and the unions.

The Richmond High School team was known as the Oilers and the coach was a World War I veteran named Ivan Hill. "He had been a major and he came in as head of military reserves," said Lefty. "He was also head of sports. In other words, there was one coach for all team sports. I don't know how he found the time to do it all, but he did. I owe him a lot."

Coach Hill brought his soldier's attitude to the field. "He demanded a positive attitude from his ballplayers," Lefty said, "and he got it. At my first tryout with the Seals, Nick Williams told me to gain weight if I wanted to play pro ball. My later tryouts were the same, Nick always droning on with the same advice. I was down in the dumps and went to talk to Coach Hill. Sometimes for fifteen minutes, sometimes for an hour. 'Give up and Nick wins,' he'd tell me. 'Get the contract. That's all that counts.'"

6.

"HIS NAME'S GOMEZ. GO WARM HIM UP"

WHEN LEFTY GRADUATED FROM HIGH SCHOOL IN 1926, HE CAME TO a crossroads. He had been offered a scholarship to St. Mary's, a small Lasallian Catholic college five miles west of Oakland at which the academics were excellent but sports something of an afterthought. For Coyote, here was the opportunity for his son to pursue excellence—and without even costing the family any money. What was more, Linus Claeys was about to enroll, as would Reder two years later.

Lefty refused to go.

To Coyote, there could be no worse sin than refusing to be educated, so he issued an ultimatum. "No baseball," he said. "No more. Runnin' here, there, and everywhere. You're a bum. It's over. You're goin' to college and be an engineer like your brother." With that, Coyote turned Lefty over to Milfred for the summer with the understanding that by autumn baseball would have fallen away and Lefty would agree to attend college. This last attempt by Coyote to pry his youngest son away from the diamond would ultimately ensure Lefty's ascension to the major leagues.

By this time, Milfred had a degree in electrical engineering and was working for Pacific Gas & Electric as foreman of a two-hundred-man crew erecting the power lines that would bring electricity to towns throughout northern California.*

Lefty was livid but was not again willing to openly defy his dad. Grum-

---

* Milfred would go on to work for an international oil company, traveling the world. He would experience a variety of cultures on four continents and teach himself whatever language was appropriate to his assignment, including Arabic during his stay in the Persian Gulf.

bling every minute, Lefty joined his brother's crew in Yuba City, north of Sacramento on the Feather River. "I thought my brother, being a big shot with PG&E, would at least give me a soft job without much work to do for good pay. I guessed wrong."

Instead of the cushy assignment he had been expecting, Lefty was assigned to be a groundsman, two dollars for a ten-hour day, digging post holes, two feet wide and six feet deep. Milfred warned Lefty to toe the line, or else.

The work turned out to be less ghastly than mucking around in petroleum stills but hardly idyllic. "There were no augers for digging. Milfred handed me a pick and a long, wooden-handled tool called a spoon. I broke ground with the pick. When the hole was deep enough, I scooped out the dirt with the spoon. I dug my tail off, sixty hours a week, up and down the California hills in the blazing sun."

Milfred, who had taken Lefty for his Seals tryout three years before, seemed to have come over to Coyote's point of view. "He watched me like a hawk. Sometimes he'd come by and ask me, 'How's your day going, Vernon?' 'Lousy,' I'd tell him. 'I want to be a ballplayer.' "

As the crew moved through Sonoma County, Lefty had taken to muttering with each post hole. At night, the crew generally pitched tents in an open field and ate communally around campfires, greasy sausages and stale bread. Lefty shoved down the food, immune to the charms of sleeping under the stars after an honest day's work.

By July, the crew was installing power lines on the Point Reyes peninsula—later a national seashore, but at the time public land. They worked amidst rolling surf on windswept beaches that sloped up to a seemingly endless vista of pastureland.

The crew was forced to shut down one day because of rain, and finally Milfred ceased being his father's surrogate and became Vernon's big brother again. The two of them walked, on and on, twenty miles to the Point Reyes lighthouse.

"It sat on a rocky ledge, jutting out into the Pacific," said Lefty. "For whale watching, it was the best spot. Also the windiest. Northwesters howled down the coast and our hair whipped around our faces as we scanned the horizon. Sometimes we'd see a humpback leap out of the water, twist in midair, then land back in the ocean with a spectacular splash. Then we went over to a beach that was close to where Francis Drake was supposed to have passed in the *Golden Hind*. Milfred was taken with the wildflowers growing in the crannies of the cliffs. Back home, if he had a square inch of space, he'd plant something in it. In some ways, we were very much alike . . . basically shy. We found constant chatter tiresome. We just poked along, aware of what was going on around us. A time to listen."

In August, the crew moved inland and eventually stopped at Point Reyes Station, a town grown up around a railroad depot on the southern coast of Tomales Bay. The station itself took quite a bit of traffic, as many as fifteen trains per day carrying passengers and freight between San Francisco and the North Coast.

"I never tired of watching the trains pull in," Lefty would remember. "As the wheels clanked to a standstill in a whoosh of steam, the schoolchildren jumped aboard the caboose and ran through the cars selling poppies. My fascination with railroads began in Point Reyes. There would come day when train travel would take up a good bit of my life."

As the summer drew to a close, Lefty began to despair of the three months he'd been away from baseball. He didn't realize that in Point Reyes he was coming closer and closer to something he had wanted since he was six years old.

One Sunday, his only day off, Lefty hiked up a hill to check out the town ball field, which was set in a pasture, facing the railroad depot. "The infield was dirt and the outfield knee-deep grass. If a player hit a line drive, it was cut down and taken hostage by the thick meadow. The outfielders had to be grasshoppers to charge the fly balls." The entire field was on a hillside, and, according to Lefty, "it sloped in such a way that whenever a ball was hit to left field, the pitcher couldn't tell immediately if it was caught or a hit. The left fielder would momentarily disappear off the face of the earth, or so it seemed. That added naturally to the drama."

Lefty settled in to watch the game between Point Reyes and the opponent, wanting desperately to be on other side of the foul lines. Sometime during the last three innings, he heard the wail of a train whistle. When the train pulled into the station, instead of a brief halt to pick up and discharge passengers, it stopped entirely. Suddenly the passengers, conductor, and baggage men poured out of the cars and ran frantically up the hill toward the ball field. Lefty learned from another spectator that this same train had dropped off members of the other team three hours earlier, then continued north to the fishing villages along the Russian River. Now, on the return, the passengers had descended en masse to crowd along the foul lines, screaming and cheering at the last outs of the game. Afterward, the opposing team would hop on board for their journey home.

A fan told Lefty it happened all the time, and Lefty thought, "Holy cow, baseball is a big deal in this town."

After the last out, with the visiting team and train's passengers hustling on board, Lefty ambled down to the field. He struck up a chat with some of the Point Reyes infielders while they were gathering up their equipment. They were older, in their mid-twenties, but friendly enough. They told him they practiced every day after work and on Saturday mornings. Lefty also learned that Point Reyes played in a more competitive league than he had experienced with Al Erle; they went up against the best town teams from Marin and Sonoma counties, and even some of the city boys from San Francisco. The most important piece of information he obtained was that the team was managed by a man named Dante Muscio and his two sons, who, like almost everyone else in town, worked for the Grandi family.

The Grandis, two Swiss-Italian brothers, Louis and Salvatore, were the S. J. Claeys of Point Reyes: aggressive, forward-thinking entrepreneurs who recognized opportunity when they saw it and understood there was as much potential wealth above the ground as under it. They had arrived from Lugano around 1880, just after the railroad line was completed, and began buying up land. By 1926, they owned the biggest hotel in town and the Ford dealership. The Grandi Feed and Lumber Company occupied an entire block of downtown and housed a grain warehouse, a livery stable, the post office, the telephone company, and the town's only grocery.

Lefty filed away the name "Muscio" and, a few days later, when Milfred decided another visit to the general store was in order, he called Lefty away from his post holes to ride along. Inside, Milfred struck up a conversation with a thickset man sporting an extravagant handlebar mustache. After some idle conversation about PG&E, Milfred wandered off to browse. As he was leaving, he introduced his kid brother to the mustachioed man. Dante Muscio.

Muscio asked what such a skinny kid was doing with a road crew and Lefty replied that he'd been digging post holes. Before Muscio could turn away, Lefty asked for a tryout with the team. Muscio did not seem at all impressed but, his curiosity piqued, finally told a clerk to go and fetch Bud Farley, the team's catcher. Lefty thought Farley was somewhere in town but he was actually working at his family's dairy farm in Nicasio, nine miles away. Milfred had disappeared and Lefty cooled his heels waiting, wondering if it was all a joke. But Farley finally arrived. Muscio said, "His name's Gomez. Go warm him up."

Farley and Lefty walked across the tracks to the field. He gave Lefty a glove, then told him to get on the mound and throw some pitches. Fifty years afterward, Bud Farley still remembered what happened next. "He went out to the mound, went into his high-kick delivery, and unleashed his fastball. *Whack!* He burned my hand. But I wouldn't let him know it. I yelled for him to throw me some more. What smoke!"

Bud Farley walked back to the general store to report to Dante Muscio, Lefty in tow.

"How did Gomez look?" Muscio asked.

"He'll do," Farley replied.

" 'He'll do'?" Lefty said much later. "I never let Bud live that one down. Then Muscio said, 'You'll be pitching for room and board. At Farley's and my house. First game is in two weeks.' "

Lefty didn't bother to mention the tryout when he next saw Milfred. "Why spoil a perfectly good day? I had two weeks to break the news."

Landing a spot on the Point Reyes staff was a far more significant step than simply pitching against better hitters. With Point Reyes, Lefty would, for the first time, pitch against teams from San Francisco, which meant sometimes pitching *in* San Francisco. And San Francisco meant scouts.

Without bridges to ease the journey to outlying towns, the few major league scouts prowling the Bay Area in those days rarely ventured outside the city limits. They were content to trawl in areas they could reach without a half day's journey over bumpy roads to watch a bunch of kids or old-timers playing on town or industrial league teams. Except to watch the Seals, some scouts never left Golden Gate Park where as many as ten games might be going on at the same time, featuring the best young players around. Anyone with aspirations to the majors, therefore, wasn't going to find fulfillment in East Bay or on Al Erle's circuit.

Lefty returned to his sixty-hour week with PG&E with, if possible, less enthusiasm than before. Milfred got so sick of his brother's complaining about post holes that he reassigned Lefty to tagging the poles, pounding in nails imprinted with the month and year the pole was installed. Lefty threw most of the nails away. Milfred tried him at other jobs, with a similar lack of success. Finally Milfred had had enough. "He was so vexed, he could hardly catch his breath," remembered Lefty. "He grabbed hold of my shoulders and shook the living daylights out of me. He told me to stop the tomfoolery or I was fired.

" 'Fired?' I yelled back at him. 'I quit! I made the ball club. I'm goin' to the big leagues.'

" 'The big leagues? What about Pa?'

" 'What about me?' I shot back. 'Nobody's listening to *me*! I can pitch!' "

Milfred pressed but Lefty would not be moved. No one was going to stop him. Not his father. Not Nick Williams. He told Milfred he'd pitch so well that Nick would be forced to give him a try. "I wanted Nick to hear my name till he couldn't stand it anymore and he'd forget my weight and sign me up." When Milfred asked what would happen if Lefty couldn't make the grade, Lefty replied, "I'll take the chance."

When they returned to Rodeo, Lefty faced down his father. He intended to live in Point Reyes and play baseball. Lefty was seventeen, two years older than Coyote had been when he'd left home to pursue *his* dream. "I'll never forget the hurt in his eyes when he told me I was making the biggest mistake of my life. At the time, I didn't understand his anxiety. What kid does?"

To his surprise, Lefty had an advocate in the room. "Milfred came to my rescue when I ran out of words. 'Let him run,' he said to Pa. 'You can't keep him off the diamonds. Let's see where his arm takes him. He's got a lifetime to sit in a classroom.' Pa wasn't convinced and I didn't waste his time or mine. If he could make decisions about my life, I could too. I had to pitch."

7

"I HAD TO STOP GOMEZ"

"I KNEW THERE'D BE TOUGH DAYS AHEAD," LEFTY SAID LATER. "DAYS I'D long for Rodeo. I also knew my father yearned for the day my dream of being a big leaguer would run its course and I'd pick up the career he'd chosen for me. But my dream never died. Not for one second."

During the week, Lefty lived in a sprawling white farmhouse with Mary and Frank Farley and their six kids. He and Bud milked cows twice a day: once at three in the morning and once at three in the afternoon. Unlike the Gomez dairy, the Farleys had no retail customers. The ten-gallon milk cans had to be filled by sunrise, before the milk truck showed up to haul them off to the creamery in Point Reyes. Lefty and Bud then got to sleep a bit before Frank had them out practicing, hours every day. Unlike Coyote, Frank Farley loved baseball and was determined to help the town put its best team on the field.

Lefty discovered another attraction in the Farley home, Bud's younger sister Cecilia, who one of Lefty's friends described as "a petite, high-spirited Irish lass with jet-black hair and blue eyes." Lefty saw Cecilia on and off for three years.

On Friday nights, Lefty packed up his glove and spikes in a sack and bummed a ride to Point Reyes Station to spend the weekend with Dante and Gilda Muscio. The Muscios also treated him like a member of the family, although the only space available in their home was in an unheated attic.

"Papa and my brother Buzz," recounted Ethel Muscio, "closed in the end section of the attic with paneling to keep the wind from blowing Vernon away. Then Vernon and my younger brother Gam laid linoleum on the floor and dragged an old iron bed up the narrow-neck staircase. Vernon loved it.

"He had only one pair of pants to his name when he came to live with us. Corduroys. When they got too dirty, he had to stay upstairs in the attic, reading in bed, until Mama washed them and they dried on the clothesline. When she brought him the pants, Vernon got out of bed for the day."

Lefty had a long history with corduroys. When he was a kid, they had been an aspiration. "Cream-colored corduroys were what jeans are today. A top-quality pair cost $2.98. My friends and I didn't have any. Our parents said bib overalls were good enough. We were jealous of the kids who wore cords. They could walk down the street and, by rubbing their knees together, they could make their pants whistle. Awesome. I got my first pair in high school and wore them day in and day out. No soapsuds. On wash days, I sprinted past Ma.

"Every night, I put the cords between the mattress and the springs of my bed. Then I jumped in under the covers. While I slept the night away, the caked dirt was pressed into the nap of the fabric. After five months of perspiration, grease, and grime, the cords developed the 'black sheen' that symbolized laid-back class. I was in. One of the guys. The cords were perfect one year later, when they became stiff. I could lean them against the wall and they stood up by themselves."

There were chores at the Muscios' as well, but Dante and Gilda were often lax in enforcement, since Lefty's real weekend job was pitching for Point Reyes. Still, even then it was no free ride. "Saturday morning, at the crack of dawn, I left the Muscio house and hitched a ride back to the Farleys' ranch to help Bud clean out the cow barns so he'd be ready to catch the game. Sometimes Bud's father stood in the doorway, shouting at us, 'Hurry up, the two of you. Get out there and practice plays at the plate.' Pa could never understand the baseball fever of Frank Farley and Dante Muscio."

It might be easy to conclude that the Farleys and Muscios were so welcoming of their new boarder solely because of a live fastball. While certainly neither family took in just anyone, each was motivated as much by a genuine sense of hospitality and the desire to care for a stranger in their midst as for whatever benefits might accrue to the town team for having Vernon Gomez as its pitcher. "There was so much love and tenderness in families around Point Reyes," Ethel Muscio said. "We pulled together on everything." Mary Farley even insisted Lefty go back to Rodeo periodically to visit his family. There were no trains between the towns, so Mary let Lefty borrow the family's ancient Model A for the trip. Frank was not completely pleased about that part—without a car in Nicasio, he and Mary were more or less marooned—but Lefty always returned the Ford in running order. As a result, Lefty, through a brilliant baseball career and future associations with presidents, movie stars, and luminaries in virtually every field of human endeavor, would remain close to both families for the remainder of his life.

Even so, neither the Farleys nor the Muscios overlooked his skills. "Point Reyes was a baseball town. We couldn't let a pitcher like Vernon get away. Monday morning after the games, the first thing Mama did was scrub Vernon's dirty flannels on a washboard. She pressed them with an iron she warmed on a wood-burning stove. 'Ethel,' she told me, 'your brothers' uniforms can wait until the end of the week. Vernon is the pitcher.' "

And Dante Muscio soon discovered that his boarder could fill another team vacancy. "When Papa found out Vernon played the sax, the Muscio band had a new member," Ethel said. "Vernon was tenor man, Gam was on alto. Buzz blew trumpet and I played keyboard. Joe Elwood, the manager of the Western Hotel, banged drums. We could play anything, but specialized in ragtime. Vernon was crazy for the blues. He liked to improvise. We played for parties, weddings, and dances at Foresters' Hall."

Foresters' Hall was Point Reyes's social center, a two-story Victorian at the edge of town. Tom Keena came from Novato. "Anyone living near Point Reyes came to the dances, even though most of us lived on ranches miles and miles apart. We didn't have electricity, gas, heat, radios, or phones. When the wind blew hard, the kitchen linoleum lifted up. We lived like hermits."

In addition to the locals, the crowd included lumberjacks who hitched rides from the logging camps on the coasts and miners on their way back from the Alaska goldfields. Everyone came to dance, listen to family bands, and partake of refreshment, some of which was obtained outdoors. "They served nothing but coffee and cake at Foresters'," Keena said.

"That was it. Prohibition. Whenever the bands stopped playing, the old men and the young hounds ran out of Foresters' into their Tin Lizzies and pickup trucks, all with blinds on the windows, to slug down the hard stuff. Old Grand-Dad was stuffed into the hay in back of the trucks or a gallon of wine under the hood of a car. A lot of the folks had some of that homebrew on hand too."

Foresters', not surprisingly, jumped a good deal more than a coffee-and-cake joint ordinarily might: music and moonshine have always made a compelling combination. Although those who heard him play extolled his talent, Lefty's description was somewhat less glowing. "The Grandis paid me five dollars for playing sax at the Saturday night dances. The band made a lot of noise we called music. But no one fell asleep."

Often Lefty came to the dances with Cecilia. When he wasn't playing, she dragged him out to the dance floor. But she had competition for her beau's attention. Lefty would more often than not drift over to the sidelines to talk baseball, leaving Cecilia to dragoon another partner.

At Foresters', the action didn't really begin until about 1:00 a.m., but that was the time of the curfew Dante Muscio had set for his sons and his new pitcher. When they ended their set, the boys were marched home. "Buzz and Gam were stuck," a friend recalled, "because they slept on the second floor with their parents. But Vernon sometimes climbed out of his attic window and shimmied down the drainpipe from the porch roof and went off to see Cecilia Farley." Sneaking out was one thing, sneaking back in another. "The Muscios locked the front door thinking I was sound asleep in the attic," Lefty noted. "Climbing back up the porch pole was murder."

Still, the main business in Point Reyes was baseball and in that there was no dispute. Although the Muscio family was rounded up on Sunday and hauled off to church, Ethel Muscio always suspected that "Vernon and my parents knelt in the pews praying for a win in the afternoon game." With Lefty on the mound, the prayers were usually answered. Word got around about Point Reyes's new flamethrower and the town games drew 4,000 fans every time he pitched.

Lefty's decision to leave home, his conviction that his road to major league baseball passed through the town in North Bay, seemed to be vindicated on a spring afternoon in 1927 when Dante Muscio suggested he try out with the Sausalito Merchants, one of the top semipro teams in Marin County and one that played regularly in San Francisco proper. It is a testament to the decency of Dante Muscio that he was willing to ship Lefty to a competitor to give him a better shot of being spotted by a scout.

Dante sent Lefty off to Sausalito with Cy Thomas, a relative of the Farley family. They walked into the general store to see the manager, Fred Perry, who also happened to be the manager of the Merchants. Perry had married a Nicasio girl and was acquainted with the Farleys, so Cy was the perfect go-between.

"I was working behind the grocery counter when they walked in," Perry said. "I can still see Vernon standing there, tall and skinny in his corduroy pants with the dirt caked into them. I'll never forget those pants of his. I don't think he ever washed them. Cy introduced me and they continued to hang around the store. I knew they wanted to talk baseball. Finally Cy asks me, 'Any chance for Gomez as the starter in today's game against Mill Valley?' Ah! Vernon was trying to win a spot on my team. I told Cy sure, to bring Gomez down to the field, to my catcher Larry Cohn. He was working with my pitchers."

Another pitcher was also working out, someone named Soares. "I gave Larry Cohn ten minutes to pick out the starter in the Mill Valley game. Soares was a helluva pitcher. Right-hander, a local Portuguese boy. My grandfather came from the Azores in 1868, so I'm background Portuguese and partial to Soares. But Cohn had the final say. 'Take Soares,' he told me. 'The Mill Valley club has six right-handed hitters. A right-hander will be better against their lineup.' Poor Lefty. He had already been told he had the wrong body to be a successful pitcher. Now, apparently, he had the wrong arm and the wrong nationality."

Lefty was disappointed when Fred Perry pulled him aside to give him the news. "If I had to do it all over again," he said later, "I'd have let it slip into my conversation that my father's mother was born in Lisbon and spoke only Portuguese."*

---

* Fred Perry had another story about the Bay Area sandlots, this one about a future teammate of Lefty's. "We all lived baseball in those early days. There came a time when I was player-manager of the Merchants that my legs were always like a toothache. Ballplayers quit on account of their

As it turned out, Soares didn't make good on his opportunity. He developed a drinking problem that ultimately killed him and never made it beyond semipro.

For Lefty, instead of pitching in a big game in front of major league scouts, it was back to Point Reyes. But sometimes being at the right place at the right time is a matter of being at the right place all the time. In October he got another shot.

Point Reyes was scheduled to play against archrival Novato and Bill Gnoss, the Novato manager, was bent on vengeance. When the two teams had met a few weeks earlier, Gnoss had boasted how his boys were going to knock Point Reyes around. "I know just how Gomez pitches," Gnoss sneered, "and we're gonna beat the pants off him." Gnoss turned out to be less than prescient. Point Reyes won 9–0, Lefty hurling a complete-game shutout, striking out twenty-two batters.

Gnoss walked around for weeks, muttering and plotting. He signed some new players to improve his lineup. "I told my boys," Gnoss related, "that we were gonna get even with Point Reyes and we were gonna do it on our home grounds. I arranged a big game on a Sunday to end the 1927 season. I told them we'd hit a lot of home runs, make money at the game, and then have a victory party." Despite Novato's previous humiliation, Gnoss possessed the motivational skills to convince his players. He was eventually elected Novato's mayor.

"Bill Gnoss was determined to win at any cost," a Point Reyes player noted. "Any cost" included stacking his team with ringers. Gnoss scoured the area for top players, whether they lived in Novato or simply worked nearby. When he heard that Moch Lucchesi, the barrel-chested, hard-hitting third baseman for the Petaluma Spartans, Sonoma County champs, had been hired as a barber in a Novato shop,

---

legs. I gave my spikes away but kept my glove and bat, just in case. One Saturday morning I went from Sausalito over to the San Francisco markets to pick up produce for the store. When I got there, everyone ran up to tell me that Joe Gregarro's looking for me. Joe was a fireball, manager of the John D. Martini team, one of the best in San Francisco. So I find Gregarro and he says to me, 'You got to help me out with tomorrow's game, Fred. I need a shortstop.' I told him I'd hung up my spikes. He kept at me, so I finally told him I'd play. Then I asked what the problem was. 'Joe DiMaggio's quit playin' baseball,' Joe told me. 'His father doesn't want him to mess up his hands for the accordion.' "

Gnoss found himself in need of a shave and nabbed Lucchesi on the spot.

Bill Gnoss was less sanguine about Novato's chances with Lucchesi than he had been with his players. "While I'm in the chair, Moch moaned that we had to have the game," he noted. "I told him, 'Yeah, but we got to be careful. The trouble is, we can't give up more than one run against Gomez. If we give him two, we're beat before we start.'"

Lucchesi then told Gnoss that he'd heard Point Reyes had recruited a couple of ringers on their own, to say nothing of Lefty himself, who was hardly Point Reyes born and bred. Though by this time half the Novato town team lived somewhere else, Gnoss expressed outrage at such an underhanded tactic. He told Lucchesi that he now had no choice but to "strengthen up" Novato's team. "The only way I can do it," Gnoss told Lucchesi, "is to get a good pitcher. We gotta stop Point Reyes from making runs."

Gnoss's next stop was to consult with the local umpire, Joe Stutt, who had once been a player with Tacoma in the Pacific Coast League. Stutt was knowledgeable and resourceful and, as a town resident, would help in any way he could to defeat the enemy. A few years earlier, when Gnoss had sustained a painful knee injury as a player, Stutt contacted his longtime friend Nick Williams and arranged for the Seals' team trainer to work on Gnoss's knee at Recreation Park. Since then, Gnoss and Williams had gotten to know each other.

Stutt listened with sympathy to Gnoss's lament. Everyone, he told Gnoss, was "buzzing that Novato's gonna get slaughtered." But he suggested Gnoss call Nick Williams. Williams, it seemed, had a young pitcher named Gus Oliva whom he might be willing to lend out. "Hiring a professional to pitch against a semipro town wasn't exactly according to the rules," Gnoss admitted. "But I had to stop Gomez."

Williams was happy to help. As long as Gnoss was willing to pay Oliva to pitch, they had a deal. Gnoss offered $25, but only if Oliva won. Williams agreed, then asked Gnoss to tell him what he thought of his young pitcher. Nick assiduously avoided discussing Gomez.

On game day, the grandstand at Novato's tumbledown stadium was packed and fans were lined up along the foul lines. Lefty and his Point

Reyes teammates arrived in an old farm pickup truck. "The diamond was in pastureland," Lefty recalled. "Before the game the Novato players mowed the perimeter of the field and cows chewed in the power alleys during the game."

Bill Gnoss's promise to his players that they would make money by hitting a bunch of homers was not idle. Whenever the two teams played, fans stuffed money into the chicken wire backstop with each round-tripper; as the hitter crossed the plate, he transferred the bills from the chicken wire to his pocket. Other fans tossed silver dollars from the stands when a run scored. After the game, a fan passed the hat through the crowd and the nickels and dimes would be given to the managers and players. Obviously, when Novato did well, its fans were prone to increased generosity. And since the Point Reyes team, in theory, had no idea that Oliva was a ringer, Gnoss was hoping for a big payday.

Before the game Bud Farley had wandered off, so Lefty asked Tom Keena, the Novato catcher he knew from Foresters', to warm him up. "Gnoss and Oliva were watching us carefully from the Novato bench," Keena said. "Gomez's fastball was whistling like the wind, hopping all over the strike zone."

But Oliva could pitch as well, and not too much money was pulled from the chicken wire that day; going into the bottom of the eighth, Point Reyes was nursing a 1–0 lead. That didn't mean money wasn't changing hands, however; spectators were betting on every pitch.

Lefty held Novato in the eighth and Point Reyes didn't score in the ninth. Bill Gnoss sat on the Novato bench, gnashing his teeth at the prospect of being shut out again by Gomez. But in the ninth, Novato managed to get a man to second with two out. The next hitter was Gus Oliva. Lefty, who assumed that the opposing pitcher wasn't going to be any better a hitter than he was, grooved a fastball. But Oliva could hit and he put the pitch into orbit. Novato won 2–1.

Novato fans were giddy, but Bill Gnoss knew his baseball and was fully aware that the victory had been a fluke. Lefty had made a kid mistake. "Forget about Oliva," Gnoss told Nick Williams afterward. "He's a good pitcher but he's not going to the bigs. You'd better go out right away and sign Gomez."

Williams responded as he had for three years. "He's got a great arm, Bill, but he's a bag of bones. I've got a two-hundred-game season. He'll be dead halfway through."

But Gnoss was adamant. "Stop fooling around, Nick. Get his name on a contract. He's hurling bullets. If you don't, someone else will."

It evidently hadn't occurred to Williams that his prejudice against skinny pitchers might not be universally shared. The idea of Lefty pitching for a competitor finally got Williams's attention. "Okay, okay, Bill. I'll go down and sign him up."

It had taken three years, but Lefty had indeed worn Nick Williams out.

8.

PING, BABE, DUSTER, SLOPPY . . . AND LEFTY

———

Bᴜᴛ ʟᴇꜰᴛʏ ᴡᴀꜱ ɴᴏᴛ ʏᴇᴛ ᴏꜰ ᴀɢᴇ, ꜱᴏ ʜᴇ ɴᴇᴇᴅᴇᴅ ᴀ ᴘᴀʀᴇɴᴛ ᴛᴏ ᴄᴏ-ꜱɪɢɴ the Seals contract. Coyote refused, so Lizzie signed instead. Contract negotiations took place at Claeys's Meat Market; Lizzie got the details on the telephone while Lefty bought pork chops.

Coyote's refusal to make his mark, surprisingly, did not create a rift between father and son. They seemed to understand each other, these two indomitable men, forty-five years apart in age. The Gomez family remained close-knit and, in the important things, fiercely supportive of one another despite the ongoing war of wills between its oldest and youngest members.

And even at this point Coyote's apprehension was hardly baseless. For all his talent, Lefty was still raw, and pitching semipro was not the same as facing professional hitters. What's more, the 1928 Seals roster was loaded. The pitching staff was led by another lefty, Dutch Ruether, who had spent eleven years in the majors, winning 137 games. Ruether had pitched for the Yankees the previous year, winning 13 games for the world champions. In fact, he was something of a World's Series magnet. He had also been on the Yankees during their 1926 series appearance, after coming over from the Washington Senators and their World's Series team in 1925. Six years before, he had started two games for Cincinnati in the infamous 1919 Black Sox World's Series against Chicago. But even at thirty-four years old and back in the Pacific Coast League, Ruether would maintain sufficient guile to win 29 games in 1928. Three other Seals starting pitchers had or would have extensive major league experience: Elmer Jacobs, Walter "Duster" Mails, and the wonderfully named Hollis "Sloppy" Thurston.

With position players, the Seals were even more impressive. Earl Averill, whose major league career overlapped Lefty's almost to the year, would end up in the Hall of Fame.* Other future major leaguers included Frank Crosetti, Smead Jolley, Babe Pinelli, Ping Bodie, Gus Suhr, and Buckshot May.

Seals players were as quirky as they were good. Pinelli, in particular, was an oddity. When his playing days were over, he turned to umpiring and ended his career calling balls and strikes for Don Larsen's perfect game in the 1956 World Series.

"If ever there was an umpire hater," Lefty said, "Babe Pinelli was the man. He used to take off on a slide and ten feet from the bag, he'd start screaming, 'No! No! I'm safe!' Then he'd come up madder than a landlord during a rent freeze and wail for twenty minutes. It wasn't a surprise when Pinelli turned into a good umpire. He'd umpired twenty years before he ever put on a blue uniform."

Ping Bodie was another character. His real name was Francesco Stephano Pezzolo, but he adopted "Ping," for the sound of a ball hitting his 52-ounce bat, and Bodie for the old prospecting town in which he grew up. He stood only 5 feet 8 but weighed almost 200 pounds, with long arms, a prominent chin, and a more prominent nose. He was the first Bay Area Italian American to make it to the majors, blazing a trail for Tony Lazzeri, Ernie Lombardi, Frank Crosetti, and the DiMaggio brothers. Ping had been Babe Ruth's first roommate after Ruth's sale to the Yankees. He said of the carousing slugger, "I don't room with Babe. I room with his suitcase." Ping was not shy about his own abilities with the bat. "I really hemstitch the horsehide," he was fond of observing. Although no one knew precisely what that meant, the gist seemed clear. He could also "whale the old apple" or "smack the old onion." When he was seventy-three years old and asked if he could still hit, Ping replied, "Give me the mace and I'll drive the pumpkin down Whitey Ford's throat."

Lefty remembered him well. "When he played ball at Old Rec, he brought his two pigs with him to the ballpark. While Ping shagged flies in the outfield, they did lunch beneath the grandstand, eating the peanuts

---

* But Averill would be best remembered for hitting the line drive in the 1937 All-Star game that broke Dizzy Dean's toe, ultimately ending the great Cardinal pitcher's career. Lefty would be the winning pitcher in the same game.

and candy bars the fans threw down on the field. After the game, Ping led the squealing swine out of the park and back to their pens at his home in the Cow Hollow section of San Francisco. 'How can I keep them down on the farm,' Ping asked me, 'after they've seen Old Rec?' " He also found time to oversee an automobile service station he owned near the Seals' ballpark.

Then there was Sloppy Thurston. He got his name because he was perhaps the most impeccably dressed man in baseball, a trait he was convinced made him more attractive to female fans. Sloppy had won 20 games for the White Sox in 1924 and later, as a scout, would discover a young power hitter named Ralph Kiner.*

If the Seals players were quirky, they only reflected the team owners. In 1918, then owner Henry Berry fell victim to a series of bad investments and put the team up for sale at a bargain price. Charley Graham, a former minor league catcher, manager, and erstwhile Latin and Greek teacher at Santa Clara University, wanted to buy the club but lacked the means. He recruited Alfie Putnam, sports editor of the *Sacramento Bee,* but even together, they only had enough for a down payment.

Demonstrating either great confidence or enormous stupidity, Graham and Putnam signed an agreement to purchase the Seals, putting up everything they had to secure the contract with not the slightest notion of where to get the rest of the money. They then announced that the team was theirs, waxing on about the glorious future of the franchise to local sports editors.

While shuttling between newspaper offices, Graham happened to notice a large billboard proclaiming the dental services of one Dr. Charles H. Strub. Similar signs were planted all over town, which had caused Dr. Strub to be labeled the "advertising dentist," a term not necessarily used in admiration. Graham grabbed Putnam by the arm. "That's our man."

---

* The debate as to which era of baseball boasted the best players will never resolve but in nicknames the players of Lefty's era beat later generations flat. During Lefty's first year with the Seals alone, along with the usual complement of Dukes, Babes, Docs, and, yes, Leftys, the Pacific Coast League sported—in addition to Sloppy, Ping, Duster, Buckshot, and Junk—Ox Exhardt, Frenchy Uhalt, Monk Sherlock, Cuckoo Christiensen, Skinny Graham, Pug Cavet, Bevo Lebourveau, Dud Lee, Truck Hannah, Boot Nose Hoffman, and Yats Wuestling.

Strub, it seemed, had once been a left-handed-hitting infielder who had played in college and briefly in the low minors. He quit baseball to set up his dental practice, just in time for the earthquake. When the dust cleared, his new practice was in shambles, so Strub approached the manager of the Sacramento Cordovas and asked for a job. The manager, the very same Charley Graham, had expressed sympathy for young Strub's predicament and signed him up. Strub had played out the season, then returned to San Francisco to reestablish himself as a dentist. By 1918, in addition to his widely visible practice, Strub had made a small fortune in real estate.

Graham and Putnam went to Dr. Strub's office and offered him a third of the club. All Strub had to do was put up almost all of the money. As reported in the *Sporting News,* "Dr. Strub removed his white professional jacket, put on his hat and coat, and the three marched to the *Chronicle* building and had their pictures taken as the new owners of the Seals. It was puzzling to the lads on the sports staff. Two owners one hour; three owners the next. But the story was explained in detail and it made excellent reading the following morning."

The three were well suited to one another. Graham was a top baseball man, Putnam a natural promoter, and Dr. Strub as sharp a businessman as could be found in any sport. Strub purchased a bottling plant so that the team got full revenue for all the soft drinks sold at Old Rec; he bought another plant to roast peanuts, which were then bagged and sold to the fans. But mostly what Strub did was raise the price of players sold to major league teams. In 1922, he sold Willie Kamm, a solid but hardly brilliant infielder, to the White Sox for $100,000, the same price the Yankees paid for Babe Ruth. Strub eventually took in well over a million dollars peddling players while Graham and, later, Nick Williams provided a steady stream of new talent to fill the holes. For his first four years as an owner, Graham managed the Seals as well.*

That such revenues could be garnered from the teams back east was, as Graham and Strub were well aware, because baseball was a game in

---

* Charles Strub didn't stop with baseball. Horse racing was legalized in California in 1933, and he immediately applied for a permit. He then built Santa Anita, one of the largest and most beautiful racetracks in the world. Some wags scoffed that Strub could not tell an infield from an outfield, but he attracted the world's best Thoroughbreds to his track by offering large purses and rendered it, as with almost all of his ventures, an enormous success.

transition and there was a shortage of players with skills for the more modern game. In standard baseball lore, the "dead ball" era ended in 1920 and a new home-run-crazed period began. Certainly, with batters seeing the ball better, they could hold the bat closer to the knob at the bottom and increase torque and thus the power the swing generated. To the disgust of purists such as Ty Cobb, an offense based on bunting, squib hitting, and the Baltimore chop had without question passed into history. But the cork-centered baseball, the "live ball," had been introduced in 1909. True, a new model came into use in 1920, one in which a tighter yarn was used over the cork center, but this was tested against the ball used the previous year and found to carry no farther.

Rather than the decade of the home run hitter, Babe Ruth notwithstanding, the 1920s were actually the decade of the line drive hitter. In 1927, for example, when the Babe hit his 60th and Lou Gehrig finished second in homers with 47, the third-place home run hitter in the American League hit only 18. The more significant increases were in batting average and other extra-base hits.

Between 1915 and 1919, National League batting averages ranged between .248 and .254. In 1920, the league average jumped to .270, then to .289 in 1921, and it did not drop below .283 for the remainder of the decade. In 1930, National League batters hit an astonishing .303 against National League pitchers, the highest league average in history. In the American League, results were similar. From 1915 to 1917, the league average remained at a measly .248, rising to .254 in 1918 and .268 in 1919. In 1920, American League batters hit .283, then for the remainder of the decade stayed in the .280s and .290s. Between 1911 and 1920, only three men had hit .400, with Ty Cobb doing it twice. Between 1921 and 1930, seven men would achieve the same feat, with Rogers Hornsby doing it twice.

And batters were not fattening their averages only with singles. In 1919, major league hitters stroked 2,922 doubles, 1,048 triples, and 447 home runs. By 1921, those numbers had jumped to 3,981 doubles, 1,364 triples, and 937 home runs. In 1927, major leaguers hit 4,148 doubles, 1,150 triples, and 922 home runs. In 1927, despite Ruth's and Gehrig's output, National Leaguers actually hit more homers than American

Leaguers. There were 3,333 more runs batted in during 1927 than there had been in 1919. Between 1900 and 1920, forty-nine no-hitters were pitched in the major leagues. Between 1921 and 1940, that number dropped to seventeen.

But pitching was evolving every bit as much as hitting was. While some young hurlers, notably Carl Hubbell, would become stars based on breaking balls or trick pitches, many of the new crop—Lefty Grove, for example, of whom it was said "could blow a lamb chop past a wolf"— threw smoke.

As a result, with an astute eye for talent and some first-class salesman-ship, Graham, Putnam, and Strub turned the Seals into the most success-ful franchise in minor league history. The three became known as "The Vanderbilts of Valencia Street." Not only did the Seals make money and watch a parade of players go off to the majors, but the team won four PCL pennants in the decade.

So for all the oddballs, both between the lines and in the front office, the dilapidated ballpark, the Booze Cage, and the Gamblers' Section, the Seals were big business. And if Lefty thought his new contract was going to vault him instantly to the mound at the Old Rec, throwing fastballs past a string of former or future major league hitters, he was mistaken.

9.

CLASS D BASEBALL SEVEN DAYS A WEEK

"SO HERE I AM," SAID LEFTY, "THE SKINNIEST MAN ON THE CLUB AND I can't even hit my weight. On the mound, I knew only what I'd picked up from the bush league diamonds, which wasn't much. Charley Graham was one of the most wonderful men I've ever met in baseball. Like other club owners in the PCL, he made his living peddling ballplayers to the majors, but he always had my best interests at heart. The ink wasn't dry on my contract when Nick Williams said he wasn't going to slot a greenhorn into the pitching rotation. He wanted veterans on the mound, guys who would keep fans in the stands and players in the money."

Charley told Lefty that he needed to hone his craft, someplace where he "could learn something every time out," and he couldn't do that "riding the pine boards in San Francisco." Graham told the press that Lefty would be a sensation the following year, but for the 1928 season, the Seals were farming him out to the Salt Lake City Bees of the Utah-Idaho League, where he could gain professional experience. "Nick Williams also hopes he'll pick up some weight and stamina," Charley added.

The Utah-Idaho League consisted of six teams: Salt Lake, Pocatello, Ogden, Idaho Falls, Boise, and Twin Falls. Lefty's teammates would be teenagers like himself, sent to these outposts to learn fundamentals and the nuances of the game. The manager was another baseball lifer, Bob Coltrin. Only thirty-seven years old, Coltrin had retired as a player two years before, never making it past the very level in the low minors in which he was now managing after fifteen years of trying to break through. He would remain in the game, shuffling around the West as a low minors manager and scout, working virtually until the day he died in 1945. But anyone on the Bees who wanted to move up could do so only with Coltrin's approbation.

For his last weekend before leaving for Utah, the first time in his life he would be out of California, Lefty invited Jake Jorgensen, the Point Reyes first baseman, to join him in San Francisco. Lefty had been given temporary accommodation at the Hotel Royan, the Seals' lodging facility, across the street from Recreation Park. All Lefty could hope was that he would be back here on a more permanent basis.

After a day in town, Lefty and Jake drove back to Point Reyes to watch a Sunday doubleheader against Mill Valley, the team Lefty did not get to face in the spring of 1927. But Lefty was returning as a professional and he received a huge cheer from the crowd. Jake had arranged for dates for both of them and after the games the girls wanted something to eat. Unfortunately, Lefty and Jake were both broke. They even needed to borrow ten dollars for gas from friends just to get the girls home. A hungry date is not a happy date and the two glumly rode back to San Francisco. The next morning, Jake saw Lefty off and they agreed to see each other after the season. They got together sooner than they planned.

After Lefty's train left, Jorgensen returned to work. The construction crew he was working with was grounded because of heavy rains, so Jorgensen took a job driving a Caterpillar. "One morning, my sheepskin jacket got caught on a pulley and spun me around. My head hit the tractor three times and knocked me unconscious."

Jake Jorgensen lay in a coma for eleven days. When Lefty got word in Salt Lake, he left the team he had tried so hard for three years to join. "He came by bus," Jorgensen said, "and sat by my bedside at Ross Valley Hospital." Only when he was certain Jorgensen was out of the woods did Lefty return to the Bees. Lefty himself refused to discuss the incident but Jake Jorgensen never forgot the risk Lefty took and remained grateful for the rest of his life.

SALT LAKE CITY had been a Pacific Coast League club, also called the Bees until 1925. But the owners of the other PCL teams balked at the travel costs to Utah, so those Bees had moved to Hollywood and renamed themselves the Stars. The new Bees, after the Mormon symbol of industry and hard work, were a good deal further down the baseball ladder.

During Bob Coltrin's pep talk as they stepped off the train, Lefty learned pretty quickly that he had not entered paradise. "If we're gonna win games," Coltrin railed, "we gotta pull together. But we're on a shoe-string. No pitching coach or any other type coach. We don't even have a ballpark yet."

A ballpark was, in fact, under construction, invitingly named Community Field. Rocks still abounded in both the infield and outfield, so the players, with the aid of convicts sent over from the state prison, helped clear the area so that spring training could commence. Six weeks later, the season got under way, albeit in a ballpark where carpenters often outnumbered the players.

Bob Coltrin was undaunted by the lack of first-class accommodations. "This is pro ball!" he yelled, sending the players to batting and fielding practice, or having them run laps or wind sprints with tires around their bellies.

The players at least expected to have people watch them while they tiptoed around the rocks at Community Field, especially since admission was only fifty cents. In this too they were disappointed. To make matters worse, the empty seats necessitated a bit of cost cutting. "Faced with a turnstile count of minus zero, the directors of the club decided to carry only three pitchers. Believe me, whoever started had the other two pulling for him to go nine because today's relief pitcher was tomorrow's starter."

The team directors decided that of the three, only one would be a left-hander. The choice was between Lefty and his roommate, Thornton Lee. The one who didn't make the club would be shipped out to someplace even more primitive. The directors told the two left-handers that the decision would be made the next day when each of them pitched one end of a doubleheader. Lefty pitched a shutout in the first game. In the second, Lee lost 1–0 and was released.*

---

* After knocking around the minors for four more years, Lee was eventually called up by Cleveland and pitched fifteen years in the majors, mostly for the White Sox. His best year was 1941, when he went 22–11, with a 2.47 earned run average.

For all its inconveniences, the Utah-Idaho League was an effective incubator. "There were so many great ballplayers with me. Dolph Camilli, Ernie Lombardi, Woody Jensen, outfielder for the Pirates, New York Giants third baseman John Vergez, Ed Coleman of the Athletics . . . we all did time on the rock pile, traveling the day-coach, upper-berth circuit. A bunch of kids playing Class D baseball seven days a week and loving every minute of it." Every one of those players held on to his dream of making it to the majors, all the while "thinking the other guy's performance on the field was more skilled and polished than his own."

In theory, each player's salary was $125 per month but because so few fans were paying their way into the ballpark, the checks were generally two to three weeks late. And no paychecks often meant no food.

"One time we had a good series in Twin Falls. The Bees cleared $180. Coltrin took us all out to dinner and we ate up the profits. Then we went hungry for another week. I learned to pitch on an empty stomach."

By midseason, Lefty's weight had dropped to 120 pounds, too light even for him. "I was so skinny, I had to put the bat down and rest on my way from the dugout to the plate for batting practice."

Batting practice in Lefty's case would never make perfect. At a time when there was no designated hitter and starting pitchers were expected to be in long enough to get at least three turns at bat, he would go through his career a notoriously poor hitter on every level. A friend once said that Lefty had a sweet swing but almost never made contact. But since Bob Coltrin's job was to prepare players for higher levels, he kept trying. "Coltrin was the first of my managers to suffer the delusion that I could be a .400 hitter," Lefty noted.

The players all boarded at the Tuxedo Hotel on North State Street in downtown. "The Tuxedo was the fancy name. My teammates knew it as 'Mom's' . . . a rooming house upstairs over an undertaker's parlor."

Mom was Mom Edgeworth. "What a dear. Mom was a widow and a rabid fan." She was also an official of the Bees. "When she put up some of the money to run the ball club, she automatically became a director. If any fans razzed us during a game, she had them thrown out. Mom refunded their ticket money herself. When we forgot our spikes, she sent the shoes along on the next train."

Since most of the players were essentially kids, she ran her rooming house like a dormitory. "Mom rented 'baseball alleys' to the players, rooms off long corridors, dimly lit by bulbs hanging off high ceilings. We each paid Mom seventy-five cents a day, two to a room, for an iron bed, a wooden chair, and a view of the Wasatch Mountains. The guys on the second floor were in luck. Their alley ended with the Tuxedo's only bathroom.

"She saw every home game. Before the seventh-inning stretch, she phoned back to the Tuxedo to warn the other hotel guests to get their baths in. There were no showers at Community Field and only one tub at the Tuxedo. Mom told them, 'My boys will be in soon from the ballpark.' After the games, we walked back to the hotel in our wool flannels, soaked with sweat."

But Mom was no pushover. "You're here for one reason and one reason only," she told the boys. "To play baseball. You want to have fun after games? Go to the silent pictures, but be back in this hotel by ten o'clock." Lefty and his crew didn't own wristwatches, but it didn't matter. Salt Lake City had a 10:00 p.m. curfew, enforced by an earsplitting whistle that rang out from the Mormon Temple.

"We walked the eight blocks to and from the movie house. We couldn't scrape up two bits for bus fare and take in the picture on the same night. When we returned for curfew check-in, she kissed each of us hello on the cheek. God help you if she smelled bootleg beer on your breath."

Punishment for drinking was to be grounded for a week and to work in the funeral parlor downstairs. "We polished coffins. We scrubbed the linoleum in the embalming room. We rode in the hearse to pick up a corpse. 'Dead as a doornail,' Mom warned. 'All of 'em stiff from cirrhosis. Don't you dare. Not my boys.' "

Mom Edgeworth dealt with other issues common to teenagers. "Our rooms were a mess. Mounds of muddy uniforms peeled off and dropped on the floor, smelly socks draped over windowsills, jockstraps hanging off glass doorknobs. The stench of perspiration in the cramped little rooms nearly bowled us over. But clean up the mess? Nah. We were professional ballplayers. It might destroy our image. My roommate slept the season out with a clothespin on his nose."*

Meals were taken not at the Tuxedo but at the State Street Café up the street. "It was owned by a wiry fellow with an engaging, toothy smile named Alex Pistolas, another director of the ball club. Our first time away in organized ball and we're surrounded by directors! We couldn't sneeze without everyone knowing it." The players bought a coupon book for $3.75 with a $5 credit line for meals at the café. On the rare occasions when they were paid on time, they bought two books and ate well for a week. But Mom had first dibs, so when the pay was late, sometimes by three or four weeks, they had to pay off rent and eating became something of a luxury. "Let's face it," Lefty said. "We were starving."

But the Bees players had gone to Salt Lake not to live well but to learn to play well—and for that, the accommodations were perfect. "At Point Reyes, I never worried about *how* to pitch to a hitter. *How* to strike him out. I just reared back and fired. The players in the Utah-Idaho League were too savvy for that. They pasted my ball up against the fences. In a game against Ogden, Ernie Lombardi hit me so hard, the ball was still going when the game was over. 'How in hell could he hit me so hard?' I muttered, and threw my glove down on the mound.

"Bob Coltrin was the first one to teach me how to throw my mind into gear before I threw a pitch. He yelled out from the dugout, 'Hey, Gomez. You're not pitching semipro. Put that glove back on and get back in there.' On the train ride back, he slipped into the seat next to me. 'You gotta get the book on the hitters,' he said.

" 'Huh,' I said. 'Where do I buy that?'

" 'Are you kiddin' me, or what? You don't buy the book. You write it in here.' He tapped my forehead with his index finger."

---

* Mom didn't forget the boys once they moved up. "She wrote letters to us all the time," Lefty said. "She came to New York to see me pitch in a World Series. She traveled to Shibe Park, Ebbets Field, Comiskey Park, Wrigley Field. Wherever my Salt Lake teammates played major league ball, Mom was in the stands, cheering them on. We were always her sons." For years afterward, Bees alumni checked with one another to see how Mom was doing and when any of them went out west, they stopped to see her. "Anyone who drove through Salt Lake without stopping to say hi to Mom got grief from the others."

Coltrin told Lefty that every time he pitched to a hitter, he had to remember every trait and quirk about every batter he would ever face. "Does he like them high? Low? Does he look for a curve? A fastball? Does he take the first pitch? And you can't go by what somebody else says . . . how the guy hits Biff Jones or Pete Smith . . . you gotta know how the guy hits Gomez and where he hits Gomez and . . ."

Lefty was staring at Coltrin wide-eyed. Coltrin sighed, leaned back in his seat, and closed his eyes. Lefty almost let it go at that, but he wanted to know what the manager had left unsaid.

"Gomez, you ain't gonna strike Lombardi out with the lucky charms you got dangling out of your back pocket. A guy goin' to the mound relies on his arm and his noodle . . . *or he's a dead pigeon.*"

Lefty found that the more he learned about pitching, the less he felt he knew. He struck out a lot of hitters, but a lot connected. He lost more games than he won. And, with his high-kick delivery, he couldn't hold runners on base. "By the end of the season, players were sending me thank-you notes for their career-high stolen base records."

By the end of the year, Lefty had led the league in strikeouts with 172, but his record was only 12–14, albeit with a respectable earned run average of 3.48.

"Charley Graham came to Salt Lake at the end of August. I thought he was in town to hand me my unconditional release. I had a lousy record and any ballplayer knows it's the wins that count. Graham had signed many a ballplayer in his day and knew why I was shaking like a leaf. 'Gomez,' he said, 'I need winning ball. Coltrin said you've got ice in your gut. That no pitcher in the league is cooler under fire. Next spring, report to the Seals.'"

10

BIRDLEGS AND WALTER THE GREAT

————

WHEN LEFTY REPORTED FOR THE 1929 SEASON, SAN FRANCISCO HAD become the home of two Pacific Coast League franchises, the Seals and the Mission Reds. Until 1925, the latter had been the Vernon Tigers, but Vernon, in northwest Los Angeles County, couldn't support a franchise so the following season a San Francisco banker named Herbert Fleishhacker bought the franchise for $300,000, moved it up the coast, and renamed it the Mission Bells. Two years later he changed the name to the Reds but everyone referred to them as the "Missions." Under any name, the team hadn't finished higher than third. The Seals on the other hand were perennial powers, winners of the 1928 PCL pennant, their third in five years.

But 1929 promised to be different. "The Seals," Jack McDonald reported, "were ripe for picking. The owners had sold star outfielders Earl Averill and Roy Johnson to the majors. The only thing preventing them from disposing of their entire outfield was economics. Nick Williams told the right fielder, hard-hitting Smead Jolley, they had to keep him for another year because he was their only drawing card. The Missions promised to be tough. Their pitchers included Bert Cole, a native San Franciscan who had spent six years with Detroit, and Dutch Ruether, who had moved from the Seals in a contract squabble. The Missions had a solid lineup of hitters."

Both teams used Recreation Park. With its two-hundred-game season, Pacific Coast League teams played six-day series on the road, stopping up and down the coast from Los Angeles to Portland and Seattle. Monday was a traveling day. When the Seals left town Sunday on the midnight train, another coast team came in to start a weeklong series with the Missions. When the Seals came home, the Missions left town—except when they played each other, of course.

Old Rec held about 16,000 and was generally full on weekends. During the week, when most fans were working, the games drew smaller crowds but Seals' management opened the gates during the seventh inning and men getting off work charged through to watch the last two innings.

"Coming out of Salt Lake," Lefty recounted, "I couldn't believe the luxury of the hotel accommodations of PCL ball. I went from my home in Rodeo with a commode on the back porch to Salt Lake with a communal bath for the entire team to a hotel room with a private bath. What a big deal. I didn't have to get completely dressed to walk down the hall."

At Old Rec, the facilities were less agreeable. Each team had a separate section in the dilapidated wooden cottage with a peaked roof in center field that passed as a clubhouse. The Seals used the upstairs, the Missions the downstairs, with only two showers for each. Gus Suhr, the Seals' first baseman, noted, "If you weren't one of the first two guys in, you got cold water."

Medical services were equally primitive. Leroy "Doc" Hughes, who began with the Seals maintaining the scoreboard and then became the team trainer, recalled, "There were a lot of injuries on the field but I didn't have much money for supplies. The ballplayers from the old days played hard and they played hurt. They had to. A doctor at every ball game? Ha. We had to phone out to a doctor at his office. 'Come quickly! A guy's hurt bad.' Whatever ailed the player, he got back quick in the lineup or else he lost his spot. With modern surgery, the careers of the old ballplayers could have been prolonged and the record books would be very different. I saw firsthand how pitchers suffered. Their days were filled with agonizing pain and frustration because the doctors didn't know how to help them."

Uniforms—heavy flannel with a full, bloomer-type leg—were an issue as well. Players were issued one home uniform and one for the road and wore them for an entire home stand or road trip before they were cleaned. "They got so heavy with sweat and dirt," Lefty said, "they'd drag you down." Uniforms came only in small, medium, and large, so for Lefty, the pants were so big in the waist that he had to hitch them up after every pitch. Fans thought pants-hitching was an eccentricity, part of his reper-toire, but the gesture was purely functional.

The field at Old Rec was as eccentric as the players. Although the dimensions—left field 311 feet from home plate, center 325, right a pop-up-length 235—would certainly have classed it as a hitter's park, wind was an equalizer. A gale blew in almost constantly from left and cen-ter, and a fifty-foot-high wire fence extended from center to the right-field foul line. Smead Jolley, a line drive hitter, swore the fence cost him thirty home runs a season.

Balls sometimes hit soft spots in the outfield and stuck, or ricocheted off the hard spots in the corners. Jolley could often field a line drive off the right-field screen, wheel, and throw the batter out at first. The grounds-keeper for the park was a goat, employed by team management to keep the grass short. How the goat got along with Ping Bodie's pigs is unknown.

And there was more to the menagerie. "The team even had a mascot," Lefty said. "A real live seal. Smead Jolley fed him fresh fish from a wooden bucket near the foul lines. The seal clapped his fins and balanced a red rubber ball on his nose whenever a Seal hit a home run. He went hungry when I went to bat."

With two teams, one of which was always at home, San Franciscans became even more fanatical about the game. Paddy Cottrell was one of a number of local kids who used the crowds at Old Rec to put some change in their pockets.

"On my way to school at St. Peter's, I sold newspapers for two cents each on the corner of Sixteenth and Guerras. I only sold eight or nine a day and was told that I'd sell a lot more if I went to Recreation Park. I could slip in during the seventh-inning stretch when they opened the gates. Not many people owned radios then and the fans at the games would want to read the personal-interest stories about the players in the afternoon edition that they tucked under their arm as they left the park. Some days there'd be extra innings and I'd sell maybe twenty-five, thirty papers."

Paddy eventually worked his way into a job inside the park. "I used to give the batboy for the Missions a free paper and once in a while he'd give me a new baseball. One day he said, 'Paddy, I want to sell hot dogs when the Seals and Missions play their doubleheader on Sunday. The other batboy had to be let go because he was caught stealing money out of the players' pockets. If I'm going to sell hot dogs, I need someone to take my place as batboy.' I jumped at the chance." From there, Cottrell spent more than a half century in the game, which included stints as a major league scout and head baseball coach at Santa Clara University.

ALTHOUGH LEFTY WAS NOW officially a member of the team, Nick Williams still refused to believe that this human cornstalk could be a starter.

During the 1929 exhibition season, the Pittsburgh Pirates, who trained at Paso Robles, were barnstorming through California. The Pirates' lineup was loaded, led by three future Hall of Famers: Pie Traynor and the Waner brothers, Paul and Lloyd. One Sunday, the Pirates played an exhibition against the local team. The Seals' starting pitcher got bombed, allowing a bucketload of runs in the first inning while retiring only one batter. Lefty was all over Nick Williams even before the manager had left the bench to yank the starter. "Let me go in there. I can stop this club." Williams said later that Lefty practically walked out to the mound and grabbed the ball out of the other pitcher's glove. Nick wasn't averse to the idea. The Pirates had already put the game pretty much out of reach, the bases were still loaded, and here was a chance to see what this kid who had been badgering him since he was fourteen could do under pressure.

"Okay, go ahead," Williams said. "Show me."

The Seals lost the game, but the Pirates got no more runs. For eight and two-thirds innings, Lefty pitched a two-hitter.

He started the season out of the rotation but he was never far from Williams's ear. Lefty made it a point to sit near the manager whenever a starting pitcher was running into trouble. Then he'd say, "Lemme in there. I'll stop those bums." Sometimes Williams would look down the bench before the game and say, "Who's got the guts to challenge the enemy?" Lefty was always the first to yell back, "I'll challenge 'em."

Finally, in early May, acutely aware that Gomez would never leave him in peace, Williams let him start a game. Lefty promptly tossed a five-hitter. The next time Williams gave him the ball, Lefty won again. Lefty kept winning, and the West Coast press began to make quite a bit of it. Between Lefty's streak and a three-way fight for the PCL pennant between the Seals, Missions, and Hollywood Stars, fans followed the fortunes of the players breathlessly.

Of course, not every breed of fan was breathless for the same reason.

Each Thursday when they were at home, the Seals held a Ladies' Day promotion at Old Rec. And to make sure the ladies actually showed up, the Thursday starting pitcher was generally Walter "Duster" Mails, a local boy born outside the walls of San Quentin who had gone east to pitch for the Dodgers and Cleveland, eventually returning to become one of the team's top pitchers. Mails was a strapping, square-hewn Adonis who had acquired his nickname by throwing fastballs under batters' chins. Occasionally Mails got dusted back. Once during the season, Mails had aimed one directly at Missions second baseman Neal Finn's ear. Finn, only about 160 pounds, hit the deck, then bounced up and calmly completed his turn at bat, apparently having accepted the knockdown. When the inning ended, Finn trotted out to his position. Mails, striding off the mound, shouted at him, "And you're gonna get the same thing the next time and I won't miss." Finn stopped short and casually turned around. "I'm sorry, Walter," he said matter-of-factly, "what was that you said?"

"You heard me," said Mails. "I'm gonna stick it in your ear."

"That's what I thought you said," replied Finn politely, and busted Duster right on his square jaw, planting him in the infield. Finn then leisurely trotted off to take his position.

The incident did little to dissuade the Thursday afternoon ladies. After all, Duster had always claimed, publicly at least, that he was "a lover and not a fighter." To further this image, Mails had chosen to refer to himself not as Duster but as "Walter the Great," and boasted regularly of how glorious he looked in his baseball uniform.

As Paddy Cottrell put it, "Walter sure packed in the fluttering-heart crowd on Thursdays. He'd strut out to the mound on those long, trim legs of his and tip his hat to the ladies. The ladies, in turn, would wave their lace handkerchiefs and chant, 'Walter! Oh, Walter!' Overcome with such adulation, Mails would turn completely around on the mound so all those feminine eyes could behold the charm of his physique. I was only seventeen but I could see why the other players envied his charisma. There were some good-lookin' chicks in those stands. Gosh. Walter was even going out with my English teacher at St. Peter's."

Distractions aside, by early July there was a pennant race on. The top three PCL teams were separated in the standings by only two games and Vernon Gomez, not Walter the Great, was now the Seals' best pitcher. So that Thursday, on Ladies' Day, Nick Williams left Duster on the bench and put Lefty on the mound.

"At first there was total silence in the stands," Paddy Cottrell reported. "The ladies stared in disbelief. 'God sakes, what's that?' they asked themselves. 'That lead pencil takin' the hill? That thing out there with long spindly legs and no hips who kept hitchin' his pants up between pitches?'

"The women didn't care a fig about the pennant and Gomez's fastball whizzin' by the batters. They wanted their big, strapping Walter with the sweat of the big leagues clinging to his flannels. Hadn't they paid $1.25 a head to see the Great One pitch? A wail of protest washed over Recreation Park. 'Birdlegs!' they screamed. 'Take him out!'

" 'Birdlegs.' That's what the ladies called him. From then on he was known as Birdlegs up and down the California coast, and boy, the opposition rode him with that one. Gomez got so burnt up he wore two pairs of stirrup socks to make his ankles look fatter. No such luck. The ladies still screamed 'Birdlegs!' Come every Thursday, they were out there to see the wind blow Gomez away. But Gomez blew the hitters away."

Walter the Great was not forgotten, however. After he retired, the Seals' owners, never ones to miss a trick, hired Mails to be the team's official greeter.

OFF THE FIELD, Lefty began to get a taste of city life. After games, more often than not he would drop by Kenneally's, sax slung over his shoulder. Before Prohibition, Kenneally's had been a tavern; after, it became a smoke shop and pool hall. When the Seals played a weeklong series in Seattle or Portland, the results came over the telegraph wires too late for the afternoon editions of the *Chronicle, Call-Bulletin,* or *Examiner.* Neal Kenneally set up a chalkboard inside his establishment, posting scores and winning and losing pitchers. Fans eager to get the details of the day's game jumped off the trolley on their way home from work and dropped by to check. Kenneally's was also a players' hangout, home and visitor alike, so fans and players mixed with a casualness that would be unthinkable in later generations. Lefty generally stayed for a while, chatting with whoever happened to be there, then left to play a gig at a vaudeville theater or with a speakeasy band downtown.

By early August, Lefty was working on a winning streak of ten straight and was being touted as the best southpaw in the loop. On August 5, he was scheduled to pitch against the Missions and Dutch Ruether, who, with some justification, thought of *himself* as the best southpaw in the loop. Ruether felt no personal animosity toward Lefty. Before he left the Seals, Dutch had even taken his fellow left-hander aside and showed him some tricks of the trade. But that didn't mean he didn't want to beat the pants off the kid.

Red Killefer, manager of the Missions, was so certain Ruether was the better pitcher that he had held him out of his scheduled start just so he could face Gomez. Twelve thousand customers jammed into Old Rec, one of the largest weekday crowds in the park's history. In the crowd were nine major league scouts, all to watch the pitchers duel it out.

The grandstand contained two other notables. Lizzie and Coyote Gomez had taken the ferry from Rodeo, the first time they had ever seen their son pitch. Milfred, who had done so much to get Lefty there, had insisted they watch Vernon in the most important game of his life.

Lefty was famously cool before a game but Nick Williams was a bundle of nerves. He kept giving advice to his young pitcher, not all of which turned out to be helpful. Jack McDonald was in the dugout. "Just before he went into the game, Nick cautioned Lefty to take his time. Lefty tried so hard to take his time with Missions on base in the first inning that he committed two glaring balks, one of which fortunately escaped the umpire's eye.

"Meanwhile, Ruether was the Dutch Master of old for the first four innings. He toyed with his former Seal teammates. He slow-balled Jolley, cross-fired Suhr, and change-of-paced Caveney, creating a lot of frustration in the Seals ranks. But in the fifth, something snapped in Ruether. He walked Bob Reed on four straight balls. Then he walked Crosetti on four straight. That was the tip-off that the bloom was off the flower for Dutch. He himself would tell you that control was 90 percent of his pitching success."

In the end, Lefty beat Ruether, pitching a six-hitter to run his streak to eleven straight. The scouts made a beeline for Charley Graham. Cy Slapnicka got there first and secured a ten-day option for the Cleveland Indians to purchase Lefty's contract for $50,000 and three players. But it turned out that Lefty's weight was not the only physical attribute that would work against his getting to the majors. As San Francisco *Examiner* sportswriter Abe Kemp recounted, "I'm sitting up in the tower talking to Charley Graham. Slapnicka . . . he's the guy who later signed Bob Feller . . . comes in and he says, 'Charley, is it all right if I go down to the clubhouse where the players are dressing?' Charley said, 'Sure.' After Slapnicka left, Graham says to me, 'What the hell do you suppose he wants to go in the clubhouse for?' I told Charley I had no idea. About a half hour later Slapnicka comes back and says, 'Charley, I'm going to forfeit my option on Gomez.'

"Graham asks him why he would change his mind from the time he left here to the time he came back. 'Well,' Slapnicka says, 'I'll tell you, Charley. I just saw Gomez undressed in the clubhouse and anybody who's got as big a prick as he's got can't pitch winning ball in the major leagues.' Slapnicka ducks out and I start to laugh like hell. Graham says, 'What do you find so amusing?'

"I said, 'This is the best goddamned story of my life and I can't write a word of it.'"*

For others interested in Lefty, it was back to the stamina bugaboo.

Bill Essick was the chief scout for the New York Yankees. He had played and managed in the Pacific Coast League as "Vinegar Bill." As

---

* Lefty never knew about Cy Slapnicka's option until he read about it in 1973 in Chicago sportswriter Jerry Holtzman's book *No Cheering in the Press Box.* "I had to laugh," he said. "Abe Kemp only tells the story when I'm sixty-three years old. But Abe won't write about it when I'm twenty and it would have made a big difference on my road trips."

soon as Slapnicka passed, Essick—"one of the ivory hunters," as Jack Mc-Donald described him—stepped into the breach. He talked with the Seals' owners in private, then left town without speaking with anyone else.

Being bypassed by Cleveland would turn out to be an enormous stroke of good luck for both Lefty and the Yankees.

II.

A DEATH IN NEW YORK

TWO EVENTS CHANGED BASEBALL FOREVER AND HELPED TURN THE YANKEES into a juggernaut. One occurred in 1919 and the other in 1920 and each involved a vile-tempered, widely detested pitcher named Carl Mays.

Going into the 1919 season, Mays, who sported a wicked submarine delivery, was considered the best pitcher on the Boston Red Sox. He had won 22 games in 1917 and 23 in 1918, including two victories in a 4-games-to-2 World's Series triumph over the Cubs. The winning pitcher in the other Red Sox victories was a brilliant young hurler named Babe Ruth, who was by then also the club's top slugger.

But almost from opening day Mays seemed snake-bit. Although he pitched well, sometimes brilliantly, his teammates refused to hit for him. Even the mighty Ruth appeared to save his off days for when Mays pitched, which Mays chalked up to their competition for the role of number-one starter on the pitching staff. Almost two months into the season Mays had a losing record, although his earned run average was a gaudy 2.50.

Mays was also known to throw at batters' heads. On Memorial Day he extended that practice to the heads of opposing fans. In Philadelphia, an Athletics rooter named Byron Hayes unleashed a steady flow of invective at the fulminous hurler from the third row of Shibe Park. Mays suddenly whirled and, showing the pinpoint control for which was he was famed, whistled a pitch that caught Hayes high on the forehead, breaking his skimmer and raising an egg-sized lump on his head. After the game, Hayes swore out a warrant for Mays's arrest but the Red Sox had left town before it could be served.* On their next trip back, July 1, constables were waiting at the train station. Red Sox manager Ed Barrow was tipped off and kept Mays on the train. Barrow then hustled his pitcher onto another train and back to Boston.

American League president Ban Johnson announced that Mays would be fined $100 for the incident and suspended him until the fine was paid. Mays categorically refused to pay up and turned his wrath to the team that he had decided was sabotaging his season. After some unpleasant comments about the Red Sox, Mays asserted he would not "stand for the withholding of his salary," then announced to sportswriters that he planned to go fishing.

Barrow was livid; he had risked a confrontation with the Philadelphia police to smuggle Mays out of town just days before. Moreover, he insisted that only because of his pleas to Ban Johnson was the punishment not more severe. Not only would Mays pay the fine, Barrow insisted, but his salary would indeed be withheld until his suspension was lifted. Barrow added that Mays could go fishing or anywhere else as far as he was concerned. Red Sox owner Harry Frazee announced that he supported his manager entirely.

Mays was eventually coaxed back to the team, though conflicting accounts exist as to who ponied up the $100. On July 14, Mays pitched and gave up four runs in the first inning to the White Sox. In the second inning he was hit in the back of the head with a ball launched by his own catcher, who later claimed he was trying to throw out a runner at second base. After the inning Mays stormed out of the dugout and disappeared. Two days later he surfaced in Boston and declared that he would never again throw a pitch for the Red Sox. Then he actually did go fishing.

Harry Frazee was in a bind. He had a star pitcher on strike and a season fast going down the drain. On top of that, his finances were tenuous, as always. Theater, not baseball, was his first love and he was always pulling money away from the club to back Broadway shows. So Frazee began to entertain offers to sell Mays. Charles Comiskey of the league-leading White Sox offered $25,000, then raised it to $30,000. But the new, ag-

---

* The team did buy Hayes a new hat.

gressive owners of the heretofore wretched New York Yankees, Jacob Ruppert and T. L. Huston—each of whom called himself "Colonel" although only Huston was—bid $40,000 and threw in two pitchers. On July 31, Frazee made the deal. Ban Johnson, who had little use for Frazee, Ruppert, or Huston, suspended Mays indefinitely for leaving the Red Sox without permission.

Ruppert and Huston insisted that the suspension was simply a ploy to muscle Mays to the destination of Johnson's choice. "He had two weeks to suspend him. Why wait until we got him?" Ruppert asked. The Yankees went to court. After some wrangling, not only did the court uphold the deal but Johnson was required personally to bear the legal fees.* Mays was allowed to pitch for the Yankees and went 9–3 for the remainder of the season, establishing the team as a coming power in the American League.†

Ban Johnson tried to redeem his authority by prohibiting Frazee from doing business with anyone but the traitorous Yankees and White Sox. Frazee didn't care. The Yankees and White Sox were the league's richest teams. So after the 1919 season, still in need of funds to finance his other endeavors, Frazee offered for sale baseball's best young player, an act unthinkable just one year before. Charlie Comiskey, fresh off a World's Series defeat to the unlikely Cincinnati Reds, offered $60,000 and Shoeless Joe Jackson, who had been a disappointment in the Series. The Yankees offered $100,000 straight cash. Frazee took the money—a wise choice since Jackson would soon be banned from baseball for life—and Babe Ruth moved to the New York Yankees where he rejoined his old teammate Carl Mays. The Yankees then lured Ed Barrow from the Red Sox and appointed him general manager. Although Babe would be credited for the coming surge of Yankee fortunes, Ed Barrow, a genius at spotting talent, was the real architect of the team's rise.

The 1920 season began well for both Mays and the Yankees. By August, the team was contending for the pennant and Mays was on his way

---

* Robert F. Wagner, the future senator from New York and father of a future New York City mayor, presided.

† It seemed like a good deal for Mays as well. Had he been sold to the White Sox in midseason, there is every reason to believe he would have eagerly joined the conspiracy to fix the 1919 World's Series.

to a 26–11 record. On August 16, Mays was facing the Cleveland Indians at the Polo Grounds on an overcast day. In the fifth inning, Indians shortstop Ray Chapman was at the plate, standing close as was his style. Chapman was as popular as Mays was not, excellent in all phases of the game and the backbone of his team. Mays unleashed a fastball, high and tight. Chapman never saw it, never moved. The ball struck him in the temple with such a resounding crack that Mays fielded the ball as it rolled toward third and threw to first, thinking it had hit the bat. Chapman lay still for a few moments, then got up with the help of his teammates. "Tell Mays I'm all right," he mumbled. But Chapman's legs gave out from under him as he walked toward the clubhouse. He was helped from the field and taken to St. Lawrence Hospital. By morning he was dead.

Mays claimed to be devastated but the rumor that he had thrown intentionally at Chapman's head was so rife that players throughout the league briefly threatened a boycott if Mays was not banned from the game. Ban Johnson predicted Mays would never pitch again. But Mays was back on the mound eight days later and threw a shutout against the Tigers. The following year, when veteran players refused to have anything to do with him, Mays counseled young pitchers to throw up and in if that's what it took to win a game. "He says this after killing a man!" fellow Yankee pitcher Bob Shawkey said later. "He was a stinker. That's what he was. A stinker."*

In the wake of Chapman's death, major league baseball made two important rule changes. The first was to ban the spitball, which caused the ball to behave erratically. Seventeen pitchers who were then making their living with the pitch were grandfathered. The second was to require that baseball be played with a white ball. Of course baseballs always started out white but up until then they had ceased being so the instant they were put into play. They were smeared with mud, licorice, tobacco juice, or even tar. Balls were scuffed, sanded, pounded out of shape, even punctured. Baseballs were expensive, so one ball was often used for an entire game; club employees were placed in the stands to ensure that any ball

---

* This particular story was related by Lawrence S. Ritter in *The Glory of Their Times,* but Shawkey often referred to Mays as "a stinker" in other contexts.

caught by a fan would be returned. By the middle of the game, the ball was a brown, misshapen mess, hard to see and even more difficult to hit with power. Most of the legendary hitters of the day, most notably Ty Cobb, therefore choked up on the bat and hit with a short, quick swing, waiting as long as possible in order to maximize the chance of making solid contact. That Babe Ruth could hit the ball so solidly with his long, powerful, fully committed cut was considered remarkable.

With erratic movement so easy to achieve, it was unnecessary for pitchers to throw with velocity. With the exception of Walter Johnson, none of the greats before 1920 were noted for speed. Christy Mathewson, Cy Young, Eddie Plank, Grover Cleveland Alexander, Three Finger Brown, and the others relied on guile, trick pitches, and foreign substances to get batters out. After 1920, however, a clearly visible ball would approach the plate on each pitch, its movement restricted to whatever a pitcher could produce with arm action.* As it became increasingly difficult to thwart batters' reflexes with sudden drops or dances, the obvious solution was to get the ball to the plate quicker. A powerful, moving fastball thus became more important than ever and youngsters such as Vernon Gomez who could deliver the pitch with movement and control became valued commodities.

In 1921, the year after the Black Sox scandal broke, New York finished first in the American League, the first of three consecutive titles and one of six the team would win in the decade. They were led at bat by the Babe, who batted .378 while hitting an incredible 59 home runs and driving in 171 runs. Add to that his 145 walks and Ruth was on base, or around the bases, more than half of his appearances at the plate. On the mound, the team was led by Carl Mays, who won 27 games. Their only blemish was a 5–3 defeat in the World's Series to John McGraw's Giants, in which Mays, after winning the first game, seemed to pitch just well enough to lose in his next two starts.

The 1921 World's Series was first to be played entirely in the same stadium, the Polo Grounds, the home park of both teams. After the series

---

* Pitchers would still load them up, of course, but with nowhere near the effectiveness as in previous decades. Lefty's rejoinder when someone complained to the umpire about him was: "Tell him to hit it on the dry side."

was done, the competition between the two franchises and the animosity of their respective owners made continuation of the arrangement untenable, although they would repeat both the Series and the result the following year. The two colonels decided to build their own facility just across the Harlem River in the Bronx—the two venues would be in sight of each other—and call it, of course, Yankee Stadium. To accommodate the Babe and fans who flocked to see him launch his prodigious blasts, straightaway right field was only 350 feet from home plate and the right-field foul pole only 295. To gild the colonels' lily, the Yankees won their first world championship that year, a 4–2 Series victory over the Giants. The three games at Yankee Stadium averaged 60,000 fans.*

With its new three-tiered ballpark and luminescent slugger—soon joined by the equally potent Lou Gehrig—the Yankees vaulted over every other franchise. The rest of baseball would chase them not only throughout the 1920s but for much of the next eighty years as well. By the time Lefty was plucked off the Seals' roster the Yankees had become baseball's most glamorous team, representing America's most glamorous city, and played in the nation's most glamorous ballpark.

"In the clubhouse," Lefty recounted, "Nick Williams pulled me aside and said, 'Charley Graham wants to see you.' When Charley told me the Seals had sold my contract to the Yankees my first thought was, 'I am so lucky!' My parents were at Old Rec that day. From sandlot to pro ball, it was the only Coast League game Ma and Pa saw me pitch and so they witnessed my lucky break.

"You know, the kids I played with in high-school, semipro, and minor league ball were talented. Good all-around ballplayers. When I or somebody else got to the majors, they were happy you made it. They may have wished it for themselves but we all knew it wasn't just talent and determination. A player had to have luck. That's why keeping fame in perspective

---

* Carl Mays did not hang around with the team long enough to appreciate the facility's charms, however. Mays's erratic performance, especially during the World's Series, had left a number of club officials, Ed Barrow and manager Miller Huggins in particular, with the distinct impression that the bad outings were not coincidence. Although no one ever uncovered proof that Mays had profited from his defeats, he was benched early in 1923 and shipped out to Cincinnati the following year. There Mays seemed once again to miraculously recover his form, finishing 20–9 in 1924.

is very easy for me. I always figured I was lucky. Of course I had talent, but God was good to me. I was a New York Yankee."

Lefty's impending trip to the majors garnered him some immediate perks. As a rookie, he had been an object of disdain to veterans no matter what his record and was denied some basic privileges. "In our clubhouse, I was given a single nail near the showers to hang up my clothes. The day I was sold to the Yankees, Nick Williams got news of the deal and my locker-room privileges were instantly doubled. Nick called out to trainer Denny Carroll, 'Drive another nail in for the kid!' "

The next day the story of Lefty's acquisition by the Yankees broke and Jack McDonald, only three years on the beat, had it. "The sale of a local player to a club like the New York Yankees was big news in San Francisco and scoops were the vogue. My rival Tom Laird and I were sitting on the bench while the players were taking batting practice. Laird was a veteran newspaperman with the *News*. I was little more than a cub reporter for the *Call*. Along about noon, Nick Williams called me over. 'Jack,' he said, 'the Yankees just bought Lefty Gomez. I was there in the tower offices when Bill Essick made the deal. Nobody knows it. The story is yours.'

"In those days there was no Guild. The newspaper could hire you one day, fire you the next. Nick was trying to help me out. So I filed the story with the *Call* and returned to the game. Laird and I were sitting together in the grandstand. I'm a rookie and I'm sweating bullets—gearing myself up for the inevitable fistfight. I knew a story that big wouldn't be buried in the sports pages. When they let the newsboys into the ballpark to sell the afternoon editions to the fans, Laird glanced at the papers. There on page one in big black type was the *Call* headline, 'Yanks Buy Gomez.' Laird was outraged. A rookie had scooped him. He jumped up, screaming obscenities at me. A second later Laird scored a knockdown, driving his fist into my jaw. But I didn't care. I had my scoop."

Essick had paid the Seals $35,000 for Lefty's contract. Ordinarily, a pitcher of Lefty's potential would have commanded a higher price but—although Lefty had ballooned up to 147 pounds—the Yankees remained incredulous that he could hold up under the rigors of a major league season. Essick had agreed to let Lefty finish out the season with the Seals and report to the Yankees the following spring. He ended with twenty-one complete games and an 18–11 record, impressive for a kid playing his first year of big-time ball.

The Seals' owners had an even better year. In addition to the $35,000 for Lefty, they collected $75,000 for Frank Crosetti; Smead Jolley finally got his chance, going to the White Sox for $65,000; Gus Suhr, who had hit .381 with 51 homers and 299 hits, fetched $45,000 from Pittsburgh; and Sloppy Thurston went to Brooklyn for another $45,000. Graham, Putnam, and Dr. Strub were going to need the money. Old Rec was doomed, heading into its last year. In 1931, a new ballpark, Seals Stadium, would open. It would be the first steel-and-concrete stadium built for a minor league team and would be home to the Seals for the remainder of their existence.

Lefty's trip to the majors after only one season in the high minors was exceptional for that era. Spots on the sixteen big league clubs were at a premium. Young players could spend as many as six or seven years in the minors honing their talents before they got a call from a major league club.

Although he was months away from his twenty-first birthday, Lefty was widely reported as being just nineteen. Frank Crosetti explained why. "When we both were playing for the San Francisco Seals, Nick Williams told him, 'From now on you are so-and-so age,' and he cut two years off Lefty's right age for his sale to the Yankees. It was done all the time." Lefty himself added, "You did what the manager told you to do. He had no way of knowing how long it would take you to stick in the major leagues and they weren't going to buy an old ballplayer."

The move to New York meant putting thousands of miles between Lefty and his family. There would be no visiting on weekends as had been the case with Point Reyes. "When I broke the news to Ma and Pa that I was a New York Yankee and going east, they were happy for me because I was happy but they thought they'd never see me again. I remember my mother saying that my feet would be the first to touch eastern soil since her mother, Mary Jane Williams, left Missouri in 1857 as a young girl in a prairie wagon, her family hell-bent on striking it rich in the California hills. A six-month journey of sweat and tears over the Oregon Trail and the Rockies. 'Yes, Ma, and now I'm chasing my dream in New York and I can hop aboard a train.'"

12

HOLLYWOOD, GOAT'S MILK, AND SPINACH

———

BUT THE TRAIN HAD TO BE PAID FOR AND BILL ESSICK HAD NEGLECTED to provide a ticket for his new young pitcher to get across country. When the Seals' season ended, so had Lefty's paycheck and he was, as usual, broke. A one-way coach ticket to Chicago and then on to New York with a transfer at Grand Central to the Orange Blossom Special for St. Petersburg cost $120. Lefty figured $2 a day for meals for the five-and-a-half-day trip, meaning he was already $132 in the hole as a major leaguer.

Ordinarily Lefty played winter ball, but the Florida trip left that out of the question. There was no way he could save $132 in three months pitching on the circuit—meals and hotels would eat up everything he earned. Nor would he go to his family. Asking his parents or siblings to front such a sum was unthinkable.

With only months to come up with the dough, Lefty cast about for a job. The solution to his problem came from an unlikely source—the Old Rec swineherd, Ping Bodie. "I buttonholed Ping, who was an electrician in the off-season, and asked him where I could get a job." Ping told Lefty to come along with him to Los Angeles, where he was going to spend the winter as he usually did, working at Universal Studios.

"I was Bodie's 'assistant.' I carried the ladder onto the movie sets, changed lightbulbs, and gawked at the starlets. Punch in, punch out, 8:00 a.m. to noon, $2 a day. Then we went out and played winter-league baseball on Sundays for the Hollywood Hills club, which was backed by Universal. They paid $5 a game. So I got to play baseball with a job attached to it, a way of making money and staying in condition. I worked three months at Universal and saved the $132 for the train fare back east."

While Lefty was working on the set, Universal was filming *King of Jazz*, starring the very same Paul Whiteman who had led the navy band through Rodeo in 1917, and Whiteman's new crooner, Bing Crosby. *King of Jazz* was the second all-talking picture, after *The Jazz Singer*, and contained the first Technicolor animation sequence ever filmed, created by famed cartoonist Walter Lantz, later to be best known for Woody Woodpecker. It was also the first Technicolor film to win an Oscar—for art direction—although it was filmed only in red and green. For all that, *King of Jazz* was a enormous flop in the theaters.

"So all these great musicians were on the movie set and I engaged them in conversation, but no way did I hobnob with Crosby, Whiteman, or the band members off the studio lot. They were making big bucks and played golf on the links of the swanky Lakeside Country Club. But since the studio backed the Hollywood Hills ball club, there was talk on the set about me pitching, and Bing, Paul, and jazz violinist Joe Venuti came out to watch. I would cross paths with these men throughout my life."

Living conditions in Hollywood weren't luxurious, but they were cheap and functional, and there were those starlets to ogle to take one's mind off poverty.

"Ping Bodie and I lived like we were back in the bushes. To cut living expenses, we asked Del Webb, a carpenter out of Oakland who was banging two-by-fours on the movie sets, to join us in renting two rooms in a Hollywood bungalow, a fancy name for a boardinghouse. Ping had one bedroom, Webb and I shared the other, flipping a penny to see who got to sleep in the one bed. Heads won, tails was the floor.

"I don't know what the studios paid Webb. Whatever it was, it wasn't enough to put him in the black. Del was always moaning about coughing up his $3.50 share of the weekly rent. At night, Del and I sat on the porch wolfing down sandwiches while Ping talked to us about the big leagues.

"Del Webb and I were close friends since high school. We met on the East Bay semipro diamonds. Del had a good arm till it came up sore and a severe bout of typhoid ended his hopes of a pitching career. He moved on, going from carpenter to construction tycoon in Sun City, Arizona, and owner of a Las Vegas hotel empire. In 1939, Jake Ruppert died. His three heirs put the club up for sale in 1945. Del Webb, Dan Topping, and Larry

MacPhail bought the Yankees. The trio later sold the team to CBS for $13 million."*

After the Hollywood gig was up, Lefty had another assignment. It seemed Nick Williams was not the only baseball man who equated weight with stamina; now Jacob Ruppert himself ordered that Gomez fatten up. Unlike Nick, however, when Colonel Ruppert made a ruling, there was no appeal. To ensure that the necessary bulk would be added to his new signee's scrawny frame, Ruppert paid to have him spend January at a health farm in Saratoga, California, just south of Santa Clara. Only then, with his new manly physique, could Lefty journey across country to join Babe Ruth, Lou Gehrig, Tony Lazzeri, and the rest of his new teammates.

Lefty was booked into the health farm for four weeks. This would be the first of his three off-season stays until, after 1931, Ruppert either gave up or came to realize that a pitcher who had just won 21 games and pitched 243 innings, as Lefty would do that year, was probably fine just as he was.

A life of spa luxury was not totally to Lefty's liking. "I got out of bed at 7:00 a.m., sat around in the sunshine all day with a bunch of old ladies, drinking goat's milk and stuffing myself with spinach till the lights were turned off at nine. Jake Ruppert paid the bill."

Mark Koenig, the Yankee shortstop and another San Francisco product, was home for the off-season. One afternoon he took his wife for a drive. Along a narrow road near Saratoga, Koenig saw "up ahead, walking towards us, a skinny kid with a mop of straw-blond hair. As soon as we passed him, I recognized him as Vernon Gomez. We hadn't met but I'd seen his picture in the New York papers and I'd heard the players talking about his fastball in the clubhouse. I also knew that Jake Ruppert had sent him to a goat-milk farm in Saratoga. So I parked the car on the side of the road, then yelled back at him, 'Vernon, come here. I want to talk to you.

* Ping Bodie worked on Hollywood movie lots for more than thirty years after he retired from baseball, mostly as an electrician but occasionally as an extra. He was as popular with movie people as he had been with ballplayers. He formed friendships with Hollywood stars such as Charles Boyer and Carole Lombard. Ken Smith, a reporter with the *New York Daily Mirror*, once went to do an article on Ping. As he entered a set, Smith saw Lon Chaney Jr. come out of some jungle foliage, transformed into a gorilla. The director yelled "Cut!" and suddenly there was Ping wearing a Yankee cap, pulling a sound track wire out of the thicket.

It's Mark Koenig of the Yankees.' He walked towards me, grinning, and we shook hands. Then I asked him, 'What are you doing here, wandering down the road?' He gave me a sly look. 'You won't tell anyone, will you?' I laughed and said I wouldn't. 'I'm planning my escape,' he said. 'You are?' 'Yeah. Look at me. Doesn't work. Not an ounce of fat.' I wished him luck on his breakout from the farm and went back to the car. My wife asked what I was laughing about. 'I can't wait to get to spring training. Gomez is as skinny as ever. Ruppert is sure in for a shock.' "

PART **2**

"WHAT DO YOU THINK OF MY BOY VERNON NOW?"

13.

"I DON'T TALK TO BUSHERS"

WHEN LEFTY BOARDED THE TRAIN FOR HIS TRIP ACROSS COUNTRY, he had with him one change of clothes and very little money. "All I knew about Florida was that it was a state hanging off the East Coast. It was like going to the moon.

"I left on a Monday afternoon in February. The news that I was going spread like a grass fire across Rodeo and the nearby towns. Old and young alike came running down to the town depot where I stood, cardboard suitcase in hand, headed for the big time. I was the first kid ever to go east. They were there to give me the big send-off.

"Cattleman Claeys, in his business suit and cowboy hat, came over and said, 'A buckaroo who worked for me can rope a pennant by the horns, Vernon.' Mrs. Smith, the town librarian, handed me two horse operas to read on the train. Harry Kronick, from the general store, gave me a bag of gingersnaps that I stuffed into my coat pocket. Coach Hill and the Richmond Oilers baseball team gave out with some rousing cheers, their fists to the sky, while my band blasted the air with their syncopated beat. Mr. Del Turco asked me why my sax wasn't slung over my shoulder. I told him if I stuck to the Yankees, the sax would be there the following season. Old Lady Dean, the school principal, put in a surprise appearance, this time, thank God, without her wooden ruler in hand.

"The local pulled to a stop. Pa and my four brothers grabbed hold of me, each giving me a hug. My two sisters kissed my cheek and Ma brushed back her tears to say good-bye."

After the local to Oakland, Lefty settled in on the Overland Limited to Chicago. For his $120.89, he got a coach seat, an upper berth, and use of a public toilet. Dinner alone cost about $2, which was Lefty's entire daily food budget, so he doled out his money for a small breakfast and lunch and nursed the gingersnaps.

"I'll never forget the horrible hunger pangs on that trip to Florida. There were times they doubled me over. To get my mind off food, I walked the length of the train whistling 'Happy Feet,' the hit tune I'd heard Crosby sing on the set of *King of Jazz.*"

In Chicago, he switched to the Twentieth Century Limited and then, at Grand Central Terminal in New York, boarded the Orange Blossom Special. When he finally arrived in St. Petersburg, almost a week after he'd left home, he trudged from the station, dilapidated suitcase in hand, to the recently built Princess Martha Hotel, where the Yankees lived during spring training. Most of the Yankees, at any rate. As was generally the case with the team, there was an exception: the Babe.

"Mother, Daddy, and I stayed out at the Jungle Hotel," Julia Ruth recalled. Babe had married Claire Merritt Hodgson the year before and immediately taken Claire's daughter, Julia, then twelve, as his own. Julia never thought of Babe as anything but her father. Claire is generally credited with saving Babe, preventing him from squandering both his money and his talent. "Claire was the best thing that ever happened to Babe," Tony Lazzeri's wife, Maye, said. "She made a beautiful home and devoted her entire life to him."

"Mother brought her cook down from New York because Daddy got so sick and tired of hotel meals," Julia added. "Mother tended to watch Daddy's diet because he didn't. Daddy couldn't go to a restaurant to eat. He would be recognized and surrounded by fans. He couldn't go anywhere really."

After Lefty checked in and unpacked, he returned to the lobby to find the new Yankee manager, Bob Shawkey. A former Yankee hurler known for precision and control, Shawkey had been named pitching coach for the 1929 season then was installed in the manager's slot after the sudden death of Miller Huggins in September. From the first, the easygoing Shawkey was considered an odd choice to replace the combative Huggins; he seemed unlikely to be able to impose discipline on men who had once been his teammates. That the contingent would be led by the ungovernable Ruth did not help.

Lefty arrived in time for breakfast, so Shawkey led him to the hotel restaurant to introduce him to some of his new teammates, men who, to this point, he had only read about in newspapers. The kid from Rodeo was about to shake hands with legends.

"Waite Hoyt, Bill Dickey, and Tony Lazzeri were cutting into their bacon and eggs when Shawkey and I stopped by their table. Hoyt didn't even lift his eyes from his plate. He just growled, 'I don't talk to bushers.' "

That most veterans refused to talk to rookies was not an affectation. With only sixteen major league teams, every up-and-comer was a threat to veterans playing the same position. Young ballplayers had a longer upside and cost the club a good deal less money. In Hoyt's case, a skinny left-hander said to throw smoke was most certainly the competition.

In the clubhouse before practice at the newly renamed Miller Huggins Field, Shawkey tossed Lefty a shirt. He was six foot two and a half and 147 pounds, and a large hung on him like a shroud. When Lefty mentioned that the shirt didn't fit, Shawkey shrugged. "You ain't made the team yet." Shawkey then told the rookie to pitch batting practice; he wanted to see what the kid had.

The very first man to step into the batter's box was Babe Ruth himself. Herb Pennock, another veteran pitcher, strolled to the mound. "Nothing but fastballs right down the pipe. If you hit the big guy, you're done."

After Pennock's helpful advice, Lefty went into his high-kick windup and threw his first pitches as a Yankee. He didn't hit the big guy. He did, however, grab the attention of everyone watching. "We couldn't believe what we were seeing," fellow rookie Ben Chapman said. "A skeleton firing bullets. He's nothing but a bag of bones and Ruth and all of us are thinking, 'Where's this coming from?' "

Of course, no one bothered passing any of this along to Lefty. When practice was over, he remained in the clubhouse after the other players returned to the hotel. "I was sitting on a bench, fretting. Was I going to make the team? If I didn't stick, how would I get home to California? The train fare was $120 and I had two or three dimes in my pocket. Suddenly, Waite Hoyt burst in. 'Hey, you!' he shouted. I looked around to see who he was talking to. It couldn't be me. I'm a busher. But there was no one else there. 'My wife, Dorothy, and I like to go to Tampa for the nightlife.

We need you to babysit the kids whenever we go. Harry's five and a half, Susie's four.' " With that, Hoyt marched out.

The babysitting assignment was the best news Lefty could have gotten. " 'Oh my God,' I thought, 'I'm a Yankee!' Hoyt would never tell me to babysit his kids through spring training if I wasn't going north with the team. So, mornings I pitched batting practice to Ruth and Gehrig, and in the afternoons I made mud pies with Harry and Susie Hoyt."*

Little did Lefty know that he would be with the team longer than Susie's dad. Hoyt, of the 1920s generation of fastball pitchers, had won 22 games in 1927 and 23 in 1928 but had tailed off to a 10–9 record in 1929. Jake Ruppert and Ed Barrow saw him as a pitcher on the decline and they offered him a contract for 1930 not especially to the right-hander's liking. Hoyt made little secret of his dissatisfaction, so Barrow offered him around in a trade before spring training opened but found no takers. They would finally unload him at the end of May, sending him to Detroit for three players. Hoyt would hang around the majors for eight more years, all but one lackluster, then go on to become a beloved broadcaster for the Cincinnati Reds.

FOR A ROOKIE IN spring training, life was constricted. The salary was $400 a month for the six-month season but did not begin until opening day, the second week of April. In St. Petersburg, players got $4 a day meal money, but even that was on the tab of the Princess Martha. "The hotel changed from year to year," Lefty said, "but not the $4." Veterans, of course, could afford to eat downtown when the mood was upon them. After the team broke camp to head north, meal money was upped to $7 a day, this time in cash. "The pay scale sounds rugged but still in all I could drop into a drugstore, sit at a counter, and get a breakfast of juice, eggs and bacon, toast, and coffee for 75¢. I didn't eat breakfast or lunch when I pitched, so those coins stayed in my pocket."

Once the players saw how much potential Lefty had, some of them

---

* Even fifty years later, Susie Hoyt remembered that spring fondly. "One of my treasures is a snapshot of Lefty and me at the beach. I had run out of the water dripping wet and asked Lefty for a ride. He swung me up on his shoulders and my mom took our picture."

opened up. Herb Pennock—like Lefty, a tall, thin left-hander with a high leg kick—was famously generous with young pitchers and took the rookie aside to help him with mechanics. Pennock, by then in his late thirties, was known for pinpoint control. He had come up with the Athletics, but owner Connie Mack, like Nick Williams, liked his pitchers burly, so Mack traded him to the Yankees where he won more than 200 games and eventually made it into the Hall of Fame.

Pennock told Lefty, "Never throw a baseball without a purpose, even when you're shagging flies in the outfield to get in shape. When you toss the ball in, throw it slow or fast, see how close you can come to a marker, like second base or an individual player. Practice location with every pitch."

"In my book," Lefty said later, "Pennock was one of the greatest left-handers in the history of the game. His curve didn't amaze anybody and he could scarcely break an egg with his fastball. But he had impeccable location and he could psych out the hitters. The ongoing battle in the center of the diamond. His pitches never arrived at the plate when or where the batter expected them. Each pitch meant something. He taught me how to recognize the strength and weakness of every opposing hitter in the American League."

Pennock, in addition to his skills on the mound, dressed well and spoke well. He raised silver foxes and rode to the hounds. Lefty could handle oratory on his own, but Pennock's sense of style, how to look like a major leaguer, caught his eye. As soon as Lefty began to receive paychecks, he visited a clothier. Lefty adopted self-improvement with the same complete and unself-conscious commitment as he had the saxophone. Six weeks into the season, he sent Lizzie and Coyote pictures of their youngest son decked out smartly in a three-piece summer suit and wingtip shoes. In two years, he would be named to New York's best-dressed list.

The other veteran who more or less adopted Lefty was Babe. Unlike many of his teammates, Babe liked the rookies and he was particularly drawn to Lefty's combination of wit, irreverence, and indefatigable urge to win. "Babe taught me the basics of baseball," Lefty asserted. "Win the game for your teammates and know that without the fans, you're nothing."

Babe also taught Lefty card tricks and told him to go pull them on Gehrig. "He drove Lou crazy," a friend said later, "because Lefty wouldn't show him how to do the tricks."

For all the potential, however, Lefty was still a rookie, prone to rookie mistakes. Control would bedevil him the entire season, as would a tendency to give up hits in bunches. During a three-inning stint in an exhibition game against the Boston Braves, for example, although he showed what a sportswriter described as "a brilliant fastball and good curve," he walked five men and gave up eight hits.

There were other adjustments. "Benny Bengough was behind the plate flashing signs, but I couldn't read them. So I just threw Benny a fastball when he was looking for a curve. The ball went over his head and, fortunately, missed the umpire and hit the backstop. Benny recovered the ball and, with a great flourish, called time. He stormed out to the mound, hollering at me all the way. 'Gomez, in the big leagues, the catcher knows what's coming.'"

Unfortunately for Lefty, he didn't always know what was coming. In a thirteen-inning game against the Cardinals on March 20, with both teams anxious to put an end to the affair and go home, Lefty offered a fastball down the middle that was slammed directly back to the source. He stopped the line drive, as he put it, "with my teeth." Lefty dropped like a stone, white lights flashing in his eyes. He got up and staggered around the mound, spitting blood. Bob Shawkey ran out and, after discerning that his pitcher wasn't going to die, proceeded to lecture him about how the old Baltimore Orioles were so tough that they didn't even rub when they got hurt.

Lefty was sent to a local dentist who capped his broken top teeth. Without even seeing New York, he had given bodily to the team and had toughed it out, major league style.

To no one's surprise except perhaps his own, Lefty survived the spring training cuts and was on the roster when the team broke camp on March 26. The team never traveled directly north, but rather barnstormed its way to New York. In 1930, the tour was sixteen days and would involve exhibition games as far west as Texas. Whenever the team traveled, the star attraction was the same.

"When Babe walked up to the plate to take his cuts at batting practice, the vendors quit selling hot dogs, the guards and ushers stood still in the stands. They were as quiet as the fans. Even the players on the opposing team leaned forward on the bench to get a good look.

"One night, on the train coming out of Knoxville, the porter came up with a mess of spareribs, sauerkraut, and a case of beer. At one late stop, a crowd gathered and demanded Ruth come out to the rear platform, which he did . . . in shorts, bedroom slippers, spareribs in one hand and a bottle of beer in the other. The crowd loved it."

But soon the sportswriters discovered that the Yankees had another good source of ink. "We were on the train, headed to Washington, D.C. There was a lot in the papers about the upcoming patent for Albert Einstein's new invention, a refrigerator that required no electricity. Buck O'Neill, a baseball writer, asked me if I knew who Einstein was. 'Sure,' I said. 'He's an inventor . . . like me.' 'What did you ever invent?' O'Neill asked. 'A revolving fishbowl for tropical fish. They stay in one spot as the bowl turns. The fish conserve energy and live ten years longer.' The next day, O'Neill pinned the tag of 'Goofy' on me in the *New York Journal*."

"Goofy" was soon ethnicized to "El Goofo," or occasionally "Señor Goofy." Lefty hardly minded. After his playing days were over, he would order a license plate that read GOOF.

Once in New York, Lefty roomed with Jimmie Reese, seven years his senior but also from the West Coast. Jimmie had finally made it to the majors at twenty-eight after seven years with the Oakland Oaks of the Pacific Coast League. They stayed at the Concourse Plaza Hotel, in the Bronx near Yankee Stadium, a popular spot for players.*

When the regular season began, as tempting as it was to pitch someone with overpowering stuff, the Yankees were chasing the world champion

---

* Jimmie's real name was James Herman Solomon and he was one of the only Jewish major leaguers. In those days no ethnic trait went unpunished, so in the clubhouse Reese was Hymie. Although his major league playing career would be done in 1932 after three seasons as a part-time infielder, Reese, who began as a fifteen-year-old batboy, remained in baseball as a coach, manager, and scout virtually until the day he died in 1994 at age ninety-two. For the last twenty years of his life he was in charge of conditioning for the California Angels. Nolan Ryan named a son for him, and after his death his number was retired by the Angels and his locker encased in Plexiglas.

A's and didn't feel they had the luxury of letting a kid pitcher work out the kinks in real games. On opening day, as it had been with the Seals the year before, Lefty was in the bullpen.

In the first major league game Vernon Gomez ever saw, another Lefty, Robert Moses Grove, struck out nine Yankees in a 6–2 victory for the A's in Philadelphia. In the coming years, the two Leftys, both among the most ferocious competitors in the game, would find themselves inexorably linked by sportswriters and would develop a friendship based on mutual respect.

Lefty was again in the bullpen on April 19 in Boston, where 25,000 fans had packed Fenway Park for a Patriots' Day doubleheader. "I remember thinking there weren't that many people in all Contra Costa County. Pennock was pitching for us. I was nervous, praying that he would go the distance. In the seventh inning, somebody rapped a line drive through the box that Pennock just got a glove on before it banged off his knee. Down he went. Shawkey came out, talked to Pennock, then waved me in from the bullpen. I was so scared, my knees were knocking like castanets. When I finally got to the mound, I said, 'I know what the situation is . . . two men on, one out,' then stuck my hand out for the ball. Shawkey said, 'Gomez, the line drive broke the webbing in Pennock's glove. Give him yours and go back to the bullpen.' "

Ten days later, Shawkey called on him for real. He relieved in a game against the Senators in which the Yankees scored seven runs in the first three innings, only to give up the lead by allowing Washington to score seven runs in the bottom of the third. Lefty came on, gave up a run in the fourth, then blanked the Senators for three more innings. But the Yankees didn't score, so he was the loser in his first major league decision.

One week later, on May 6, Lefty got a start against the White Sox, whose cleanup hitter was his old pal from the Seals, Smead Jolley. Batting right behind Jolley was another Seals alumnus, Willie Kamm, the third baseman Charles Strub had sold to the Sox for $100,000 in 1922. Lefty struck out the side in the first inning, got Jolley to start the second, then watched Kamm park a home run in the left-field bleachers.

From there, in what the *New York Times* described as a "brilliant major league debut," Lefty pitched shutout ball. He scattered only four more hits, walking none while striking out six. The *Times* added, "In one day he stepped from the awkward squad to full standing on Bob Shawkey's pitching staff." And Lefty had to be good because, for six innings, forty-two-year-old Urban Faber, one of the last remaining legal spitballers, held the Yankees scoreless, striking out Babe twice. But the Yankees touched Faber for three runs in the seventh without hitting a ball hard and Lazzeri added a long home run in the eighth. Lefty had his first major league win, 4–1.

Five days later, he started against the Tigers. He couldn't match his opening effort, giving up five runs on eight hits, but he didn't have to. The Yankees scored fourteen runs. But the game wasn't a rout until the end. After seven innings, the teams were tied 3–3, the Tigers starting their own rookie sensation, Elon "Chief" Hogsett, billed as a full-blooded Cherokee Indian, although only one grandparent was actually Native American. The Yankees finally blasted Hogsett with four runs in the seventh and then pasted relief pitchers with another seven runs in the eighth. Lefty gave up two meaningless runs in the ninth to go 2–1. Perhaps even more satisfying, he went two for four at the plate and scored his first major league run.

The Tigers game also provided Lefty another opportunity to play El Goofo. At second base for Detroit was future Hall of Famer Charley Gehringer, whom Lefty would later nickname "The Mechanical Man." "They wind him up at the start of the season and he never runs down. He hits over .300 on opening day and he hits over .300 for the season." Before the game, Bill Dickey overheard Bob Shawkey tell Lefty, "Don't give Gehringer anything good. He'll hit it out." So, Dickey recalled, "the third man up for Detroit was Gehringer, and he parked one in the stands. When the half inning was over Gomez said to me, 'Bill, warn me when that Gehringer comes to bat. I wanna bear down on him. I hope he isn't any tougher than the guy who just poked one into the bleachers.'" Dickey never did figure out if Lefty had been serious.

Road trips were long and arduous but, thanks to the team's resident iconoclast, they were also fun. Perhaps never in sports history has a player hogged so much of the spotlight as did Babe without arousing the antipathy of his teammates.

"We traveled by train and the stars, the regulars, and the utility players were all thrown together," Ben Chapman said. "We played cards all the time. Hearts. I was just coming up and yet I found myself in a game with Lou Gehrig, Bill Dickey, and Babe Ruth. The Babe would get a pint of Old Grand-Dad and the card table and we'd begin. He'd drink the Old Grand-Dad, but rookies couldn't drink. That was his rule for us. One time, the conversation was moving along and I was moaning about only making $2,500 a year. Ruth was shuffling a new hand and he looked up at me and said, 'Listen, Chapman. If it wasn't for me, you wouldn't even be making the twenty-five hundred.' "

When they reached their destination, Jimmie Reese was assigned as Babe's roommate. Babe adopted Jimmie much as he had Lefty. Babe and the two rookies often prowled around at night, or Babe prowled, and Lefty and Jimmie trotted along after him.

"To eat, we mostly went to the speakeasies," Reese said. "We walked down the side of a brownstone and rapped our knuckles on a locked door with a peephole in it. A bouncer looked through, checking to make sure we weren't federal agents out to bust the place. Believe me, when the guy saw the Babe, he couldn't open the door fast enough. Then it was all we could eat and all we could drink."

Lefty didn't drink—he literally tossed his drinks into the potted plant—but he did eat. Even so, he couldn't crack 150 pounds. Ruppert and Barrow decided his inability to acquire major league heft was due to inferior dental work and so they asked members of the New York medical community for solutions. What they got back was pure quackery.

"Ruppert was told that the dentist who capped my teeth didn't drain the pus first, and I didn't gain weight because my body was waging a losing battle with the 'poisoned pus' draining from my abscessed teeth into my bloodstream. What malarkey, but in the thirties, yanking teeth was an accepted medical procedure for a ballplayer who ate well but remained skinny. So Ruppert and Barrow demanded that my upper teeth be yanked out."

Such was the state of sports medicine in 1930. Four years later, Lefty Grove would have teeth yanked for the same reason. And teeth were not all that came out. "The Yankee team doctor had two remedies whenever a player was injured on the playing field," Ben Chapman grumbled. "First he took out your appendix. If that didn't cure what ailed you, he removed your tonsils. Doc took out my appendix in 1930. I was a rookie and didn't know any better so I went along with it."

The list of players who were required to endure addition by subtraction is extensive. Joe Sewell, who would join the team the next year, also woke up in the hospital one morning to find his appendix was no longer attached. When Schoolboy Rowe, a 24-game winner for the Tigers in 1934, lost his fastball, he had his tonsils removed in 1937 and was disappointed that the procedure did not increase his velocity. Even Lou Gehrig had teeth pulled in the mid-1930s.

After the team returned from a long road trip in June, Lefty, whose dental work had been perfect, had his top teeth pulled and replaced by an upper plate. "By mid-June, I was still a skinny twenty-one-year-old rookie wearing ceramic choppers and the Yankees were holding the mortgage on them to the tune of $1,500." Still, Lefty found a bright side. "To a young man who had been brought up on 50¢ tooth pullings and $2 fillings, a $1,500 dental bill was very impressive. You can understand, then, why I felt a trifle proud being worth so much money to the Yankees when I'd hardly even won a ball game."

John Kieran of the *New York Times* reported a more dramatic version of the same story. Referring to a relief appearance in which Lefty couldn't get the ball over, Kieran wrote, "Before they could drag him off the mound, he had handed out four or five passes in a row. The very next day, the Yankee authorities sent him to a dentist and the dentist neatly removed all of his teeth. Colonel Ruppert didn't issue any formal statement, nor did Bob Shawkey say, 'Let that be a lesson to you.' But Gomez is still suspicious and doubtless will warn newcomers on the Yankee pitching staff to avoid wildness if they value their teeth."

From late June until mid-July, the aftereffects of losing half his natural chewing power and the pain of getting used to the upper plate sufficiently diminished Lefty's effectiveness and stamina that Shawkey rarely called on him to pitch. But false teeth did not prevent El Goofo from further cultivating the press. When asked by a reporter after an especially rough outing if he had a special pitch, Lefty replied, "Sure. Nobody else uses it, either. I call it a go-fer ball." When the reporter asked what the go-fer ball was and how it was thrown, Lefty told him, "I just throw it natural. You saw it go-fer two bases, go-fer three bases, and three times it went for a home run." Which is how the term "gopher ball" entered the language.

On July 25, the Yankees announced that they were shipping Lefty to St. Paul in the American Association, a AA ball club, just like the Seals.* The published report said that the young left-hander was to "work himself into pitching condition, a dental operation having incapacitated him almost entirely for mound duty for the past five weeks." While there was some truth in this, the team also recognized that Lefty needed steady work as a starter to refine his craft and he wasn't going to get that with a team in the middle of a pennant race. Lefty had walked more than four batters per nine innings, more than he'd struck out, and given up a disquieting sixty-six hits, including twelve home runs, in only sixty innings of work. With all of his potential, a kid fireballer with an ERA of 5.55 was going to spend most of his time on the bench.

Lefty claimed not to be worried by the demotion. "The New York Yankees were a business organization," he later told a reporter, "and they were too smart to let me out of their clutches while I was wearing $1,500 worth of their teeth."

Lefty pitched for the Yankees for the last time as a rookie the next day—"a farewell inning," as the newspapers put it. "Its features," the article went on, "were two dashes from third to home by two Tigers while Gomez was taking a leisurely wind-up." In fact, the first runner was out but the catcher dropped the ball, while the second was a clean steal. Seven years later, Lefty used his demotion as fodder for a tale and also to get in a dig at Bob Shawkey, who had by then gone into the fur business, dated Lefty's sister-in-law, and become a close friend.

In 1937, in an interview by J. G. Taylor Spink of the *Sporting News*, who billed him as "one of the prime wits of the major leagues today," Lefty gave a slightly altered account of that fateful inning.

"One afternoon Henry Johnson was pitching," Lefty told Spink. "The

---

* AA was the highest classification in 1930. Leagues were not designated AAA until 1946.

bases were loaded, nobody out, the game tight.* Shawkey stopped the game and told Henry to watch out for the guy on third. Right away that player stole home. Bob stopped the game and told Henry to take the rest of the day off. Shawkey said, 'I'm going to put in a man who will hold those guys on the bases.' So he sent word for me to come in. First one runner stole home, and then the other. Shawkey looked disappointed. He called me into his office and he gave me a long railroad ticket. I thought I was going to China, but it was only St. Paul. I won eight and lost four with the Saints and came back to the Yankees in 1931, when Joe McCarthy became manager of the club. I won 21 and lost 9 that season and here I am."

In truth, Lefty reported to St. Paul in early August and he was back with the Yankees five weeks later when the AA season ended. But he had gotten in the work he needed. He appeared in 17 games and pitched 86 innings, ending with the 8–4 record. He still gave up more hits than innings pitched, had an ERA over 4.00, and walked too many, but he had struck out almost seven batters per nine innings.

The stay in St. Paul was noteworthy for two other events. First, on the team was another pitcher, Johnny Murphy, who would become both a close friend and Lefty's late-inning alter ego at the tail end of his career, when his arm was going and nine innings were too taxing.

The second event was, to Lefty, of far greater significance. On August 8, 1930, he became one of only three pitchers to sign a contract for his very own autographed Louisville Slugger. The others were Walter Johnson and Charley "Red" Ruffing. The contract was for twenty years and Lefty even designed the bat himself.

"I always believed I had the potential to be a great hitter," he said. "So when Henry Morrow, the rep for Hillerich & Bradsby, came to St. Paul, I convinced him my first home run was right around the corner, and wangled an autographed bat contract for myself. A G100, 34½ inches, 32 ounces, made of ash. I received $1, two bats, and a set of golf clubs. Anything is possible when you're a rookie."

But Henry Morrow wasn't completely fooled. "We didn't make many

* In fact, Detroit was already leading 10–6.

bats for Lefty. For one thing, he didn't play every day, and second, he didn't break too many. As I recall, Lefty said he only broke one bat in his life and that's when he drove over it in his driveway."

When Lefty rejoined the Yankees in September, he was just in time to watch the team end up in third place, its worst finish in a decade, except for the largely Ruth-less 1925.

The team had been done in by a dearth of quality pitching. Despite a total of 348 runs batted in from Ruth, Gehrig, and Lazzeri, and an offense that led in virtually every category, the pitching staff's ERA was 4.88, second-worst in the league.* Hoyt was gone; Pennock, at thirty-six, was not the pitcher he had once been; and George Pipgras, the other mainstay of the staff, managed only a 15–15 record. Only Charley Ruffing had turned out to be a pleasant surprise. Ruffing had been a disaster in six years with the Red Sox, who were something of a disaster themselves, and was traded to the Yankees in May with an 0–3 record and an ERA over 6.00. With the Yankees, however, he finished 15–5, showing he could pitch well for a team that could actually hit a baseball.

So while Lefty might have had to wait his turn with Washington or Philadelphia, he was firmly in New York's plans for 1931, and in November they put him on their reserve roster. He returned to California still needing to pay for his own ticket to return to spring training, but as a major league baseball player with a bright future.

But first, he would be required by Colonel Ruppert to enroll for another six-week stint at the Saratoga Health Farm.

---

* Only the 64–90 St. Louis Browns were less effective on the mound.

14.

THE DOCTOR AND THE DICTATOR

Two men came into Lefty's life in the 1930–31 off-season, each a model of how to approach life and craft. One was a relative, one a stranger; one was quietly benevolent, one ferocious and complex.

The first came to Lefty's rescue at the Saratoga Health Farm.

"Once again," said Lefty, "it's in bed every night at nine and I have to drink at least six quarts of milk a day. I drank so much milk, I couldn't walk past a cow or a goat without bleating. After a month, my cousin, Dr. Arthur Gomez-Lumsden, came down to Saratoga and signed me out. He told the staff I was thin by nature and that Ruppert was nuts. Doc Lumsden had clout. He was a respected surgeon and owner of the Petaluma General Hospital. I was only too happy to follow him out the door."

Juan Enrique Gomez had been killed in an explosion in 1901 while at work at the gunpowder factory in Hercules, two miles southwest of Rodeo. Accidents there were not uncommon, and as a boy Lefty had sometimes felt the tremors from the powerful blasts. Juan Enrique's wife, Magdalena, soon remarried, to a millwright named Williams Lumsden. Lumsden paid for Magdalena's son Arthur to go to college and then medical school. Out of respect for a stepfather who financed his education, Arthur added Lumsden to his last name.

"As we sped away in his car, Doc said, 'From now on, Vernon, you're working for me. We're making house calls together.' He'd spoken to Coyote and both agreed it was a good way for me to earn the train fare back to St. Pete. So I spent the winter in Petaluma. When an emergency call came into Doc's home office, I went out to the barn and hitched the horses to the buggy. He came out, carrying his medical bag, jumped in, and off we went. Many times the emergency calls came in at two, three, and four o'clock in the morning. While Doc tended to the patient, I stood along-side, handing him the instruments. His patients often paid him with chickens and a bottle of wine."

Lefty had returned to an East Bay struggling to cope with the Depression. Life with the Yankees in New York, and even his stint in St. Paul, had not prepared him for the ravages that were overtaking the rest of the country. But Lizzie and Coyote witnessed the full brunt. There was always enough to eat at the largely self-sufficient Gomez house, but everyone in the family understood the need to help others out.

"Hoboes walking the tracks had heard about Lizzie's home cooking and followed a well-worn path to the rambling two-story house above the shoreline. The men weren't bums or drifters looking for a handout. They wanted to work but no one was hiring. Lizzie admired them. They were broke but not broken. She paid them to do chores around the dairy or to hoe a row, oil the windlass, or build a chicken coop. At sundown, she in-vited the men to join the family for dinner. They dived into the pork chops and the scalloped potatoes. The dinners didn't eradicate their problems, but at least they left Rodeo knowing they did a good job and someone cared."

THE SECOND OF LEFTY'S mentors was waiting for him in Florida when he reported to spring training.

For baseball, 1930 had been a false dawn. Major league attendance had topped 10 million for the first time ever, and the prevailing view of some owners was that in bad times Americans would seek relief from day-to-day worries by coming to the ballpark. But with more and more Americans out of work, fear of spending that extra 50¢ or $1, even for tickets whose price hadn't gone up, overwhelmed the need for a few hours of recreation. In 1931, the great wave of the Depression would break over baseball. Attendance league-wide dropped 20 percent. It would decline an additional 10 percent in 1932, then crash in 1933. Some franchises were decimated. Attendance at Wrigley Field plummeted from 1.4 million in 1930 to less than 600,000 three years later. In 1933, the St. Louis

Browns, hapless as they may have been, would draw only 88,000 fans for the entire year, an average of just over 1,100 per game. As the season and then the decade wore on, many owners changed focus from winning the pennant to keeping their franchises afloat, none more tragically than Connie Mack.

The Yankees, as was often the case, were the exception. Jake Ruppert had never been a speculator and had hung on to most of his personal fortune—unlike Mack, who had lost heavily in the market. And, with the most recognizable team in the game, albeit no longer the best, a steady stream of fans continued to pay their way into Yankee Stadium. The stream would diminish, certainly, but would still dwarf those of other franchises. In 1931, attendance at Yankee Stadium dropped to 912,000 from the record 1,169,000 in 1930, but even that figure was more than double the average attendance for the other seven American League teams and 300,000 more than their closest competitor.

For ballplayers, just being in New York helped insulate them from the nation's grim reality. "I knew Tony when he was playing minor league ball," Maye Lazzeri said. "I married him when I was sixteen. Tony said he'd quit if I didn't go with him to New York. He'd never been far away from home and neither had I. I told Tony, 'I don't care where you play. I'll go to China. But I don't want you to throw your money away on silly stuff or drink yourself out of a baseball career. If you're not going to do it right, then let's not go.' So we went to New York and we loved it. I could never understand the wives who came from small towns and said they didn't like New York. Couldn't they see it was a great city?"

Great city or no, a franchise still had to put a winning team on the field and for the Yankees that meant finishing first. Ruppert and Barrow were all too aware that the pitching would need a drastic upgrade for the team to challenge for the pennant.

Defense was the other big problem. The 1930 infield had been a shambles. Ben Chapman, who could hit and run but not field ground balls, was moved to the outfield, which would also help cover the defensive liabilities of an aging Babe. Lazzeri was moved from third base, where his throws had often pulled Lou Gehrig off the bag, back to his natural position at second. Joe Sewell, a smooth fielder and solid hitter who almost never struck out—and who, for the moment, was still in possession of his appendix—was acquired from Cleveland to man third.*

The biggest change in the 1931 Yankees, however, was not between the lines but in the dugout. As many had feared, Bob Shawkey had been bulldozed by the veterans. After the 1930 season he had been shabbily and unceremoniously dumped and would spend the season managing the Jersey City Skeeters. To replace him, Ruppert and Barrow hired Joe McCarthy.

McCarthy had been in his own political storm, fired by the Cubs in late September despite taking the team from cellar dwellers to first- and second-place finishes in his five years at the helm. The move was instigated by the irascible nonpareil Rogers Hornsby, who wanted to manage the team himself, as the Babe wanted to do in New York. Unlike Jake Ruppert, however, who refused to knuckle under no matter how many home runs Ruth hit, Phil Wrigley and Bill Veeck Sr. caved in. In fairness to the Cubs, Rajah had managed previously, leading the Cardinals to a stunning World's Series defeat of the Yankees in 1926; then again, he was so difficult to get along with that he was traded to the Giants immediately afterward. This time around, Hornsby would last but a season and a half before being bounced in the middle of a year in which the Cubs won the pennant, while McCarthy would remain at the helm of the Yankees until 1946.

Ruppert gave McCarthy a two-year contract and told his new skipper that he didn't demand a first-place finish in 1931 but he expected to see his team in the World's Series in 1932. From his first day on the job, McCarthy made it clear that the rules would change. He was a stickler for fundamentals and drilled his players constantly—double-play pivots, hitting the cutoff man, positioning. "Joe was a tough guy, but he really knew the game," Lefty said. "He tried to be perfect in everything. That's why we rarely missed signs. You'd be sitting in a hotel lobby on the road when McCarthy would come into the hotel, walk up to you, and ask you for the sign for a hit-and-run, a take, or other signs. But when a mental mistake

---

* Sewell's first game had been at shortstop in 1920, as Ray Chapman's replacement, after Chapman died earlier in the day.

did occur, McCarthy didn't chew you out in the dugout. He had too much respect for his players. He talked to you in his office."

Off-the-field behavior would change as well. "Joe didn't let guys smoke a pipe, and you had to wear a tie and jacket on the road and keep your shoes polished. He thought playing for the Yankees called for being the same type of gentleman who would work in a bank."

McCarthy instituted a midnight curfew and, with it, a novel means of enforcement. "Every night of an away series," Lefty noted, "Joe gave a baseball to the elevator operator in the team hotel. As the guy took a player up to his room, he asked the player to autograph the ball. When the clock struck twelve, he collected no more signatures. We all knew what Joe was doing but we still had to get our signatures on that baseball." After it was checked, of course, the operator got to keep the ball. Also on the road, players were required to be downstairs for breakfast at eight-thirty, thus guaranteeing a short sleep to anyone who had succeeded in sneaking out after he'd signed in.

At Yankee Stadium, the clubhouse was transformed into a place of business. Players were required to talk only about baseball, and McCarthy had the card table removed; some sportswriters insisted, apocryphally, that he had ordered the table to be smashed with an ax.*

McCarthy's dicta promised to become a direct challenge to the mammoth presence of one George Herman Ruth. Babe was already livid at being passed over for a shot at managing the Yankees himself, and despite fading skills, he remained the team's dominant presence both on the field and off. Most of the players loved him, not the least because he helped make the Yankees the wealthiest and most successful franchise in the game. Had McCarthy been hired four years earlier, Ruth might have fomented open revolution. Instead, as long as the Bambino didn't threaten team unity—and Ruth never did—he and the new manager cut each other

---

* Joe McCarthy was one of the most successful managers in baseball history and was inducted into the Hall of Fame in 1957, but it is difficult to imagine him functioning effectively in the modern game. The essence of his success was that he didn't care if the players liked him as long they followed his rules. In later generations, his style might well have incited player walkouts, grousing about playing time or mistreatment, or formal complaints to management or the players' union.

a wide berth. Babe did not stay at the Princess Martha during spring training nor did he follow each of the new rules, but McCarthy was content, at
least for the moment, to indulge Babe's many idiosyncrasies.

"Babe called everyone 'kid,' " Lefty said. "He said he didn't want to fill
up his memory with names. He needed space for the pitching mechanics
of every hurler in the league. I was sitting on the porch of the Princess
Martha in '31 when Babe and Claire drove up. He was going to play golf
with Lazzeri. 'Hey, kid,' he said, 'have you seen the dago?'

" 'He's in the lobby,' I told him and, still sitting at the wheel, Babe hollered, 'Daaago!' "

And Babe didn't sit behind the wheel of just anything. "The sixteen-
cylinder Cadillac was as long as a Pullman car. Three coughs and it was
out of gas. The sudden showers that drenched the Florida streets gave the
rookies plenty of exercise. Babe dashed through the puddles and shorted
out the ignition system. When the car stalled, Babe unloaded a few of the
rookies he was transporting and they pushed the vehicle until it started.
You might have a million-dollar arm on the diamond, but on the street it
was, 'Hey, kid. Push my car.' "

One of the reasons Babe always got along with his teammates—and,
almost certainly, one of the reasons Babe got along with McCarthy well
enough—was that, unlike a lot of stars, Babe could take it as well. "One
morning," Lefty said, "Lazzeri goes into Babe's locker with a pair of cutting shears. When Babe gets into his street clothes after the game, the right
pants leg on his white slacks is sheared off at the knee. Later, I see Babe
standing out in the parking lot signing autographs for the kids, his right
leg bare from the knee down to a black sock and a shoe."

Lazzeri, the team's most prominent prankster, was an epileptic. "Mc-
Carthy told me to room with Tony at spring training and on the road.
Tony told me if a seizure occurred I should stuff a towel in his mouth so
he wouldn't swallow his tongue. There was one incident in a taxi and another on the train, but his seizures usually happened in our hotel room.
When one came over him, he fell to the floor. Being a lightweight, I
couldn't pick him up and carry him to the bed. I had to get my hands
under his armpits and drag him across the floor, then inch his body up
onto the mattress. All the while he would be foaming at the mouth. I ran

to Charley Ruffing's room for help. Charley was a steam engine and he picked Tony up like a banana peel. I hightailed it to McCarthy and told him Ruffing should be Tony's roommate, so Charley moved in and I moved out.*

"Henry Gehrig, Lou's father, was an epileptic, and the doctors at the Mayo Clinic told Lou his father would only have an attack when he was relaxed. Lazzeri lived in fear that he'd have a seizure in front of the fans. That's probably why Tony never had an attack on the field. Who could be relaxed playing second base for the Yankees?"

WHERE BOB SHAWKEY had fiddled with his lineup a good deal, trying to find a formula that worked, as spring training wore on McCarthy made it clear that, barring injury and the occasional day of rest, he believed in putting the same eight position players on the field. Being a reserve infielder, as Jimmie Reese was, meant developing strong hindquarters. With pitchers, however, McCarthy was much more likely to ride a hunch or a hot arm, or to juggle his rotation to get the right matchups. Any pitcher who performed for "Marse Joe," as the sportswriters called him—likening McCarthy to a pre–Civil War plantation owner in the stunningly racially insensitive mood of the day—would be guaranteed a lot of innings and the chance to make himself a star.

But not every sportswriter saw Lefty leaping into Yankee history. "Red Ruffing is about the only pitcher who goes along at an even pace," wrote John Kieran during spring training. "Sherid, Gomez, and Johnson are brilliant on some days, terrible on others."

After the team had made their pilgrimage north, Lefty started life as a second-year man by relocating to the theater district in Manhattan, a more appropriate location for a guy who had that year come east with his sax. Myril Hoag, an outfielder also from the Bay Area, had joined the team, so he, Jimmie Reese, and Lefty went thirds on a suite at the Edison Hotel. The Edison was $2 a day each. A subway to Yankee Stadium cost a nickel.

---

* Lazzeri would die tragically in 1946 at age forty-two. "Tony had an epileptic seizure while I was away from the house," Maye Lazzeri remembered. "When I returned home I found him dead at the bottom of the staircase."

"Once in a while," said Reese, "we'd take a cab for $1.50. If we could put five players in a cab, it would only cost us a quarter each."

For the season Lefty was given a new uniform number, 11, which he would wear for the remainder of his career.* As in his rookie year, Lefty started 1931 in the bullpen. McCarthy agreed with John Kieran about Charley Ruffing: He called on the big right-hander to pitch the opening-day game against the Red Sox in front of 70,000 fans. Mayor Jimmy Walker threw out the first ball, the Babe hit his first home run, and the Yanks, Red Ruffing, and Joe McCarthy, who had never before seen a game in Yankee Stadium, got their first victory.

In the second game of the season, another victory over the Red Sox, Henry Johnson got the start; the crowd was 60,000 less than the day before. Herb Pennock pitched the day after, running the Yankee record to 3–0, a far more agreeable start than the 0–5 in 1930.

Lefty's first appearance was on April 20, relieving Henry Johnson, who had been shelled for four runs in three innings by the Athletics. In three and two-thirds innings, Lefty walked two but allowed only one hit while striking out five. He got his first start five days later against the Red Sox. His performance was all too reminiscent of 1930. In seven innings, before being removed for a pinch hitter, Lefty gave up seven hits and three runs, struck out seven, but walked five. He left on the bad end of a 3–2 score. The Yankees tied it in the eighth, only to lose in ten.

From there, it was back to the bullpen. Lefty pitched five innings three days later, giving up the tying run in the ninth to the Senators in a game ultimately called for darkness after fourteen innings with the scored tied.

McCarthy gave Lefty another shot at starting on May 4. It was a disaster. He gave up two runs in the first, then, after four scoreless innings, fell apart in the sixth, yielding five runs, although the old Yankee bugaboo of shoddy defense contributed in no small manner to the onslaught.

Another manager might have moved Lefty to a less conspicuous spot on the staff but McCarthy had total confidence in his own judgment and

---

* The temptation is to assume that he was given 11 because it was the narrowest two-digit number that could appear on a jersey, but he had been assigned 20 in 1930.

he saw in Gomez—young, skinny, and wild as he may have been—the perfect complement to Charley Ruffing. He stuck with the kid and, to some significant extent, each made the other's career. McCarthy would later say, "Gomez had as much to do with my success as any man who ever played for me." Possibly as a result of their intertwined fortunes, Lefty and the taciturn McCarthy developed a unique relationship.

Tom Meany, who traveled with the team, described it. "McCarthy knew that a ball club needed relaxation and that Gomez was invaluable in providing it, but Joe preferred to pretend that Lefty's pranks were being performed behind his back."

Lefty, who was also described as "the only Yankee who could needle McCarthy," parried jibes with his manager for eleven years. "Joe chewed gum in the dugout when he got nervous," Lefty said. "I sat down next to him one day and bent over to pick something off the dugout floor. On the underside of the bench was a mound of chewing gum as big as an eggplant."

With mock innocence, Lefty asked McCarthy what made him chew all that gum.

"Your bases on ball are responsible for half of it," McCarthy shot back.

None of that would have been possible, of course, if Señor Goofy couldn't pitch, and any doubts anyone might have harbored on that score were dispelled on May 26. Pitching in Philadelphia against Connie Mack's astounding machine, who were then riding a seventeen-game winning streak, Lefty held the Athletics to one run over eight innings, gave up a meaningless solo home run with two out in the ninth to Al Simmons—a blast that exited Shibe Park over the left-field roof—and allowed the Yanks to come away with a 6-2 victory. Lefty gave up only seven hits, five of which were singles, and, most significant, walked only one. That night in the hotel lobby, Tom Meany overhead McCarthy telling another reporter that the win was vital to his team, since "it brought the A's up short and let them know that the Yanks weren't dead."

The most telling statistic that day, however, did not emanate from the playing field. To see perhaps the most complete and powerful baseball team ever assembled go against its only real rival in an attempt to win its eighteenth straight game, Shibe Park on that Tuesday afternoon was less than half full. Attendance was optimistically announced at 15,000, though decidedly fewer fans were actually in the seats.*

With that appearance, Lefty also began his decadelong duel with Double X, Jimmie Foxx. Listed at 6 feet and 195 pounds, none of which was fat and only about four ounces of which was water, Foxx was also called "The Beast." He would be the subject of one of Lefty's most famous quips—"He has muscles in his hair"—and would also inspire Lefty to note that Foxx "hit a home run off me that broke seats in the third deck at Yankee Stadium. You can't walk that far in an hour and a half." The Beast made such an impression on Lefty that when Neil Armstrong landed on the moon in 1969 and was reported to have come across a white object, Lefty said, "That was the home run Jimmie Foxx hit off me in 1937." Jimmie didn't hit any homers off Lefty in 1931, but as a harbinger, he did launch two monstrous triples.

Even so, from the middle of May until the end of the season, Lefty won 21 games while losing only 8. He finished the season with an earned run average of 2.67 and struck out 150 batters in 206 innings. He walked only 85. He was especially effective against the dazzling 107–47 Athletics, winning his first three decisions before losing to 31–4 Lefty Grove after the Yankees had effectively been eliminated from the pennant race. With that meeting, he began another of his great personal rivalries. Although each was among the game's most intense competitors, their styles were very different. When Gomez lost, he turned stonily silent, while Grove would batter whatever he could lay his hands on. When asked why he never smashed up a locker room, Lefty replied, "I don't have the strength."

Lefty won one additional game in 1931. It appeared neither in the

* Eventually, the inability or unwillingness on the part of fans to pay their way into the ballpark six days a week—baseball was banned on Sunday in Philadelphia—would force Connie Mack to once again dismantle a brilliant squad, trading away Grove, Simmons, Mickey Cochrane, and even Jimmie Foxx, in essence selling his team for parts in order to keep the franchise running. Mack had been forced to sell away most of another great team after the 1914 season when the upstart Federal League drove up players' salaries and the A's had no money to pay them. Mack's team went from a 99–53 record and first-place finish in 1914 to a 43–109 eighth-place finish the following year. The Federal League folded after two seasons when a quixotic federal district court judge with a wild shock of white hair named Kenesaw Mountain Landis refused to issue an antitrust injunction in its favor, but that was too late for Connie Mack.

standings nor on his record, but it did epitomize the changes overtaking both baseball and its fans. On September 9, the Yankees and Giants played an exhibition game, for which 60,549 paid their way into Yankee Stadium to see the cross–Harlem River rivals meet for the first time since the 1923 World's Series. All proceeds, more than $59,000, went to benefit those out of work, funneled through the Mayor's Unemployment Relief Fund, although the mayor himself, Jimmy Walker, was not present. Walker had resigned in the midst of a scandal nine days earlier and fled to Europe. An investigatory commission had exposed widespread corruption in city government—they hadn't had to look far—and the mayor himself had been accused of profiting from an extortion scheme in which innocent people were arrested by crooked cops, threatened with prosecution by crooked DAs, and then had to pay hefty "fines" to avoid conviction by crooked judges.*

Lefty went nine innings to beat the Giants 7–3, with Babe hitting an eighth-inning homer. A round-robin series, with the Yankees, Giants, and the Brooklyn Robins, was played at the Polo Grounds two weeks later and raised another $44,000. Beau James—as the mayor was known—had returned for these games after receiving assurances that he wouldn't go to jail.

Although the Yankees finished the season in second place, 13½ games behind the Athletics, the gap on the field was closing. Red Ruffing could not match his 1930 success, finishing at 16–14 with an ERA over 4.00, but his future was unquestioned. Philadelphia's big three—Lefty Grove, George Earnshaw, and Rube Walberg—were all over thirty. The Yankees' two best pitchers were Gomez, age twenty-two, and Ruffing, twenty-six. Largely thanks to Lefty, the team ERA had dropped by almost half a run per game. With the Babe still hitting, and Gehrig, Dickey, Lazzeri, and Ben Chapman in their prime, the Yankees were positioned to make 1932 a dogfight—and Lefty was positioned to become an ace of their pitching staff.

---

* The *New York Times* delicately noted that "Mayor Walker's European excursion prevented him from presiding at the September 9 game."

15.

JUNE IN JUNE

EVEN DURING A DEPRESSION, WEALTH, CELEBRITY, ENERGY, AND GLAMOUR thrive in great cities. Not two years after Lefty had debarked in St. Petersburg with a cardboard suitcase, the almost quintessential hayseed—in fact, his nickname in Rodeo *was* "Hayseed"—had slipped into the life of a New York cosmopolite. He met, impressed, and charmed businessmen, show people, politicians, and other sports figures. Between starts, he swam or played racquetball at the New York Athletic Club. At night, he often visited the hottest nightclubs with Jimmie Reese or Myril Hoag, toting his sax along with him.

"Eddie Duchin played at the Central Park Casino in New York and at the Hotel Brunswick in Boston, where the Yankees stayed on the road. Eddie dazzled with his fancy finger work, especially his upswing arrangement of a Chopin étude that was his calling card. In New York or on the road, I'd drop into a supper club and talk with the musicians in the house bands. Sometimes Duchin, Joe Venuti, or Jack Teagarden would ask me to sit in with their bands as a sideman, tootle a few bars on my sax. What a thrill for me to play alongside these marvelous men."

He even bought a car. Frank Cuccia, who owned the General Motors dealership on West 57th Street, was a rabid Yankee fan and always gave the players a good deal. Lefty put down a payment on a yellow two-door, five-passenger LaSalle convertible, complete with radio, heater, and tire covers. The car listed for about $2,800, but Cuccia let him have it for $2,000.

Most stunning about Lefty's metamorphosis was that it occurred without arousing animosity or envy, without anyone calling him a phony, and, most important, without him changing a note of his personality or style. What appealed so much to so many, from sportswriters to Joe McCarthy to Mayor La Guardia to a hat check girl, was not the false face of a social chameleon but Vernon Gomez, who was the same Vernon Gomez in New York as he had been in Rodeo.

There did turn out to be one exception. One Sunday night in early June, when the three roommates ventured north to the Woodmansten Inn in the Bronx, Lefty met someone who saw a slightly different Vernon Gomez.

The Woodmansten was one of New York's in spots, the kind of place where celebrities, politicians, the idle rich, and gangsters rubbed elbows. Its owners preferred to say that the club was in Westchester, but the ground on which it stood, on Williamsbridge Road and Pelham Parkway, had been annexed into New York City in 1895. It had been padlocked for nine months in 1929 for Prohibition violations, suffered a probable arson attempt a year later, was raided regularly, and finally burned down in the mid-1930s under suspicious circumstances.

In addition to the regular band, entertainment was provided by noted singers, dancers, and musicians moonlighting to pick up publicity and sometimes extra money, hot tickets such as Benny Goodman and Russ Columbo. On Sunday nights, cast members of Broadway musicals ventured north to sing and dance for the eclectic gaggle of onlookers. The performers weren't paid for their turns; they were there simply to drum up interest in the show.

That Sunday, with Jimmie Reese, Myril Hoag, and Lefty at a ringside table, one of the performers was a stunning brunette who had just landed a lead role in the Harold Arlen musical *You Said It.* "She sang and danced and we were awestruck," said Jimmie. "Our mouths hung open. What a beauty. After the show, she came down into the audience and greeted the guests. She stopped by our table, smiling brightly. 'I'm June O'Dea, and who are you?' The three of us just gawked at her. We couldn't even remember our names. Finally I stammered, 'Uh, we never met a showgirl before.' June moved on. But from then on, that's all Lefty talked about. He was smitten."

JUNE O'DEA WAS BORN Eilean Frances Schwarz on December 18, 1912, in Revere, Massachusetts, then "a hurly-burly resort town near Boston, with the oldest public beach in the United States." Her father, William Schwarz, was a German Lutheran from Ohio, and her mother, Nellie Grady, a second-generation Boston Irish Catholic. Eilean's sister, Elizabeth, who would later be known as Sunny Dale, had been born in May the year before.

Nellie's father, Milo Grady, was a house painter and cardsharp; his brother, Bart Grady, was a theater impresario; Nellie herself would turn out to be an indomitable showbiz mom. By age five she was improvising on the piano. As a teenager Nellie studied composition with private teachers and by her twenties she was a published composer of marches, rags, and two-steps. One pop tune, "I'll See You Later, Dearie," was written with a lyricist prophetically named Joe McCarthy. McCarthy would go on to a distinguished career as a Broadway lyricist among whose credits was *Kid Boots,* a Ziegfeld comedy about a crooked caddy. June would play in a revival of that show in St. Louis in 1936 that would have enormous significance for both her and Lefty.

Eventually Nellie got a job as a song plugger at Siegel's Department Store in Boston. "Before radio," June recalled, "in order to buy sheet music, a customer had to hear the songs. A song plugger had to play the tune with such élan that the customer grabbed the music and ran over to a cash register, where a clerk rang up the sale."

At Siegel's, Nellie met Bill Schwarz, a buyer of books, stationery, and toys. They were married in 1910. "Daddy grew up speaking German at home. He had hoped that Sunny and I would be fluent in German. But when he married our mother, his parents refused to welcome her into the family because she was Irish Catholic, so Nellie would have none of it."

Bill Schwarz was as conservative as Nellie was mercurial. He dressed in tweed suits with bow ties and was rarely seen without his meerschaum pipe. His shirt cuffs, however, were fastened with oval pictures of his daughters that Nellie had fashioned into cuff links. Bill Schwarz valued education. At one point in his life he would write in his memo book,

"Without a love of books the richest man is poor, but endowed with this treasure, the poorest man is rich."

In 1914, just before the outbreak of the First World War, he got a job at Bloomingdale's and the family moved to a six-room white clapboard house in Elmhurst, Long Island. "Daddy told the management to put in a year-round toy department on the first floor, down front, as the customers walked in from the street. 'Toys can be sold all year,' he said, 'not just at Christmas.' The toy shop was an instant success. He added a soda fountain with marble counters and high stools, so families could eat ice cream while they pondered what toys to buy."

Soon after the move to New York, a third child was born, a boy named William, a perhaps unfortunate choice, since the German kaiser had the same name. "During World War I, there was mistrust against Americans of German heritage. Even sauerkraut was renamed liberty cabbage. One day, hate mongers painted 'Schwarz Huns, Go Home!' in red paint on the side of our house and littered the yard with trash."

But the arrival of a male heir had the potential to heal the rift between Nellie and her in-laws. "Grandma and Grandpa Schwarz came east to see their first grandson born in America. Daddy Schwarz picked them up at Grand Central in his Chevrolet touring car. He believed that his parents, upon meeting the charming Nellie, would understand why he had married her.

"When they arrived, Nellie was buttoning her dress. She had just nursed the baby. She greeted her in-laws with a smile and said, 'Come, Mother and Father Schwarz. Baby William is awake and cooing.' Daddy led the family down the hall. He quietly opened up the nursery door and went to the crib. 'My God, Nellie,' he yelled, 'what's the matter with the baby?'

"William was dead. A crib death. Nellie scooped William up in her arms and ran up and down the deserted street crying, 'Somebody help me. Somebody help me, please!' The neighbors ran out of their houses, trying to console her. Nellie couldn't stop sobbing and she wouldn't let anyone take the dead baby out of her arms."

After William's funeral, Nellie threw herself into songwriting and playing the piano. The motion picture industry had yet to move west, and she found work at two studios, Vitagraph in Brooklyn and Paramount in Astoria, playing background music for silent films. "Her young daughters couldn't be left alone in the Elmhurst house, so Nellie took us along. Sunny and I were bitten by the showbiz bug. Nellie took on the challenge of getting her daughters on Broadway."

She also became a suffragette. June remembered her mother "parading down the streets with hundreds of other women in long white gowns with sashes that read 'Equal Justice.' "

Nellie was indefatigable. When June was in first grade and Sunny in second, "we were already on the vaudeville stage doing three shows a day, billed as the 'Famous Schwarz Kiddies.' We sang, danced, laughed it up in comedy sketches, and recited poems from *Little Diddy-Dids,* a book Nellie wrote. Away from the theaters, our days were filled with tap and ballet classes. Sandwiched in between the classes, we auditioned for the theatrical agents in New York City who booked the Keith-Albee and Orpheum vaudeville circuits across America."

Vaudeville conflicted with school, of course, so whenever absences were likely to occur Nellie wrote what amounted to a form letter to the principal: "I regret to inform you that Elizabeth and Helene Schwarz will be absent from school," with the number of days filled in. "It was against the law not to attend school, but the truant officers never came to our house."

The girls got their first taste of the big time in 1917. "When America entered the war, President Wilson asked Americans to buy government bonds. The organizers of the Liberty Bond rallies asked everyone to support our troops overseas. The department store where Daddy Schwarz was working erected an open-air pavilion for a bond rally. Sunny was six and I was five. As soon as the band played the opening bars, 'When Yankee Doodle Learns to Parlez-Vous Français,' Sunny and I ran out onto the stage, whirling and twirling in our red-white-and-blue-spangled costumes. When the war ended, many Broadway theaters put on variety shows for wounded veterans. Sunny and I got to sing and dance in a show emceed by George M. Cohan, Mr. Yankee Doodle Dandy himself. After the show, Cohan took Sunny and me by the hand and walked us down into the audience to welcome the veterans back home."

As the 1920s began, Nellie stepped up her efforts. The girls took dance lessons in Manhattan with top instructors, then pursued their careers in other important ways. She took them to be seen in show business haunts such as Lindy's, the St. Regis Café, or Murray's, "where a theatrical agent might glance our way and say, 'Oh, look over there. Aren't they lovely? Who can they be?' "

And it happened. "One Saturday, at the St. Regis Café, Evelyn and Kenny Delmar stopped by our table. 'We've been admiring your two lovely daughters. I'm Evelyn Delmar, and I'd like you to meet my son, Kenneth.' 'Sit down,' Nellie said, 'and join us for dessert.' "

Evelyn Delmar was a character actress who read prologues at David Belasco's theater and understudied Lenore Ulric, Belasco's big star, noted for her portrayals of sexpots. "Evelyn orchestrated our climb up the ladder from vaudeville to the Broadway stage. Kenny was nine, already with a gift for dialects. We started a three-kid act, Kenneth & the Kay Sisters, doing Klever Komedy in Klassy Kostumes. We were no longer the Schwarz Kiddies. Sunny was now Elizabeth Kay and I was Helene Kay. Evelyn became our agent and publicist. Nellie traveled the vaudeville circuits with us while Evelyn stayed grounded at her apartment on West 84th Street, always in touch by telephone."

Kenny Delmar would go on to a major career in radio, part of Orson Welles's famous broadcast of *War of the Worlds*, but would be best remembered for his hilarious, over-the-top portrayal on *The Fred Allen Show* of Senator Beauregard Claghorn, on whom any number of future blustering, stentorian characters were based.* At nine, however, the Senate was in the distant future and Kenny was enrolled in the Professional Children's School on Riverside Drive and 72nd Street, along with such future stars as Martha Raye, Ruby Keeler, Milton Berle, and Lillian Roth. Sunny and June—still Elizabeth and Helene—enrolled as well. The girls took classes in arithmetic, spelling, English literature and composition, reading, history, geography, science, and French from eight-thirty to three-thirty.

---

* Including Foghorn Leghorn, the truculent, blustery rooster in the Looney Tunes cartoon shorts.

Once in the Professional Children's School, the girls were free to audition during their off-hours, but only if they could pull off some sleight of hand. The Society for the Prevention of Cruelty to Children, known as the Gerry Society, although a private organization, was charged with enforcing child labor laws in New York. Those laws stated that children in the theater must attend school and that any child under sixteen could not perform after 7:00 p.m. So two girls who were barely ten instantly became teenagers.

"We called our mother 'Nellie' and referred to her as the wardrobe mistress, so no one knew she was our mother. Only a kid actress needs her mother along. But our nerves were frayed when we walked out onstage because we were always running from the Gerry Society, the officers hot on our trail. If we were caught, we were pulled out of the show, a fine was levied on the producer, and the Gerry Society officer threw us in the clink until Nellie posted bail. If Sunny or I got caught using one stage name, or the trail was getting hot, we signed contracts with new names, so that we couldn't be traced by the officers of the Gerry Society who scrutinized the theater playbills."

Nellie moved the family to Manhattan, to an apartment on 188th Street and St. Nicholas Avenue in Washington Heights. When the girls were on the road, they brought a packet of schoolwork and Nellie drilled them during free hours in the hotel so they could pass their exams when they returned. "We were doing two, three shows a day and we loved it. Kenny, Sunny, and I had wonderful childhoods . . . every moment was glorious."

Bill Schwarz did not share the enthusiasm. "My father wanted his daughters to follow a more traditional path . . . go to college, get our credentials, and along the way acquire an air of respectability." But Nellie was having none of it. "She said she would do her best to bring us up properly, but her daughters wanted to be in show business and she was determined it would be so." Soon Bill took a job on the road. "But when he returned from an out-of-town book fair at the same time that Sunny and I were in New York, Daddy took us to the opera or a concert. There was never any doubt in our minds that our father adored us."

The kid act broke up when one of the kids got a break. In late spring

1923, Sunny, just turned twelve, was with Evelyn buying a new pair of toe shoes when "suddenly, at Times Square, we were swallowed up by a swirling mass of breathtakingly beautiful girls in colorful sundresses as far as the eye could see. The stage door of a theater on the corner of 41st Street opened and the girls began elbowing their way forward, a stampede of determined lovelies. Evelyn and I were literally swept off our feet and propelled through the narrow passageway. We moved with the flow down an iron staircase and found ourselves in a huge dressing room in the basement. From tiny satchels, the girls pulled out leotards with thigh-high ruffled skirts in hot tropical colors. Evelyn whispered, 'It must be an audition. Don't ask. Do what the girls do.'

"I was in street clothes, but Evelyn was wearing a pair of black lace bloomers. She stepped out of them and handed them to me, told me to roll them up high and tight. Then she said, 'Show a lot of leg. With your red sweater and black toe shoes, you'll be fine. Follow the girls, Elizabeth Kay,' and she left to find out what was going on."

What Sunny had stumbled into was an audition for the Ziegfeld Follies, the most prestigious and successful revue on Broadway. The other girls had been given cards letting them know when to go onstage, but Sunny had none. The stage manager inexplicably gave her one and asked her to write her name and address on the back. The auditions went on for hours, but eventually she heard, "Elizabeth Kay, step out, please." Sunny stood on the bare stage, "in my red sweater and black lace bloomers, rolled up high and tight, showing a lot of leg." She had no music with her but asked the pianist to play "Dance of the Sugar Plum Fairy."

"Even though the footlights were bright, I could see a tall man standing behind the orchestra pit, in the first row of the theater. I recognized him from press photos. When the music started, I began twirling on my black satin toe shoes. When I was done, Ziegfeld called out in a gravelly voice, 'Do it again!' When I completed my routine the second time, Ned Wayburn, the dance director, called me down to the footlights and asked me some questions . . . my name, where I lived, where I was studying dance. Then one of Ziegfeld's assistants told me to report to the New Amsterdam Theatre on Monday for a 10:00 a.m. rehearsal.

"I was in the Ziegfeld Follies. Of the 3,200 girls who auditioned, Flo Ziegfeld chose three. I was one of the three."

But Sunny's coup was short-lived. Eighteen weeks after she began, Ziegfeld's secretary told her that a letter had been received from the Gerry Society stating that Elizabeth Kay was under sixteen. The lunch lady at the Professional Children's School, it seemed, was a paid informant and had blown the whistle. Sunny tried to bluff her way through by using Evelyn Delmar's niece's birth certificate but the society knew all the tricks. And just like that, Sunny was out of the show. When she went to pick up her belongings the next day, "on my makeup table I found a long white box tied with pink ribbons. Inside lay a dozen American Beauty roses and a handwritten note: 'Tomorrow's a new day. Dance through it with a happy heart. Good luck to you.' There was also an autographed picture: 'To Elizabeth Kay with best wishes, from your Jewish friend, Fanny Brice.' "

But Ned Wayburn was not done with Sunny. After the girls spent a few weeks in Lexington, Massachusetts, where Grandma and Grandpa Grady had bought a Victorian cottage, Wayburn got in touch with her and offered her a part in a revue called *Honeymoon Cruise,* which would play the vaudeville circuit from New York to San Francisco. She couldn't be Elizabeth Kay anymore, of course, so she combined a childhood nickname, Sunny, with that of a local undertaker, W. J. Dale, and became from then on Sunny Dale.

Sunny joined the revue in rehearsals, which were held in Wayburn's theater on West 59th Street. June went along to watch. But June could never just watch. "She sat in a chair in the back, with her ankles crossed, swinging them back and forth . . . just a little kid, eleven years old. But then she got bored and started practicing her dance routines in the aisle. June was not a bit theatrical-looking . . . just a healthy, well-complexioned girl with dark brown hair cut in a Dutch bob. But her eyes sparkled and every time you came her way she smiled at you. With just a fleeting glance, you were smitten with June."

Which was exactly what June had intended. "I wanted to be in *Honeymoon Cruise.* A musical comedy playing across America. But Wayburn was too busy to notice me. One night I made sure he'd notice. I bounced out of my chair in my tap shoes and danced as loud as I could in the back of the theater, slapping the taps down, pounding the wooden floor. I really went at it. *Wham! Bam!* Then I turned cartwheels down the aisle. Suddenly a long shrill noise pierced the room. Wayburn had blown his legendary silver whistle. It meant only one thing: He was *exasperated.* 'Stop the damn racket! Right now!' He marched over to me and thundered, 'This is a rehearsal! What's the matter with you? Are you nuts?' 'No, sir,' I said meekly, 'I love to dance.' He took a look at me. 'What's your name?' 'Helene.' 'Okay, Helene, if you *love to dance,* go up onstage.' That's how I crashed *Honeymoon Cruise.*"

"So Ned Wayburn had two Gerry Society fugitives," Sunny said. "Sunny Dale and Helene Page. We both dropped 'Kay.' Radioactive. Backstage, no one knew we were sisters except Wayburn, who signed the contracts with Nellie." Nellie completed the picture by getting herself hired as wardrobe mistress. Her sewing was only fair, but she could make fabulous hats.

Honeymoon Cruise was a huge success, even playing the legendary Palace Theatre in New York. June, as she often did, had learned every part in the show and, on opening night at the Palace, came out of the chorus to sub for the leading lady, who had come down with laryngitis. The audience loved her, marveling at the skill and stage presence of the sixteen-year-old, who was in fact only eleven.

Bill Schwarz finally came to accept that his daughters were not leaving the stage. "Because Sunny and I spent so much of our childhood on the road, my father decided we needed somewhere we could call home. We told Daddy the best place in the whole world was Grandma and Grandpa Grady's house in Lexington. So Daddy Schwarz bought a bungalow on Oak Street, a few steps away from the Gradys', across a terraced croquet lawn that lay between the two houses." In the next decade, the house in Lexington, 83 Oak Street, would turn out to be a second home to a good many baseball players, including Babe and, later, Joe DiMaggio. Bridget and Milo Grady became Lefty's surrogate grandparents.

"We had plenty of space at number 83 for the Yankees to stay overnight," June said, "and if the get-together ran late into the night and Babe was at the party, he was the short-order chef for breakfast the next morning. . . . Ham and eggs with a side of pancakes. Grandma Grady would come to the back door from her house, bringing eggs over in the skirt of her apron from the hen coops in her yard. One morning she tripped running along the path. 'All cracked and gone to waste,' Bridget said woefully. Babe noticed the tears in her eyes and said, 'That's fine, Grandma,' and he scooped the eggs out of her apron and went along to the kitchen and whipped them into an omelet.

"And then there was the time Babe saw a kid's bike on the side of Oak Street, picked it up, and pedaled up and down the hill. Lefty watched in horror as the God of Baseball crashed into the boxwood and lay sprawled, moaning, on the street. If Babe had broken his legs, Lefty said, his days as a Yankee were over."

The Oak Street house didn't turn out to be simply a stopover, however. Bill Schwarz put his foot down and insisted that the girls spend at least one year in a regular school. "Daddy Schwarz wanted us to know what a 'normal' childhood was all about. Nellie couldn't see the sense of it: 'What an outlandish idea.' But Nellie decided to give Daddy his say for one year of our lives. Exactly one school year. Not a day more."

So the sisters again became Helene and Elizabeth Schwarz and enrolled in Marycliff Academy where the two German-named girls were taught exclusively in French by Parisian nuns. "French in the classroom. French cuisine for lunch. That's how Daddy Schwarz finally sold Nellie on the idea. She figured we could take a year abroad in our own backyard."

The girls did well at Marycliff, each winning honors. But the day after their June 12, 1925, graduation, Bill Schwarz drove them to Grand Central Station in New York to rejoin the road tour of *Honeymoon Cruise.* When they returned, they reenrolled in the Professional Children's School, Gerry Society spies and all.

Then Evelyn Delmar told them that Jake Shubert and his brother Lee had hired her as dialogue coach for *Princess Flavia,* an operetta based on the Anthony Hope bestseller *The Prisoner of Zenda.* The production was being mounted at the Century Theater, where perfect diction was a must, because the acoustics were so poor that only the most accomplished actors could be understood beyond the first ten rows. Evelyn, always looking for an angle, had an idea how the former Kay sisters could use the operetta to further their careers. The Shuberts were also opening a musical called *A Night in Paris*. Casting for that show had been completed. Jake Shubert had wanted to book a sister act but had been unable to find anyone suitable. Evelyn hatched an elaborate plot whereby Sunny and June would audition for the operetta—even though neither of them sang opera and most of the singers would be doing Puccini or Verdi—and thus be discovered by the casting director as a new find for *A Night in Paris*. Both sisters, and even Nellie, thought that was the most idiotic thing they'd ever heard.

Until it worked.

June, desperate for something to sing at the audition that wasn't pop, chose a Russian folk song. When the casting director asked her name, "Evanthea" popped out of her mouth. "Exotic names were all the rage," she explained later. Then she asked the casting director, "Would you like to see what my sister can do?" Sunny ran onto the stage, plopped a baseball cap over her blond ringlets and sang a rousing rendition of "Don't Take Your Sweetie to the Ballgame or You'll Never See the Game at All." Both girls were hired for *A Night in Paris*—after assuring everyone they were both sixteen.

But even after that display of chutzpah, the road to fame featured a few bumps. When they reported for rehearsals they discovered that, without telling them, J. C. Huffman, who was staging the show, had replaced them with the Fairbanks twins. The twins were being pursued by Flo Ziegfeld, and hiring them away from the Follies had been considered a coup.

Shubert himself was about to sail for Europe. Evelyn wrangled Nellie an invitation to the bon voyage party aboard ship. Nellie "buttonholed Jake over crackers and cheese" and asked why her daughters had been fired. Shubert knew nothing about it, and while the Fairbanks twins would get the sister act, Jake promised to see what he could do for Sunny and Evanthea.

"So Sunny and I went into *A Night in Paris*, two acts, thirty-four scenes of songs, dances, and broad comedy. At rehearsals, Sunny and I did what we could get. We were singing and dancing extras in the French café scenes or walk-ons with a few lines here and there. We did anything to get our feet on the stage."

By the time the show opened in New Haven, Jake Shubert was home from the continent, *Princess Flavia* was losing money, Jake and his brother Lee were warring, and the Fairbanks twins had bolted for *George White's Scandals*. Jake took over the show himself, desperate to cut costs and shut his brother up. Sunny and June couldn't step into the sister act because all the numbers had been written for identical twins and had been eliminated. Jake screamed at everyone and got into a fistfight with comedian Jack Osterman. June, who had learned every part and understudied everyone, even got to play the lead at one performance. But in the chaos, when the show headed for New York, all of June's actual appearances on-stage were eliminated. She had only one thing to do: a scream from offstage. "When the curtain went up I stood in the wings, where no one could see me, screaming my lungs out. A sound effect. Not even a walk-on."

This time it wasn't Nellie but Sunny who went to Jake, a far riskier proposition because Shubert was in a foul temper. "But when you're fourteen, you have a lot of nerve because you don't know any better."

" 'Mr. Shubert,' I said, 'do you know my sister has nothing to do in this show?' Jake was already at wit's end, and I come prancing in complaining about my sister's part in his show.

" 'Well, Sunny,' he said, 'I'll see what I can do.' "

At the next rehearsal, Shubert suddenly called Evanthea to center stage and asked her to sing and dance a number that had been cut. After June was done, Shubert yelled, "That's it. She's Evanthea, the Powder Puff Girl. Get her in satin and feathers. I want a goddamn first-act finale for New York."

A Night in Paris, the first musical of 1926, was a runaway hit. The critic at the *New York American* wrote, "The beauty of beauties in *A Night in Paris* is conceded to be Evanthea, the most versatile girl in the revue."

The Powder Puff Girl was June's big break. From there, not yet fourteen, she was cast in two other hit shows, Laurence Schwab's *Queen High* and Rodgers and Hart's *Peggy-Ann.* The day before the signing of the contract for *Queen High,* Schwab called her into his office. "Evanthea? Your name sounds like a disease. We're in the month of June. Do you like the month of June?"

After Eilean/Helene/Evanthea admitted she did, Schwab closed his eyes, opened a phone book, and pointed at random to a name. "Evanthea," he said, "you are now June O'Dea." June was happy with the choice, and relieved. "I was hoping," she later said, "his finger wouldn't land on Brickenpooper."

In 1928, June was cast in *Here's Howe*, which closed after seventy-one performances, but its early demise gave June a shot at working with another of Broadway's iconic figures. Auditions had just begun for the George M. Cohan musical *Billie*. "About five hundred actors tapped the boards for that call. Cohan was up to his eyeballs in hoofers. He was pacing behind the pit, looking everywhere but up front. I was dancing my brains out in cut time and he's not even looking at me. So I stopped right in the middle of my routine and yelled at him, 'Listen. If you'd sit down you'd see what I can do.' Cohan burst out laughing and hired me on the spot.

"We broke the show in at the Colonial in Boston and the Grady clan was out front. We lived at the Charlesgate Apartments in Harvard Square, so the cast found itself caught up in Harvard football. We'd sit in the stadium waving our victory banners, chrysanthemums pinned to the lapels of our camel-hair coats.

"The Charlesgate Apartments were also one subway stop away from the New England Conservatory of Music. I wanted to tweak the squeak out of my violin playing, so I enrolled in a technique class. While I was there, I had the good fortune to sing for Maestro Arturo Vita, an operatic coach from La Scala, who said he was moving to New York. We began working together, and in October 1928, when Cohan brought *Billie* to New York, I caught up with the maestro again at his new address on 57th Street. The study of opera meant I had to add Italian to my French, so back to the grammar books for me."

During the run of the play, June reached a milestone.

"Two months after *Billie* opened at the Erlanger, I turned sweet sixteen. I had run from the Gerry Society for ten years, constantly changing my name, looking over my shoulder for an undercover agent, and, if I saw one or was told one was in the theater, leaping onto the fire escape outside the dressing room window or exiting through the tunnels in the basement that emptied out onto the alleyway. What a darn nuisance. But now, in *Billie,* I was an old lady of sixteen, dancing at the legal age. The cast and the stage crew threw a party for me backstage. Everyone, including George M., sang 'Happy Birthday' as I made a wish and blew out the candles on my cake.

"George M. was fun to work with but very demanding because he wanted his shows to click on Broadway. High-voltage. I knew he was obsessed with fast pacing so I did my tap routine in double time. It was so fast, I collapsed into the arms of the stage manager every time I danced off stage. I lost fifteen pounds in that show."

After a national tour of *Billie* and featured parts in other shows, June's career continued to flourish until, one night in 1931, still only eighteen but a rising Broadway star, she wandered north to the Woodmansten Inn and met a ballplayer named Lefty.

16.

A PITCHER'S PITCH

——

LEFTY BEGAN TO CHASE AFTER HER, BUT AS HE SOON DISCOVERED, June would not be wowed by a Yankee uniform. In the first place, she was a bigger star at the time than he was; in the second, she had never been to a ballpark, didn't know the first thing about baseball, and didn't give a fig about learning. Not only was June as ardent about the theater as Lefty was about pitching, she was also every bit the match for him in brains and will.

Always prepared to do whatever it took to achieve a goal, Lefty decided that if he was to successfully court a dancer, it might be a good idea to learn to dance. So for a week, he enlisted Myril Hoag to practice in the apartment at the Edison. "Hoag had the smallest feet in baseball," Jimmie Reese said, "a size 4 on the right foot and 4½ on the left. His cleats were special-order. Gomez, with size 13, had the biggest feet. It's a wonder Hoag could take the field after that week of being stepped on. I wonder what McCarthy would have thought if he knew these two were prancing around in the apartment, doing the foxtrot and the tango."

Armed with his new ballroom skills, Lefty began to pop up at Chanin's 46th Street Theatre, where June was starring in *You Said It*. He would become quite a presence over the next months. "I was at her show so many times, I could have acted in it." He invited June to Yankee Stadium for a Sunday game—when Gomez, that irresistible left-hander, would be on the mound—and a night of dancing afterward.

June accepted but since, as everyone knew, baseball players were just a bunch of lechers and drunks, mother Nellie insisted on coming along with Bill Schwarz to chaperone. Lefty agreed to leave three tickets for them at the gate. On June's first visit to Yankee Stadium, she saw Lefty face the Detroit Tigers before a crowd of 30,000. Fortune seemed to be playing Lefty's way: Charley Gehringer wasn't in the lineup, and the Tigers didn't have much hitting without him.

For seven innings, Lefty and the bespectacled Vic Sorrell fought each other to a 1–1 tie. In the bottom of the eighth, the Yankees took the lead on an RBI single by Joe Sewell. All Lefty needed to do was to retire the Tigers in the ninth to seal the win. But as Sewell gaveth, he tooketh away. After an infield single, he bobbled a perfect double-play ball; instead of two out and none on, the Tigers had two on and none out. The Tigers' best hitter, Dale Alexander, then stroked a single and the game was tied. In the tenth, the Tigers scored twice, on a single, a triple, and a squeeze bunt. The Yankees went one-two-three to Sorrell and Lefty and the Yankees lost.

Blowing a lead in the ninth, error or no, and then giving up two in the tenth put Lefty in an unpleasant mood. June, who understood a bad notice as much as anyone, tried to be cheerful and supportive. "Don't worry," she said, blissfully ignorant that starting pitchers took the mound only once every four days, "you'll beat them tomorrow."

"But she became a great fan and a second-guesser," Lefty said. "In August . . . it was Lou Gehrig's one thousandth straight game . . . Gehringer hit a single in the eleventh to beat me. 'Gomez,' she growled, 'how long do you have to be in the big leagues before you learn to pitch Gehringer high, not low?' I thought, 'Oh my God. It was better when she thought I pitched every day.' "

After that first game, Jimmie Reese recalled, the pursuit intensified. "Once June and Lefty started dating he went to see her as often as he could. The Yankees only played day games then, so he could catch the evening shows. He'd take a bunch of ballplayers and of course he sent flowers backstage. Roses, orchids, bouquets of tulips and daisies. I never knew him to go out seriously with a girl before June."

On August 31, Lefty and June returned to the Woodmansten Inn to celebrate their engagement at a party thrown by the famed Prohibition mistress of ceremonies, Texas Guinan. They were lucky not to have been present six days earlier. Guinan's show had been halted at 1:00 a.m. and six waiters and the proprietor arrested in a raid in which all of two quarts of gin had been confiscated. The five hundred patrons present stood on tables and jeered until the dry agents left.

Sunny and June had first met Guinan on the vaudeville circuit, then ran into her again at the Silver Slipper speakeasy on West 48th Street. "Sunny was fifteen and I was fourteen. It was our first gig as scantily dressed showgirls, and it ran from 11:00 p.m. to 5:00 a.m., featuring wise-cracking comics and girls, girls, girls." Guinan not only hosted Lefty and June's engagement party but picked up the tab as a wedding gift. "Fabu-lous eats, dancing, and bootleg brandy. The guest list included Lefty's Yankee teammates and Joe McCarthy, guys in the newspaper game, and my friends from Broadway.

"My one regret," June added, "is that Sunny missed the celebration, but that's what happens when a career opportunity comes up. Sunny's comedy act, Conville & Dale, had been booked for fifty-two weeks on RKO stages across America and Canada with George Burns and Gracie Allen after George's agent saw Sunny and Frank Conville onstage with Cab Calloway at the 86th Street Coliseum Theatre in New York."

To top off the evening, Harold Arlen played songs from *You Said It* on the piano and Fred Waring led the band. "With my costars Lou Holtz, Lyda Roberti, and Stan Smith all at the engagement party, we were more than happy to sing song after song. Broadway hams, all of us. A few years later, Arlen became world-famous with his score for *The Wizard of Oz*."

During the party, flushed with love and newfound stardom, Lefty pre-sented June with a specially designed engagement ring from Tiffany's, an immense three-carat job, marquise cut with a platinum band, which cost $5,000 in Depression-era dollars.

Before June and Lefty announced their engagement, however, they broke the news to their families. When June called Grandma Grady and said she was engaged to Lucky Lefty, Grandma thought June said "Lucky Lindy" and ran around Lexington telling the neighbors her granddaugh-ter was going to marry the famous flier. She was disappointed when she learned June was only engaged to a baseball player.

Grandma Grady was not the only one who had issues with the an-nouncement. The Yankee brass were more than a bit leery about their star pitcher getting involved with a showgirl. Ed Barrow threatened to ship

Lefty to the Yankee farm club in Newark if he married her. Walter Winchell, the legendary gossip columnist, tossed some gasoline on the embers by predicting that a marriage between a dancer like June and a ballplayer like Lefty wouldn't last six months.

If Barrow couldn't dissuade his pitcher, he could at least keep tabs. "One night I picked June up after the show," Lefty said, "and took her to the Roof Garden at the Park Central Hotel. We dined and danced and I took her home. The next day I went to the Stadium and there was a message to go to the office. Ed Barrow wanted to see me. I went upstairs and he said, 'You didn't get much sleep, did you?' I said, 'No, and neither did that guy you had following me.' "

Joe McCarthy, on the other hand, couldn't have cared less what Lefty did as long as it didn't affect his performance on the field. If that was threatened, however, McCarthy was right on it. "Joe never missed anything," Lefty said. "In September of '31, the Yankees had an off day on a Wednesday. *You Said It* was opening in Buffalo, so I drove up to see the show, then turned around and drove home. I didn't tell anyone I was going. The next day, I pitched against Washington and got beat when I muffed a bunt and three runs eventually scored. The next spring in St. Pete, Joe said to me on the bench, 'Lefty, how many did you win last year?'

" 'Twenty-one.'

" 'Well,' he said, 'it should have been twenty-two. Remember that game against Washington when the bunt rolled under your glove? You didn't get much sleep the night before. You were driving back from Buffalo after seeing *You Said It*.' "

But June's career soon became a genuine bone of contention within the relationship. He worked days and if she continued on Broadway, working six nights a week in a play, he would virtually never see his wife. The subject of her giving up the stage arose regularly.

Lefty pushed; June pushed back. "I've been in front of the footlights all my life and I have no intention of standing in front of a stove," she said. And that was expected to be that.

Jimmie De Shong, a pitcher, was present during a later exchange that typified the ongoing battle. "Most times when I went out to dinner in New York, it was with Lefty and June and we had a whale of a good time. But one night they fell into an argument because their careers were putting demands on their time together. June wanted to stay on the stage and Lefty said, 'Hey, wait a minute. I make enough money. You don't have to do that,' and June said, 'It has nothing to do with money. I love the stage.' Then they turned to me and asked, 'What do you think, Jim?'

"I told them, 'If I agree with Lefty, June will be angry, and if I agree with June, Lefty is going to say, "What kind of a guy are you?" So I'm gonna pass and just eat my dessert.' They were in love but trouble was coming down the pike."

In the fall, June finally informed Lefty that if he brought the subject up one more time, the engagement was off.

Lefty was undaunted. A few days later, after a matinee, he arrived at June and Sunny's apartment in the Greystone Hotel at 91st and Broadway and once again insisted June stop working after they were married. "You can leave the show and relax at home with what the Yankees are paying me."

June did not yell. She did not protest. She merely raised an eyebrow, stood up, and walked to the bathroom, Lefty in her wake. Once inside, rather than close the door, June calmly removed the three-carat Tiffany ring from her finger and dropped it into the toilet. Then, after making certain that Lefty was watching, she reached up and pulled the chain.

Lefty too said not a word. He turned and marched from the apartment. Once in the hall, he tore down the stairs to the manager's first-floor apartment and pounded on the door.

"Turn off all the water!" he screamed when the manager appeared.

When the manager heard the reason, he rushed to the basement and shut the valves. Plumbers were summoned to drain the system and go through the pipes and the traps. It was hopeless, they said, but Lefty made them keep looking. The next day, astoundingly, the ring, covered in muck, turned up in one of the traps.

Another man would have taken the hint, or at least breathed an immense sigh of relief, then either given up his demands or returned the ring to Tiffany's with his bankroll, if not his dignity, intact. Lefty did return to

Tiffany's, but only to have the ring cleaned. To Vernon Gomez, watching three carats flushed down the toilet represented only a temporary setback. He was in love with June and there was no doubt in his mind that she would marry him.

Two weeks later, the engagement was on again. To commemorate the occasion, Lefty presented June with that very same three-carat ring.

This time she didn't take it off. The two stayed married, bumpy though it sometimes was, for fifty-six years.

FOR THE TERM OF the engagement, however, they were apart more than together. For one thing, the team spent half its time on the road.

"In my day, teams didn't travel coast-to-coast. The furthest west a major league team traveled was St. Louis, but because the teams were limited to train travel, it still took us longer. The two fastest trains from New York to Chicago were the sixteen-hour New York Central's Twentieth Century and the nineteen-hour Broadway Limited. A trip to steamy St. Louis meant twenty-seven hours aboard the American. Without air-conditioning, the railroad cars were stuffy and suffocatingly hot. We tossed and turned in the upper berths, always too short for any ballplayer over six feet. All we did was count the beads of perspiration falling on the floor.

"To while away the time, we played card games like hearts, bridge, or poker. If the stakes ran too high, Joe McCarthy curbed our avarice by only allowing Old Maid. We all knew when Babe got the old crone. He bellowed furiously."

After the season had concluded, Lefty had to make his way home to Rodeo while June remained in New York. At the end of the 1931 season, to make some money and stay in condition on the way across the country, Lefty hooked on with a barnstorming tour organized by Earle Mack, Connie's son, which would play across the United States and end up in Juarez, Mexico.

"The roster included Bill Dickey, Tony Lazzeri, me, St. Louis shortstop Red Kress, and White Sox first sacker later turned boxing palooka Art Shires. A bunch of pro ballplayers playing games against semipro teams. We traveled by train and played exhibition games in the towns coming up along the tracks—Omaha, Kansas City.

"After the last game in Juarez, we went to a Mexican restaurant where everything was on the house. The owner and the city dignitaries honored us with a toast and the owner added that he was putting a case of bourbon onto our train. Right after the toast, the owner leaned over to me and said, 'Mr. Gomez, where exactly were you born in Mexico?' I looked up in surprise. 'I'm not Mexican. I'm Spanish.' Two seconds of stunned silence, then boom, bang. The party is off. No case of bourbon. After we're out the door, my teammates jumped me, shouting, 'Son of a bitch, Gomez. You could have been a Mexican for another two hours.' "

The reception in Rodeo was more amicable, especially from a surprising source.

"Coyote became a baseball fan because his son was pitching for the Yankees," said Lefty's niece, Vivien Sadler. "I don't think he truly knew what the game was all about, since he couldn't read the newspapers. But when Coyote opened the papers and saw Vernon's picture on the sport pages, a grin spread across his face. He'd point to Vernon's picture and say, 'My boy Vernon. In the papers again today. Pitching for them Yankees back east.' And I can still picture Lizzie sitting in her parlor with the coal-oil lamp light falling on her hands as she crocheted a pillow. Vernon had written and told her he had been initiated into the Order of the Elks. On one side of the pillow Lizzie crocheted the Elks emblem, and Vernon's initials, VLG, on the other. It was on his bed for his entire life. Lizzie was not one to show much emotion. She kept her thoughts to herself, but her eyes sparkled when she talked about Vernon pitching ball in the majors."

"Coyote and Lizzie listened to the Yankee games on the radio," Lefty noted. "If I pitched and we won the game, the radio announcer in San Francisco wrapped up his national news broadcast with, 'And for that little old couple in Rodeo, the Yankees won today.' "

While Lefty was in California, June landed a leading role in George Gershwin's Pulitzer Prize–winning *Of Thee I Sing,* where her dancing partner would be future United States senator George Murphy. With Murphy, she introduced the hit song "Love Is Sweeping the Country," which stopped the show every night with a standing ovation. Gershwin himself played piano at the rehearsals, spelled by Oscar Levant. Gershwin was so fond of his "Junie-Bug" that she and Murphy often tried out new numbers at Gershwin's West Side apartment.

After some fine-tuning, *Of Thee I Sing* opened in Boston in early December and audiences loved it. What could be more appealing than a send-up of American politics with Gershwin's music as a backdrop? Critics predicted a big hit, but in a Depression market, nothing was a certainty. Not until December 13 did the producers finally decide to open in New York on the night of Saturday, December 26. In late December, Lefty departed California for the premiere, the first time in his life he would not spend Christmas in Rodeo.

17.

"THE GREATEST THRILL OF MY CAREER"

———

AS THE 1932 SEASON APPROACHED, PROHIBITION WAS CREAKING WITH age. Unemployment, however, was in full flower. Herbert Hoover was so widely reviled that when he threw out the first ball of the season, he was jeered. But for the Yankees, 1932 was a year of promise.

The team's optimism was engendered not simply by its strong finish the season before but by the fact that the A's were decidedly weaker. Connie Mack was insisting to anyone who would listen that he had no plans to break up his team, which only made his players more certain that he did. Mickey Cochrane, the best catcher in the league, had dropped so much money in the crash that he was said to be losing focus during games. Other A's players had lost heavily as well, and with Mack's own net worth only a fraction of what it once had been, they were unlikely to recoup their losses in salary. Nor was attendance likely to improve, as Philadelphia's city fathers stubbornly maintained their ban on Sunday baseball.

New York was a different story. The only significant lineup change was at short, where Frank Crosetti, Lefty's old pal from the Seals, would displace Lyn Lary, but with budding stars Bill Dickey, Ben Chapman, Charley Ruffing, and Lefty Gomez to supplement Gehrig, Ruth, Lazzeri, and Earle Combs, the Yankees were one year better and the A's one year worse.

For spring training, Lefty joined the team in St. Petersburg, traveling south from New York on the Seaboard Airline train. The team had abandoned the Princess Martha for the stunning, luxurious Don CeSar. The hotel was pink stucco and built on a spit of land on the Gulf of Mexico in the historic Pass-a-Grille district. The rooms were large, the view was magnificent, and an orchestra played at dinner.

Unfortunately for the players, these virtues were overshadowed by the Don CeSar's location—across two causeways and fourteen miles from the attractions of downtown. The players were bused each day to practice, then bused back to the hotel. Nightlife was decidedly lacking. "There was nothing," Lefty said. "And I mean nothing. The only exciting thing near the hotel was a couple of tackle shops for fishing. Ted Williams would have loved it."

Jerry Mitchell, a beat writer, was marooned with the team. "There wasn't much for the players to do after dinner except play cards, write home, or listen to the chamber music aimed at the old gaffers in the lobby chairs. Most of them got into the habit of repairing to the quiet of their rooms early where the only noise came from the sound of the surf breaking on the beach below."

But if Señor Goofy's job was to keep the team loose, he would do so—even at times unwittingly. June, now a headliner in a hit show, had given Lefty the backstage number at the Music Box. At eleven-thirty, without fail, he called and transmitted what Mitchell termed a "nightly message of love." All up and down the seventh floor, transoms were opened wide, the better to eavesdrop on the cooing. "One night, as soon as Lefty's phone hit the cradle, a mighty chorus of 'Good Night Darling, Good Night Sweetheart' filled the hall. Transoms slammed shut up and down the hall as Gomez charged out."

June eventually charmed everyone, including Joe McCarthy, whose wife was called, without irony, "Babe." "Joe and Babe caught me in *Of Thee I Sing*. They came backstage to tell me how much they liked the way George Murphy and I tap-danced. Joe told me he liked to soft-shoe, and I said, 'Show me.' He laughed and did an 'Off to Buffalo' exit step out the door. Joe also had a fine baritone voice. Lefty heard him singing Irish melodies in the showers, although even Lefty knew not to let on."

Lefty's lack of skill as a hitter had also begun to receive increased attention among his teammates, in the press, and especially from the man himself. By modern standards, his hitting was actually not all that bad. He would finish his career at .147 and in one year, 1937, actually hit .200. In the coming season, he would drive in 15 runs. In the 1930s, however, pitchers were expected to go nine innings and Lefty would therefore have a sufficient number of plate appearances to guarantee that he would look utterly inept at least once per game. Charley Ruffing, on the other hand, finished his career with a .269 batting average and hit .330 in 1931, with 8 doubles, a triple, 3 home runs, and 12 RBIs. For Lefty, getting an extra-base hit seemed to require an act of God.

The previous season, Babe began a running bet, $50 at five-to-one odds, that Lefty would not get ten hits in the entire season. It had come down to the wire, but Lefty scratched out a single against the Tigers on September 13, then lashed a dribbler through the infield on September 26 to finish with eleven singles for the season and a batting average of .133, which nonetheless forced Babe to fork over $250. This was no insignificant sum for a man making less than $7,500 a year. Of course, Babe was at $80,000 in 1931, so he could afford it. Babe had taken a cut in 1932, to $75,000, while Lefty was raised to $10,000, a hefty sum at a time when prices were dropping everywhere.

While Babe remained iconic among his teammates, Lou Gehrig, although no one talked about it, was by then accepted in the clubhouse as the team's best player. The astonishing numbers he put up year after year would have guaranteed him iconic status on any other team. In 1931, he had batted .341, with 46 home runs and 184 RBIs. He had drawn 117 bases on balls while striking out only 56 times, a stunningly low number for a slugger. Lou drove in more than 150 runs eight times in his career, three of those topping 175. Babe had a huge year in 1931 as well, but he was eight years older with bad knees and had become almost stationary in the field.

Lou was different from Babe, different from most major leaguers. He had attended an Ivy League college, was quiet, determined, and introspective, and when the Yankees were in New York continued to live at home with his mother and father. He was not a leader the way Babe was, but he set the sort of example McCarthy favored. Perhaps he didn't join his teammates for nights on the town, but Lou did invite them over for some home cooking.

Lefty was a frequent guest. "Whatever German food Lou liked best, that's what Mom Gehrig served. Her dishes were heavy with cream sauces and noodles, but if Lou liked it, we liked it, according to Mom. Everyone was bilingual in the Gehrig family. Even the Gehrigs' German shepherd answered to commands in German and English. After dinner, we were at the sink. We had to scour the frying pans and wash the dishes, dry them, and stack them neatly back into the cupboards. When Mark Koenig was with the team, though, he'd duck out and disappear down into the damp basement with Pop Gehrig to sample Pop's bootleg brew. Koenig didn't bother with a glass, just stuck the tube in his mouth."*

But Lou was simply never good copy, especially on a team where sportswriters had so many appealing choices. Between a 21-win season in 1931, an impending marriage to a Broadway star, and his ripening El Goofo persona, Lefty got the most ink of all the Yankee pitchers that spring. Ruffing was a distant second, and the aging veterans Pennock and George Pipgras were consigned to third-paragraph status. When the team arrived in New York on April 7, Lefty was facing higher expectations than ever before in his life.

He would face them with a new roommate, Frank Crosetti. Among the changes in personnel had been the sale of Jimmie Reese to St. Paul as payment for an infielder named Jack Saltzgaver, who arrived with a big reputation but who ultimately could not displace either Lazzeri or Sewell. He played in twenty games, batted .128, and was shipped to Newark. Jimmie went to the Cardinals, where he would spend one solid season before returning to the Pacific Coast League. Even though he was with a contending club, no one blamed him for choosing the minors instead. St. Louis was widely considered the worst place to play in the majors.

"On the theater circuit, everyone said the same thing," June recalled. " 'Stay away from St. Louis in the summer. Hottest place in the country. Washington, D.C., is next.' Something about St. Louis being in a valley. The heat gets in and the city steams."

---

* Later in his life, watching *Pride of the Yankees,* Lefty noted the scene in which Gary Cooper, who played Lou, appeared for his first major league game. "A hawker selling souvenir programs approaches Mom Gehrig saying, 'Lady, you need a scorecard to know the players.' Mom retorts, 'I know my own son, Louis. The rest are not my business.' That was Mom Gehrig, all right. She was always calling out from the stands, 'My Louie! My Louie!' " Many thought Cooper had been miscast in the lead but not Lefty. "Coop was taller and thinner than old Biscuit Pants but his shyness and dogged determination were exactly right. Coop was a terrific baseball fan and came out to Yankee Stadium many times. He gave June and me our white Sealyham terrier, Colonel."

Lefty said, "When the Yankees played the St. Louis Browns in the thirties, before air-conditioning, the ballplayers checked into a hotel, stripped the sheets from their beds, and soaked them in cold water in the bathtub. Then we wrung the sheets out, spread them wet on the beds, and crawled between them to sleep. During the night, when the sheets dried out, we got up and did it all over again. It's a wonder we could pitch and hit after being clammy all night." The ballpark was little better; the pitching mound was essentially a pile of rocks. "They'd have to paint the place before they could condemn it," Lefty observed.

With Reese gone, Lefty went in with Crosetti and Myril Hoag on an apartment at 91st Street and West End Avenue, conveniently close to June's place at the Greystone Hotel. The rent was $100 a month and, as the year before, they split the chores. "Myril and I did the shopping and I arranged a small breakfast every morning," Crosetti said. "The day Lefty was pitching he never ate breakfast. He was too high-strung, like a racehorse going to the barrier. And Myril and I would have starved if we waited for Lefty to do the housekeeping."

The three macho major leaguers did encounter one problem they had not anticipated. "One day, when I was a kid back home in Rodeo," Lefty recounted, "driving the cows to the milking barn, there was an electrical storm and a bolt of lightning killed two of our cows. I was thrown to the ground with a scorched shirt. I wasn't hurt, but from then on I was petrified of lightning. So when I'm rooming with Myril Hoag and Frank Crosetti in the West End Avenue apartment, I find out Hoag and Cro are scared of lightning too. Then Lazzeri tells me that anything electrical draws lightning to it during a thunderstorm. That's all we needed to know. If a storm broke when we were in the apartment, we shut off all the lights and stumbled around in the dark until we rammed into the beds. We jumped in and stuck our heads under the covers. How dumb could we get? Big leaguers. The lightning may not have hit the apartment house, but we almost broke our shins stumbling around in the dark."

Fear did not stop at the portals of Yankee Stadium. Joe Cronin's wife, Mildred, witnessed a game between the Yankees and the Senators when, during a sudden, violent thunderstorm, "to my amazement and everyone else's at the game, Lefty ran off the mound into the dugout followed closely by Crosetti from short."

Although tales of the perils of apartment dwelling didn't make the papers, many other Señor Goofy stories, some of which were at least partially true, popped up regularly during the 1932 season, penned by sports page luminaries Tom Meany, Will Wedge, Dan Daniel, and even Damon Runyon and Grantland Rice. Lefty quickly got the idea and learned to plant his tongue in his cheek if it helped make a good yarn. When asked to write a short piece about himself, "How I Broke In," he began, "When I was a kid, I had no particular desire to be a ballplayer. My parents wanted me to be an electrical engineer. I wanted to be an aviator more than anything else in the world. In the end, I crossed up everybody, including myself." Lefty went on to write that he only played baseball in high school because the other kids did, and that he became a pitcher "because I was left-handed and everybody thought left-handers could pitch." Finally he observed, "Although I had no particular interest in baseball, I got by all right." In this one case, it was probably a good thing that Coyote couldn't read.

As the Yankees' ace, Lefty was given the ball on opening day, April 12, at Shibe Park, to face the A's, although his opponent was George Earnshaw and not Lefty Grove. Once again, the Philadelphia crowd was sparse, announced at 16,000, and those few witnessed a harbinger of a disappointing season. The Yankees scored four runs in the first inning and five more in the fourth to take a 12–4 lead into the bottom of the ninth. When Lefty gave up two more runs, Charley Ruffing finished up. In the seventh inning, Jimmie Foxx had sent a drive to dead center field that not only cleared the fence but passed the flagpole halfway up. But the Yankees had a huge lead at that point, so the homer did no damage except to Lefty's ego. The Yankees had hit five home runs themselves, two by Ruth and one by Gehrig.

In the second game of the series, played two days later, the champion A's rallied in the bottom of the ninth to win 9–8 in front of 6,000 fans.

Midway through the season, Lefty had an important visitor, although the two did not get to speak. Milfred, who had done so much to help his kid brother, found himself in New York, strolling down Broadway, waiting to board a ship that would take him to one of the many far-flung locations at which he would spend his working life. He had never seen Lefty pitch in a major league game. He noticed a billboard that read, "Baseball Today. Yankee Stadium. 2 p.m. New York Yankees vs. Chicago White Sox. Gomez Pitching." Milfred just had time to hop in a taxi to make it to the ballpark for the game. He got close enough to the field to get a big smile and a wave from an astonished Lefty. Milfred watched his brother pitch for a few innings but he had to leave lest his ship sail without him. Instead of being escorted to the clubhouse after the game to meet Babe Ruth and Lou Gehrig, Milfred settled into a stateroom for a long voyage. He would never see Lefty pitch again.

THE 1932 PENNANT RACE turned out to be an anticlimax. The Yankees won 19 of their first 25 games and never looked back. The 1932 results were almost an exact reversal of 1931. The Yankees finished 107–47 to win by 13 games over the 94–60 A's. Washington, as it had in 1931, finished third, also winning more than 90 games. Jimmie Foxx had a stupendous year, batting .364 with 58 home runs and 169 RBIs, edging out Lou Gehrig for most valuable player.

Placing fifth in the MVP race and tops among pitchers was Lefty. He finished 24–7 with 21 complete games, striking out 176 in 265 innings. Although his ERA went to 4.21, many of those runs came in the late innings of games the Yankees had well in hand. Lefty had become the team's top big-game pitcher; Charley Ruffing, who became the first Yankee ever to lead the league in strikeouts with 190, was close behind. George Pipgras, near the end of his career, chalked up 16 wins, and volatile Johnny Allen went 17–4. But Lefty was the one who got the ball in the key games. If McCarthy didn't give it to him, he demanded it.

"Lefty loved to pitch against the tough clubs," Joe McCarthy told the *Sporting News*. "When he thought he should pitch, he would give me that look . . . put the bead on me. Even if my back was turned, I could feel his eyes boring into me. I may have figured on pitching somebody else but when Gomez gave me that look I had to go with him. In 1932, we were on our way to winning the pennant, but the Yankees still had to knock off the

A's. We were playing a doubleheader and, after Lefty beat them in the first game, he wanted to pitch the second game. In the clubhouse, between the games, he came to me and said, 'Joe, I can beat them again. Let me pitch the second game.'

" 'No,' I said, 'I'm not doing that. But go down to the bullpen and if I need you, I'll call you.' Fortunately, I didn't need him, because we won easy. I knew if we got into trouble, he would have coming running out of that bullpen without being called. I only sent him to the bullpen to keep him from driving me crazy on the bench."

Lefty could be a target as well. Late in the season, he started a game by giving up three first-pitch singles. With the bases loaded and no one out, McCarthy came out to the mound. Bill Dickey, the catcher, came out as well.

"I'm standing there," Lefty said, "and McCarthy asks Dickey, 'What's Lefty got today?' 'How do I know?' Dickey said. 'I haven't caught one yet.' "

On September 29, Lefty had the opportunity to fulfill the ultimate dream of millions of boys all across America, a dream that had once been his own. He strode to the pitcher's mound at Yankee Stadium, in front of an announced crowd of 50,709, to begin the second game of the 1932 World's Series against the Cubs.

The Yankees had won the first game 12–6. Red Ruffing had given up two runs in the first, but the Yankees had scored three in the fourth when Gehrig hit a huge home run, and five more in the sixth off Guy Bush to put the game away. The crowd, which in previous years would have been in excess of 60,000, perhaps 70,000, was announced at a Depression-induced 41,459. World's Series games tended to have more accurate attendance figures, since the players' share was based on the gate.

For the second game, Lefty would face the Cubs' best pitcher, Lon Warneke, "The Arkansas Hummingbird," who had finished the regular season with a record of 22–6 and an earned run average of 2.37. Joe McCarthy never explained his pitching order, but it had become common practice during the season for Lefty to face the top hurler on the opponent's staff. For his part, Cubs third baseman and manager Charlie Grimm said, "We're a long way from losing the series. Warneke will stop the Yankees tomorrow."

Warneke did not.

The Cubs scored in their opening at-bat on a double, an error by Crosetti at short, and a short sacrifice fly on which the Cubs took advantage of center fielder Earle Combs's notoriously weak arm. The Yankees scored two in the bottom of the inning on singles by Gehrig and Dickey. Both runners who crossed the plate were on base by virtue of walks. The Cubs tied the score in the third, when Babe allowed a ball to fall in front of him, then skitter past him for a double, the runner then scoring on a single that Babe could not charge fast enough. That was all the Cubs got. The Yankees scored three more and took a 2–0 Series lead.

Lefty lost four pounds during the game, even in the cool of late September. He gave up nine hits, but struck out eight and walked only one. Afterward, the most profuse praise came from Cubs manager Charlie Grimm. After what the *New York Times* termed "dazed admiration," Grimm extolled, "One of the greatest pitchers I ever saw. He beats Lefty Grove with me. Why, he was just as fast as Grove and what control." When asked about the nine hits, Grimm replied, "We didn't get any real hits when it meant something."

The Associated Press also ran an article with reactions to the game. Datelined "Rodeo, California," the piece noted that "while the Yankees were beating the Cubs today, one of the citizens of this little town strutted up and down the main street . . . proudly greeting his fellow townsmen." Coyote Gomez proclaimed to one and all, and perhaps even to himself, "What do you think of my boy Vernon now? I knew he could do it. He really showed those Cubs something."

June was not at the game. *Of Thee I Sing* had a matinee that afternoon, so whenever she was offstage, she dashed for the radio—as did George Murphy and the other members of the cast. They were all laying bets on the Yankees. They would have driven her crazy if Lefty didn't win.

Lefty said later, "The greatest thrill of my career was my first World Series win. A World Series game is not like any other game, and winning the World Series is the crowning event of a team's season. If you ask most ballplayers, they'll tell you the same thing. The winner of a short series is the club that has power, pitching, and luck. It's peak performance under the maximum tension possible on a baseball diamond. The team can't afford to get rattled, and in a World Series that's tough, because the pressure is at the boiling point. And who dominates a series? The pitchers.

"Funny thing was, I wasn't nervous from the time the game started until about an hour or so after it was all over. Before a game, I'm fidgety, walking up and down the bench. But once I started to warm up I felt okay and I was that way all through the game. In the clubhouse, after the win, I answered all the press questions and called June and asked her to meet me at Penn Station, where the Yankees would leave for Chicago. Then I walked out to the parking lot, got in my car, and started to drive downtown from the Bronx. I must have gone about twenty or thirty blocks when I suddenly realized I had pitched in a World Series and won it. I began shaking all over and had to pull over to the curb to let the shakes wear off."

The third game, in Chicago, became one of the most famous in World's Series history, not so much for the outcome but for an immortal piece of baseball lore. About all that is not in dispute about that fifth inning was that Babe Ruth hit one of the longest home runs anyone had ever seen. Whether he "called his shot," as many, including Lefty, insisted until the day they died, or merely waved his bat in some contemptuous but unspecified gesture was never established. Film of the event unearthed years later would seem to indicate the latter. Lost in the rumpus was that Gehrig followed with an even harder-hit blast that put the nail in the Cubs' coffin. The Yankees won in four straight, their first Series victory in four years.[*]

Afterward the Yankee players chipped in and bought Babe a humidor with all their names engraved on it to commemorate his tenth World's Series. In the heady atmosphere of a winner's clubhouse, few would have realized it would also be his last.

---

[*] For Bill Dickey, winning the World's Series was just the beginning of an excellent off-season. He was scheduled to marry Violet Arnold, a showgirl in *Earl Carroll's Vanities,* on October 5 in New York. "June and I were in the wedding party," Lefty said. "After we beat the Cubs, I offered to drive the car Bill had just bought in Chicago back to New York. He handed me the keys and went to sleep in the passenger seat. I got to Cleveland in no time at all, then drove for six more hours. Bill woke up and asked me where we were. I stopped at a gas station to find out how far we were from Scranton, Pennyslvania. The gas man guffawed. 'You boys are only thirty-two miles from Cleveland.' Somewhere I had made a wrong turn and gone around in a circle for six hours. Bill damn near missed the ceremony."

18.

"NO LIPSTICK FOR LEFTY"

With the world's series victory, Lefty had become a full-fledged celebrity. Word of his comedic skills had gotten around as well. "Shortly after my World Series win, Nicholas Schenck rang me up at the Ansonia. Schenck was president of the Loew's theater chain and his brother Joe was chairman of the board of Twentieth Century Fox. I had met Nick and Joe at the Stadium through Sunny. He offered me $3,000 a week, three shows a day, for a twelve-week booking in and around New York. The vaudeville stage acts were live entertainment between the showings of the Hollywood films. How could I refuse?

"I opened at Loew's State, Broadway at 45th. Edgar Bergen and Charlie McCarthy were on the bill. So was Russ Columbo. Russ was suave and handsome, just a year older than me. He sang his hit tunes, 'Prisoner of Love' and 'You Call It Madness.' "*

The first part of the act was simple. With the band in the theater pit belting out "Take Me Out to the Ball Game," Lefty walked onstage in his Yankee uniform and did a ten-minute monologue on big league life. "Gomez had impeccable timing," June recalled, "and the audience roared." The second segment was not so simple. He was part of a three-minute skit with slapstick comedians Mills, Kirk, and Martin. Physical comedy turned out to be a less gratifying experience. After his first performance, Lefty rushed into the wings where June was waiting. "It's

---

* Two years later, at age twenty-six, Columbo died while visiting a friend in Hollywood who was fidgeting absentmindedly with an antique pistol that he kept on his desk as an ornament. Columbo was in an armchair, and when the pistol fired, the lead ball shot into his left eye and lodged in his brain.

too long," he exclaimed. "I'm not an actor. Why can't I just run across the stage with those guys in pursuit?"

June tried to calm him down. "Why, honey, you were swell in that skit. The audience called you back for three bows and this is a tough house."

"What's tough about it?" Lefty retorted. "All those people clapping for nothing at all."

Lefty quit after five weeks, but not because of the skit. Schenck told him, "Under the stage lights, you look like a ghost. You have to wear rouge and lipstick on Broadway."

"No lipstick for Lefty," he replied, and a $3,000-a-week contract came to an end. Still, it was quite a year. With his $15,000 from Schenck, $5,232 in World's Series money, and $10,000 in salary, he grossed more money than anyone on the team except Babe Ruth.

After his precipitous retirement from the stage, Lefty drove the LaSalle to California; in an era before interstate highways, the trip took a week on roads of varying quality. June remained in New York in the Gershwin show. The winter of 1932 would be the last for Lefty as an unmarried man and, mercifully, the last during which he would see the inside of the Saratoga Health Farm. Most of the time he spent with Lizzie and Coyote.

"With the children grown, married, and moving on with their lives, my parents were rattling around in a big empty house. My brothers and I decided to remodel the old homestead into four apartments. Coyote and Lizzie could live in the first-floor flat with the original country kitchen, parlor, bath, and bedroom and rent the other apartments for income. Earl and Lloyd built it, Milfred wired it, and I paid for it with my 1932 World Series money. With tenants in the house, I suggested it was time to lay sidewalks. Earl laid them out in front of the house and told me to press my left hand into the wet cement. Then Milfred took a stick and scratched 'VLG 11/22/1932' next to the hand imprint. Some people are in Grauman's Chinese Theatre. Hell, I'm in Rodeo cement."

"Vernon looked real sharp when he returned home in the off-season," said George Lakeman, who had been a volunteer catcher when Lefty was a teenager. "No more bib overalls or dirty cords. Vernon wore flannel slacks and tailored silk shirts. He loved to come home. He was a Californian. When he arrived in town, after seeing his parents, he drove over to the school, pulled up in the parking lot in that snazzy yellow convertible, and banged the horn. All the students ran from behind their desks over to the windows yelling, 'Lefty's home. Lefty's home.' We ran to the parking lot, crowding around him. 'Lefty, how's Babe? How's Lou?' And all the time we were running our hands along his LaSalle. Wow! The teachers closed up classes for the day. We ran out to the ball field, dragging Lefty along with us. Next thing you know he was playing sandlot with us. A New York Yankee. After that, he came by most every day, watching our games, coaching us in the fundamentals. He was like a big brother to us all. A nice man and a great man."

On another occasion, Stan La Fontaine, five years old, was with his father and sisters, driving on Richmond's main street on the way to buy clothes. "At a traffic light, we see Vernon driving by in his convertible. He stops right smack in front of us, then stands up and yells to Dad, 'Hey Curley, I want to talk to Marion and Joyce.'

"My dad doesn't know what to do. All the traffic is bunched up now with Vernon in the middle of it. So, of course, here comes the burly traffic cop walking over all steamed up and he bawls my dad out but good. Then he spies Vernon. 'Oh, hi there, Lefty, when did you get back in town?' And a big bull session goes on with the cop asking about baseball back east, and what's going on with the Yanks, and then the irate drivers stop their honking and cursing and they leave their cars in the middle of the street and they run over and surround Lefty's car and everyone's talking Yankee baseball.

"Well, what Vernon wanted to do was take my two sisters flying at the Oakland airport, the one Amelia Earhart was using at the time. But my dad says, 'But, Lefty, I'm taking the kids to buy clothes,' and Vernon says, 'Never mind the clothes. They can buy shoes anytime. Come with me.' Anyway, in the middle of the traffic tangle, Vernon has my sisters leave my dad's car and jump into his. So off they go. I'm in the backseat of the car, five years old, wishing I was old enough to go with them instead of buying long pants for school."

19

PITZY AND FUNG

O N FEBRUARY 26, 1933, VERNON GOMEZ AND JUNE O'DEA WERE MARRIED. The ceremony took place at the Church of the Blessed Sacrament on West 71st Street in New York City. June wore a full-length pale blue dress and matching hat; Lefty wore a dark suit. Sunny was maid of honor and Frank Conville, Sunny's partner in Conville & Dale, the best man.

Planning for every wedding has its challenges; for this one, some were unusual. "The priest came to me a couple of days before and told me he was having trouble. When I asked what the matter was, he said, 'All the altar boys want to be part of the service. They're all Yankee fans. If I pick two of them, the other six are sure to be mad at me.' So I told him, 'I have a bunch of baseballs over at my place autographed by the entire team. I'll bring over six tomorrow and you can give them to the other kids. That should make everything okay.' "

After the priest distributed the balls, a different complication arose. "Now I don't have any altar boys for the wedding," he told Lefty. "When they heard what had happened they all wanted the baseballs instead."

There would be no idyllic getaway to celebrate the nuptials. "We had a one-night honeymoon in Atlantic City," June said. "The next morning Gomez said, 'So long, sweetheart, I'm off to spring training.' *Of Thee I Sing* had moved to Philadelphia, so I headed there. We didn't lay eyes on each other for six weeks."

Nellie and William Schwarz were present to see their daughter married, but Lizzie and Coyote Gomez were not. Both were by now over seventy, and attending the wedding meant ten days of cross-country travel to a freezing city in the midst of winter, a season with which Lizzie and Coyote had little experience. Worse, with Lefty and June leaving immediately after the ceremony, the two would have remained stranded in New York with not a single person they had ever previously met. So, after some discussion on each coast, everyone agreed that Lizzie and Coyote should send their blessings and congratulations from afar. They would not, in fact, meet their daughter-in-law for almost two years.

With the prospect of a new wife, Lefty wanted a new salary. Although the Yankees claimed Gomez was one of two players to be offered a raise that year—Babe was asked to take a $25,000 cut to $50,000, and Gehrig, who was pounding the ball everywhere, was asked to go from $27,500 to $20,000—whatever the club was offering, Lefty wasn't accepting. It didn't help the club's bargaining position when McCarthy announced to the press that Lefty might win 30 games. At least ten other players resented having their salaries cut after winning the World's Series and either held out or threatened to, but Ruppert and Barrow were equally insistent that, with plummeting gate receipts both home and away, the players were lucky to have jobs at all. After some dickering, Lefty finally signed for a reported $15,000, although it was likely to have actually been $13,500. Babe, after threatening to quit if he didn't get $60,000, signed for $52,000; Gehrig signed for a reported $21,500.

Lefty drove into St. Pete three days late but threw hard in his first sessions. One by one, the other disgruntled Yankees straggled into the monastic Don CeSar. The players were adamant that their umbrage at tightfisted management would not carry over to the ball field, but without a doubt, the team went into the 1933 season with less élan than a Series winner should have.

After another dull stay watching the Gulf of Mexico ebb and flow, the team moved north. Lefty's road roommate was Red Ruffing. If a bolt of lightning had hit their hotel room, the Yankees' pennant chances would have been finished.

Lefty and June took an apartment on West End Avenue in the 70s, not far from Babe and Claire's on Riverside Drive. The Ruths entertained an eclectic group, including writers, show people, other sports figures, and businessmen. Conversation was more likely to be of world events than of baseball. As with Lefty, Babe's private persona was a far cry from what fans and sportswriters witnessed in public.

"It drives me up a wall when sportswriters write all these things about Babe secondhand," Maye Lazzeri said years later. "Babe didn't play ball for all those years and set records because he was a drunk. No alcoholic could play like Babe did. The sportswriters exaggerated everything. It just kills me when they write what a bum he was. Babe was anything but that. He and the whole Yankees club had too much respect for Ruppert and Barrow and what the Yankees meant to the fans.

"Tony and I and June and Lefty were always up to Babe and Claire's for his birthday parties on February 7. He'd sit there in his smoking jacket and slacks sipping one or two drinks all night long. He was really a very pleasant man to be around. Good conversationalist. The Lazzeris and the Gomezes went on family picnics with Babe and Claire. My son David idolized him. Babe kidded around with him, played catch or tag. What a lovable guy. Never a braggart or a show-off. I never did hear him talk about himself in nine years. And when we went on family picnics, he'd have two or three beers, but we never saw Babe drunk. June and I didn't see him every day, but we saw him a lot more than the sportswriters did."

Certainly Maye's portrait is as incomplete as the reporters', but it does indicate the sort of complexities that newspapermen of that era, and perhaps every era, chose to overlook.

The Ruths were totally hospitable. "As a new bride," June noted, "I could only boil water. When the telephone rang in our apartment and it was Claire inviting us to 'drop everything and c'mon over for crab cakes,' Lefty was out the door in two seconds flat."

As close as they were, Lefty wasn't dependent on Babe for social introductions. Sometimes, in fact, it worked the other way, once through the unlikely catalyst of a barely five-foot-tall, wisecracking, cigar-chomping ex-vaudevillian named Irving "Pitzy" Katz.

Pitzy Katz was one of Lou Gehrig's closest friends. Katz could make Lou guffaw at jokes in dialect or with general antics. Katz had purchased a janitorial service with his vaudeville earnings, and Lefty remembered Lou asking, "Pitzy, when you contract out to clean these office buildings, how do you give them an estimate for the work to be done?" Pitzy replied, "With my nose, Lou. I walk in, take a big whiff, and say, 'This will cost you four hundred a month.'" It must have worked, because Katz's janitors cleaned, among other skyscrapers, the Chrysler Building and Empire State Building.*

Katz played in a weekly poker game held at the apartment of cartoonist Paul Fung, who lived in the same Riverside Drive complex as Babe, although they had never met. Lou introduced Pitzy to Lefty, and Pitzy invited Lefty to the game. Weekly poker games weren't Lou's style; his passion was bridge.

Like Pitzy Katz, Paul Fung was another of the fascinating, off-center characters Lefty was drawn to. At one point, Pitzy gave Fung's son, ten-year-old Paul junior, a baby alligator, which he named, of course, Snapper, and kept in a back bathtub. Father and son fed Snapper either mice they'd trapped for the alligator or fed it raw eggs and chopped meat.

"I'd lift him out of the bathtub," Junior recounted, "and Snapper would waddle around the apartment. I could keep his mouth closed with a clothespin on his nose, but I didn't need to. He didn't bite, because he didn't know any other alligators, only people. If I turned him over on his back and rubbed his belly, he'd go to sleep. I used to play with him. When guests came to the door, Snapper opened his mouth wide and gargled a big toothy greeting." When Snapper got to be four feet long, however, the Fungs gave him to the Bronx Zoo.

The Fung family also liked tropical fish. More than two thousand of them were housed in various locales about the apartment. Paul's wife, Mae, spent a good deal of time maintaining fish tanks.

Paul Fung himself was born in Seattle in 1897, son of a Baptist missionary, at a time when discrimination against Chinese Americans was virtually as intense as that foisted on blacks. He attended school in China where he studied orthodox Chinese art, decorating dainty fans with cherry blossoms and following the designs prescribed by Chinese master painting textbooks. He excelled, but became fascinated by the Sunday

---

* Lou's friendship with Pitzy was neither casual nor ephemeral. Katz visited Gehrig through the entire course of his illness and was one of the few people allowed to be with Lou at the very end, when the great iron man was fully paralyzed and could not swallow.

cartoon supplements sent to him from Portland by his sister. When he returned to Seattle to attend high school, he took a correspondence course in cartooning. Around that time, his father died and, forced to fend for himself in hostile white society, Fung got his start designing posters for theater lobbies. That brought him to the attention of the editor of the *Seattle Post-Intelligencer*. Fung thereafter attended high school in the mornings and worked at the paper in the afternoon. By the time he was twenty, he had gained national recognition for his patriotic depictions of World War I, and he eventually moved to New York with the King Features Syndicate where he drew a series of comic strips, the most famous being *Dumb Dora*, which featured a ditz based on Gracie Allen.

Fung's social circle included fellow cartoonists Chic Young of *Blondie* fame and Billy DeBeck of *Barney Google* and *Snuffy Smith;* Robert LeRoy Ripley of *Believe It or Not!* and writers Damon Runyon and Grantland Rice. Another poker regular was insurance executive Morris Silverman, whose four-year-old daughter Beverly was about to begin a professional singing career. Beverly would later shorten her name to Sills and become one of America's best-known sopranos. Paul junior would follow in his father's footsteps at King Features and also become an award-winning cartoonist.

Lefty and Paul senior became fast friends. Whenever Paul drew a car in a panel, he used Lefty's license plate. (By that time, Lefty had traded the LaSalle for a Pierce-Arrow.) "Lefty surrounded himself with entertaining and knowledgeable people," Junior said. "He liked being in the flow of their conversation. He was a terrific listener and he asked a lot of questions. My father and Lefty got along famously because they were quick-witted and constantly challenging each other. It was the Depression, so politics and what FDR and Congress were doing to ease the financial pain took up a good share of the conversation. Lefty sought out friends who could verbally challenge him, fashion the unexpected phrase."

At one point, Lefty suggested that those assembled at the Fungs go over to the Ruths'. The Fungs were precisely the sort of quirky folk that Babe enjoyed as much as Lefty did. "On any given night during the week, a bunch of us, June and Lefty, Paul and Mae, June's sister Sunny if she was back from the road and playing a New York theater, would go to Babe and Claire's," Junior recalled. "At Babe's, if he served you a drink, you got six ounces of scotch or rye, one ice cube, and a thimbleful of soda. Most times Babe was in his pajamas, or slacks and a smoking jacket. The Ruths came to our apartment, but not too often, because Babe didn't like dressing up and going to someone else's place. He wanted to relax at home among friends. Babe's fame was suffocating. If he put his nose out the door, people grabbed at him."

"In the early thirties," June added, "only movie houses had air-conditioning. On a blistering summer night, the heat in a New York City apartment would melt lead. To catch a breeze off the Hudson, Babe and Lefty carried the dining room table and chairs up the back stairs to the roof of Babe's apartment house. Most of the roof was filled with clothes-lines and tenants' laundry strung up to dry, but Babe and Lefty made a space and set up the table and chairs. After we ate, Lefty put a record on his portable crank-up phonograph and we danced the night away under the stars. Dancing with Babe was a delight. He was light as a feather on his feet. I'm here to tell you that Babe Ruth was one of the best dancers I ever danced with. Sometimes, though, he would stop, look across the river at Palisades Amusement Park, and sigh, 'Oh, how I wish I could go there.' "

THE PLAYERS ALWAYS tried to top each other. One night at dinner, a bunch of them were discussing the odd occurrences that seemed so prevalent in the minor leagues. After Babe had finished waxing on about all the outrageous conduct he had witnessed, other than his own, Lefty told this tale: "When I was in the Coast League, Los Angeles had a pitcher named Harry Child who had glass eye. He'd have to turn all the way around to hold a guy on second base. So Child is pitching against us at Old Rec Park, and in the fourth inning he suddenly calls time. Then he's down in the dirt fishing all around the mound. Fred Haney, the L.A. third baseman, runs over and asks, 'What are you looking for?'

" 'My eye popped out,' says Child. 'What do you think I ought to do?'

" 'Go get your spare,' Haney says. So Child runs into the locker room, gets his spare, puts it in his eye socket, and continues pitching.

"In the eighth inning, after a couple of pitches, Childs calls time again and bends over and brushes his hands in the dirt. Haney rushes over to the mound again. 'Whatsa matter now?'

" 'I just found my other eye,' Child says. 'What d'ya think I ought to do with it?'

"Haney says, 'Stick it up your ass so the guy on second can't get a lead for third.' "

Babe didn't question Lefty as to whether or not the story was true. (It almost certainly wasn't.) He just laughed and said, "Goddamn, I can't beat that."

"Lefty made Babe laugh," June said. "Zinged him with wisecracks. He treated him like any other teammate and that's what Babe wanted. To be one of the boys, not an icon that other players couldn't relate to. So if Lefty let off a crack, Babe just laughed and waited for his chance to slap Lefty with one of his own. But Lefty didn't say unkind things. He took baseball seriously but not himself."

As the 1933 season approached, Lefty decided the team needed a mascot, and Paul Fung Jr. was just perfect to fill the bill. The duties were hardly arduous.

"When the Yankees were home, Lefty arranged a pickup time with my dad, usually around 10:00 a.m., and he swung by in his convertible," Junior recalled. "Lefty gave me a Yankee baseball cap, one of his, with 'V. Gomez' sewn in script inside the visor. I still have it. There were always two or three Yankee ballplayers sitting in the backseat.

"After Lefty parked his car, we walked through the players' entrance and then into the clubhouse. The ballplayers yelled, 'Hiya, Paul,' or 'Hey, Junior.' I sat on a bench, watching the players get rubdowns, their ankles taped, listening to them talk amongst themselves and to me. Then they'd leave the clubhouse for batting practice and I'd go with them, down a flight of stairs, through a dark passageway, and up into the dugout and out onto the field. This was before the ruling that strangers couldn't be on the field. Later on, as a teenager, I pitched for my high-school team. I was a left-hander. I had great teachers . . . Lefty, Spud Chandler, and Red Ruffing. They showed me how to throw a slider and helped me with my curveball and my changeup. Then they'd tell me to practice what they preached, and called over Bill Dickey or Joe Glenn to go behind the plate and catch me. Because so many of the Yankee players were part of our family life, it seemed very natural to me. I just grew up having fun with the Yankee ballplayers out on the field."

For the games themselves, Junior repaired to the stands. "I sat with June, my parents, a bunch of cartoonist friends, and baseball wives . . . Claire Ruth, Maye Lazzeri, Violet Dickey, and, later, Dottie DiMaggio. Fans in the stands dressed to the nines in those days. It wasn't the vogue to appear in public looking rumpled or sloppy. It didn't matter if you were sitting ringside at Madison Square Garden, down center at a Broadway theater, or grabbing a sandwich at the corner deli. Guys wore suits or sport jackets, slacks, shirts, and ties. In the summer they wore straw hats and, come the fall, fedoras. No slacks for the gals. They wore dresses and stacked heels, or skirt suits, gloves, jewelry, and hats adorned with silk flowers and veils."

"June was lucky," Maye Lazzeri added. "Her mother, Nellie, not only designed hats, she made them from scratch, so June wore a new hat to die for at every ball game." But Nellie was good with another kind of needle as well. "Lefty's trials with his mother-in-law were priceless," Maye added. "Nellie never shut up."

The wives had different levels of knowledge of the game and different reactions to the play on the field. Pauline Ruffing, Charley's wife, cried through all the games he pitched, whether he won or lost. One day June asked her, "Pauline, how can you be weeping? Charley's winning," and Pauline sobbed, "I'm crying because I'm so happy."

After the game, Junior got to tag along with the adults. "We all went out for dinner. Beer and charcoal-broiled steaks at the Dutchman's, Paul Darby's steakhouse in the Bronx, or to Chinatown for cocktails and fantail shrimp at Shavey Lee's at 32 Mulberry Street or Lum Fong's at 220 Canal. Shavey Lee was the mayor of Chinatown, jolly and fat like a Buddha . . . a character. He was also a bookie. He loved to play the horses and he placed bets for my father." Babe couldn't join the crew at a restaurant, of course, but had to content himself with holding court on Riverside Drive.

The season itself began with optimism. The A's, with Jimmy Dykes, Mule Haas, and Al Simmons sold to the White Sox, were fading quickly.

To make matters worse for Connie Mack's team, Mickey Cochrane would have a dreadful year. Little impediment seemed to exist between the Yankees and the 1933 pennant and they began like champions, opening 5–0 and finishing April in first place with an 11–4 record.

Lefty might have had a moment of immortality just afterward if only he had listened more closely to June's instructions on how to pitch to Charley Gehringer. On May 4, in Detroit, he took a no-hitter into the ninth, only to have Gehringer lead off the inning by parking a low fastball in the right-field bleachers. Lefty later claimed to have been under the impression that he had already given up a couple of hits before Gehringer's shot and that all he cared about was winning the game, but soon afterward he gave up a double and uncorked a wild pitch to let a second run come home.

Although Lefty and the Yankees did win the game, Gehringer's home run seemed to precurse the season. From then on, no matter what the Yankees did, someone else did it better. They fell to 14–9 in May, then 18–12 in June, finishing the month in a tie with Washington. By August, the Yankees trailed the Senators by a game, and by September 1, Washington's lead had grown to nine.

By the end of June Lefty was 9–5, but for the next two months he went only 4–5, not notching a single victory for three weeks in August as the team dropped further and further behind. In one particularly atrocious outing, he blew a 3–1 lead in the eighth inning and walked nine men in losing to the Athletics 8–3. The A's victory allowed them to sweep a three-game series and virtually end the Yankees' pennant hopes.

But scorecards never tell the entire story. "I used to get blood blisters on the tips of my fingers. Make them raw or bleeding and it was painful to grip the ball. But it was against the rules to use a Band-Aid or tape. It was a foreign substance . . . doctoring the ball. I know my location suffered but if Joe had me in the rotation, then I was pitching, blisters or not." A newspaper reported, "Vernon Gomez is handicapped with lacerated fingertips, yet the young southpaw insists on taking his turn during the present Western trip of the champions."

In the end, Washington won by seven games. The Yankees played well in September, after they were out of it, and thus their 91 wins were deceptive. Lefty finished 16–10 with an ERA of 3.18, third-best in the league, just ahead of Lefty Grove, but like the team had let opportunities slip away. Three of his complete-game wins came in September. Charley Ruffing did even worse, finishing 9–14 with an ERA of almost 4.00. The Yankees hit as they always did, but again not as well—particularly Babe, who barely hit .300 and drove in only 103 runs.

Lefty never complained or made excuses from the time he was a boy until the day he died, but the 1933 season got to him. He had been on teams that didn't win a pennant, but never before on one that had given one away. On a trip home from Detroit at the end of August, he came as close as he ever did to showing his real feelings when beat writer Frank Graham caught him at an introspective moment. "You don't know how badly I wanted to win at least twenty games this year. Just as I was better last year than I was the year before, I wanted to be better this year than I was last. And now I suppose I'll be lucky if I win fifteen. You know what's the matter with me? I've been getting too smart. I was a better pitcher when I was just a dumb cluck and just reared back and powdered the ball. But I didn't want to be just a thrower. No. I was going to be a real pitcher, figure all the angles, and learn all the answers . . . when you lose, it's so disheartening."

The woes were shared by baseball itself. Although the year had begun with a feeling of promise, 1933 marked the low-water mark for the sport. Attendance at Yankee Stadium dropped to 728,000, less than 10,000 fans per game, leaving an average of 50,000 empty seats when the team played at home. As bad as those numbers were, the average attendance for the other seven teams was a woeful 314,000, or only 4,000 fans per game.

Baseball executives and even Judge Landis finally became aware that not only was the league itself in trouble, but simply waiting around for things to return to normal might not be enough. In the boardrooms of baseball, some creativity was finally sought. It was found in midseason.

20.

GAME OF THE CENTURY

———

I N JANUARY 1928, TO CAPITALIZE ON A BOOMING ECONOMY THAT EVERY-one knew would simply continue to improve, Ernest T. Trigg, executive chairman at the Philadelphia sesquicentennial exposition, spoke at a luncheon at which he told a group of Chicago businessmen and civic leaders that "all the countries of the world were waiting to participate in a world's fair and Chicago is the proper place to hold it." His audience consisted of trustees for the newly chartered Chicago World's Fair Association, formed to create just such an event to commemorate the city's centennial. Although this would be the city's second fair, after the wildly successful Columbian Exposition in 1893, Trigg assured the trustees that "the world would be a-raring to come a-fairing by 1933 . . . that this civic urge ran in short cycles of about ten years and that Chicago was certain to hit it just right." With money burning in the pockets of common citizens, Trigg concluded, such an extravaganza would draw at least 100 million visitors and deposit untold wealth into city coffers.

Not everyone agreed. A society columnist who wrote under the alluring moniker "Madame X" reported that some of Chicago's "thoughtful and able citizens" asserted that staging such an event would be "tempting fate." Madame X's warnings notwithstanding, officers were chosen and plans initiated. Chicago even bid for the 1932 Olympics, which would be pushed back to 1933 to coincide with the rush of visitors.*

In July 1929, the fair was given its official name, "A Century of Progress," and the plans were every bit as grandiose for the four-hundred-acre

---

* Chicago lost. The Olympics were held in Los Angeles as scheduled in 1932.

section of new parkland along Lake Michigan as those for the San Francisco fair at which six-year-old Vernon Gomez saw Lincoln Beachey plummet to his death. The vast majority of the funds needed to mount such an effort was to be raised with a $10 million bond issue, which was brought out on October 28, 1929. The bond was snatched up, mostly by prominent Chicagoans. The next day, the stock market crashed.

As the country sank into the Depression, the organizers pressed forward. They had little choice. Construction at the various venues was keeping thousands of local workmen drawing paychecks. But that didn't mean organizers were not worried that the fair could degenerate into the biggest boondoggle in the city's history. In March 1933, Mayor Anton Cermak, one of the fair's biggest boosters, was assassinated while shaking hands with President Franklin Roosevelt in Miami. Which man was actually the target has been a subject of conjecture. After a power struggle among Chicago's various shady political factions, Edward J. Kelly, a former sanitation commissioner, succeeded to the office.

Faced with a potential fiscal and public relations disaster, Kelly cast about for a means of promoting the coming fair. One of the men he consulted was Colonel Robert Rutherford McCormick, publisher of the *Chicago Tribune*. McCormick called in Arch Ward, the newspaper's sports editor, McCormick's bedfellow in ultra-right-wing politics, and a man of big ideas with a promoter's flair. Ward had cut his teeth on hyperbole at Notre Dame, where he had been Knute Rockne's publicist.

Ward almost immediately suggested a one-time-only "dream game" between the best players of the American League and the best of the National. The managers would be legends: Connie Mack and the recently retired John J. McGraw. Fans would choose the players—Chicago fans, of course. *Tribune* readers. Only fair, since Ward had talked Colonel McCormick into underwriting the cost. In addition to its obvious attractions, such a game would give Chicago baseball fans another shot at Babe Ruth, who had humiliated them in the World's Series just six months earlier. Kenesaw Mountain Landis might be a problem, of course—innovation was hardly his long suit—but that could be overcome by not asking the commissioner at all, and instead going directly to the league presidents.

To make the proposal irresistible, proceeds from the game would be given to help indigent former players.

Eventually everyone was brought around. Judge Landis harrumphed but did not intervene. Even he understood that anything that would bring fans into a ballpark was not to be eschewed. Ward lost one battle, however: Fans from around the nation were allowed to vote, not just McCormick's subscribers. And if any egregious error was made, Mack and McGraw could overrule the fan vote. The game was scheduled for July 6, 1933, at Comiskey Park (Wrigley Field had lost in a coin flip) six weeks after the Century of Progress opened and over half a million ballots clipped from fifty-six newspapers were mailed in. Tickets for the 48,000-seat stadium sold out in two days.

On June 27, Connie Mack announced his squad, making no changes to the fans' vote. Six Yankees made the team—including, of course, Babe, Lou, and Lefty. Lefty lucked out, because June was in Chicago, touring with *Of Thee I Sing*. Babe, as he always did, took Claire and Julia along.

Although June was barely five years older than Julia, as a married woman, June qualified as a "chaperone." "It was my senior year in high school," Julia said, "and before the all-stars arrived, I took a train out to Chicago and June met me there. We had so much fun touring the Century of Progress exhibits. At the Streets of Paris concession on the Midway, we saw Sally Rand and her ostrich plumes dancing to 'Clair de Lune,' her fans her only costume. June and I had a ball."

Although the game was an exhibition, both managers were determined to win. Rick Ferrell, the American League catcher, was surprised at the seventy-one-year-old Mack's intensity. "He was out to make toast of the National League, to beat John McGraw. He told us, 'We came here to win. Some of you may not get to play today. If the American League gets a lead, I'm going to stick with my original lineup.' And that's exactly what he did."

Mack planned on using only three pitchers, three innings each. To start, he chose not his own Lefty but Joe McCarthy's. Rick Ferrell said it was to give the National League a jolt.*

---

* Mack must have given the hypercompetitive Grove, who would finish 24–8 with a mediocre team, a jolt as well, but not nearly the jolt he would transmit when he sold the great left-hander to the Red Sox before the 1934 season.

John McGraw gave all his position players a shot but Mack used just one pinch hitter and a defensive replacement for Ruth in the ninth. Before his exit, Babe had stolen the spotlight with a two-run home run in the third but had also struck out twice and misplayed a routine fly ball by Lon Warneke into a triple.

In the end, the American League triumphed 4–2. Lefty pitched three innings of shutout ball after hurling a complete game just two days earlier and was the winning pitcher. Since this was the inaugural All-Star game, every "first" remained so in perpetuity. Thus, for as long as there is baseball, the man who drove in the very first All-Star run will, as Henry V extolled, be remembered:

Vernon Gomez with a single to center in the second.

FOR WANT OF AN INNING

BUT THE ALL-STAR GAME WAS A RARE HIGH POINT IN WHAT WAS PERHAPS Lefty's most disappointing year since he started throwing a baseball. When the season ended, he once more got into his car and drove to California. With *Of Thee I Sing* still a hit show, June remained behind.

Home, as always, provided a respite. On November 5, he got to relive a treasured moment from his youth and, in doing so, unwittingly got a glimpse of his future. A team of major and minor leaguers had been recruited to play an exhibition against an all-star team from the Refinery League—shades of the Screwbeanies. For this game, of course, the executives would have done anything to claim Lefty as an employee, but they would instead face him in the batter's box. Another local alumnus destined for the Hall of Fame, Ernie Lombardi, was Lefty's catcher. A third future Hall of Famer was on the field as well, a converted minor league shortstop playing in left. His name was Joe DiMaggio.

Either 1,500 or 3,000 fans, depending on which newspaper one read, turned out to see the game. Lefty did not disappoint. He began by throwing twenty-two straight called or swinging strikes before a batter succeeded in getting a bat on the ball, a foul tip that elicited an ovation from the crowd. In the end, he struck out eight of the nine men he faced. DiMaggio hit a home run and the professionals beat the amateurs, although by a surprisingly respectable 3–0 score.

In January 1934, when Ed Barrow mailed out the contracts, Lefty learned that the Yankees had responded to his 16–10 record with a salary cut. Gomez refused to sign and didn't agree to terms until early March. He told reporters that the contract he signed was "better than last year's" but, in fact, he'd taken a $1,000 cut, to $12,500. He came to camp determined not to let that happen again.

The salary cut put him in good company. Ruppert and Barrow were becoming increasingly restive about Babe Ruth's place on the ball club. His numbers at the plate were still impressive, but he had missed twenty games in 1933 and gave back almost as many runs in the field as he drove in. Still, Babe was Babe, an institution, and after some dickering he agreed to sign for $37,500, the least he had been paid since 1921. But Ruppert did little to suppress the rumors that 1934 would be Babe's last with the Yankees on the field.

Change was coming on another front as well. At the end of the previous season, Lou Gehrig had finally gotten married, to Eleanor Twitchell, the daughter of a Chicago restaurateur. Lou lived with Mom and Pop Gehrig until the very last minute and the wedding took place in the New Rochelle apartment into which Lou and Eleanor were in the process of moving. The mayor of New Rochelle officiated. Lou had traded one strong-willed woman for another. "What Lou needed badly," his new wife would say later, expressing sentiments that had already been transmitted to Mom Gehrig, "was confidence, building up. He was absolutely anemic for kindness and warmth."

Lou was also anemic when it came to negotiating skills. Eleanor was not. She couldn't do much about 1934, but in subsequent years she made certain he never signed for less than $30,000.

Eleanor was different in other ways as well. "She went to the opera, the Philharmonic, and art museums," Lefty recalled. "At first she had to drag Lou along but then Lou started buying the tickets. He'd come into the locker room, all excited about a performance: 'They're doing Wagner.' Lou loved Wagner, because he could follow the German. 'Wanna go to the Met?' A low moan would run along the benches and the excuses would start flying. 'Big date.' 'Tonight's the fights.' 'Hitting golf balls.' Lou was such a sweetheart of a guy. Took life so seriously. Seeing his disappointment, someone would call out, 'Hey, Lou. Don't give up on us. We need that culture.'"

But Eleanor could also create friction. "There were times when we were sitting together at the ballpark," June said, "and Eleanor came out with these highfalutin remarks, not being sociable at all, and I had to ask myself 'Where is she coming from?' "

"There were times," Maye Lazzeri added, "when Eleanor was impressed with the fact that she was Mrs. Lou Gehrig. She could fabricate outlandish stories. I remember four or five of the wives were out at the ballpark and she said something about Lefty and I almost turned inside out. Eleanor is going on and I finally said, 'What do you know about Lefty? You weren't even here. You just married Lou. Some stupid story that's not true at all.' But Eleanor kept it up, and that's when I gave her hell because I'm honest and up front and she's talking down to us from a pedestal. 'Listen, Eleanor,' I said, 'I'm only married to Tony Lazzeri. I have nothing to do with all the home runs and the honors. I'm just lucky I've got him. And the quicker you learn that you're not Lou Gehrig, the better off you're going to be.'

"Looking back, I realize Eleanor was young and it was easy for her to lose perspective. Her every step met with adulation from the fans and the press. To be fair, she was marvelous to Lou. They enjoyed the opera, reading fine books, and most of all they liked to be with one another. When Lou was sick, Eleanor was by his side every moment. Eleanor and I grew closer after the deaths of our husbands. We were both young widows and shared a bond. Whenever I came to New York from San Francisco, I stopped off at her apartment. Since I was in business and she kept up with the financial markets, sometimes we talked about buying and selling stocks. Once she asked me, 'Well, are you all right, Maye?' meaning, 'Are you going to starve to death?' I said, 'Yes, I'm all right, Eleanor. Don't worry about me.' And she said, 'Buy IBM.' Okay, it was only $48 at the time, but it didn't pay enough dividends. I told Eleanor that with a child to support, I had to buy income. I knew IBM was good but David and I couldn't eat paper while I waited around for it to pay off. But Eleanor was savvy and made a lot of good investments."

In a rare concession, Yankee management relocated spring training headquarters from the Don CeSar to the Swanee Hotel, just down the street from the team's old headquarters at the Princess Martha. For the first time, Lefty didn't travel to Florida by train, nor stay at the team hotel.

June had secured an engagement to do a one-woman show at the Hollywood Yacht Club, and she and Lefty and Claire and Babe rented adjoining beach cottages on Treasure Island. When Lefty drove back north, June and Nellie came along.

Lefty's road roommate was now Jimmie DeShong, a rookie. "In those days, veterans usually wouldn't give rookies the time of day," DeShong said. "But not Lefty. He made me feel a part of the team. Once I had a run-in with one of our veteran players and Lefty told me, 'Don't bother with him. He's just a jerk.'

"One time in Detroit, Lefty and Charley Ruffing and I were walking in downtown and passed a clothing shop. I looked in at the window display and said, 'Boy, isn't that a beautiful suit?' Lefty tells me to go in and try it on. I told him it was $45 and I couldn't afford it. 'Come on, Jimmie,' Lefty said, 'try the suit on. We've got time.' So the three of us go in. The suit looked great and the salesman asked me if I wanted it. Lefty called the tailor over and said, 'Mark it up. We'll take it.' 'Wait a minute, Lefty. I can't . . .' but he's paying no attention to me. He's talking to the tailor. 'Get it ready. We're leaving town in two days.' Lefty pays cash for the suit. But I wouldn't be a charity case. I insisted on paying him the $45 in two installments over two paydays, but believe me, it took a lot of persuasion on my part to get that money into Lefty's pocket."*

Lefty's generosity was legendary, not just to friends and teammates but to strangers as well. Sunny was sometimes a witness. "The thirties were hard times, but with Lefty, the old cliché came to life. Once when we were walking down Broadway, I saw him take the coat off his back and give it to a guy who was penniless on the street. When the kids on the sidewalks of New York crowded around him for autographs, Lefty bought them ice-cream cones. Another time, he and I were bicycling through Central Park and this ragged kid said to him, 'Oh, what a bike. I wonder how it feels to own a bike like that.' Lefty said, 'You want it? Take it.' And he walked back to his apartment."

* In 1988, when Jimmie called Lefty to wish him a happy eightieth birthday, Lefty said, "Hey, you cheapskate, when are you going to pay me for that suit?" Jimmie laughed, "I had forked over the dough years ago, but went along. 'Damn. And I thought I got away with it.' "

THE YANKEES ONCE again were good out of the gate. At the end of May, they trailed Cleveland by 1½ games with a record of 22–16, but the Indians were expected to fade and did.

The bigger threat would come from a Detroit Tiger team that had added Mickey Cochrane as player-manager and Goose Goslin from Washington and that, in addition to Charley Gehringer, featured a slugging second-year first baseman named Henry Greenberg. Player-managers were all the rage in the 1930s—Charley Grimm, Frankie Frisch, and Rogers Hornsby, among others—since doubling up allowed financially embattled owners to save the cost of one player's salary.

In those first weeks of the season, Bill Schwarz was admitted to the hospital. "Two years before, Daddy Schwarz had been diagnosed with an obstruction in his esophagus and an intestinal ulcer. When he ate solid food, the esophageal obstruction became inflamed and the food wouldn't pass into his stomach. The doctors suggested a salt-free diet and a shot glass of pure cream every two hours to soothe the alimentary tract. But he craved salt. Everything would be going along well and then he'd insist on a plate of pigs' knuckles and sauerkraut and he'd be back in the hospital again." The "obstruction" turned out to be esophageal cancer, and on May 16, Bill Schwarz died.

"Sunny and I were stagestruck," June said. "Nellie did her best to make our dream a reality. The challenge cut into her relationship with her husband. At the end of her life, Nellie said how badly she felt that she hadn't provided a home for Bill."

BY THE BEGINNING of July, the Yankees led the Tigers by a game and whatever Lefty had been doing in 1933 that had caused him to lose his edge was a memory. When the teams broke for the second All-Star game, his record was 14–2 and he was largely responsible for keeping the team in first place. He was again chosen to be the starting pitcher, this time by player-manager Joe Cronin of the American League champion Senators. American League president Will Harridge hadn't wanted to continue the

All-Star game, thinking that one "game of the century" was enough, but baseball was hardly in the position to eschew the proceeds from a big crowd. Harridge agreed to make the game an annual event.

The game would be played at the Polo Grounds on July 10. As they had the previous year, the fans voted for pitchers as well as position players. When the final tally was announced on July 1, Lefty had 84,712 votes, more than a 30,000-vote margin over any other American League pitcher, although 1,000 less than the Giants' Carl Hubbell. Babe, despite a lackluster year, drew 114,000 votes. But the most lopsided tally was for the American League second baseman, where Charley Gehringer outpolled Tony Lazzeri 120,700 to 2,600.

Lefty's resurgence made him, if anything, more popular with the press. On July 9, just before the All-Star game, he was the first pitcher ever to be on the cover of *Time*. After the first sentence, however, virtually everything in the accompanying article was wrong: "Carl Hubbell of the Giants and Vernon Gomez of the Yankees are indisputably the best pitchers in their leagues. Vernon Gomez has succeeded in his profession largely by accident. His father, Francisco Gomez, was a rancher and rodeo performer who settled in Rodeo, Calif. There Vernon was born in 1910. At 13, Vernon Gomez hoped to be a rodeo performer also. He fell off a horse and broke his right arm, took to throwing baseballs with his left. The next spring while a freshman at Richmond High School, he became so expert that a Pacific Coast League team offered him a contract. A member of his high-school basketball and swimming teams for three years, he also played football. Instead of going on to college he played baseball with the San Francisco Seals, went to Salt Lake City for a year's seasoning, returned to San Francisco for the season of 1929, when he struck out 159 batters. The New York Yankees hired him in 1930, sent him to St. Paul for one year." In another widely distributed interview, June was purported to assert that Lefty had gained fifteen pounds because she insisted he eat steaks for breakfast. In fact, he was as thin as ever.

One piece of news that was not apocryphal was Lefty's participation in a unique experiment. "Before the radar gun, it was conjecture as to exactly how fast a pitched ball was moving. Up at West Point, the army came up with a way to measure the velocity of a pitched ball and Carl Hubbell, Van

Lingle Mungo, and I were asked to participate in the trial. We held a base-ball and a West Point cadet held a rifle standing side by side. The very instant one of us threw a pitch, the cadet fired a bullet at a target, and the velocity of the pitch was compared to the velocity of the bullet. Of the three of us, Van Lingle Mungo was the fastest, but my fastball was clocked at 100 miles per hour. Hubbell had a good fastball but he was mostly a breaking-ball pitcher . . . curves and his famous screwball."

FOR THE SECOND All-Star game, the Polo Grounds was filled to its 50,000-seat capacity, raising $53,000 for the players' fund. Lefty barely missed achieving additional notoriety in the batter's box. After letting the first two American Leaguers get on, Carl Hubbell proceeded to strike out Babe Ruth, Lou Gehrig, and Jimmie Foxx to end the first inning. He opened the second inning by fanning Al Simmons and Joe Cronin before Bill Dickey stroked a single. Lefty, who struck out next, was annoyed with Dickey afterward. "If Bill had struck out, Hubb would have struck out seven of the greatest hitters in history."

Gabby Hartnett, the National League catcher, had a different take. "I walked up to the plate," Lefty said, "and Hartnett growled, 'Are you trying to insult Hubbell?' I said, 'Whattaya mean?' He said, 'You coming up here with a bat.' " But Hall of Fame infielder Frankie Frisch had a better line. The bat flew out of Lefty's hands as he flailed at a Hubbell offering and it sailed out near second base. "Leave it there," Frisch yelled when the bat-boy came to retrieve it. "It won't do him any good."

On the mound, however, Lefty got knocked around. Frisch led off the game with a home run into the upper deck, and two innings later Joe Medwick parked another immense upper-deck shot with two on. Lefty departed after three innings, having given up four runs on three hits and one walk. The American League, however, scored two in the fourth and six an inning later to win 9–7.

When regular play resumed, Lefty picked up where he had left off, winning his next ten decisions. On July 31, the Yankees swept a double-header from Boston and took a slim lead over Detroit.

The team began August winning five of six, including Lefty's one-hit shutout over the A's. Then, as they had the year before, the Yankees began to fall off the pace, losing four of five, only Lefty's win over Boston breaking the string. Meanwhile, the Tigers wouldn't lose. On August 14, riding a twelve-game winning streak with a four-and-a-half-game lead, Detroit came to New York for a five-game series, beginning with a doubleheader. In front of 79,000 fans in Yankee Stadium—the largest paid crowd in the stadium's history, with an additional 20,000 turned away—Lefty took the mound in the opener against Al Crowder.

The Yankees started the game by scoring three runs in the first and another two in the third. Lefty set down the Tigers in the first four innings without a hit or a walk. The Tigers scratched out a single with two out in the fifth to break the string. In the sixth, after another ground-ball single, Charley Gehringer again proved he was much more Lefty's nemesis than Jimmie Foxx by sending a long home run into the right-field bleachers. Four hits followed and suddenly the game was tied. Jimmie DeShong put out the fire, but the Tigers scored another four runs in the eighth to seal the win. Red Ruffing gave up seven runs in the nightcap and the Yankees had suddenly lost seven games in the standings to the Tigers in two weeks, which would prove to be the precise margin by which the Tigers would win the pennant six weeks later.

Other than one bad inning, Lefty had the finest season of his career. He finished a sparkling 26–5, with a 2.33 ERA, 25 complete games, 6 shutouts, and 158 strikeouts, in 281⅔ innings, each of which led the American League. He had even recorded 13 hits, one of which was a double, to take another $250 from Babe. He finished third in the voting for most valuable player. Even so, he likely would have traded it all for a strike-out of Charley Gehringer in that sixth inning.

Charley Ruffing pitched well, winning 19, and a burly rookie named Johnny Murphy, Lefty's teammate at St. Paul, added fourteen more. But for the first time in memory, the Yankees had only one player drive in more than 100 runs—Gehrig, with 165. The Yankees led the league in ERA by a wide margin, but were only fifth in batting and did not even finish first in home runs. Lou had another superb year, winning the Triple Crown with a .363 batting average and 49 homers to go along with the RBIs, but the Babe was done. At thirty-nine, with knees that balked at supporting an ever more massive torso, Ruth hit only .288 with a paltry 22 home runs and 84 RBIs. He said after the final game that he hoped to land a manager's job and felt good enough to play two or three times a week. Later, after meeting with Ruppert, he announced that he would not sign a player's contract with any club. Babe claimed that Ruppert's assertion that he was satisfied with Joe McCarthy was "fine by me." Frank Graham, on the other hand, claimed Babe's response was, "Well, I'm not."

In any case, the Yankees, certainly without meaning to, had become a pitchers' team.

Hard as it would be to imagine, however, in 1934 another pitcher not only had a better record than Lefty but also out-goofed El Goofo. Over in St. Louis, an Arkansas farm boy named Jay Hanna Dean finished 30–7, with 7 shutouts, 24 complete games, and 195 strikeouts in 311⅔ innings, was first in the MVP voting, and led his team to a seven-game World's Series victory. After being hit between the eyes with a thrown ball in game four, dropping like a stone, and then being rushed to a hospital, Dizzy had observed, "They took X-rays of my head, but didn't find nothin' in there."

The competition between Dizzy Dean and Lefty on and off the field wasn't lost on either hurler. When sportswriters asked Lefty who was the best pitcher in the National League, he replied, "Well, Dean must be. He's won 30 games and pitched the Cardinals to the pennant." Then the writers asked Dean who was the best pitcher in the American League. He asked them, "Who said I was the best pitcher in the National League?" They said, "Gomez." And Dizzy said, "Well then, Gomez is the best pitcher in the American League. He is the best left-handed or right-handed pitcher in baseball except me."

For baseball, 1934 was its best season in five years. Attendance rose by almost 1 million. With Prohibition a quixotic memory and the New Deal programs beginning to inject money into the economy, the mood of the nation, and its pocketbooks, had begun to swell. Baseball franchises, with more fans paying for tickets—and now for beer—made some tentative moves toward profitability.*

---

* This was too late for Connie Mack, though. He had sold off half his team, Philadelphia continued to ban both Sunday baseball and beer sales in the stadium, and the A's began to look less like the Yankees and more like the St. Louis Browns, ahead of whom they finished just two games in the standings.

The Tigers-Cardinals series was considered one of the great post-season affairs in baseball history. St. Louis, the major leagues' farthest southern and western venue, was populated, or so it seemed, by a bunch of country boys: dirty, plainspoken, and even profane, qualities that would earn them the moniker "Gas House Gang," although not until the middle of the following season. Actually, the team was more a product of evangelical teetotaler Branch Rickey's development of a farm system and conservative management than of Dizzy, Daffy, Ducky, Pepper, and Ripper. Still, the defeat of the Tigers by this populist bunch was celebrated by Americans who either remained out of work or were just emerging from financial ruin. Each of the seven games drew sellout crowds and millions more were glued to the radio. So widespread was the focus that, almost obscured, was the inglorious end in New York for Babe Ruth.

22

LET LOOSE TO RUN AROUND THE WORLD

———

HOWEVER HIS ON-FIELD PERFORMANCE MIGHT HAVE DECLINED, BABE remained a renowned figure, particularly in baseball-crazy nations such as Japan. As it happened, a tour of that very nation by a team of American Leaguers had been planned for the upcoming months. The team would be led by Connie Mack, who turned out to be willing to cede his position as manager, in public at any rate, to that other aspiring manager, Babe Ruth. For Mack and the other organizers, principally John Shibe of the A's and Matsutaro Shoriki, owner of the *Yomiuri Shimbun,* Japan's most widely read newspaper, Ruth's presence would ensure a huge success in Japan. Babe would get to remain in the public eye and the stunt would draw attention to his managerial skills. A rumor even got started, source unknown, that the seventy-two-year-old Mack was retiring and Babe was to replace him on the A's. Babe claimed no knowledge of it; Mack made no comment.

When Babe signed on, so did Lefty. Other than the barnstorming stop in Juarez, he had never been out of the country, and he was voraciously curious to experience other cultures. Claire Ruth was to go as well, as was Julia, so Lefty took June. The trip would serve as the honeymoon their careers had not allowed them. Lefty brought along his newly purchased 16mm film camera to commemorate the journey.

Other stars followed, including newlyweds Lou and Eleanor Gehrig. Lou, who had been part of a 1931 tour that included Lefty Grove, had wanted to return to Japan ever since, and like Lefty he decided the tour would be a perfect honeymoon. The entourage would sail from Vancouver on the *Empress of Japan* on October 20. After a short stopover in Honolulu, the *Empress* would then continue across the Pacific.

Although six baseball tours had been made to Japan, the first by a team from the University of Chicago in 1910, the 1934 version would be the grandest yet. The team consisted of fourteen players and included six future Hall of Famers.

Shibe and Mack filled out the team with solid if not spectacular players, many drawn from the A's roster. Three other pitchers, Earl Whitehill, Clint Brown, and Joe Cascarella, were on the squad, as well as two catchers, the Athletics' Charlie Berry and a backup journeyman named Moe Berg. Berg, who became well known after World War II for having been a spy, took lots and lots of photographs in Japan, some of which may or may not have been used to plan bombing raids during the war. (He claimed they did; most others insisted they did not.)*

In addition to the players and their wives, the tour included an umpire, a trainer, and a business manager. Bud Hillerich of Hillerich & Bradsby and his wife, Rosie, went along as well, although there is no record of whether Bud tried to renegotiate Lefty's bat contract.

Instead of traveling directly to Canada, however, Lefty and June headed for Rodeo, so June could finally meet Lefty's family and see where he'd grown up. But before Rodeo, Lefty and June stopped in Salt Lake City.

"We checked into Mom's Tuxedo Hotel for three nights. I was afraid to check into the snazzy Hotel Utah up the street. Mom would have been heartbroken. Here I am, in the big leagues, making good dough, with a new bride, and we check into a baseball alley. Even when our children came along, if June and I were traveling through Utah, we bundled the

---

* Whether or not Berg's photographs were used by War Department, the 16mm films that Lefty took on the tour certainly were. "Late in the 1936 season, during batting practice in a game against the Red Sox," Lefty said later, "I was in the bullpen warming up when Moe Berg asked to talk to me. He was interested in the films I had taken of Yokohama harbor and asked if I had any of Shanghai and Hong Kong. I didn't have a clue what he was driving at. Moe gave me an address in Washington and asked me to send my pictures there. He told me they'd be sent back. I mailed the film to Washington. I don't know specifically who received them. They kept the film for seven or eight months, and then it was returned with a letter that expressed thanks."

kids and the dog into Mom's. I was more afraid of Mom Edgeworth than my own mother."

When June and Lefty arrived in Rodeo on October 6, June began a diary that she maintained for the entire trip.

"I arrived on the western frontier wearing the last gasp in traveling attire . . . a pearl gray slim-skirt suit, oxford shirt and man's tie, high heels, and a gray fedora worn over one eye. That's how I descended on my new Rodeo relatives, up to their elbows in rawhide fringe. Lizzie and Coyote's eyes went wide."

That first afternoon, they all sat around the radio listening to the World's Series, then Lizzie cooked what June termed a "grand dinner." American Leaguers to the core, everyone pulled for Detroit. Three days later, when the Cardinals won the seventh game, June wrote, "Poor Mickey Cochrane."

For a woman who had not met her in-laws in a year and a half of marriage and had walked in the door as if she were backlit, June fit immediately into the Gomez family. She continually wrote with affection and gratitude of the hospitality she received and from the first called Lizzie "Mother" and Coyote "Pa." (June still referred to her own mother as "Nell.") She might have worn Broadway clothes, but she was totally without Broadway pretension. June sat on the porch and talked with Lizzie and Coyote, went to Mass with the family, swam in the bay, went to a local dance, sucked down milk shakes at the ice-cream store, went fishing with Lefty's childhood friends, and visited Gomez relatives around the area. "We had oodles of fun and caught twenty big ones and fifty small ones," she reported after one trip to the lake.

George Lakeman was older now and trying to get work. On October 9, he went to the Civilian Conservation Corps camp, but, June reported, "they only took 25 men so we had to go get him. He felt terrible, poor kid." George later received a card granting him five days of work per month. At one point, Lefty and George played tennis. "Lefty beat him 3 sets to 1. George was wild. They came in telling how each one cheated."

The entry for October 14 gives a flavor of the trip. "We went to ten o'clock Mass in Rodeo. Mrs. Claeys invited us to dinner tomorrow night. We dressed in our riding clothes and went out to Claeys Ranch. Linus saddled the horses for us and we rode for 1½ hours. I enjoyed it immensely. I certainly love to ride in the hills. Linus roped a cow for me and I got quite a thrill seeing the horse hold the cow while the men rode it. We came home at 2:30 and boy did we feast on chicken. We could hardly move and Gomez made us go swimming. The water was freezing. Lefty threw water and mud at George and so I threw his dressing gown in. Was he mad! We went to visit Lefty's cousin and Irene. Arrive home at eleven o'clock. I raided the chicken."

Ten days later, Lefty and June left for Seattle; almost all of Rodeo came to see them off. Lizzie cried but promised to come to New York next summer for a visit. After a short trip by ferry, they arrived in Vancouver. Lefty and June were given a large stateroom between Babe and Claire's and Julia's. The voyage did not begin well. The sea was rough and stormy and there was no shortage of intensely seasick passengers.

Joe Cascarella, who was counted on to do a quarter of the pitching, wasn't in shape to do much of anything when the ship finally docked. "I was sick most of the time. Lefty too, but he was better off than me. I lost twenty pounds. Connie Mack wanted to put me on a ship and send me home. I told him, 'Another ship? I'm only going to get sicker going home, so I might as well stay.'"

Cascarella, who was single, was also unlucky in shared accommodations, drawing Charley Gehringer, one of the two other unmarried players on the tour. Gehringer was just as difficult for Joe as for Lefty, but for a different reason. "I hated him because he was always healthy. Charley was sort of a phlegmatic person, but every morning he got up, punched his chest, and said, 'I feel great! I'm going down and eat a big breakfast.' I'm sick and I can't get up out of bed. That was Gehringer's idea of humor."

June was spared—she won a $5 bet with Babe that she wouldn't get sick on the trip—as was Eleanor Gehrig, but Claire and Julia Ruth couldn't get out of bed. The Ruth family did have one healthy member, as June noted. "Babe never gets sick. He smokes, drinks, and eats like a horse. Three steaks for breakfast, lunch, tea and a huge dinner. He is superhuman, I think. I have never seen anyone like him."

The seas eventually turned calmer, so except for severe cases such as Cascarella, most of the party began to enjoy the voyage. Julia recovered more energetically than most. "She dated Moe Berg and Frank Hayes on the trip, and from then on Julia and Frank were an item back in New York."

Sometimes Babe would wake June and Lefty up at 7:00 or 8:00 a.m. to engage in whatever shipboard activity the big fellow favored that day. The Japanese crew did everything possible to see that the passengers enjoyed themselves. "The stewards wait on you hand and foot," June wrote, "but it's tough to get them to understand you. They say yes but don't know what you're talking about."

Lefty was also feeling better, as Julia Ruth attested. "After dinner, there was dancing to a swing orchestra. We all sat ringside . . . Daddy, Claire, me, and the other ballplayers and their wives. June, so elegant in her evening gown, and Lefty would be out in the center, cutting fancy dance steps, and June couldn't understand why we were all laughing our heads off. She didn't know that when Lefty spun her around, he pushed his upper plate out with his tongue, and gave us all a big toothless grin."

One source of friction, however, had become apparent. "There was a little bit of an unsatisfactory situation with Eleanor Gehrig and Ruth's wife, Claire," Cascarella said. "It never flared out but was obvious to most of us." After the trip, it was widely reported in the press that Babe and Lou were no longer speaking and the rift had to do with their wives. Subsequently, reports surfaced that Babe had become furious with Lou because Mom Gehrig had accused Claire of treating Julia better than Dorothy, the daughter Babe adopted with his first wife, Helen. Babe was reported to have told Lou never to speak to him again off the ball field, a dictum he maintained until July 4, 1939.

Whether or not Claire and Eleanor did or did not like each other, Lefty always insisted that the war between Lou and Babe was vastly overblown by sportswriters. "You keep hearing these stories about Babe and Lou not hitting it off. When you consider ballplayers are together from February until October, there are going to be squabbles. But Babe and Lou enemies? Not a chance. Babe was an extrovert in the extreme and Lou was an introvert. Babe threw his money around and Lou counted his pennies. Babe liked the high life and Lou enjoyed the opera and the philharmonic.

Babe was glib with the press; Lou found it hard to come up with a snappy quip. There may have been comments here and there that caused temporary chagrin, but Babe and Lou were teammates and friends on and off the field. The press created a feud between Ruth and Gehrig that I never saw. Babe and Lou were both dear friends of mine as well as teammates, and I respected the fact that they lived life their own way. Nothing more, nothing less."

An entry in June's diary after the team had been in Japan for a week suggests the same. "Claire and I went by Eleanor Gehrig's room laughing, so she called out and invited us in for a drink. We sat and talked until 1 a.m."

THE EMPRESS OF JAPAN docked in Yokohama on November 1. The next day, upward of 500,000 people lined the streets to welcome the Americans to Tokyo. Wide boulevards were shrunken to narrow alleys with barely enough space for the automobiles to pass through. The main attraction, of course, was Babe, who led the procession in an open limousine, waving and smiling to the adoring crowds.

"When we walked off the train at the Tokyo station," Lefty recalled, "the Japanese spectators awaiting Babe's arrival rushed forward, almost crushing him. Babe had to push his way through the crowds as they were running by, tearing at his clothes for souvenirs. The fans were desperate to have a memento of something that Babe was wearing. They pulled at his jacket, his pants, his hat, and the crowds and their passion about Babe never let up for one second wherever he went."

The tour was not popular with everyone in Japan, a nation already simmering with ultranationalist fervor. In February of the following year, a young army officer attempted to behead Matsutaro Shoriki as he was leaving his home. But Shoriki, short and bald, was also a judo master and took only a glancing blow with the sword. He spent fifty days in the hospital, but recovered and lived until 1969.

The first game was played in Tokyo in front of 55,000 fans. To face the American juggernaut, Shoriki had assembled the best players in the country, the All-Nippon team, including eleven that would make the Japanese hall of fame. For the first game, however, the Americans played a team of former college players and won, 17–1.

When the All-Nippon team played, the results were little changed. The Japanese lost all eighteen games on the schedule by a combined score of 189–39. Still, on November 20, a seventeen-year-old pitcher named Eiji Sawamura lost 1–0, the only run scoring on a Lou Gehrig seventh-inning home run. Sawamura struck out nine, including a Hubbell-like streak of Gehringer, Ruth, Gehrig, and Foxx.*

"I pitched twice against Sawamura," Lefty said. "He was young, but he instinctively knew how to take command when he was on the mound. He was fast with good location and a tantalizing curve ball."

Connie Mack immediately offered Sawamura a contract, but Sawamura, still in high school, did not want to leave home. He died almost ten years later to the day, when his ship was torpedoed in December 1944. The Japanese equivalent of the Cy Young Award is named for him.

When a game wasn't scheduled, Lefty and June got to experience Japanese culture, usually with Babe and Claire. June wrote of visiting a Meiji-era sacred shrine, where millions of visitors tossed coins; sitting on pillows shoeless as they ate sukiyaki served by geishas with pomaded hair; riding in rickshaws; and having massages. Then there were the toilets. "The funniest yet . . . a hole in the floor, and you have to practically lay down to go. Lefty was in one when a Japanese girl came in and asked him for his autograph."

The cuisine was predictably exotic—a good deal of sushi and sashimi, of course, then virtually unknown in the States, but also some even more unusual items. "One dish that caused dismay among the wives was baked woodcock," June said. "The little brown bird was served on a dish with its head still on. None of them would eat it, except me. I said, 'Oh, I love that!' so they dumped their birds on my plate and I sat there whacking their heads off and ate them all. But that was the exception. The Japanese food in '34 was tasty and elegantly served. The geisha girls never let the sake cup be

---

* Many American newspapers incorrectly credited Ruth with the seventh-inning blast, thus epitomizing the subordinate role Lou played to Babe through the early 1930s.

empty. Once we dined at the famous club which was known to only serve dignitaries like Queen Mary, Queen Elizabeth, and Charles Lindbergh."

Still, a vegetarian on the trip might have had a difficult time. "Then there were the 'honey-wagons,' horse carts carrying pails of human manure that the Japanese used to fertilize their plantings. When the ballplayers and their wives became aware that all the vegetables were fertilized by human manure, nobody wanted to eat them."

On November 10, a cold, damp day in Tokyo, Lefty struck out nineteen in a 10–0 victory in front of 65,000 fans, including an imperial prince. Lefty wasn't supposed to pitch that day. He had gone nine innings just two days before. But Joe Cascarella still had trouble standing up for nine innings, let alone pitching them, so Lefty stepped in.

Sometimes the Americans went to the dignitaries instead of the other way around. Cascarella reported on a sumptuous banquet at the royal palace. "Emperor Hirohito was the 'Son of Heaven,' a god, and mere mortals like us were not supposed to cast an eye on him. Most Japanese had never heard or seen him. And yet, here are the ballplayers and their wives in his presence in a magnificent reception hall, exchanging pleasantries through an interpreter. Protocol demanded that we be respectful and stand facing the Emperor and there was a lot of bowing. Suddenly, we heard Moe Berg conversing with Hirohito in Japanese, and the Emperor was hanging on his every word. I don't know what Moe said, but the Emperor's face broke into a smile." Berg was famously known as a man who could speak ten languages but was unable to hit a curveball in any of them.

When the players made trips to outlying cities, the wives remained in Tokyo. Once away from the capital, both the crowds and the conditions deteriorated. Spectators sometimes numbered as few as 5,000 and Lefty remembered playing games in pelting rain. In some cases, a layer of snow ringed the field.

Joe Cascarella remembered the conditions as well. "The dugouts were freezing. We sat on the benches, huddled together, shivering in the overcoats we wore over our uniforms. On the dirt in front of us were braziers, little boxes of fire, the length of the bench."

Players slept on straw beds in primitive hotels, four to a room, and had beer for breakfast. "In Hakodate, we stayed at a hotel that was so cold, we had to keep our overcoats on in our rooms. I remember sitting up all night playing bridge with Earl Whitehill, Charley Gehringer, and Jimmie Foxx because it was too cold to sleep."

"The games were mostly one-day trips," Lefty said, "and the only one who had a bed on the train was Babe. The rest of the players sat up at night or slept on the floor. Babe's portable bed was set up next to the toilet. The toilet was just a hole in the floor, so of course it stunk, and Babe complained about the smell. The rest of us just laughed at him, 'Babe, you're complaining? You're the only one with a bed.' "

On November 28, in Kyoto, Lefty pitched for the seventh time in the series. June remembers him being ecstatic. "He won 10–1 and he also got three hits and two walks. A perfect day. He told Mr. Mack he had found his league at last." But although Lefty made light of it, the overwork had become palpable. On one occasion, two days after pitching a complete game in cold, damp weather, he pitched again, this time finishing by pitching the ninth inning for both teams. But Lefty kept going out there every time Connie Mack called on him.

And all the time Lefty was pitching, he was also eating. For the first time in his life, he gained weight, eventually twenty pounds' worth. "They were giving us two banquets every morning, then you'd go out and play a game and there'd be two more banquets before you'd get to bed. And you had to eat if you wanted to be polite . . . everybody is polite in Japan. I guess I was too darned polite for my own good."

The tour ended with as much pomp as it had begun with, and after one last banquet the Americans sailed from Yokohama on December 2. The event had been such a success that Matsutaro Shoriki kept the All-Nippon team together and renamed them the Tokyo Yomiuri Giants. The following year, he organized a league and professional baseball in Japan was born.

The team headed south for stops in Shanghai, Hong Kong, and Manila, where they would play four more games. Shanghai was a teeming, boisterous city, and June regretted leaving. "It's a shame we couldn't stay at least one night and take in all the clubs. The nightlife is very wild."

Manila presented a new brand of exotica, as Lefty noted. "The steward told us today that in the Philippines they eat dog. They starve it for days and then feed it rice and roast it alive. Claire won't eat meat in Manila. And I'll never forget the hotel. I woke up and heard a noise like squack-squack, something like a frog. I jumped out of bed and turned on the lights, and on the ceiling were lizards about six inches long. I was afraid of them so I ran into the bathroom and soaked a towel in water and began heaving it at the ceiling. I hit about three of them. Next morning I told the hotel manager about it, and he said not to tell anybody else or nobody would want my room because the lizards killed the mosquitoes."

Most of the group then headed home. Some members of the tour, however, decided to make other arrangements. As June wrote on December 13, "I stayed in bed until 8:30, then dressed and went to Claire's to talk about the next trip. We decided to take it." The Ruths, the Hillerichs, and the Gomezes decided, strictly on impulse, to instead head south, to Java, Bali, and Sumatra, and from there to continue west until they had circled the globe. Lou and Eleanor had also decided to extend the trip to a world tour but would travel by themselves.

"June and I were like schoolchildren let loose to run around the world," Lefty said. "We were in our twenties and there was nothing but laughter every moment of every day. Because our trip took place before airplane travel and computers brought the world to your back door, June and I were fortunate to experience life as it had been lived for centuries in these countries."

After a calm, relaxing voyage south, the first stop was Bali. They arrived the day after June's twenty-second birthday. She described a setting far removed from the island paradise of today.

"The women wear skirts but nothing from their waists up and carry huge bundles on their heads. The men and women chew something red and black like our tobacco. The little boys run around in the nude with enormous stomachs. They are so emaciated and the women are so wrinkled from the sun. Very few are attractive.

"It was excruciatingly hot and Lefty got deathly sick after eating a can of sardines imported from Monterey, California. He was doubled over with cramps and couldn't even keep water down. The very same day, the guide told us that a famous one-legged Balinese dance would be performed in the temple that night. 'Lefty,' I said, 'no matter how sick you are, you've got to come to the show. How many one-legged dancers do you know?' 'Not many,' he groaned, and he dragged his body to the temple. It's a wonder he didn't die right there."

For the next two weeks Lefty and June island-hopped through what was then the Dutch East Indies and made it as well to Singapore, still under British rule and steeped in the prewar colonial mood that would disappear forever a decade later. They saw the world's largest orangutan in Surabaya, drank champagne and danced on Christmas Day in the Des Indes Hotel in Java, drank at Raffles, visited the sultan's home in Sumatra (complete with ten wives, one of whom was German), and visited the temples of a variety of Eastern religions. In an era when travelogues were by and large restricted to grainy black-and-white film, the Asia that Lefty and June experienced was utterly beyond the reach of most Americans.

Their steamship made its way across the Bay of Bengal to Ceylon, then through the Arabian Sea toward the Gulf of Aden, the Red Sea, and the Suez Canal. They were sailing toward Marseilles but had no formal plans once they landed. The Ruths decided to head to St. Moritz to ski, then to London and Paris. June and Lefty had met a Dutchman on the ship who had traveled extensively and suggested a different itinerary that the Gomezes and the Hillerichs found irresistible.

"Rosie and Bud Hillerich were the perfect traveling companions," June said, "peppery, with the same 'Do it now!' attitude. Rosie was fifty-five, tall and angular, with auburn hair, and Bud sixty-seven. Lefty and I were twenty-six and twenty-two, and Lefty's an athlete and I'm a dancer, and the Hillerichs ran us ragged. What vitality."

Passage through the Suez Canal took twelve hours, and the ship's fee was £5,000. To arrive at the south end, the ship passed Mount Sinai and the biblical location of where the Red Sea parted. Camels, Arab fishing boats, and villages dotted the route. At the north end of the canal was Port Said. "One of the worst places in the world," June wrote. "Criminals and thieves who think nothing of taking you sightseeing and then robbing you. The streets are so dirty and they can't grow any flowers. Also, the veiled women won't pose for you and it was maddening."

Two days later, the ship docked in France. "Lefty made all the travel arrangements once we left the ship. He took care of the train tickets, the hotel reservations, the meals, the foreign exchange, and the sightseeing junkets. Plus, he took care of the daily hassles that always crop up with traveling from one country to another. It was a masterful job and Lefty was just off the Rodeo ranch with a few years of New York living under his belt."

The north coast of the Mediterranean was more appealing to June than the south. "Monte Carlo and Nice are the two most beautiful places I have ever seen. The southern coast of France is for me."

There were unanticipated expenses, however. "The desk clerk at the Cannes hotel said they only served a Continental breakfast of juice, toast, and coffee," June said. " 'But,' the clerk added, 'if you wish an imported American breakfast we can provide one for an extra charge.' We thought, 'Why not? We can certainly afford fresh grapefruit, bacon and eggs and coffee.' Babe told the clerk, 'Sign us up for the American breakfast.' The next morning, room service knocked on the door of our suites with the American breakfast. It looked marvelous until the waiter asked us to sign the hotel tab: $145. From then on, we ate Continental."

The Gomezes and the Hillerichs then bid farewell to Claire, Julia, and Babe, who headed north. The foursome spent the next five weeks in Europe.

"We had an extensive itinerary. We went to London with its theaters and shops; Buckingham Palace and the changing of the royal guards and saw the crown jewels; Paris, Cannes, Marseilles, the gambling casinos of Monte Carlo; Amsterdam and the Hague; to Volta, where the people wore wooden shoes; to Czechoslovakia; Belgium; Rome; the canals of Venice; Florence, Tuscany; Munich, Berlin, and the Unter den Linden, the big arch that the soldiers walked under in World War II; Dresden. There were sporadic Nazi demonstrations and the flying of the swastika on the streets, but it was early in Hitler's rise to power and his horrific actions were still clandestine and not center stage."

They added some impressive wrinkles to the initial plan. Lefty managed to wangle a private audience with the Pope, using the bishop of Salt Lake City, who was then in Rome, as an intermediary.

"I found out that a woman must wear a floor-length black dress with long sleeves and a black veil covering her hair to meet privately with the

Pope. We were getting low on dough but found a shop that sold inexpensive black. When Lefty spoke with the Holy Father, he actually knew about the New York Yankees and that Lefty was a World Series winner. Wow."

Lefty and June also visited the Colosseum and walked past Mussolini's residence. During the trip, they would visit all three Axis powers. Many of the other countries would be occupied during the war by the Nazis.

"In Paris, the Hillerichs and Lefty and I spent the day with Sparrow Robinson, head of the *New York Herald* Paris bureau, who wined and dined us and showed us the sights. We walked the Champs-Élysées, went to the top of the Eiffel Tower, dropped in to the Gothic cathedrals, and stood in awe in front of the *Mona Lisa* at the Louvre. On to the nightclubs and the Folies Bergère. Finally, at 3:00 a.m., Lefty and I were pooped. Not Sparrow and the Hillerichs. Bud said, 'Okay, you two, grab a cab and go to bed.' They kicked up their heels till dawn."

Lefty and June finally sailed for home on the SS *Majestic* on February 21, 1935, five days before their second anniversary. The trip ended as it had begun, with violent storms. "Lordy, what a night," June wrote on February 25. "The ship rolled you from one end of the bed to the other. At one o'clock, Lefty put the light on as the bottles and books were falling off the dresser."

They docked on March 1, three days behind schedule. Lefty and June were photographed as they left the *Majestic*. "Lefty and I had both gained a lot of weight. I went from a hundred to a hundred twenty-five pounds. Twenty-five pounds of tasting everything set before me. In the news photos, I look like a butter tub. My face is completely round. I could get my clothes over my head but I couldn't pull them down over my hips. I ate my way around the world."

23.

"THE YANKEES PAY YOU
EVEN WHEN YOU LOSE?"

Wᴴᴇɴ ʟᴇꜰᴛʏ ᴀʀʀɪᴠᴇᴅ ʜᴏᴍᴇ, ʜᴇ ꜰᴏᴜɴᴅ ᴀ ᴄᴏɴᴛʀᴀᴄᴛ ꜰᴏʀ ᴛʜᴇ ꜱᴀᴍᴇ money as he had been paid for the previous season. He refused to sign and demanded $27,000 per year. "I don't know what you have to do in this league to get a raise," he said after speaking with Ed Barrow. He also announced he would not leave by train for St. Petersburg with three other pitchers, as he was scheduled to do that day, but rather would remain in New York until the dispute was resolved.

As further proof of his worth, Lefty cited fulfillment of Jake Ruppert's five-year wish. The new Vernon Gomez checked in at a stamina-inducing 180 pounds but told the sportswriters he was in better shape than the year before. When asked what he had done to stay in shape, he replied, "I haven't thrown a ball since we left Manila." Sports cartoonist Willard Mullin portrayed him bulging out of an overcoat with a Ruthian figure, in a panel with the caption "Goofy Returns Home, Fat and Sassy . . ."

Babe was also in the news. When Connie Mack returned in early January, he praised Ruth for the quality of his play and his role in establishing good feeling in Japan, but scotched any thought of Babe replacing him in Philadelphia, either then or at any time in the near future. The Yankees initially retained Babe on their reserve list but tendered him only a nominal contract. When he returned from London in late February, he waited to meet with Ruppert, but succeeded in speaking only with Ed Barrow. On February 26, Babe received a terse note from Colonel Ruppert that read, "You are hereby notified as follows: 1. You are unconditionally released." The same day Babe signed with the Boston Braves as a player, vice president, and "assistant manager." The signing turned out to be largely a publicity stunt—on the Braves' part, at any rate—and Babe's tenure in Boston was brief. He would never be given the chance to manage a major league club.

Gomez was a different story, however, and the day after his meeting with Barrow, the newly hefty Lefty signed a two-year deal for $20,000 per year. Red Ruffing also held out, eventually settling for $13,000 after spring training was almost two weeks old. Lefty Gomez was now the highest-paid pitcher in baseball, exceeding the contract for $17,500 Dizzy Dean had signed the previous month and Carl Hubbell's rumored $19,000. With the contract signed, Lefty got in the Pierce-Arrow and drove to Florida with June and Nellie.

"Lefty and I went on crash diets," June said. "We worked out and drank gallons of Florida orange juice and grapefruit juice in St. Pete, which only cost 50¢ a gallon in the thirties. Lefty had to get in shape to pitch and I needed a good shape to open with the Lou Holtz show, *Hold Your Horses,* that I had left to travel to Japan."

Crash diets are not the optimal method by which to get in shape. The fat might go, but the muscles don't get toned. Nonetheless, Lefty pitched four sparkling innings against Babe's Braves on March 19, giving every indication that he would justify his contract. Three days later, however, his tune-up was postponed. Lefty was in the hospital, for the first time in his career, from soreness in his left shoulder. The soreness, he said, was due to a "side-arm pitching style he acquired in the Orient." Ruppert and Barrow had been none too keen on the trip to begin with and were thus doubly displeased that they might have just been hoodwinked into giving an extremely generous two-year deal to a pitcher who had left his fastball across the Pacific.

Japan had certainly taken its toll. Although pitching mechanics was not the science it has become in the modern game, pitchers of Lefty's era understood the importance of precision, efficiency, and disguise in delivering the ball. Without any one of those elements, major league hitters would soon make them aware of the shortcoming. And, of course, when a pitcher changes his delivery, different muscles experience strain.

For Lefty, the need for precise consistency was more acute than it was for, say, Charley Ruffing. Back in his Seals days, Paddy Cottrell had described Lefty's motion as "snaky arm." "What Paddy meant was that there was fluid movement through my arm as I delivered a pitch. My arm looked like a snake. I was considered to have great rhythm. Bill Dickey said that, not me, and Dickey caught me, so he should know."

Satchel Paige was the same. He generated velocity and movement not with muscle—Paige's arm was no more beefy than Lefty's—but by transferring torque from shoulder to elbow to wrist with fluidity and then creating spin as the ball rolled off his fingers. Each had a high kick to initiate the sequence maximally in the lower body.

One of the tips that Herb Pennock had given Lefty in his rookie year was never to sidearm a hitter. When he came overhand, his fastball moved up and away from right-handed hitters. "But when he dropped down," Joe Sewell said, "the ball would stay flat, wouldn't take off. He'd be out there pitching sometimes and I'd be playing third base and all I'd have to do was holler, 'Up and over,' and as soon as he did he'd start striking them out."

One of the reasons an overhand pitcher drops down, of course, is muscle fatigue. Paige was a wonder. With all the innings he pitched from his teens through his fifties (and maybe even his sixties; the record is unclear), except for one episode in the late 1930s his arm never gave him trouble. For everyone else who has ever thrown a baseball, however, different rules applied. Lefty never complained when Connie Mack had him pitch so frequently, but the effects of the extra work in cold weather coupled with four months of eating, drinking, sightseeing, and no real exercise would linger for two years.

And there was also no getting him into shape gradually, because Lefty wanted to pitch. "Gomez was calm and collected on the mound, but a nervous fellow on the bench," said McCarthy, "boiling over with energy and enthusiasm. He was always trying to get my okay to go to the bullpen if we were losing or in a tight game. He'd pound his glove, mutter about going in there and stopping them, and pretty soon he'd be almost sitting in my lap. It never mattered to Gomez if he pitched the day or night before or an extra-inning game two days ago. He always wanted to pitch if the Yankees were in a tight spot." At the end of the previous August, Lefty had volunteered to pitch every third day, if that was what it took to get the team into the World's Series. McCarthy had refused.

Lefty was out of the hospital and on the mound four days later, but had to leave after five innings when his shoulder got worse. He was treated by Doc Painter, the team trainer, which from a sports medicine point of view was not a good deal better than not being treated at all. Perhaps worse.

"Doc was a nice guy who did the best he could with what he had to work with," Lefty noted. "He never threw an empty bottle away. He rinsed them out and recycled them for other lotions. If a player was injured, Doc had two liniments: Martin's and Rubifax. Rubifax would take varnish off a table and Martin's would remove black marks from linoleum. It was safer to forgo the 'medical treatment' and instead pray for recovery. The odds were the same."

On April Fools' Day, Lefty was back again, facing Paul Dean in an exhibition against the Cardinals, and all seemed well. He dominated for six innings and reported no pain in his shoulder. But in his next outing, he was pounded for seven runs and eleven hits by a minor league team.

Lefty remained erratic for the remainder of the exhibition season, but on opening day in Yankee Stadium, he tossed a six-hitter at the Red Sox, giving up but a single run. Unfortunately, the Sox's Wes Ferrell gave up only two hits and no runs, so Lefty lost 1–0.

As the season progressed, he didn't pitch badly, and even had moments of brilliance, like the four-hit, 2–0 shutout against the Senators on April 29. In many of his outings, however, he was just that little bit off, especially in the late innings. On June 23 against Cleveland, for example, he took a 5–4 lead into the bottom of the eighth, only to give up the tying run in that inning and the winning run in the ninth on two wild pitches.

Six days later, against the Senators, McCarthy took no chances. For seven innings, Lefty pitched shutout ball, the Yankees staking him to a six-run lead, but he gave up a run in the eighth, then walked two in the ninth and gave up a run-scoring single. The Yankees still led 6–2, and in other years McCarthy would simply have let his ace pitch out of the jam. On this occasion, however, McCarthy saw that Lefty had lost his stuff and brought in Johnny Murphy to close things out. Even the newspapers noticed, observing that "Gomez weakened perceptibly in the eighth and staggered around alarmingly in the ninth."

As Lefty struggled and even Gehrig's numbers were off his usual Olympian standards, Jake Ruppert fumed. He was convinced that the Japan trip and its aftermath were the cause of subpar years by his best pitcher and best position player, and he was probably right. But the Colonel's wrath was tempered by the Yankees' fast start. After a blistering May, the team was 25–15 and one and a half up on the White Sox. Lefty hadn't given up many runs, but wasn't getting a lot of wins either. And, midway through the month, he had something else to think about besides how far Jimmie Foxx's home runs off him traveled: He was having visitors.

THE DEPRESSION HAD HIT the East Bay hard. Almost everyone had a vegetable garden and most had livestock, so residents didn't go hungry, but there was no work to be had and everything that couldn't be produced became a luxury. Even the most unpleasant jobs at Union Oil were unavailable, so locals scuffled around for whatever work they could find.

Frank Wilson was a few years older than Lefty but they had spent a good deal of time together as kids. He had stayed in Rodeo and was hired as a pipe fitter at the Union Oil refinery. But even though he had a mechanical engineering degree, his salary was not enough to make ends meet, so he took extra work when he could. In the spring of 1935, he landed a part-time maintenance job on U.S. 40, which cut through the town. He would be one of a crew of three assigned to dig a water line in Pinole. Frank was lean and strong, thirty-two years old. Each of the other members of the crew was seventy-one: Mike Kerns and Coyote Gomez.

For Coyote, this was a second job as well, perhaps a third. He continued to work for S. J. Claeys, although his sons had taken over some of the load. Coyote also owned a grain ranch in the Christie hills beyond Franklin Canyon, where he and the boys raised oats, barley, and hay. But whenever the chance to earn extra money came along, Coyote was at the front of the line.

"Digging ditches is backbreaking work," Frank Wilson related, "and I wondered how these old men could dig alongside of me. But they kept up the pace. I know I didn't dig any more than Coyote and Mike did. Jack Williams, the boss, complimented us all. After a week of work, we went our separate ways."

A few nights later, Frank Wilson was surprised to see Coyote in front of his house, dressed, as always, in faded jeans and tan leather vest. Frank noticed that the grizzled old cowboy had tears in his eyes. He'd been as hard as nails on the job. "You know something, Wilson?" he asked.

"No, Coyote, I don't."

"I'm goin' to Yankee Stadium."

"How are you going to get from here to Yankee Stadium?"

"Well," Coyote said, "I've just come from talkin' with Vernon on the telephone down at Claeys's butcher shop. My boy is sending Lizzie and me railroad tickets."

"Congratulations. Like you say, you and Mrs. Gomez are finally going to see your boy pitch at Yankee Stadium in New York."

Coyote smiled, then the two stood in silence.

"Coyote was remembering Lefty as a boy, like I was," Frank said later. "And how Vernon had gone on and made good back east, just like he told his pa he would. So I clapped Coyote on the shoulder and said, 'It ain't everybody can have a son like Lefty. You should hurrah a little bit.'

" 'So, *hurrah!*' Coyote shouted into the night. *'Hurrah!'* I'll never forget how that old man's face lit up when he spoke of Yankee Stadium."

"THE YANKEES WERE in Detroit when Lizzie and Coyote arrived by train at Grand Central Station on May 13," June related. "I picked them up in a taxi during rush hour, and as the cabbie darted in and out of the traffic it didn't take them long to realize that New York was not Rodeo. We went to Broadway for a sandwich at Lindy's and then to bed."

Coyote and Lizzie's arrival in New York coincided with the docking at Pier 55 of the *Ile de France.* Sunny and Frank Conville were on the passenger list, returning from a five-week engagement with Maurice Chevalier and the Ballets Russes in London, Paris, and Edinburgh.

Conville was Sunny's partner only onstage. Offstage she had become engaged to a bandleader, Rutledge Hawn, known as "Rut," a direct descendant of Edward Rutledge, the youngest signer of the Declaration of Independence. Rut, June, Nellie, and the Gomezes met Sunny when the ship docked at 5:00 p.m. on May 14.*

"With Rut in town, terrific on the sax and the clarinet, it was a foregone conclusion that we would wind up at the Famous Door, an after-hours musicians' club, featuring Louis Prima and his New Orleans Gang. It was Rut's treat to Lizzie and Coyote, sitting ringside at their first jazz gig, wide-eyed as Prima and his band were swinging hot with Pee Wee Russell on clarinet, running through 'Sweet Sue,' 'Dinah,' and 'Lazy River.' "

The pace didn't slacken when the Yankees came home. "Lefty returned on May 16, and we were off and running to the top of the Empire State Building, where Lizzie and Coyote got a bird's-eye view of the city's skyscrapers from the 102nd floor. Getting to the building by walking down a flight of stairs to an underground train called a subway was a ho-hum experience to Lefty and me, but so distant from anything his parents had witnessed back home that I think their nerves were jangled. Afterwards, we split up for a shopping spree. Lefty, Rut, and Coyote dropped into Ben Brooker's men's shop. Lizzie, Nellie, Sunny, and I went to the garment district because Lizzie did all the sewing back home and wanted to see the showrooms of the famous labels and fabric wholesalers she had read about in fashion magazines. She bought tons of fabrics and trimmings that I sent on to California.

"We met back at the Greystone. Coyote showed off the suit and shoes Lefty had bought for him and then he asked, 'And guess what else?' Before we could answer, Coyote dropped his pants and said, 'Silk shorts!' Lizzie was shocked that he's standing there in his underwear, but we could all understand how great silk would feel after a lifetime of wearing cotton flannel.

"On May 18, we all went out to Yankee Stadium to watch Lefty pitch against Cleveland and win 3–0. How exciting for Lizzie and Coyote to see

---

* Rut Hawn eventually married Laura Steinhoff, but he and Sunny remained friends. Years later, Rut asked Sunny's advice on how to get his daughter Goldie into show business.

Lefty pitch winning ball on their first time to the stadium. Coyote pointed to the mound and said, 'That's my son,' and his face broke into a wide grin."

Lizzie and Coyote saw Lefty pitch five times during their two-month visit. They watched him win and they watched him lose. Mostly what they saw was the culmination of a lifelong dream. The economics of the game, however, eluded them. Coyote once exclaimed in disbelief, "You mean the Yankees pay you, even when you lose?"

After the 3–0 shutout against Cleveland, June reported, "Pitzy Katz joined our gang, along with Lou and Eleanor Gehrig, and we went to Paul and Mae Fung's for dinner. Coyote was speechless when he saw Snapper, the Fungs' baby alligator, waddling around the rooms, and Paul's thousands of tropical fish. After chop suey and fortune cookies, we went to the theater to see *The Great Waltz*. One of the violinists, Freddy Fradkin, ran with our crowd and had left tickets. Freddy was also a prankster. I don't know if Coyote was into the Strauss music, but he certainly had a belly laugh with the rest of us watching Freddy fiddling his way through the waltzes in the orchestra pit. The violinist next to him wore a toupee, and the guy kept jumping around in his chair because he knew that Fradkin was trying to pick the toupee off his head with his bow. Lefty said to me, 'Oh geez, I have some crazy wonderful friends.'"

Lefty and June were determined to cram as much into the visit as Lizzie and Coyote could take. "Then it was on to meet the Gradys in Lexington. Grandma Bridget and Lizzie talked recipes, and Coyote and Milo, the two card sharks, played blackjack. When the Yankees came to town for a series against the Red Sox, Lefty's parents, Nellie, and the Gradys were in the stands. Nellie took Lizzie and Coyote by car to see the Old North Bridge in Concord, where the first shot of the American Revolution was fired in 1775, a battle against the British that many baseball fans would say was never as intense as the Yankees' rivalry with the Red Sox. Over the remaining weeks, Lizzie and Coyote went to Radio City and saw the Rockettes, more ball games, and celebrated Sunny's twenty-fourth backstage with us at Loew's Theater in Jersey City, where Conville & Dale were on the bill."

Despite a .500 record, Lefty was again the starting pitcher in the All-Star game on July 8. In front of 70,000 fans in Cleveland, including his parents, he threw six innings of three-hit ball and was the winning pitcher in a 4–1 American League victory—Jimmie Foxx helping him out by blasting a two-run homer in the first inning. Lefty said later that Mickey Cochrane kept him beyond the traditional three-inning stint so he would be unable to pitch against the Tigers in a series that began immediately after the break.

On July 17, Lizzie and Coyote boarded the Broadway Limited for Chicago, where they would make a connection to San Francisco. When Lizzie returned home, she told a niece that the trip was the highlight of their lives. Lefty and June were gratified to hear that news, all the more so because, as they knew, both Lizzie and Coyote were ill and neither might have long to live.

WHEN THE SEASON resumed after the All-Star game, the Yankees were still in first place, two games ahead of the league champion Tigers. But once again the Yankees faded in the heat. By the end of the month the Tigers had turned the two-game deficit into a three-game lead. In August, the Tigers extended their lead to eight and a half games.

But, unlike in the previous two seasons, the Yankees made a run in September, closing within four games with a week to go in the season. The Yankees remained a long shot and needed to win almost every game. The pressure took its toll on both the players and their wives. "During the pennant race, if I went to the game on the days Lefty was pitching," June said, "he asked me not to sit with the wives of his teammates because in the tension of a game, if a teammate booted a ball or mishandled a catch and a run scored and the Yankees lost, I might spontaneously say, 'Now look what happened. Your husband cost us the game.' So when Lefty was on the mound, I sat high in the grandstands with opera scores on my lap for the down moments like the seventh-inning stretch."

In the end, Detroit won the pennant by only three games, the tightest American League race in a decade. The Yankees, at 89–60, finished second for the third year in a row, and the fifth time in the last seven. While the Tigers played the Cubs in the World's Series, Yankee Stadium was converted to a 92,569-seat prizefighting arena to host the upcoming heavyweight championship between Joe Louis and Max Baer.

In the eyes of an owner and general manager who had just made him the highest-paid pitcher in the game, Lefty bore much of the blame for the second-place finish. He ended 1935 with a losing record for the first time in his life, 12–15. He finished fourth in ERA, however, at 3.18, precisely the same number he had recorded in 1933. Charley Ruffing finished just ahead of him at 3.12, and Ruffing didn't have such a great won-lost year, either, finishing 16–11. The Yankees' two other main starters, two Johnnies, Broaca and Allen, finished 15–7 and 13–6, respectively, both with an ERA around 3.60. The entire pitching staff, at the same 3.60, led the American League.*

Offense had again done the Yankees in. They finished fourth in batting, third in home runs, and scored 101 fewer runs than Detroit. Again, only Gehrig had driven in more than 100 runs, and his 119 was his lowest total since 1926. Without Babe hitting in front of him, Lou had drawn 162 bases on balls, a career high. The sad truth was that no one else in the Yankee lineup scared anyone. Not one other player hit as many as fifteen home runs. Worst of all for Ruppert and Barrow, with yet another second-place finish attendance slipped to a paltry 657,000—400,000 less than Detroit.

Still, with their pitching and an essentially solid lineup, the team was probably just one player away from greatness. Of course, the player would have to be great as well. And for that player, three thousand miles away, the drumbeat had already begun.

LEFTY AND JUNE remained in New York at the season's end. June was doing a nightclub act at the Hotel Elysée and, after the previous whirlwind off-season, planned on spending some time in the city before heading to Rodeo for the holidays, this time by a new form of cross-country travel,

---

* Both Johnnies were among the oddest men in baseball. Allen, who had been raised in an orphanage, was so bad-tempered that, despite a ton of talent, he bounced from one team to another. Umpires loathed him. After his playing days were over, he of course became an umpire himself. Broaca was even more bizarre. He'd attended Phillips Andover and Yale, where he starred in three sports. In 1937, after three promising years, he walked off the mound in the middle of a game and disappeared for eighteen months. After a failed comeback in 1939, Broaca spent the rest of his life as a common laborer.

airliner. The five-day train trip had been shrunk to twenty-five hours, albeit with numerous stops to refuel and change planes along the way.

"Then Milfred called and asked June and me to come earlier. 'No alarm, Vernon, but Pa's in the hospital. Heart disease. Dr. Weil said he'll be home for Christmas but Lizzie wants you to come out earlier in case he takes a turn for the worse.' So June and I flew out on December 16, a night flight to Oakland. Milfred picked us up at the airport and we went directly to Richmond Hospital. When we walked into Coyote's room, Pa was propped up against the pillows. His face was pale but a smile was twitching around the corners of his mouth.

" 'How'd you get here, Vernon?'

" 'Plane, Pa.'

" 'Where you goin' after this?'

" 'Home to Rodeo with Milfred.'

" 'Good. Your ma will be happy having June here. Holidays 'round the bend.'

" 'Yeah, Pa. All of us together at the table.'

"The next morning, around 7:00 a.m., Milfred and I came back to the hospital. After Pa jawed awhile about Claeys's cattle, he began reminiscing.

" 'You know, when Lizzie and I were courting, I took her for a spin in my horse and buggy and we lost track of time. Lizzie was living at a boardinghouse close to a wooden bridge and her landlady didn't look kindly on her coming in late from a date. So I put socks on the horses' hooves to quiet the clattering coming across the bridge.' Coyote began laughing. 'And the old lady was none the wiser.'

"Listening to these shenanigans from a father who made us toe the line all the time, Milfred threw me a wink. A few moments later, we took our leave. As Milfred and I left the room, Pa said, 'Goodbye, sons.'

"We were halfway down the hall when a nurse leaned over the railing and called out for us. Milfred and I rushed back. Pa was gone, split seconds after he had said, 'Goodbye, sons.' "

24.

"HE CAN'T HIT IT, IF I DON'T THROW IT"

THE YANKEES HAD TWO NEW ADDITIONS IN SPRING TRAINING.

The first, a kid just turned twenty-one, arrived by car after a trip across the country, escorted like a Michelangelo, which in fact he was, by Tony Lazzeri and Frank Crosetti. The year before, playing for the Seals, he had amassed 270 hits in 172 games, hitting .398, with 34 home runs and 154 RBIs. In 1933, he had batted safely in 61 consecutive games. Joe DiMaggio was perhaps the most lauded rookie in the history of the game. That he would play in the media capital of the world for a team starved for a giant personality to fill the Babe's void, and that as an Italian he would bring even more of New York's vast Italian American population to Yankee Stadium, only added to the anticipation.

McCarthy later described DiMaggio. "Of all the outstanding stars I've known, DiMaggio required the least coaching. Joe would have been a famed base stealer if we played the game that way. Joe had no equal at going from first to third base on a hit into the outfield. He had an uncanny sense that told him when to go for third or stop at second. He knew every arm in the league and had the long stride and the arm action to bring out his true speed. Opposing catchers have told me that DiMaggio actually hit the ball out of their mitts just as they reached out to catch it, but it must have been an illusion for he was always out in front with his bat when he met the ball. He hit countless drives into the deep reaches of left field and left center in Yankee Stadium that would have been home runs in most major league parks. But I never heard him complain about one of them being caught. I never heard him say, 'That would have been a home run in Boston' or 'a home run in Detroit.' Joe was a near-perfect player."

Lefty's parents, Coyote Gomez and Lizzie Herring, at their California homestead.

VERNON LEFTY GOMEZ LLC

Lefty and his collie, Jack, inseparable as always.

VERNON LEFTY GOMEZ LLC

Rodeo Town team, 1923. Vernon Gomez, 14, is top row, third from right.

VERNON LEFTY GOMEZ LLC

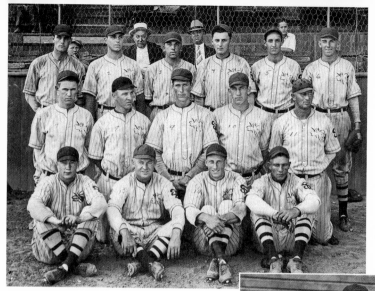

Salt Lake City Bees, 1928. Lefty is first left in the second row. He scowls his determination to make the big leagues into the camera. Bob Coltrin, manager, is down in front, second from left. VERNON LEFTY GOMEZ LLC

San Francisco, 1929. The Seals best—and skinniest—pitcher.

AP PHOTO

Lefty, the rookie babysitter, with Susie Hoyt at spring training, 1930.

VERNON LEFTY GOMEZ LLC

Herb Pennock giving Lefty pointers on hay pitching at his farm in Kennett Square, Pennsylvania.

VERNON LEFTY GOMEZ LLC

William Schwarz and Nellie Grady honeymoon on the boardwalk at Atlantic City, New Jersey, 1910.

VERNON LEFTY GOMEZ LLC

Stars of Tomorrow vaudeville act: Kenny Delmar and the Kaye Sisters (Sunny and June), working the Keith-Albee and Orpheum theater circuits, coast to coast.

VERNON LEFTY GOMEZ LLC/
NASIB, NY

June at sixteen years old—no longer a fugitive from the Gerry Society—on Broadway in George M. Cohan's *Billie*.

Sunny Dale, a 1923 Ziegfeld Follies showgirl.

Backstage, Lefty asks June to her first baseball game. Not a fan, she thinks he pitches every day. When Gomez and the Yanks lose, June says, "Don't worry, honey. You'll beat them tomorrow."

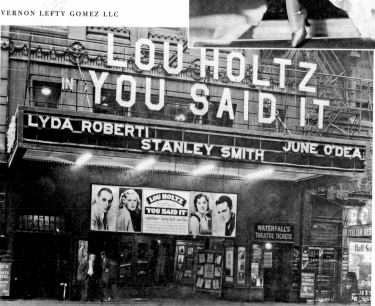

1932 World Series Champions team photo. Lefty, Babe, and Lou (second row center) are without belts and pants. They were horsing around in the clubhouse and had to rush to meet the pop of the flashbulb. PHOTOGRAPHY COLLECTION, MIRIAM AND IRA D. WALLACH DIVISION OF ART, PRINTS, AND PHOTOGRAPHS, THE NEW YORK PUBLIC LIBRARY, ASTOR, LENOX AND TILDEN FOUNDATIONS

Lefty chalks up his first World Series win in 1932 at the Stadium against the Chicago Cubs. Dickey, Gomez, and Gehrig: three reasons why the Yankees were pennant winners.

NATIONAL BASEBALL HALL OF FAME LIBRARY, COOPERSTOWN, NY

Babe Ruth and Lefty Gomez, on their swing north from spring training, take in an exhibition game in Mobile, Alabama.

ERIK OVERBEY COLLECTION, THE DOY LEALE MCCALL RARE BOOK AND MANUSCRIPT LIBRARY, UNIVERSITY OF SOUTH ALABAMA

Lefty showing pinpoint location.
VERNON LEFTY GOMEZ LLC

Lefty at Lowe's State Theatre with his $3,000-per-week vaudeville act, 1932. He quit when told the footlights demand stage makeup. No lipstick for Lefty. VERNON LEFTY GOMEZ LLC/ PHOTOGRAPHER: BARBERO & GALE

Comiskey Park, Chicago, Illinois, 1933: the first American League All-Star team.* Lefty is fourth from the right in the second row. He will be the winning pitcher and drive in the first run.

   * Kneeling (left to right): Trainer Doc Schacht, Eddie Collins, Tony Lazzeri, Al Crowder, Jimmie Foxx, coach Art Fletcher, Earl Averill, Ed Rommel, Ben Chapman, Rick Ferrell, Sam West, Charlie Gehringer, and Clyde McBride, batboy.

   Standing: Clubhouse man Art Colledge, batting practice catcher Bill Conroy, Lou Gehrig, Babe Ruth, Orv Hildebrandt, manager Connie Mack, Joe Cronin, Lefty Grove, batboy Harry Colledge, Bill Dickey, Al Simmons, Lefty Gomez, Wes Ferrell, Jimmy Dykes, and clubhouse man Eph Colledge. AP PHOTO

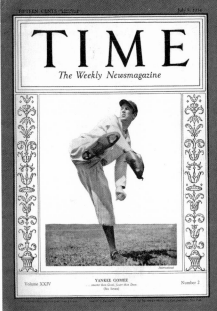

Buying a paper at a Broadway newsstand in the summer of 1934, Lefty was surprised to find himself on the cover of *Time* magazine. He was the first pitcher to be so featured.
TIME INC.

Bali, 1934: Lefty and Babe sport the latest in pith helmets and footwear.
VERNON LEFTY GOMEZ LLC

FDR and the Secret Service enter the Polo Grounds for game two of the 1936 World Series. Gomez and the Yanks win 18–4. FDR is among the 43,500 fans watching Lefty gaze at an airplane while a slugger waits in the batter's box.
AP PHOTO

The 1934 American All-Star trip to Japan.

Front row kneeling (left to right): Charles Gehringer, Frank Hayes, Eric McNair, Bob Schroeder, Joe Cascarella, Moe Berg, Bing Miller, Clint Brown, Earl Whitehill, Earl Averill, Lefty Gomez, a newspaper reporter, "Doc" Ebling, "Rabbit" Warstler, "Bud" Hillerich, Walter M. Warren, and John Quinn (umpire).

Back row (left to right): Jim Foxx, Mrs. Foxx, Mrs. Schroeder, Mrs. Warstler, Mrs. McNair, Mrs. Miller, Mrs. O'Doul, Mrs. Averill, Lefty O'Doul, Mrs. Brown, Mrs. Whitehill, Mrs. Ruth, Babe Ruth, Connie Mack, Julia Ruth, June Gomez, Mrs. Gehrig, Mrs. Hillerich, and Lou Gehrig.

★ TRIALS OF A GOOFY ONE'S WIFE ★

June in the stands at the 1936 World Series, Yankees vs. NY Giants. Emotions run high as Lefty hurls his pitches through the batter's box.

Bing Russell (behind the wheel) preparing for a jaunt with his buddies Lefty, Joe, and batboy Timmy Sullivan in St. Petersburg, Florida, 1936.

Paul Fung Jr., a good charm himself, gives Lefty a good luck Buddha.

The 1937 World Series shocker: Lefty—who said, "I had only one weakness as a hitter…a pitched ball"—belts in the winning run in game five against the NY Giants. NEW YORK *DAILY NEWS* VIA GETTY IMAGES

Cartoonist Willard Mullin's tribute to Lefty's Triple Crown in 1937. Lefty also won it in 1934.

After a bowl of Wheaties, Lefty's a champion among Champions in 1937.

World Series winner Lefty Gomez calls the pitches at Bronx vs. Manhattan, 1937.

LaHiff's Tavern, October 1937. A kiss for a two-game World Series winner at the Yankees victory dinner. A few months later, the mood would be different.

THOMSON'S
"Glove-Fitting"

June modeling lingerie, a job that led to attorney Melvin Kleeblatt and victory in the divorce court.

"Lefty, the fans want to know…
Edna Torrence or June O'Dea?"

March 1938: The movie *Rawhide* opens in St. Petersburg: Two-gun Lou won't take no for an answer. Gehrig ropes Crosetti, Dickey, Gomez, and Knickerbocker into attending the premiere.

Explosive power in the Yankee dugout, 1938: Manager Joe McCarthy, Gehrig, Ruffing, Gomez, DiMaggio, Dickey, and Rolfe.

Mayor Fiorello LaGuardia hefts the lumber between Lefty and Bill Dickey, 1938

1938 World Series: Gomez and Yanks vs. Dizzy Dean and the Chicago Cubs. June holds the 6–0 World Series record-winning ball. This photo is laser-engraved on the Gomez gravesite monument.

Roommates Lefty and Joe do the shopping scene on a Yankee road trip.

"Triple Exposure" created by Vincent Lopez on glass plates was the focal point of June's last Christmas card. The award-winning photo hung in exhibition at the 1939 World's Fair.

The Yankees try out a new catcher, two-year-old Vernona.

Sharon and Vernona on the left and Gery, far right, at the old swimming hole in Durham with their friends Deidre, Jim, and Billy.

True Comics gets caught up in the Lefty legend.

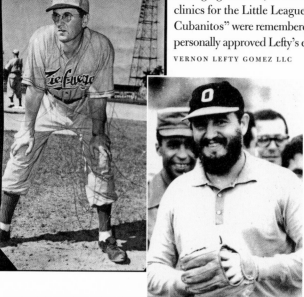

Managing in Cuba, 1947. Lefty's annual pitching clinics for the Little Leagues of Cuba, "Los Cubanitos" were remembered by Fidel Castro. He personally approved Lefty's exit visa during a later trip.

A law student who loved to pitch, Fidel attended Lefty's clinics at the Universidad de La Habana. They would meet again during the Cuban Revolution.

Lefty presents the Executive of the Year award to Bing Russell, owner of the Portland Mavericks, at Bing's induction into the Baseball Hall of Fame in 1974.

For twenty-five years, Frank Conville and Sunny Dale brought laughs to soldiers in the war-torn theatres of Europe, the Pacific, and Korea. Here, in October 1951, they entertain the 7th U.S. Infantry Division in Korea, with a Charlie Chaplin comedy bit.

Lefty Gomez, Wilson Sporting Goods ambassador, wears his top-of-the-line personal model glove.

WITH PERMISSION OF
WILSON SPORTING GOODS

Publicity shot for the Nugget Golf Classic. As Joe said to Lefty, "When you're too old to pitch, it's time to putt."

VERNON LEFTY GOMEZ LLC/WITH
PERMISSION FROM JOHN ASCUAGA OF
JOHN ASCUAGA'S NUGGET AND THE
SAN FRANCISCO LIBRARY

Duane, playmaker for Sir Francis Drake High School, one year before his death.

VERNON LEFTY GOMEZ LLC

Hall of Fame induction, 1972, with Yogi Berra, Lefty, Sandy Koufax, Buck Leonard, and Early Wynn.

NATIONAL BASEBALL HALL OF
FAME LIBRARY, COOPERSTOWN, NY

The master salesman in his
Yankee uniform sporting two
Wilson gloves. PERMISSION OF
WILSON SPORTING GOODS

April 1987: The
Lou Gehrig
Pride of the
Yankees award,
presented to
Lefty by George
Steinbrenner.
VERNON LEFTY
GOMEZ LLC/WITH
PERMISSION NEW
YORK *DAILY NEWS*

DAILY NEWS

PRIDE OF THE YANKEES

Lefty Gomez receives 1987 Award

LEFTY STILL HAS HIS FAST BALL
Vernon (Lefty) Gomez shows he still has his form with this pitch. Lefty helped the Fairfax-Sleepy Hollow Little League open its 1974 season yesterday and tossed the first ball. Behind Lefty is a sign in his honor to be erected at White Hill School. The park was named "Lefty Gomez Field" in 1972, the year Lefty, a resident of Fairfax, was inducted into baseball's Hall of Fame at Cooperstown, N.Y.

Lefty whistles in his fastball to open
the Little League season in 1974.
MARIN INDEPENDENT JOURNAL/ALFRED ARN

April 1987: Lefty accepts the Lou
Gehrig Pride of the Yankees award.
Lefty, still trim at 78, and June, still
stunning at 74. VERNON LEFTY GOMEZ LLC

Lefty, grand marshal at the
Babe Ruth League World
Series in Nogales, Arizona.
JOE VITTI/*THE ARIZONA DAILY STAR*

And he was acquired in a near-perfect deal. It wasn't often that Charley Graham got snookered, but the Yankees did just that, acquiring Joltin' Joe for the ridiculous bargain-basement price of $25,000.

Bill Essick, the same scout who had signed Lefty, had been following DiMaggio since he was seventeen, as was everyone else on the West Coast. Joe was a shortstop then, with a powerful arm, excellent speed, and preternatural baseball instincts. Essick and his fellow scouts had watched the kid mature, move to the outfield, and become perhaps the most valuable property Charley Graham had ever owned. Even in the Depression, a $100,000 sale price was considered a certainty, and there was speculation that with some deft maneuvering, Graham could get even more than that.

Then disaster struck. In May 1934, after a night when Joe may or may not have been drinking, may or may not have been trying to get into a moving car driven by someone else who had been drinking, may or may not have been coming from a nightclub, and may or may not have been heading for his sister's, he slipped, fell, and tore cartilage in his knee. In less than five seconds, Graham's $100,000 evaporated.

The question remained whether or not Charley would get anything at all. DiMaggio sat out six weeks, tried to come back, then collapsed in the dugout when his knee gave out, and missed the remainder of the season. One by one, scouts sighed and lost interest. Except Essick.

He arranged for DiMaggio to travel to Los Angeles, completely on the sly, and be examined by a specialist. The doctor assured Essick the damage wasn't permanent. The kid just needed rest. Without mentioning the trip to the doctor, Essick offered Graham $25,000 and five players for his injured Italian. Graham jumped at it. On November 21, 1934, the Yankees announced the deal. It was agreed that DiMaggio would remain in the PCL one more year while the knee healed. In that year, Joe hit almost .400, was named league MVP, and Charley Graham spent the summer kicking himself around the block.

In October 1935, after the Yankees' second-place finish, Jake Ruppert observed, "If DiMaggio provides the needed punch at the plate, we can't miss next year."

Joe might have baseball skills beyond his years, but his life skills were stunted, even by the standards of a West Coast transplant and second-generation immigrant christened Giuseppe Paolo. He was shy, moody, uncertain of himself in even the most basic social situations, untrusting of strangers, which meant everyone, and completely unprepared for the assault he was about to undergo by the New York press. He could not drive a car, and when he learned, he could not master reverse. Even a far less astute crew than Ruppert, Barrow, and McCarthy would have figured out that Joe desperately needed a mentor, someone dexterous and clever, to protect and guide such a valuable property through the minefield that was New York.

Fortunately, such a man was close at hand. World traveler, noted wit, snappy dresser, and fellow Bay Area refugee Vernon Gomez was assigned as Joe's roommate, and would remain so for seven years. In the process, the two would forge a deep and lifelong friendship, unlikely even by an opposites-attract standard.

When DiMaggio arrived in camp, he dressed totally in black: black suit, black tie, black socks, black shoes. He looked like a Sicilian widow. Lefty, on the other hand, favored checked jackets and contrasting pants, with everything from shoes to shirts custom-made.

Ben Brooker, the clothier, and Johnny Calgano, his top salesmen, were devoted Yankee fans. They were fixtures at the stadium, welcome in the clubhouse, and likely sold more clothes at games than at the clothing store. As soon as they returned to New York, Lefty took Joe to Brooker's, and Calagno sold him some casual slacks and jackets. No black. From then on, Joe looked sporty.

Lefty performed other functions for the prized rookie. After the season, Joe was invited to a banquet to honor his outstanding play. He asked Lefty to come along. After receiving the acclaim and the awards, Joe got to the microphone and said, "Thank you very much. And now my roommate will say a few words." Lefty later said he was "shocked to his shoes." But he got up anyway, gave a speech off the cuff, and left the audience in stitches. After Joe pulled this routine a few more times, Lefty realized if he was going anywhere with Joe, he had to be prepared to go to a microphone. "Thus," a writer commented, "a baseball humorist came to be."

THE OTHER ADDITION to Yankee camp that year was another kid, this one only nine. His name was Neil Russell, although everyone called him Bing.

Bing's father, Warren, known to everyone as Bud, was a pilot based in St. Petersburg. In 1936, he had been hired to fly a wealthy businessman around in his private plane. But Bud Russell was not just any airborne chauffeur. He was a six-time national stunt champion, one of a generation of daredevil aviators that had followed Lincoln Beachey.

Bing and his sister were home-schooled, mostly by their mother, Ruth, called Ooie (no one in the Russell family seemed to use a given name), who was a musician and songwriter. Bing didn't attend regular classes until high school, which didn't stop him from eventually graduating from Dartmouth. But, with a flexible schedule, he was able to hang around the airfield with his dad, helping with mechanics and learning to fly. Bing soloed for the first time when he was ten.

In late February, Bing noticed a tall, skinny guy hanging around as well, chatting with his father while Bud worked on the engine of a Stinson Gullwing. When the skinny guy heard that Bing liked baseball, he showed up the next day with a dozen new American League baseballs in a box. Until then, Bud hadn't asked who the stranger was. It was Lefty, of course, there to take the next step in aviation and learn to fly on his own.

"Lefty flew a lot with Buddy, as much as some commercial pilots did in those days," Bing recounted. "He was a good pilot. Had respect for an airplane. Good reflexes, good memory, and analyzed the situations."

Whenever Lefty landed, Bing was either playing ball or bugging some-one to do it. "Lefty saw that I loved baseball. He also knew that when Buddy was away flying I was alone down in St. Pete, fending for myself. So Lefty asked Bud, 'Would you mind if I pick Bing up every morning at a quarter of nine and bring him back at four-thirty? I'll take him with me to the ballpark.' Bud said, 'Sure.'

"So Lefty picked me up the next morning and took me up to Miller Huggins Field. I didn't know this till much later, but the Yankees had adopted a ruling that players' children couldn't be around the club in spring training, except for Earle Combs's two sons. Earle was a great ball-player whose career was shortened when he fractured his skull crashing into a wall in St. Louis in July of '34, and was on the team as a coach. Lefty walked me into McCarthy's office. Joe was behind his desk, doing paper-work, and he looked up as we stood in the doorway. 'Joe, this is Bing Russell. He's nine years old and he's gonna be with us.'

"Joe said, 'That's fine with me, Lefty.' Lefty put his arm around me and we walked out to the clubhouse. I went to Huggins Field every day after that and I was with Lefty at spring training for six years."

Bing Russell played much the same mascot role in St. Petersburg as Paul Fung Jr. did at Yankee Stadium. He loved being on the field as much as Junior. But Bing discovered early on to watch himself around certain players. "Charley Ruffing was big and gruff. During infield practice, when I was on second base and Red was walking over from third, I didn't look before I tossed the ball in. I hit Ruffing in the head. I can't blame him for not talking to me that day, but McCarthy certainly did, one of two times in six years. He growled, 'Look before you throw.' "

At twelve, Bing's two aspirations were to win an Academy Award and to be in the Hall of Fame. He went one for two, good in any league. In Hollywood, Bing had a solid career, with a supporting role on the hit series *Bonanza,* as well as appearances in more than one hundred films and television shows, including *The Horse Soldiers* and *The Magnificent Seven.* His son, Kurt, became better-known.* Decades later, Bing became owner of the Portland Mavericks in the Class A Northwest League, known for as much its *Bull Durham* style as for games won. His team set a record for the highest attendance in minor league history. In 1974, he was named national baseball executive of the year. "But I'm up on the third floor of the Hall, not down in the gallery where Lefty is."

Bing, maybe because he was a kid, saw a side of Lefty that perhaps no one else except June was privy to. "When Lefty lost a game, or got banged around for a few innings, it hurt me as much as it hurt him. There were

---

* Kurt's longtime partner, of course, is Goldie Hawn, completing an interesting coincidental loop.

times a day would go by after he had lost, and he was not funny at all, not talking much, because in his mind he was going over the game. When other people came around, though, he'd be funny and carefree. But I knew what was going on inside him and he appreciated that it had hurt me so much and kept me quiet in his company. I was alone with Lefty in some great times, but tough times too. There's no question that any happiness and success I've enjoyed is due to those years I shared with Lefty."

If Bing Russell got to revel in a kid's fantasy, Joe DiMaggio began 1936 with a series of disappointments. On March 22, he was spiked sliding into second base, a mild injury that, if left alone, would have healed in a couple of days. But Doc Painter wasn't a team trainer to let wounds heal unattended. He put Joe's foot in a newly acquired diathermy machine, a medical marvel that would bring heat to the affected area and promote faster healing. Unfortunately, Doc brought a bit too much heat to Joe's foot, and the prize rookie was scalded. So, instead of being out a day or two, DiMaggio limped around with second-degree burns and would not make his anticipated major league debut until early May.

Despite his losing record the year before, McCarthy still considered Lefty to be one of his aces. Joe sent him to the mound on opening day in Griffith Stadium in Washington in front of a capacity crowd of 31,000, which included Franklin Roosevelt, who threw out the first ball. The Senators got only seven hits and one run, and that in the bottom of the ninth. The Yankees, however, without DiMaggio, once more exhibited their 1935 offense and got only four hits and didn't score at all. So, for the second year in a row, Lefty lost 1–0 on opening day.

DiMaggio finally made his major league debut on May 3, in front of 25,000 fans in Yankee Stadium, with Lefty on the mound. The team was in second place, a half game behind the Red Sox. Joe went three for six, with a triple and three runs scored in a 14–5 Yankee win. For Lefty, however, the day was less than satisfying. Despite having his teammates put up nine runs in the first four innings, he couldn't get out of the fifth. Johnny Murphy finished up and got the win.

From there, the Yankees simply plowed through the schedule. By June 15, they had opened up a three-game lead, and by July 1 had stretched it to eight. The lead held steady through July and then, reversing the collapses of previous years, the Yankees pulled away, finishing nineteen and a half games in front of second-place Detroit.

DiMaggio had made Jake Ruppert a prophet. Despite missing the first weeks of the season, he batted .323, drove in 125 runs, and scored 132. But most important, his presence had lifted the team. Five Yankees drove in more than 100 runs, led by Gehrig's 152. Lou scored 167 runs, to go with 49 home runs, a .354 batting average, and 130 walks, all of which made him league MVP.

The pitching, almost in recognition of the ease with which the Yankees scored runs, fell off. They again led in ERA, but it had risen to more than 4.00. Charley Ruffing won 20 games but lost 12 for the worst winning percentage among the starters. Monte Pearson, who had come over from Cleveland, won 15, Bump Hadley 14, and Johnny Broaca 12.

In the face of all that success, Lefty had the worst year of his career. His record improved to 13–7, but his ERA was 4.39, and he pitched only 188 innings, his lowest since his abbreviated rookie year. He started thirty games but finished only ten, and went for the first time without a shutout. His arm was sore off and on all year, and sometimes he went five days, even six, between starts. He was on the All-Star staff but didn't pitch in the game.

But McCarthy always insisted that Lefty and Charley Ruffing were the best big-game pitchers he'd ever seen, and they backed up Joe's boast in the World's Series.

"My most anxious moments," McCarthy said later, "were in the 1936 and 1937 Series against the Giants. We knew we had to beat Carl Hubbell in either of his first two starts, and at that time he was almost unbeatable. If he could win his first two games against us, that meant a seven-game Series and our chances to win would be lessened considerably if either Series went the limit."

Hubbell had indeed been pitching about as well as anyone ever had. Paul Fung Jr., who went to the Polo Grounds to see the Giants play when the Yanks were out of town, witnessed an exhibition of King Carl's prowess.

"I sat in the grandstand with Hubbell's family and a whole mess of people related to the Giant players. On one visit, some movie people were filming a short of Carl pitching at a French door set up at home plate. The door had small panes of glass in it and the director had numbered the panes 1, 2, 3 . . . up to 8. The director held up a card with the number of the pane that he wanted Carl to break throwing a ball from the mound. Before the windup, the director called out the type of pitch he wanted Hubbell to throw . . . a fastball, curve, or a screwball. Hubbell broke every pane of glass in the French door the first time. Eight pitches. One for each pane of glass."[*]

To face Hubbell in the first game, on September 30, McCarthy sent Ruffing to the mound. Joe's prediction proved correct. Hubbell gave up only seven hits, and the Giants busted open a tight game with four runs in the eighth inning to come away with a 6–1 win. Rain had drenched New York, but the players had "slogged through," as one sportswriter put it. Lefty was to pitch the next day against Hal Schumacher. If the Giants won that one, they would become prohibitive favorites to take the Series.

The skies opened that night, leaving the outfield a swamp. Although the rain stopped early in the morning and the sun was peeking through the clouds, Judge Landis unilaterally decided the field was unplayable and put the game off until the next day, October 2.

The Yankees were furious. President Roosevelt, Governor Herbert Lehman, and New York's mayor, Fiorello La Guardia, had arranged to come to the ballpark on October 2, but the ballpark was supposed to be Yankee Stadium for game three. But the president's schedule could not be changed, and Landis brooked no interference from club owner, mayor, president, or king. So Roosevelt and his forty-eight-member entourage graced the Polo Grounds instead. To further inflame Yankee ire, the postponement gave Hubbell an extra day of rest and a potential start in a seventh game.

"This is the second time this season I've drawn the president," Lefty said before the game, "and I hope I have more luck than I did the other

---

[*] After he retired, Hubbell was asked about his greatest thrills in baseball. The man who won four World Series games and struck out those five great hitters in the All-Star game chose as his two most memorable moments stealing second on Gabby Hartnett and hitting a home run off Dizzy Dean.

time." Roosevelt had been present opening day, when Lefty lost 1–0. Privately, however, he said, "What a thrill of a lifetime to meet and chat with President Roosevelt. I'm a Democrat and I'm sure he brought me luck."

The Yankees took the field in a vile mood and almost immediately foisted it on the Giants. Schumacher—Prince Hal to Hubbell's King Carl—threw a strike to Crosetti for the opening pitch, and Gus Mancuso, the catcher, presented the ball to FDR. That was about the only thing that went right for Schumacher all day. The Yankees scored two runs in the first inning, then erupted for seven in the third. During that at-bat, Tony Lazzeri, batting eighth, just before Lefty, came up with the bases loaded. Dick Coffman had relieved an ineffective Schumacher. A Polo Grounds pigeon, showing much better accuracy than had Prince Hal on the mound—four walks and a wild pitch in two innings—landed a deposit perfectly in the center of Lazzeri's cap. Lazzeri called time and backed out to shake it off. The home plate umpire, Harry Geisel, barked, "Don't do that! Pigeon shit is good luck!" Lazzeri wasn't about to ignore the man calling balls and strikes, so he stepped back in to hit, the pigeon product undisturbed. Lazzeri fouled off the next pitch, then sent a waist-high inside fastball into the right-field seats, only the second grand-slam home run in World Series history.

The game was memorable for more than just reinforcement of the pigeon shit adage. In the seventh inning, Lefty performed perhaps the most famous act of his life and it was for a pitch he didn't throw—at least not right away.

Instead of delivering a pitch to the plate, Lefty suddenly paused on the mound. Quite an extended pause. He stood for some moments, eyes toward the heavens, watching an airplane fly by. No player before or since would have dared disturb the sanctity of a World Series game by calmly and blissfully gazing skyward. When the plane had disappeared, Lefty unflappably picked up where he had left off and polished off the Giants for a complete-game victory by the lopsided score of 18–4.

"Airplanes were still a bit of a novelty back in 1936," Hal Schumacher said, "so it was unusual to have a plane fly over the Polo Grounds. When this rickety plane was circling in the air over the ball field, Gomez just stopped what he was doing, stepped off the mound, and stood there, his head thrown back. Lefty's glove was dangling from his right wrist and he was rubbing the ball in his left. He was completely oblivious to the tension of the game. Everyone in the ballpark, including the Giants and Lefty's teammates and his manager, were watching Gomez watching the airplane."

"I heard the sputtering of an engine over the Polo Grounds," Lefty said. "From the mound it looked like an old prop plane used in World War I and it caught my attention. I called time and stepped off the mound. I forgot about the hitter, the game, and the fans. I imagined myself in the old crate, loving that carefree feeling a pilot has. As I stood there, looking skyward, my eyes followed the flight of the plane until it completely disappeared from sight."

The newspapers didn't quite know what to make of Lefty's stunt. He was terrific copy, of course, but there was the purity of the game to consider. Most papers ignored the incident.

Later, McCarthy portrayed himself as surprisingly sanguine about the affair. "It was unexpected, but a natural thing for Lefty to do. Walking down the street or driving an automobile, Lefty would stop until he identified a plane. So when he stood there near the mound, oblivious to the crowd and the game, he was doing what he wanted to do . . . scanning the plane so that he could tell his teammates what make and type it was."

At the time, however, Lefty's reaction was somewhat different. "When my eyes returned to the field, McCarthy was at my side, hollering at me, 'He could have hit a homer because you're not paying attention.' 'Joe,' I said, 'he can't hit it, if I don't throw it.' " With which, another Leftyism was born.

After the game, the mood was different. "Schumacher and I were living at the same hotel. When I got down there after the second game and the 18–4 bashing of the Giants, I met Hal in the lobby. I never saw anybody look more miserable. He had tears in his eyes. But he came back for the Giants in the fifth game and won. That takes guts, and that's what I admired about Schumacher."*

* After baseball, Prince Hal went to work for Adirondack Bats. He and Lefty, who was by then working for Wilson Sporting Goods, saw each other regularly at promotional banquets, where they were chatted up by attendees. "Invariably, after greeting each one of us," Schumacher said, "the person would turn to Lefty and ask, 'How were you sooooo nonchalant in the 1936 World Series? Holding up a game to gaze at an airplane flying over the Polo Grounds. Wow. Lefty, how could you be *that* nonchalant?' I heard this same question over and over again. A zillion times! I got sick of it. Finally at one gathering I turned to a guy waxing on about Gomez's nonchalance

In the third game, the Yankees eked out a 2–1 win, despite being outhit eleven to four, pushing across a run in the bottom of the eighth on a Crosetti single. In game four, Hubbell went again, but McCarthy saved Ruffing, sending Monte Pearson against King Carl. Pearson, who had won nineteen in the regular season, did the job, holding the Giants to two runs, while the Yankees scored three in the third inning, two on a Gehrig home run, to win 5–2. Hal Schumacher held the Yankees in game five, and then Lefty, although giving up four runs, bested Freddie Fitzsimmons behind a seventeen-hit barrage, 13–5, and the Yankees had their first world championship in four years.

Pitching the clinching game would have been a lifetime thrill to most, but to Lefty the series had a different high point. He got a single in the ninth inning of the second game and drove in a run. Arthur Daley of the *New York Times* was agog. "When Lefty Gomez hits a foul ball, the Yankees consider it a full-fledged batting rally. His hit was the last crushing indignity and akin to the man biting the dog." Lefty, of course, had his own take. "The only hit I ever got in a World Series was a ground ball that handcuffed Burgess Whitehead at second base, and that winter he had a nervous breakdown." (Actually, Lefty was being modest. He got another hit in game six, and even drove in another run. There were no reports of any psychological disorders as a result.)

Lefty's joy was tempered, however. The day of the sixth game, he had received a telegram from Rodeo. Twelve years earlier, in 1924, Lizzie Gomez had been treated for abdominal pain. Eventually she had undergone surgery performed by Dr. Manuel Fernandez, a cousin of the man for whom she was working when Coyote walked into the Pinole warehouse thirty-four years before. Dr. Fernandez could not find the cause and, according to her granddaughter Vivien Sadler, "he just stuffed her intestines back in and sewed up her." What Dr. Fernandez had missed were the beginnings of uterine cancer.

Lefty sent a return telegram saying: "I'll get that game over as quickly as I can and fly right out."

Which he did. As soon as he arrived, Lizzie improved.

---

and said, 'My God, I was pitching against him that day. Don't give Lefty all the credit. I gave him the eighteen runs so he could afford to be so damn nonchalant!' "

25.

FAREWELL TO RODEO

O N JANUARY 27, ED BARROW MAILED THE 1937 CONTRACTS TO THE Yankee players. As World's Series champions, many on the team expected substantial raises. Few got them. A rash of holdouts ensued, some of them from quite unexpected quarters.

Lou Gehrig, no doubt prodded by Eleanor, flatly refused the same $31,000 he had made for the past two years. He wanted $50,000, as befitting the man who had led the American League in home runs, on-base percentage, slugging percentage, and runs scored, to go along with a .354 batting average and 154 runs batted in. Tony Lazzeri, after a decade of clutch hitting, big numbers, and team leadership, had made only $12,000 in 1936 and wanted it raised to $18,000. Lefty, whose two-year contract at $20,000 per had expired, had expected a cut, but was aghast at the Yankees' offer of $7,500, roughly the same as he had made as a second-year man. He categorized that figure as a "batboy's salary."

The most surprising holdout was Joe DiMaggio. The young phenom wanted more than double his rookie's salary of $8,500 for his second year. Second-year players, even at DiMaggio's level, simply didn't get such treatment. The club offered the same $8,500 and DiMaggio remained in California.

Almost half the team refused their contracts and Ruppert was fulminous. He applied his wrath selectively, however, making it clear he intended to finally settle an old score. "Gomez and Gehrig seem to forget," he fumed, "that they cost us a pennant in 1935 by going off on their barnstorming tour of Japan." Ruppert accused Gehrig of ingratitude since he'd received the same $31,000 in 1935, when he had "a poor season." Of course, in Lou's "poor season," he had led the Yankees in virtually every offensive category.

"As for Gomez," Ruppert went on, "he certainly has plenty of nerve comparing what we have offered him to a bat-boy's salary. I think he is a very lucky young man that we did not cut him worse than we did." Conspicuous by its absence in Ruppert's diatribe was any reference to perhaps the most significant holdout of all, but the Colonel could not have helped but be aware of Joe and Lefty's relationship.

Lefty was vacationing in Bermuda, where he had begun to take yearly sojourns for sun and golf with June. He offered, according to John Kieran, "to return to Japan to recover what he is accused of leaving there," if only Ruppert would pay his expenses.

What frightened Ruppert and his fellow owners was not so much individual malcontents but the possibility of players organizing to improve their bargaining positions. In the wake of the bloody Flint sit-down strike against General Motors, the company had agreed to recognize the United Auto Workers, with whose representatives they had refused to be in the same room during negotiations. In his article, Kieran referred to "Capitalist Ruppert" and "Laborer Gehrig"—tongue in cheek, to be sure, but indicative of the mood of the times. As the columnist pointed out, many players had followed the developments quite carefully. The nation had also slipped back into recession when many New Deal programs had been unwound. A combination of falling gate receipts and players demanding to negotiate en masse promised to make owning a ball team a good deal less fun.

But the time for a union had not yet arrived. Players may have worked as a unit on the field but they still thought of themselves as individuals off of it. As they always did, one by one the Yankees straggled in. On February 9, Lazzeri signed for $14,000 and George Selkirk also agreed to terms for a "satisfactory increase."

Lefty, Lou, Charley Ruffing, and Joe D continued to hold out. Lefty returned from Bermuda and met with Ruppert, who raised his offer to $10,000. Lefty categorized the new number as "humiliating." He agreed that he deserved a cut, but not by half.

By mid-February, Ruppert was offering Gehrig $36,000, DiMaggio $15,000, and Lefty $12,500. He observed that he and Gomez were having "nice chats." Ruppert soon added another $500 and Lefty agreed. Ruppert and Barrow stuck in one other clause that, it is fair to say, was unique in the major leagues—a $1,500 fine if Lefty was caught flying loop-the-loops.

Joe DiMaggio received $17,000, double his salary from the year before, and the public cheered the great young player who backed down the owner. Gehrig stood firm, even signing a contract to make a movie, although he refused an entreaty to play Tarzan.* Eventually he agreed to the $36,000 with a $750 signing bonus. Lou's film debut was put off until after the season.

When everyone had signed up, things settled back into their normal routine. From Lefty's first workout, it was apparent that Ruppert had gotten a bargain. His fastball had more hop than at any time in three years, and his curve had so much break that his teammates couldn't touch it, even in batting practice.

The improvement was no coincidence. "From now on," he had told Frank Graham, "Lefty Gomez isn't going to listen to anyone but Lefty Gomez. For two years now, I've been petting good luck charms, reducing, not reducing, throwing 'em fast, throwing 'em slow. Next guy who gives me advice gets a punch in the nose." The other thing Lefty did was lose weight, about fifteen pounds' worth, and get into the best shape of his life. At spring training, he posed for a press photograph in a 1936 suit, holding out the waist of the pants with enough room to fit June in there. Finally, he said his clowning days were over. As they say, two out of three.

The Yankees again broke fast, and this time so did Lefty. He did not give up more than two earned runs in a game until June.

On May 4, against the Tigers, he took a shutout into the bottom of the eighth. The Yanks had scored eight runs, so the outcome was not in doubt. With a man on first, Hank Greenberg hit one back to the box. Lefty whirled, but instead of throwing the ball to Crosetti, standing on second,

---

* Lou did, however, pose for a publicity still in a loincloth.

he threw it to Lazzeri, ten feet away. Lazzeri just managed to get his glove up in time. "What was that?" Lazzeri demanded. Lefty replied, without missing a beat, "I keep hearing what a smart player you are. If you're so smart, I just wanted to see what you'd do with that one." No one was ever certain whether Lefty had thrown to the wrong man on purpose.

Although Cleveland, featuring irascible former Yankee Johnny Allen and a high-school flamethrower from Iowa named Bob Feller, remained at the Yankees' heels through May, by the end of June the Indians had faded and the Yankees held a three-game lead over the White Sox. Still, there was a sense around the league that the race was effectively over.

On July 1, Lefty pitched a one-hitter, only a fifth-inning home run by Bob Johnson that barely cleared the fence marring the no-hit bid. And he was pitching on short rest, because McCarthy had once again tabbed him to start in the All-Star game the following week. As a tune-up three days later, he shut out the Senators.

Three days after that, as the newspapers happily noted, Goofy went against Dizzy. Lefty pitched the first three innings for the American League and, for the third time in four appearances, was the winning pitcher. Lou Gehrig had another sterling day with a home run and four RBIs, but the game is most famous for the out made by Earl Averill against Dizzy Dean to end the third inning, so seemingly innocuous at the time that it was ignored in almost every newspaper account of the game.

"Diz and I were good friends," Averill said. "A bunch of us rode down to Washington on the train. Diz and I had breakfast together and joshed around. Diz bragged he was going to get me out with a curveball. In the third inning, he retired the first two batters. Then Gehrig got a hit, DiMaggio followed with another one, and I came up.

"Diz threw that big curve. The last thing I remember is seeing it break toward the outside of the plate. I was already into my swing. I connected and saw the ball hit him in the toe and bounce right into the second baseman's glove for the third out. We passed as Diz was on his way to the dugout, and he said, 'Hey, you didn't have to hit me with it,' and I laughed. He stayed in the dugout for about three more innings, then disappeared. They told me later that they had to carry him on the train that night because the toe was broken. I saw Diz many times after that and he bore me no grudge. It could have been anybody who did it."

Because the injury was considered minor, Dean came back before the toe was completely healed. He changed his delivery to compensate, hurt his arm, and effectively ended a brilliant career at age twenty-six.

Lefty added a footnote. "Around twenty-five years later, Diz and I were the starting pitchers in an Old-Timers' Game. Averill comes to bat and hits a ground ball. Diz ran over to cover the bag and sprained his ankle. The same hitter and pitcher. There's a believe-it-or-not for Mr. Ripley."

Unlike in the doldrum years, the Yankees got stronger as the season went on. Red Ruffing had an outstanding season, as he had the year before, but this time Lefty matched him. Ruffing won twenty, Lefty twenty-two. Lefty led the league in wins, ERA, strikeouts, and shutouts. The two would finish eighth and ninth in the MVP voting. For winning percentage, however, no one could touch Johnny Allen. He finished the year 15–1 for a team only twelve games above .500.

At the plate, the Yankees were a juggernaut. Gehrig drove in 159 runs but did not lead the team. DiMaggio drove in 167 while leading the league in homers with 46, while Bill Dickey, now thirty, drove in another 133 while batting .332.

Lefty won his thirteenth game on July 19, an 8–5 victory in Cleveland over the Indians. This game in many ways epitomized the differences between a manager's approach to pitchers in Lefty's era and in the contemporary game. The Yankees led 8–1 going to the bottom of the eighth inning, with Lefty having retired thirteen batters in a row. In the eighth, the Indians scored three runs and added one in the ninth. Anyone hearing just the score would assume that Lefty did not pitch all that well. After all, his earned run average for the game was an inauspicious 5.00. In today's game, once a win was in the bag, the manager would have brought in a reliever to save wear and tear on the starter's arm. Lefty likely would have been pulled, after seven innings perhaps, with a game ERA of 1.29. In 1937, however, the Yankees carried just eight pitchers and a starter was pulled only if he was getting bombed or was threatening to blow a lead. McCarthy had regained the confidence in Lefty that had waned in the previous two years, so he left him in for the entire nine and a complete-game win.

"In the thirties and forties," June said, "if a pitcher didn't go the full nine innings, and a relief pitcher came in from the bullpen, the press and the fans screamed, 'The guy got knocked out of the box.' I'm happy for today's pitchers. The front office finally realized that a guy's arm is ripped apart throwing sliders, cutters, curves, and fastballs over and over for the full nine innings. Babe Ruth always told Lefty, 'There are only so many pitches in that arm. Don't be so anxious to keep pitching.' But Lefty never learned to say no."

Five days later, Lefty faced the White Sox and his old Salt Lake roommate, Thornton Lee. In a small measure of retribution, Lee won a 6–5, ten-inning decision. That started Lefty on a personal tailspin that stretched into the third week of August. Lefty's explanation was unusual but fitting. "Finsler's Comet [which had been big news after its discovery on July 4] began to edge into the picture and I knew right off I was cooked," he told *Time* magazine. "Comets and left-handed pitchers don't go well together."

But what Lefty was not telling *Time* magazine, or anyone else for that matter, was that he had learned that Lizzie had again been stricken, and this time it appeared to be for the final time. That he would joke in public was not duplicity but simply a philosophy acquired in boyhood, a code acquired from Coyote and Earl and Cecil—and, of course, Lizzie.

Later in life, he said, "I believe that a ballplayer, or any performer in the public eye, deserves as much privacy as the person who works a nine-to-five job. Many don't agree with me. I've heard it said that the media owns the most private moments of a person in the public eye. I disagree. As a player, I was always most willing to discuss any questions that sportswriters and photographers put to me about the game on the field. They had a job to do. If I could help them do it, then it was my duty to do so. But questions whether my wife and I had an argument before or after the game or stuff like that, no, that's private. And since I like privacy, I also gave it to my teammates.

"For example, I will not answer personal questions about DiMaggio unless the questions are sent to Joe D and he calls me before the show. If Joe okays the questions, I'll answer them truthfully. Joe does the same for me. He doesn't talk personal stuff about Gomez. That's what a friendship means. That two people can talk freely in private and the confidences will be kept. It's the same with Babe Ruth. The staff is told to send the questions to Julia and Dottie. No matter who it is, send the questions to the people first and have them call me before I answer."

DiMaggio himself bore that out. "Lefty was someone I could ring up on the telephone and talk about something that was bothering me. I knew our conversation wouldn't wind up in the papers. That gave me a good feeling because I really can't talk off the record with most people. It winds up on the nightly news. Lefty kept confidences for everyone, not just for me."

But private lives inevitably become public. On August 3, Lefty pitched the second game of a rare midweek doubleheader against the White Sox in Yankee Stadium. The Tuesday affair drew 66,767 fans, many of them coming out to see Lou Gehrig honored both for winning the 1936 Most Valuable Player award and for playing in his 1,900th consecutive game. George M. Cohan presented Lou with a watch to commemorate the occasion.

Red Ruffing cruised in the first game, 7–2. Gehrig, with a brilliant sense of the moment, launched a huge, 420-foot three-run homer in the first inning off Thornton Lee, and DiMaggio matched Lou in the seventh. Lazzeri added a bases-empty shot in the fourth.

In the second game, Lazzeri hit another solo shot to stake Lefty to a one-run lead, but that was all the Yankees could manage for seven innings. Lefty held Chicago scoreless for six innings, but the White Sox scored a run in the seventh and then two in the eighth to take the lead. McCarthy pulled Lefty with two outs and the bases loaded in favor of Johnny Murphy. Murphy got the last out in the eighth and was thus the beneficiary of Bill Dickey's grand-slam homer in the bottom of the inning. Murphy retired the White Sox with only four pitches in the ninth to get the victory as Lefty's losing streak remained unbroken.

Immediately after the game, Lefty headed for Newark Airport to board a DC-3 for San Francisco. The DC-3 was a new, luxury airliner introduced just two years before that reduced the coast-to-coast flying time, including three stops to refuel, to a remarkably brief seventeen and a half hours.

He arrived in Rodeo the following evening. "When my taxi pulled up in front of the homestead, the house was all lit up with parked cars in front, up and down the street. Reporters and press photographers were camped out on our lawn. It looked like a celebration was going on inside instead of my mother dying. Pandemonium.

"The San Francisco press had pounced on the open secret that I was flying west from New York after the White Sox game to be at my mother's bedside. My sister Irene made her way through the newsmen telling me she had lost control of the situation: 'Vernon, they're everywhere. In the kitchen. The dining room and parlor.' Irene and I walked around to the back of the house. As I opened the screen door, a crowd of reporters and press photographers in the kitchen ran towards me.

" 'Lefty, how's it going?' 'What 'bout them Yanks!' The pennant . . . the Series. Some slapping me on the back. 'Please,' I said. 'No questions. I'm here for my mother.' I made my way to the door just off the kitchen that opened into my mother's bedroom, where she lay weak and in pain. I closed the door on the press, went to her bedside, and leaned over and kissed her cheek. 'Ma, I'm home.' Her wan smile clutched at my heart. Suddenly, there was a banging on the door and then it flew open. The press pushed their way past Irene into the bedroom, calling out, 'Hold her hand, Lefty.' 'We want a picture of you and your ma, on her deathbed.' 'Hold her hand!' If one said it, twenty said it. I will never forget their stunning insensitivity. Men who had mothers of their own. Pitted against getting their scoop, they didn't care that my mother lay critically ill.

" 'Come on, Lefty,' they shouted, 'one picture!'

" 'No! I'm not doing that.'

" 'Come on! Hold her hand!'

"I ran out of the bedroom and into the kitchen and came upon my brother Earl, who had just returned home from a construction site. He saw the press trailing me. Earl was easygoing until his hide was scratched. 'What's the matter, Vernon?' he asked me.

" 'They say I have to take a picture holding Ma's hand on her deathbed. I told them over and over I won't do it but they won't stop.' Earl turned to the crowd and shouted, 'The kid said no! Now, get your asses out of here or I go for the sheriff!' and he punctuated his retort by grabbing one of them by the collar and tossing him out the back door. 'And stay out!' he yelled at the guy as he stumbled down the stairs.

"The press left."

Lefty stayed with Lizzie for just over a week. She didn't improve, but neither did she worsen. Finally, she insisted Lefty rejoin his team and made him promise not to return. "She asked me to stay with the team, no matter what happened," Lefty said.

Reluctantly he returned to New York. McCarthy put him on the mound the same day he landed. Joe knew Lefty well enough to be certain it would be the best thing for him.

For six innings he held the A's to one run. Newspapers reported that Lefty was throwing so hard that Dickey was having trouble holding on to his fastball. But after seventeen hours en route, Lefty tired in the seventh, gave up three runs, and lost 4–3.

Four days later, before his next scheduled start, the first game of a doubleheader against the Senators, he got the news. "When I walked into the clubhouse on August 17, Joe came out of his office and said to me, 'Listen. Why don't you go back to California? Go on home. I'll pay your plane fare.'

" 'Something's happened to my ma?'

" 'She died, Vernon. About an hour ago. I just got the phone call. Go home. We've got that young kid that can pitch today.'

" 'No, I'll pitch my turn. I can't sit in a room and stare at the walls. I'll drive myself crazy.' "

Lefty went out and, constantly wiping his eyes on the mound, threw a three-hit 8–0 shutout. In the clubhouse after the game, he sat on a wooden stool with his legs crossed and stared at the floor, struggling unsuccessfully to hold back tears. Finally he talked to reporters. "I don't recollect that I was in a game," he said. "I don't know which batters I faced. I don't know who made the hits. My whole life at home rolled before me."

"Lefty had everything," Bill Dickey said. "I never caught him when he had more stuff."

Even Lefty's closest friends on the team knew to leave him alone, not to interfere. "June and Nellie were vacationing in Canada at Lake Louise, where there wasn't a telephone. When I returned to our apartment, I just walked through the rooms, staring at the memories on the walls. I called Paul Fung and told him the aloneness was getting to me and he said, 'Come on over and spend the night with us.' "

Despite McCarthy's offer of as much time off as Lefty needed, he stayed with the team and did not attend Lizzie's funeral. "My brothers and sisters told me not to come back because Ma kept saying, 'Tell Vernon to stay with the team.' It was her dying wish."

"Everyone knew my mother loved flowers. She got bouquets from Joe McCarthy, Ed Barrow, J. Taylor Spink of the *Sporting News,* Joe DiMaggio, the New York chapter of the Baseball Writers' Association, Mare Island Navy Yard, the New York Yankees team, Glenn Cunningham the great miler, individual sportswriters, teams in the American League and the National League. Jacob Ruppert sent a floral piece that took up one corner wall of the church."

With Lizzie's passing, in many ways the Gomez family saga ended. "Our pet deer, Betsy, was part of our family as far back as I can recall. The day she came to our back door as a fawn, she came to stay. Betsy could easily have jumped the fence around our backyard gardens and run off, but she didn't. After Ma passed away, no Gomezes would be living at the homestead, leaving old Betsy without care. I called Mayor Rossi of San Francisco and said, 'Can you help me? A tame deer can't fend for itself.' Mayor Rossi contacted the governor of California for permission to place Betsy in the Golden Gate Park Zoo. And so, whenever my brothers and I visited Betsy at the Golden Gate, we'd give out with the old familiar whistle and she'd spring over to the fence . . . so glad to see us and still looking for tidbits."

Six weeks later, the Yankees won their second straight American League pennant and would again face the Giants in the World Series (writers had begun to drop the " 's" after "World"). Lizzie had known her son: the competition was precisely what he needed to move on with his life.

In the first game, he faced Carl Hubbell. Except in All-Star games, it was the only time the two would ever go against each other. The Yankees won 8–1, pasting a seven-spot on King Carl in the sixth inning.

Afterward, Lefty had regained his wit. "Sometimes the press made me look a lot smarter than I really was. In the sixth inning, the Giants leading 1–0, I'm at bat against Hubbell and I keep getting the sign to take, to wait Hubbell out. The count builds to 3 and 2 and they're still telling me to take. I couldn't believe my eyes. I stepped out of the box and walked over to Frank Crosetti in the on-deck circle. 'Frank, they want me to take?' 'It's take, Lefty,' Cro told me. I drew a walk and the Yanks went on to a seven-run rally. The headline in the morning newspaper read, 'Gomez's Keen Eye Starts Yanks' 7-Run Rally.' "

Walter Johnson was asked after the Series who he thought was better, Lefty or Hubbell. Johnson replied, "Gomez is a great money pitcher who loafs through an ordinary game but pitches brilliantly when the chips are down. He stands the gaff better, has speed, wonderful control, and a good curve. Hubb is great, too, but when his screwball isn't working he's lost."

That praise must have been especially gratifying. The Big Train was the pitcher Lefty idolized as a boy.

The Series turned out not to be close. The Giants managed only one win, by Hubbell, when they were already down 3–0. Lefty pitched the fifth-game clincher, winning 4–2.

Afterward, he was described as "dancing in the dugout," but the source of his elation was not his pitching. "Did you see that hit I got off Melton, driving in the winning run? That's what I call hitting." When informed that the hit did not exactly knock anyone's hat off, Lefty replied haughtily, "It was a hit, wasn't it? And it drove in the run that was enough to win, wasn't it?"

But Lizzie's death had touched something fragile in Lefty. "I couldn't go home for the holidays anymore. Home for the holidays wasn't home with Pa and Ma gone. I celebrated in Lexington and New York with June's family and our friends." His siblings felt the same way. The Rodeo house was soon sold and subsequently the family scattered on Thanksgiving and Christmas.

26.

JUNE IN JANUARY . . . AND FEBRUARY

———

UNTIL LIZZIE'S ILLNESS, MAINTAINING THE DICHOTOMY BETWEEN CARE-free public person and shy, intensely private man had generally not been difficult. That the side Lefty chose to show publicly was so irresistibly magnetic made it easier to deflect the inevitable probes into his personal life.

But in August 1937, that wall began to crumble. The press invasion as Lizzie lay dying was deeply disturbing to Lefty. Remaining outwardly up-beat after she died was especially difficult. Lefty had thrown himself into the pennant race and World Series, but almost from the instant baseball was done, he began to skitter on the rails. Within weeks, his life had degenerated into a self-induced full-scale catastrophe that would persist for eight months.

The debacle began innocently enough. Three days after the Yankees defeated the Giants, Lefty, June, and a group of friends went for dinner and drinks to Billy La Hiff's Tavern on 48th Street, a saloon that catered to the sports crowd. A photographer snapped a picture of June kissing Lefty at the table, and it ran the next day, captioned "A Kiss for the Winner." The day after that, Pitzy Katz told them he was scheduled to leave for Nevada. Pitzy had become involved with a woman named Polly Klein and was going west to establish residency (which took all of six weeks in Reno) so that he could divorce his wife, Lillie.

Coincidentally, Lefty was also heading west on an extensive jaunt: first to Salt Lake City to see Mom Edgeworth, on to San Francisco, where he was slated to pitch in a Catholic Youth Organization benefit game against the Seals, and then home to Rodeo to see his brothers and sisters and help settle Lizzie and Coyote's effects. After a week in Northern California, Lefty was to drive to Los Angeles to pose for a Gillette razor ad, for which he would be paid $5,000, then hang around and play some golf with Bing Crosby, who remembered him from *King of Jazz*. Pitzy didn't know how to drive and decided to hitch a ride. The Hollywood stop was particularly appealing because it allowed him to schmooze with friends from his film days.

And if that wasn't enough, Lefty planned a return trip to Juarez, where he had volunteered to help establish a baseball clinic. He could drop Pitzy in Reno on the way back and then return to New York in the roadster in time to spend the Christmas holidays in Lexington with June, Nellie, and the Gradys.

Soon after Lefty and Pitzy drove off, June decided she didn't want to stay alone in the couple's apartment in the Ansonia, so she moved down to a brownstone on West 51st Street to live with Sunny and Nellie.

"On November 21," Sunny recalled, "we were finishing up dinner and planning for Thanksgiving, when June tuned on the radio to hear Walter Winchell's Sunday night broadcast on ABC. 'There's a divorce in the air,' Winchell began in his high-pitched, stiletto-edged voice. 'Yankee World Series winner Lefty Gomez is in Hollywood seeking a Mexican divorce on the grounds of incompatibility.' We were so stunned, we almost fell off our chairs. June turned to us and asked, 'Did he say "divorce"? Maybe we didn't hear it right.' "

Winchell, immensely powerful and just as vicious, hadn't given any details, and since he was the same man who had predicted the marriage wouldn't last six months, his pronouncement had to be taken with at least some salt. Still, hearing on the radio that perhaps your husband was planning on dumping you was more than a bit upsetting.

June had continued studying opera with Maestro Vita, and the next morning she was up early for a lesson. She made her coffee on a hot plate and ran off. "In between arias," Sunny said, "June asked the maestro if he'd heard Winchell the night before. Yes, he told her, Winchell had said Lefty was going for a Mexican divorce.

"As soon as June had walked out the door for the lesson, Nellie and I ran down to the street corner and bought the morning papers. Over breakfast at the Automat, we scanned the gossip columns and the sports pages to see if the press had picked up on Winchell's comments. Everyone had. June O'Dea and Yankee pitcher Lefty Gomez, a two-game winner in the World Series, were on the brink of divorce. There were pictures of Lefty on the links with Bing Crosby and standing outside a courthouse in Juarez. And there was endless speculation about the stunning blondes and brunettes doing the L.A. scene with him. So many stunners that the columnists asked, 'Who's the girl in the triangle?' Mostly the talk was of Edna Torrence, a dancer, and Eunice Healey, who had appeared on Broadway in Gershwin's *Girl Crazy*."

Not surprisingly, the columnists had printed the names of Lefty's paramours without making any effort to find out if they were actually involved with him. "When Edna saw her name linked with Lefty's she wired the columnists: 'No, no, no. It's terribly wrong. I'm engaged to marry Paul Schweger in two weeks. It was announced five months ago. How could I possibly be contemplating marriage with Mr. Gomez?' Schweger was a former All-American football player and an assistant movie director. Eunice also issued a resounding no. She said it was true Lefty was a friend, but that was because they had been classmates at Richmond High. 'Friends and nothing more,' she said."

But there did seem to be someone. "Whoever the girl was," Sunny said, "I'm positive Lefty wasn't going with her in New York. He was around all of us all the time during the season and the World Series. The crowd we ran with would have known about it. I don't ever remember him carousing at night in New York City. Lefty didn't do that. So the affair couldn't have started until he was in California.

"Nellie and I finished reading the papers and left the Automat. When we returned home, smoke was pouring out of the windows of my apartment. After June had made the coffee, she'd kicked the hot plate under the bed so the landlady wouldn't see it, but forgotten to unplug it. The comforter caught fire and the room was in a blaze. Everything went up in smoke. We had to pay the damages and move to June's apartment at the Ansonia until my place could be completely renovated, which turned out to be after New Year's."

June had no intention of sitting around and being walked over, but neither did she want to take any action without hearing from her husband. In order to get in touch with Gomez, however, she had to find the name of the hotel he was staying at. Sunny wired some friends who knew the lay of the land, and soon June had Lefty's hotel and room number. She shot off a telegram: "Lefty, is it true? Do you really mean it?" Lefty wired back, "What you read in the papers is true."

June was still unwilling at that point to completely sink the marriage, so she decided to file for a legal separation, a holding action until she could determine if the rift couldn't be mended. But to file the papers, she needed a lawyer and she didn't know any. So Sunny asked a friend, Bill Palazzi.

"Palazzi distributed lingerie—girdles and bras, peignoirs and sexy underwear—to high-end department stores and boutiques. June and I did fashion modeling, so that's how we met Bill. Every time we saw him, he'd hand us a box of sample lingerie to wear and complain about. He wanted our input so he could bring the complaints to the manufacturers before the buyers came to his showroom. June and I kept notes like, 'The girdle is lousy, keeps riding up . . . the bra strap stretched and fell down to my elbow . . . the garters are flimsy and the panties had holes in them after two days.' Stuff like that. It was common practice in the thirties to have customers wear and evaluate samples of clothing. There was no money in it, but June and I had gorgeous lingerie."

Palazzi told Sunny to call his own lawyer, Melvin Kleeblatt. Kleeblatt specialized in labor law and had never handled a divorce in his life; all his clients were in the rag business. But a labor lawyer seemed better than nothing.

Melvin Kleeblatt turned out to be a lot better.

June's newly hired legal representative filed a separation support suit on January 2, 1938. A summons to appear in court in New York in May was served to Lefty at his California hotel.

"That's when Lefty did something really foolish," Sunny related. "He and Pitzy drove to Reno. On January 4, he announced to the press that he was there to establish residency so that he could divorce June O'Dea."

The next day he was seen with a girl, and word filtered back east that he intended to marry her.

That was all Melvin Kleeblatt needed to hear. He announced to the press: "A Reno quickie divorce is not valid in the state of New York. The minute Lefty walks into this state with a new wife, he'll be hit with adultery and bigamy." Pitzy Katz had gone to Reno simply to get rid of a wife. Lefty, in wanting a replacement, found himself in the thorny position of being unable to bring his new bride into the state where he earned his living. Lefty would either have to give up the idea or find a way to be divorced in New York.

Sunny had a ringside seat to the lunacy. "June now knew the girl's identity, as did everyone else." It was Edna Torrence after all. "She was a dazzling brunette who did a ballet act in theaters coast-to-coast. Three years later, when the Copacabana opened in New York, she stepped out of her ballet slippers into glitzy high heels and became a Copa showgirl.

"The scandal was on everyone's lips. It was a very messy affair and Lefty doesn't like mess. Now he's fair game for the gossip columnists and it's his own doing. So he said he was misquoted. He's in Reno for Pitzy's divorce, not his. 'And what about that packet of Mexican divorce papers in Spanish that a clerk from a courthouse in Juarez sent to June at the Ansonia?' the reporters asked. In Juarez, a divorce could be granted to one party of a marriage on incompatibility even if the other party was not there. 'What was that all about?' Lefty claimed he was in Juarez to set up a baseball clinic." That last part was at least half true.

Lefty had two choices: fold or raise. He raised. Before he left Reno for St. Pete and spring training, he hired Lowell Birrell. Birrell was as famous and feared in the courtroom as Melvin Kleeblatt was unknown.

From University of Michigan Law School, where he had been an editor of the law review, Birrell had joined Cadwalader, Wickersham & Taft. By 1938, still only thirty-one, he had gained a reputation for brilliance, both in the courtroom and in the boardroom. Birrell became an expert in securities law and would eventually control numerous corporations and amass a vast personal fortune. In 1961, however, he suddenly fled to Brazil with a phony passport and, soon after, was indicted for securities fraud. Birrell eventually spent four years in prison and, after his release in 1973, dropped from sight. He now graces a number of websites that list the most crooked lawyers in history.

On Lefty's instructions, Lowell Birrell immediately filed a counterclaim for divorce and the case was put on the docket for May 3 in New York Supreme Court, Judge Aaron Levy presiding.

Filing a claim is one thing, however; winning the case is another. In order to gain a judgment on Lefty's behalf—and avoid alimony—Birrell would have to demonstrate that June was fully responsible for the breakup. There was no evidence of infidelity, the lead-pipe cinch of New York divorce actions, so Birrell turned it on its head and claimed June was frigid, incapable of sexual relations. The marriage, Birrell claimed, had never been consummated.

Why Lefty behaved in such an utterly foolish and self-destructive manner remains a mystery. But never again in his life did he act so willfully against his own interests.

When Birrell's charges were filed, the press seized on them. The Gomez divorce was front-page news, not just on the sports page. "Everywhere June turned, she heard people talking about Birrell's hatchet job," Sunny later reported. " 'Maybe there is something wrong with Lefty's wife.' It was humiliating. A good example happened at a little meat shop on Sixth Avenue when I went in to pick up the daily order for June, Nellie, and myself. There's a long line of customers. When it's my turn, the fat-jowled butcher gives a raucous laugh and asks in a loud voice, 'Are you cold like your sister? June in January?' I looked him straight in the eye and said, 'If you don't mind, I'll have four lamb chops, please.' "

Birrell's charge, absurd on its face, turned the action bare-knuckle. "If her marriage was down the drain, June was returning full-time to the theater," Sunny said. "But first, she was out to win her reputation back. She was in for the battle. June's a warrior."

And she had chosen the right lawyer for the war. Melvin Kleeblatt hadn't worked among some of the most cutthroat men on earth without coming away a fighter. When Kleeblatt filed his brief in March, Lefty would get more than a taste of his own medicine.

In late February, unaware that he and his high-priced Wall Street lawyer were about to get it right between the eyes, Lefty reported to spring training.

27

THE NOT-SO-PERFECT CRIME

———

ALTHOUGH JUST ABOUT EVERYONE IN AMERICA KNEW THAT HE WAS having marital problems, Lefty, as was his wont, behaved as if nothing were amiss. And what better way to project normalcy than to ask for a raise?

He wasn't alone. A team that had just claimed its second consecutive World Series could be expected to have a lot of players who thought they should be earning more money. After Ed Barrow mailed the 1938 contracts on January 20, the list of holdouts included, as usual, Gehrig, Ruffing, and Bill Dickey. Relative newcomers to the list were third baseman Red Rolfe, Frank Crosetti, and, marking his second holdout in two years, Joe DiMaggio.

One Yankee not on the list, or any list, was Tony Lazzeri. Toward the end of the 1937 season, plagued by a bone chip in his hand and falling production, Tony had announced that he would likely retire as a player the following year to pursue a managerial position. After an exceptional World Series, it was widely assumed he would reconsider. Before he had a chance to do so, Jacob Ruppert sent a letter to Lazzeri's off-season California home giving the second baseman his unconditional release, based purportedly on knowledge that another club wanted to pursue him as a manager. That the Yankees had a wonderful young second baseman at Newark named Joe Gordon with whom they intended to displace Lazzeri was not mentioned. Lazzeri eventually signed with the Cubs as player-coach, a deal that he could easily have been offered by the Yankees.

Modern-day baseball fans often grumble about the lack of team loyalty and continuity engendered by free agency, to say nothing of the explosion in ticket prices necessitated by funding multimillion-dollar salaries. While these complaints are often true, players of Lefty's era were utterly at the mercy of management. That a player such as Tony Lazzeri, who was described by his teammates as "a manager on the field," could be simply tossed aside by an owner and general manager to whom he had given twelve years of often brilliant service, in an era when players received no pensions, is hardly a testament to loyalty and continuity. Almost that precise description would apply a few years afterward to Lefty Gomez.

The irony is that just as players of Lefty's era accepted that their careers could end with an injury, they were equally accepting that those who had reached the end of their careers would simply be discarded with no pension and no prospect of future employment. The lack of resentment on the part of men cut adrift by other men who had made money from their labors was astonishing. Few players complained publicly, or even groused in private. Neither Lefty nor Lazzeri did. Gordon, therefore, universally seen as an improvement on the field, fit seamlessly into the club. Players in later decades, however, having seen the advantages of organization and tough collective bargaining, did not show the same equanimity.

Most of the 1938 holdouts ended quickly. Lefty, who likely very much wanted to get baseball under way to take his mind off lawyers and angry wives, signed his contract in early March for the same $20,000 salary he had received in 1935 and 1936. Red Ruffing, who was often the last to agree, signed on the same day.

As March progressed, only two players were unsigned, Gehrig and DiMaggio. Lou, refusing to play for less than $40,000, had driven to Florida from Hollywood, where he had finally made that motion picture he'd contracted for during his previous holdout. Since the producers couldn't get Lou to swing from a vine, they settled for putting him on a horse. The film was called *Rawhide,* and the plot—what there was of one—involved Lou playing Lou and quitting baseball to buy a ranch with his sister, only to run afoul of a crooked cattlemen's association. His costar was a singing cowboy named Smith Ballew who played an honest lawyer. Together, they brawled and braved their way through danger and bad guys to return peace and law to the valley. Lou wore a big hat, threw a rope, and perused his herd. During filming, when Lou showed up on the set, real cowboys had put a saddle with handlebars on his horse.

In mid-March, Lou finally signed for $39,000, just in time for *Rawhide* to open in St. Pete. "The world premiere took place at the Century Theatre," Lefty reported. "The day before, the press came out to take publicity shots of Gehrig as he moseyed around in his chaps and cowboy hat, throwing his lasso and roping Bill Dickey, Frank Crosetti, and me. Ruppert and McCarthy got into the act, pleading for mercy when Lou held them up at pistol point. We all laughed because Lou had held Ruppert hostage for more dough and Ruppert had called it 'robbery.'

"The night of the premiere, the Yankees marched in a parade down the streets of St. Petersburg, wearing our pinstripes and carrying torchlights. Lou led the way, high in the saddle on a snowy white Cayuse. Fans crowded the sidewalks, screaming and throwing streamers and confetti. There were giant posters of 'Two Gun Lou Rides Again' and the theater was bathed in the glaring white of the klieg lights. We were mobbed at the entrance and were lucky that we still had our uniforms when we settled into our seats with our boxes of popcorn. Of course, I like westerns, but Lou's debut as an actor was laudable and he could brawl with the best of the cowpokes in the barroom scenes. The Yankees had such a good time with Lou that night."*

DiMaggio, however, was not at the premiere. Ruppert and Barrow had offered him $25,000, but Joe thought that was peanuts for a player of his abilities. He wanted $40,000 or he would just stay in San Francisco. But Joe, who had been cheered for prying money out of management the previous year, had grossly misread the mood of the fan base. The recession had deepened and a twenty-three-year-old kid who wanted to be paid $1,000 more than Lou Gehrig all of a sudden looked simply like a greedy brat.

By this time, Lefty was doing all he could to demonstrate that the divorce proceedings weren't a concern. For one thing, he was sneaking off

---

* Years later, experts studied the film to try to determine if Lou had exhibited signs of muscle atrophy in his hands in January 1938, when *Rawhide* was filmed. They concluded that when the film was shot, he was still functioning normally.

to the airfield every chance he got. "The Yankees had a clause in Lefty's contract that he couldn't fly," Bing Russell said. "But whenever Buddy was in St. Pete, Gomez was in the skies. At the end of spring training, Gehrig buttonholed Lefty as they boarded the train to go north. 'You should have been here earlier.' Lefty asks why, and Gehrig says, 'Because there was a pilot over at Million Dollar Pier in an airplane just wringing it out. My God, what stunts. You'd have loved it!' Lefty asked if it was a little red plane, and Lou said, 'Yeah. You saw it?' 'No, Lou,' Lefty says. 'I was in it.' "

He also pulled the strings on any number of pranks with Joe Gordon, who had taken over not only Tony Lazzeri's position but his role as team cutup. Bing Russell, now eleven, was often the stooge.

"Gordon was always in the thick of things. I think Lefty picked him out because he was just off center enough to do what Gomez wanted. Joe tells me that in the game that day, Gehrig is playing outfield and he, Gordon, is on first. I said, 'No way. That's ridiculous.' So Flash bet me five bucks, which was a helluva lot of money in the Depression. Son of a bitch, if they don't open the game that way. I don't know how they pulled it off without McCarthy getting wind of it. All I know is, I'm in the dugout at the start of the game and Gehrig is playing outfield and Gordon is on first and I lost the five dollars. And if you hit me for a hundred thousand now it wouldn't hurt as much as those five bucks hurt. And you know the whole Yankee ball club was in on it."

Then, at the end of March, just before the team was to break camp and begin its journey north, Melvin Kleeblatt unleashed his barrage.

Vernon Louis Gomez was a drunk. He had hit his wife and blackened her eye. He had locked her in her stateroom on the 1934 trip around the world. And, for the coup de grâce, Vernon Gomez had been overheard a full two years earlier outlining "the perfect crime." He was, Kleeblatt made clear, planning to murder her.

Lefty related the details of his murderous plot a half century later. "A socialite was strangled in 1935, and the killing was played up in the newspapers. Tony La Faso, a seaman on a luxury liner and a pal, had just arrived from Australia and stopped by our apartment. He and I sat up late playing bridge and drinking beer. June went to bed around nine because she had an early morning opera class. So Tony and I are dealing cards in the dining room and, after an hour or two, our beery conversation turned into how to commit the perfect crime. La Faso asked me, 'How would you kill June and get away with it,' and, after some thought, I outlined in minute detail how I would strangle June, leave no clues, have an ironclad alibi, and walk away from her murder a free man.

"Tony and I didn't notice that in the middle of this murder conversation, June had woken up and walked past the dining room on her way to the bathroom. More to the point, we didn't realize that she had overheard me talking about my 'perfect crime.' There had been rifts in our marriage that year over our conflicting careers and my frustration with my lousy win-loss record. June put two and two together and came up with five, that I was going to strangle her to death.

"The next morning, she left for her opera class without mentioning what she had heard the night before. I went on a road trip. After I left town, she returned to the apartment and packed her suitcases and went into hiding at a friend's house in Boston. For two weeks I couldn't reach her. No one knew where she was. I didn't know why I couldn't get in touch with her because I didn't know June overheard Tony and me talking about the perfect murder.

"When June finally returned to New York and told me why she went into hiding and I explained what really happened, she didn't believe me. From then on, she was on high alert for any suspicious behavior. I bet to this day, after fifty-five years of marriage, June still thinks she was going to be the victim of my perfect crime. I was having a bad year in '35 but I hadn't thought of rubbing her out . . . yet."

"Kleeblatt's accusations against Lefty were so outrageous that even I was in shock," Sunny said, "but June was going for a knockout and she didn't care if she hit below the belt. If she had to lose, she was going down swinging."

For the first time in his life, Lefty was fully in the glare of adverse publicity. That the charges weren't true, and that June knew they weren't true, made the sting all the more painful. But Lefty was too proud to back down. He returned to New York in April, the center of a media frenzy, moved into the Mayflower Hotel with Pitzy Katz, and tried to bluff his way through the storm, remaining outwardly the same old Lefty. When opposing players took to coming to the on-deck circle with a ring of black around their eyes, or pretended to strangle each other in the opposing dugout, Lefty laughed it off. "I'll wait for them at the plate," he said. But Babe Dahlgren, whose locker was next to Lefty's for three years, said the only time Lefty didn't talk in the clubhouse was during the separation suit.

Meanwhile, although spring training had ended and opening day had come and gone, DiMaggio was still in California. The moribund St. Louis Browns offered $150,000 for Joe, a lovely publicity stunt since they probably couldn't have afforded half that figure. Finally, on April 20, Joe hoisted the white flag. Not only did he agree to $25,000, but he was forced to swallow a $1,850 fine for the time he missed. Joe swore he would never indulge in such behavior again and, just to make sure he remembered, when he made his first appearance in Washington on April 30, he was roundly booed. To make matters worse, in the sixth inning he ran into Joe Gordon while chasing a pop fly. Both players were knocked unconscious and taken to a local hospital. DiMaggio was out of the hospital the next day and began playing with his usual excellence. Gordon, however, was out for six weeks.

With the court hearing coming due, Lefty began the season with a win over the Red Sox, a loss to Washington, then lost to Boston and Lefty Grove. In his fourth start, the same game in which DiMaggio collided with Joe Gordon, he again lost to the Senators, 4–3. The Yankees returned to New York just in time for Lefty to appear before Judge Levy.

"The first witness called, Miss O'Dea testified in a sheer wool black dress, picture hat and silver fox furs," a newspaper reported. "Her sister, Sunny Dale, also an actress, and her mother, Nellie Schwarz, and her grandmother, Bridget Grady, accompanied her to court."

The Gradys had closed ranks for the court case. It probably pained Lefty as much as anything to see Nellie and Grandma Grady lined up against him. If he won in court, he'd lose not only June but house privileges in Lexington and his surrogate family.

"I came off the circuit from Houston, where Conville and I were doing the comedy act for the Texas Bicentennial Celebration," Sunny recalled.

"Bridget, seventy-four years old, came by train down from Boston to testify that her granddaughter June was a decent person. She went into Filene's in Boston and bought a new gray skirt suit and matching hat. Grandma was scared out of her wits to go to court, but she boarded a train in Boston with gumption and came. She wasn't used to living in a skyscraper. We had to make sure we kept all the windows closed at the Ansonia, even though it was May, because one day, standing next to an open window, Bridget got so dizzy looking out at the street, we almost lost Granny to the sidewalk."

The opening of the case did not look promising. Judge Levy's sister taught at a Harlem elementary school and brought her students to watch her brother preside at a real live court case. When the children saw who one of the parties was, they lined up in front of the table for Lefty's autograph. Sunny leaned over the railing and whispered to June, "I don't think we're going to win this one."

June came out fighting anyway. Her testimony was, if anything, even more lurid than Kleeblatt's filing. In 1933, June insisted, she had awakened one night to find Lefty prepared to jump out the window of their hotel room. Once, driving home from a game, he had threatened to wreck his car and kill them both. And, according to June, she hadn't overheard the perfect crime story but had been directly threatened with it. "He said he would wear gloves and choke me to death and leave," she testified. "He would come back later, discover me, and tell everyone his wife had been killed." About the black eye, she said, "After all, he's a very big boy."

Testimony in the trial was accompanied by a bevy of gleeful headlines. On the front page of the *Daily News* of May 6, for example, were pictures of a leggy Edna and an equally luscious June, with a small inset of Lefty in the middle looking like Rodin's *Thinker*. The caption read, "Will It Be Edna . . . Or June?"

Lefty pitched against Detroit on May 7, a Saturday, and got pasted, giving up seven runs, five earned, almost blowing a nine-run lead. The Yankees drew 41,000 fans, their largest crowd of the season, many undoubtedly to see how the man in the hot divorce case would fare on the mound.

On Monday, Judge Levy called both parties into his chambers. "June had written out what she wanted," Sunny said, "but Lefty wouldn't accept her terms because he didn't want a legal separation. He wanted a divorce. He'd come this far and even if he had misgivings, he was still going through with it. When it comes to June and Lefty, you're dealing with two strong-willed, stubborn personalities.

"June came out from the meeting in the judge's chambers and walked over to where I was sitting. She whispered to me, 'I don't know what to do. Lefty wants a divorce.' 'Tell him he'll get his divorce,' I said. So she went back into the chambers and said, 'I'm not being cast off as a wife with a flawed character. But, in a duly respectable length of time, you will get your divorce. You can count on it, Lefty. I will divorce you.' Lefty went along, because it was now a win-win situation."

So June withdrew her separation suit and Lefty withdrew his counter-claim for a divorce. Judge Levy stipulated that terms were not to be disclosed to the press. Lefty was now free to take up again with Edna. There was only one problem.

He didn't love Edna. He loved June.

"My sister picked up her life. Once again, she appeared at the Hotel Elysée on East 54th Street in her nightclub act. She added an engagement at a Philadelphia hotel. Her pursuit of a career in opera was serious and meant almost daily coaching lessons and building a repertoire of arias. Sandwiched in between were ongoing lessons in piano, French, and Italian, and the joy of her life, horseback riding on the bridle paths of Central Park."

Within weeks, however, a distraction emerged. "More often than not there were phone calls from Lefty at the Ansonia, asking Nellie if he could speak with June. It seemed that the bloom was off his romance with Edna Torrence. He wanted to start up again, but June's pride got in the way. She loved Lefty. Who didn't? But she never wanted to see him again. So, after exchanging pleasantries, Nellie would say, 'June's out,' whether June was in the apartment or not, and hang up the phone.

"When June wouldn't respond to his phone calls, Lefty sent her telegrams every day. Would she like to eat in Chinatown . . . at the 21

Club . . . Tavern on the Green? Golf . . . dancing at the Park Central roof? June ignored them all. Undaunted, if the Yankees were home Lefty began driving his roadster around and around the block of the Ansonia, hoping to catch sight of her coming out the front door. Lefty was out there every morning, but not having any luck. That is, until he spoke with the doorman, who said June usually came downstairs around eight-thirty.

"So Lefty was at the hotel entrance at eight-thirty. When he caught sight of her coming out the door, he drove up the block, pulling his car up alongside the curb, blowing the horn to get her attention as she made her way to the subway entrance at 72nd Street. June just looked straight ahead. Soon, to avoid meeting Lefty and his roadster, June walked out of the hotel earlier, eight-fifteen, eight, seven forty-five, but Lefty had anticipated that and he was out there as early as she was, ready to spring into action. What a scene. Of course, the press got wind of it and their pictures of the sidewalk rendezvous were splashed across the sports pages and the tabloids."

But June's strategy of avoidance was not simply upsetting Lefty. "Their friends missed Lefty and June being together. To everyone's credit, no one took sides. They thought of them as two sides of a valuable coin. They wanted the tap dancer and her witty left-hander running in their circle once again. And not just close friends, but also the fans and the guys and gals on the street, like newsboys and waitresses and cops on the beat, who knew these two who so readily struck up conversation with anyone they chanced to meet. Everyone was in agreement that June and Lefty were made for each other. But how to get them together again?"

Help was to come from an unexpected source. "Jack Dempsey was a mutual friend. He called June at the Ansonia and said he'd heard that Frank Conville and I were sailing from New York for Sydney, where we'd been booked on an eight-month tour of Australia. Before they sailed, Jack said, he wanted to give them a surprise bon voyage party at his Broadway chophouse. 'It's a swell idea, Jack,' June said. 'Sunny and Frank will love a big send-off.'

"So far, so good, Jack thought, and told June he needed her help with the invitations, which of course would include all of June and Lefty's friends . . . the Fungs, the Russells, the Ruths, the men of the newspaper game, theater folk, the Yankees. 'But, Jack,' June said, 'I don't want to see Lefty and the Yankees.'

" 'Of course, June,' Dempsey said. 'I understand. But Sunny is a close friend of Crosetti and some other guys. They're Yankees.'

" 'Jack, I'm leaving if Lefty talks to me.'

" 'June, trust me. With two hundred people at the party you won't bump into Gomez, even if he comes. He'll be talking baseball with the crowd.'

" 'Okay, Jack, if you promise.' So Jack promised he would make sure the two did not run into each other.

"Of course, Lefty showed and June did bump into him, but when she tried to leave the restaurant, she found that the door had been locked 'to prevent strangers from crashing the party.' Dempsey said he was sorry but he didn't know where the key was."

And that was that. A few weeks later, June was back at Yankee Stadium.

Lefty could laugh about the problems later in life. When asked what he thought a couple should do if they're having marital problems, he replied, "One or the other should leave home and have amnesia."

BY MID-MAY, with DiMaggio back in the lineup and batting almost .500, and the Gomez divorce off the front page, the Yankees' season took off. Lefty once again became the team's free spirit and both McCarthy's nemesis and foil. Bing Russell observed, "McCarthy would be stewed up about the team, the pennant, whatever, and say something caustic to Lefty about it, making out that it was Lefty's fault, and Lefty would laugh and the tension on the team would be eased. McCarthy knew Lefty could hold what he said in perspective, that McCarthy was letting off steam and needed someone to torch."

Lefty also picked up where he had left off with DiMaggio. "The year before, DiMag did a picture called *Manhattan Merry-Go-Round*," Bing Russell said. "It opened around Thanksgiving. In it, Joe sang a song, 'Have You Ever Been to Heaven.' He didn't sing it too badly, but he didn't sing it too well either. Joe was a little off-key, as I recall. When Lefty wanted to needle DiMag, he'd start crooning that goddamn song. You'd see the steam coming out of DiMaggio's collar. Nobody but Lefty would dare to do such a thing to DiMaggio because of the way Joe was, taking offense, but Lefty didn't care. He'd be driving along humming 'Haaaavvve youuu everrr beeeen to heavennnnn,' and Joe would fume."

After June forgave him, Lefty was once more welcome in Lexington and the Gradys' home on Oak Street regained its status as the Yankees' extended clubhouse. When the team was in Boston to play the Red Sox, Lefty and DiMaggio stayed in Lexington instead of at a hotel. If it was a weekend series, they attended Sunday Mass at Sacred Heart Church in East Lexington.

One Sunday, according to Bing Russell, "Lefty's doing the collection during Mass with DiMaggio in attendance. Lefty doesn't think Joe put in enough, so he prods Joe's shoulder with the long-handled basket. The solemn Mass is going on, but here is Lefty determined that Joe will cough up some more money for the church and for the poor. DiMag was a tight-wad and Lefty knew it, and Lefty's not satisfied with Joe's two bucks. He keeps poking him with the basket. Everyone in the church knows it's the great DiMaggio and he knows they know, so Joe reaches into his pants pocket for some more dough. He puts in another dollar, but Gomez pokes him again. Joe is getting redder and redder and going deeper and deeper into his pocket. The other parishioners are chuckling because Lefty won't be put off and keeps poking DiMag till he coughs up about twenty bucks. Course, you know, after that DiMag isn't gonna talk to him for another three weeks. Does Lefty care? Nah."

Joe DiMaggio's flaws, both real and wildly exaggerated, have by now been well documented. Certainly he was not the warmest of men, nor sometimes the nicest. But Lefty had that rare gift of bringing out the best in almost everyone he met. Perhaps because the pressure to be anything larger-than-life was so utterly absent when he was with Lefty, DiMaggio became a more relaxed and therefore more likable man.

DiMaggio himself acknowledged how unique the relationship was. "Some friendships last five minutes. I've had my share. My friendship with Lefty lasted over fifty years.

"Lefty said the same thing I did: 'Why McCarthy put us together as roommates I'll never know. Joe says nothing and I talk all the time.' But the chemistry worked and I can't tell you why except that whenever I saw Lefty across a room, I made a beeline to get in on whatever he was up to. Lefty was someone I could laugh with. There was never a dull moment. At times, when I might have been feeling a little low, Lefty would cheer me up. It was a privilege to room with him.

"I was a rookie in '36 and Lefty was a star. He introduced me to his circle of friends. That brought a lot of fun to a ballplayer who said almost nothing. I talked with my bat."

But the friendship couldn't have survived without mutual respect on the field. "A lot of guys who pitch bellyache about the plays made behind them, especially if the game is lost," Joe said. "Lefty never did. He chalked the win or the loss against his name. I never once heard Gomez complain about an error made by one of his teammates. Never. And he burned to win like the rest of us. Lefty ate the loss and moved on. He took responsibility for the game. He didn't make everyone around him miserable if the Yankees lost. I admire that. If my turn at bat wasn't what I wanted, I was silent, and I bet he'd say sour."

In that spirit, Lefty was likely the only man on earth willing to tease DiMaggio in public. "DiMag loved the *Superman* comics," Bing Russell said, "but he didn't want his fans to know that. So he asked Gomez to buy them. Lefty would leave Joe signing autographs on the sidewalk, walk over to a newsstand, and pick up the latest copy of *Superman.* He was supposed to put the comic in his coat pocket and bring it up to their room. But instead, he'd come back to where Joe was standing, waving *Superman* in front of Joe's nose, so the fans could see it, and ask, 'This what you wanted, Joe? *Superman?*' Joe would look up, ready to kill him."

Joe had acquired something besides a reputation for off-key singing on the set of *Manhattan Merry-Go-Round.* She was an absolutely beautiful blonde from Minnesota named Dorothy Arnoldine Olson, who was an extra in the film under her stage name, Dorothy Arnold. Joe started dating Dottie immediately and she became part of Lefty's extended social circle.

"Dorothy and June were both stunners," said Paul Fung Jr. "June and Dottie became close friends but, like their husbands, they had different personalities. At social gatherings, Dottie laughed and giggled, but she was more reserved than June, who was vivacious and brimming over with energy. June's enthusiasm was extraordinary. If June was determined to do something, look out, nothing would stop her. And she was outspoken. Not so Dorothy, unless she knew you very well."

ON THE MOUND, Lefty's year was as schizoid as his personal life. During the trial and its aftermath, his record was 4–8 and he was giving up runs in clumps. The last two weeks in May, when his pursuit of June was most intense, he gave up six, eight, four, and five earned runs in consecutive starts. After he and June got back together, he went 14–4 with an earned run average under 3.00.

Without the marital shenanigans, 1938 might easily have been Lefty's best year. As it was, with his 18–12 record, Lefty finished third in the league in victories, third in ERA at 3.22, and led the league in shutouts with four. He was again starting pitcher for the American League when the All-Star game was played on July 7 in Cincinnati. June was in the stands. Lefty pitched three innings. He didn't allow an earned run, but one did cross the plate on an error by shortstop Joe Cronin, and Lefty became the losing pitcher in a 4–1 decision. It was to be the only loss of his postseason career.

With DiMaggio recovering nicely from his holdout and driving in 140 runs, the Yankees plowed through to another pennant. Only the Red Sox, with Jimmie Foxx having another huge year, finished within hailing distance. The only thing that prevented a festive run to a third straight title was Lou Gehrig's inexplicable second-half decline. Although he played in every game, he seemed to age ten years in half a season. Balls that jumped off his bat were caught instead of landing in the bleachers. Routine ground balls rolled under his glove. He was thrown out at bases he should have reached easily. His batting average plunged below .300 for the first time since his rookie year in 1925. Lou was thirty-five, it was true, but his body still seemed to have been fashioned from concrete. Still, every player knew that age at some point erodes everyone's skills. His teammates simply hadn't expected it to happen to Lou so quickly.

Another factor mitigating the Yankees' joy was a deteriorating Jake Ruppert. The Colonel had come through a bout of phlebitis in April, but it was apparent that his health problems had lingered. Although many members of the team had gone to war with Ruppert over salaries, and some over their own health issues, Ruppert had built both the best stadium and the best team in the game, and to a man, the players were proud to be a part of it. The realization that Ruppert might be nearing the end hardened the Yankees' determination to send him out with a championship.

Their opponents in the World Series would once again be the Cubs, a repeat of the 1932 series, and would have the same result. It was a coin toss between Lefty and Ruffing to open. The big right-hander, who had gone 21–7 with an ERA of 3.31, got the nod and pitched the team to a 3–1 win in Wrigley Field. Lefty started the next day. Before the game, photographers snapped him standing at the railing, head-to-head with June in the front boxes. June was holding a baseball, wearing a fur, gloves, a very smart hat, and an electric smile. A reporter who was unaware that they were again a couple made the mistake of asking Lefty what June was doing there.

"I didn't bring her here to pitch," he snapped.

Indeed, Lefty needed little help on the mound. Stan Hack, the same man who had scored the unearned run in the All-Star game, scored an unearned run in the first inning. Lefty gave up another two runs in the third. Meanwhile, Dizzy Dean, reduced to slow curves and deception, was pitching brilliantly. He gave up two runs in the second but kept the Yankees otherwise befuddled for seven innings. But Crosetti hit a two-run homer with two out in the eighth to give the Yankees the lead and then DiMaggio planted one in the seats in the ninth for a 6–3 victory.

The Yankees closed out the series with two victories at Yankee Stadium and New York had its third straight world championship.

28

IMMORTALITY, ACHIEVED AND DENIED

———

THANKS TO THAT UNLIKELY DUO OF MELVIN KLEEBLATT AND JACK DEMPSEY, Lefty had family with whom to commemorate the victory. "We celebrated the sweep of the Cubs with a victory dinner at Billy La Hiff's Tavern. The following morning, Nellie, June, and I jumped into the roadster and drove to Oak Street to celebrate Grandma Grady's seventy-fifth birthday, with the neighbors and relatives laughing and kissing the blarney stone. After Bridget blew out the candles, we bundled her into the backseat for her surprise holiday trip to Niagara Falls and the fishing villages of Nova Scotia. We were back in Lexington by Thanksgiving, dropped off Nellie and Bridget, and June and I went north once more, to Maine, to spend the Christmas holidays with Bing, Buddy, and Ooie Russell in Rangeley Lakes."

This holiday season would be especially joyous. "We had found out that June was expecting a baby in July. To celebrate, in January we went by ship to Bermuda to relax and play some golf before I had to report to St. Petersburg."

On January 13, while they were gone, Jacob Ruppert died. For his funeral three days later, 4,000 people crowded into St. Patrick's Cathedral to pay their respects, and another 10,000 stood in the wintry streets outside. Mayor La Guardia and Senator Robert Wagner joined the honorary escort, and Joe McCarthy, Ed Barrow, Babe Ruth, minor league director George Weiss, and Lou Gehrig represented the Yankees.

The Colonel had a large extended family but had never married, so with his passing Ed Barrow became team president after Jake's brother George declined the post. The Colonel's will had stipulated that the Yankees be run as before. When Barrow sent out the contracts on January 20, although only Gehrig received a salary cut, few of the players who had won three straight World Series got raises. DiMaggio kept to his word not to hold out and was rewarded with a paltry $1,500 increase, not even enough to cover the fine he had been assessed the year before. Lefty was offered the same $20,000 and, with fatherhood looming, quickly accepted.

Although McCarthy was as intense as ever, spring training was characterized by the easy professionalism of a team that considered itself one of the greatest in the history of the game. The Yankees could, and almost did, field an All-Star at every position. Pranks and hijinks were in full flower, some even directed at the manager himself.

El Goofo was in the thick of the action. In return for Bing's exalted role with the team, Lefty had Joe Gordon anoint him official Yankee peanut smuggler. "McCarthy didn't allow peanuts in the dugout or the bullpen," Bing remembered. "He couldn't stand the clutter. After a game, if he saw peanut shells on the floor, he'd shout, 'No peanuts!' The players didn't mess with that little bastard. McCarthy was a tough, tough man. But every day, Joe Gordon gave me five dollars to get peanuts for the players. I know it was Lefty who put him up to it. I wore DiMaggio's warm-up jacket. Joe D told me to use it because McCarthy would never suspect Joe of going against him. So I bought the peanuts and smuggled them in.

"Finally, McCarthy caught me with DiMaggio's jacket full of peanuts. I don't know how he figured it out, but he grabbed me and said, 'Bing, if you bring any more peanuts in here, you're gone.' I was shaken. Next day, here comes Gordon again with the five dollars and he hands me DiMaggio's jacket. So what am I going to do? I went and got the peanuts. And McCarthy never growled about the peanuts again, and he didn't throw me out. He just wanted Gordon and Gomez to know they hadn't put one over on him."

Peanut smuggling had its rewards, however. "To go to the dog track in Florida you had to be twenty-one. I'm twelve. Lefty takes me aside and asks me if I want to go. Of course. Anyplace he was going, I wanted to be there. 'If you can't act twenty-one, Bing, you're going to get the rest of us in trouble. This isn't funny business. We're talking police. Do you think you can act twenty-one?' He put me in a sport coat ten sizes too big, a shirt and tie, and a fedora pulled down low over my face, with an unlit cigarette dangling out of the corner of my mouth. We're in line and I'm expecting to be handcuffed any minute. The guy at the entrance gives me a strange look, but I make it through, probably because I'm with the Yankees. We had a great time watching the greyhounds, and I know the players got a chuckle out of me so deadly serious about acting twenty-one and not being carted off to jail."

The only source of concern that spring was the continuing physical woes of Lou Gehrig. He came early to practice and stayed late. He stretched, he took extra batting practice, he ran in the outfield. But nothing made Lou's play improve. Instead, it got worse. At this point, many on the team had begun to suspect that the problem wasn't just age.

"The one and only time Lefty got mad at me was in the spring of 1939," Bing said. "Morning practice at Miller Huggins Field was eleven to one, and Gehrig was always there, trying to get in shape, work out the slump. He thought it had something to do with his legs. Lefty and I would return in the afternoon to pick up DiMaggio and many times Lou would still be going around the field trying to get his legs in shape. In the clubhouse one day, I was standing in front of Lefty's open metal-stall locker, which was next to the showers. Lou walked by me and ruffled my hair like he usually did. I just naturally watched him move into the showers because it was something for a kid to see this iron machine. Lou was a lion of a man. There was about a four-inch drop to the showers, and when Lou stepped down, he fell, went right down on his kisser, sprawled flat on the floor. Not one Yankee looked. Only me.

"The next thing I knew, Lefty had grabbed me by the collar and thrown me into his locker. He growled at me, 'Bing. Get in the car and stay there.' I picked myself up and walked out of the Yankee clubhouse to Lefty's convertible. Usually after spring practice, a bunch of pitchers rode home with us. Well, that day, none of those guys came near Lefty's car. Lefty came out, sat for a minute, staring straight ahead, then said, 'Bing. If you ever do anything like that again with Gehrig, I'm gonna have to get you outta here.' I really didn't know what I'd done wrong. But now I realize that Gehrig's teammates knew that Lou's weakness went beyond a slump. Seeing Lou's frustration and embarrassment when he fell off benches and tripped on stairs, they ignored what was happening. 'Let Lou think we didn't see it,' they thought. Me, being a kid, I had no idea. But if I was in the Yankee clubhouse, I'd better grow up or get out."

One player on the team, never named, wouldn't keep his mouth shut, and continued to make wisecracks about Lou's clumsiness. As Lefty reported, "Bill Dickey put an end to that. He socked the guy in the mouth."

But Lefty was about to have a crisis even more personal to deal with. "On March 15, I pitched three innings against the Reds. When I returned to the hotel, there was a telegram from Nellie, who was staying with June at our New York apartment. June was hemorrhaging and had been taken by ambulance to a hospital. I caught a night flight to New York and landed in Newark at 8:00 a.m. By the time I reached her bedside, the physicians had begun hormone therapy by injection, a treatment they said was unproven to stop the blood flow, but couldn't hurt, and perhaps would prevent a miscarriage. The treatment didn't stop the bleeding, but the doctor still didn't want to let nature take its course. Yet June's body was trying to spontaneously abort. Outside gynecologists were brought in throughout the day, and as they discussed new treatments, June's life was ebbing away. Twenty-four hours went by and nothing but talk from the medical staff. Nellie and I walked the halls, waiting for their decision. The following morning, when we entered June's room, her face was thin and wan, as white as the bedsheet pulled up to her chin. Her eyes were sunken, outlined with dark circles. She was too weak to speak. I took her hand in mine and it was icy cold. Her fingernails were black. I was out of that room in a flash, running the halls looking for her doctor, and when I found him, I told him I was fed up with all the talk. 'I'm losing my wife! Do something. I want June to live.' Within the hour, June was taken into surgery and the pregnancy was terminated."

June was devastated. "In the hospital maternity ward, everyone had a baby to hold and love but me."

After she returned home from the hospital, "I was so weak I couldn't stand up, even just to walk around our apartment. The doctors insisted on eight weeks of bed rest. Sunny was still in Australia, so when Lefty returned to Florida, Nellie, a live-in nurse, and room service brought me through until Lefty returned. From then on, Lefty carried me in his arms.

My feet never touched the floor. As my strength returned, I resumed my Italian lessons in the apartment. When the doorbell rang, Lefty carried me from the bedroom to the day couch and the language classes began."

On the field, Lefty's year began strangely. He gave up few runs but, despite the fact that he was playing on one of the great offensive machines in baseball history, got few Yankee runs to work with. On a team where, incredibly, seven of the eight starting position players would drive in 80 or more runs, Lefty lost two of his first three decisions by 3–1 and 2–1 scores.

Between those two starts, on May 2 in Detroit, after 2,130 consecutive games, Lou Gehrig went to the bench. He would never swing a bat again.

Joe McCarthy later told the *Sporting News,* "I can't help but grieve when I think of that day, when Lou, the captain of the Yankees, took himself out of the lineup. The whole Yankee team cried when he went to home plate to give the batting order to the umpire. There wasn't a dry eye in the dugout. I guess I cried myself. The movie writers are always writing about drama. But they missed the most moving episode of my time in baseball when they omitted that dugout scene in the picture they made about Gehrig."

After he returned, Lou sat alone amidst a thunderous ovation from the Detroit fans and began to weep. The other Yankees sat stunned, unsure of whether to go to Lou or leave him alone. Even Bill Dickey, his closest friend in the world and roommate for eight years, was frozen on the bench. After about fifteen seconds, Lefty got up and sat next to Lou. "Hell, Lou," he said loud enough for everyone to hear, "it took fifteen years to get you out of there. Sometimes I'm out in fifteen minutes." According to Tommy Henrich, "Everybody laughed, including Lou, and that broke the tension."

"Lou would have starred for five more years if he hadn't been struck down," McCarthy added. "We saw the signs, but never suspected anything like that was wrong. The spring of his final season, his old friends like Dickey and Gomez would slap him on the back and praise him for making routine plays. Lou told me after his retirement that he knew then that he was near the end of the line."

JOE DIMAGGIO WAS NOT in the dugout that day. He was lying in a hospital bed. Two games earlier, on a muddy outfield at Yankee Stadium, during Lefty's 3–1 loss to the Senators, his cleats had stuck in the turf as he tried to change direction chasing a fly ball. Joe went down and didn't get up for eight minutes, thinking he'd broken his leg. There was no fracture, but muscles in his lower leg had torn away from the bone.

Robert Walsh, the team doctor, ordered Joe to the hospital, "more to keep visitors away than because of serious injury." Walsh said Joe would rejoin the team in a week, but it took almost a month for the injury to heal.

With Gehrig and DiMaggio out of the lineup, the Yankees defied predictions and went on a tear. They went an entire month and lost only four games. They would win the pennant by nineteen games, but the race effectively ended in May.

Lefty's month was less propitious. On May 10, he had to leave with shoulder pain after pitching to just one batter. Doc Painter was quoted the next day as saying the injury was "muscular cold in the shoulder and stiffness in some back muscles." He added that it was nothing serious.

In fact, it could not have been more serious.

In that 3–1 loss to the Senators, while covering first on a ground ball, Lefty got knocked down and hurt his back. In true Lefty fashion, he didn't say anything about it. But, like Dizzy Dean, he unconsciously altered his motion slightly to compensate and wrecked his shoulder. Lefty would persevere through that season and several more, but he had, for all intents and purposes, ended his career. Still, after missing only one turn, he was back on the mound and won his next five decisions.

While his teammates were tearing up the American League, Lou went for tests at the Mayo Clinic and learned the tragic news. The disease was reported as a form of infantile paralysis. Lou could never play baseball again, it was announced, but could otherwise live a long and productive life. At what point during the progression of the disease Lou suspected the truth has been a matter of conjecture. Certainly Eleanor went to enormous lengths to convince Lou that his disease could be arrested.

But Paul Fung Jr. believes Lou knew the true state of his health and was likely sparing Eleanor's feelings as much as Eleanor was trying to spare his. "A year before he died, Lou gave me an autographed photo of himself holding his favorite bat in front of the Yankee Stadium dugout. On it he wrote, 'To Junior. I hope that you can wear this uniform when I am forced to discard it. Cordially, Lou Gehrig.' Even though Eleanor made sure the subject didn't come up at home, Lou knew he was dying."

The Yankees decided to hold an appreciation day for Lou between games of the July 4 doubleheader against the Senators. Not only would his current teammates participate, but also those who had retired, most prominently Babe Ruth, and assorted dignitaries. In addition to being the seminal event of its kind in the game's history, as well as the scene of the most quoted thank-you speech in sports, July 4, 1939, was also the first, albeit unofficial, Old-Timers' Day.

Players came from as far as California to honor Lou. One former teammate, however, did not have far to travel. Like Babe Pinelli, George Pipgras had turned to umpiring after his playing career ended. He began in the Eastern League until, in 1939, he was hired to umpire in the American League, calling balls, strikes, and outs for former teammates and opponents. On July 4, he happened to have been assigned to Yankee Stadium.

"Lou's teammates were standing on the foul lines," said LeMorn Pipgras. "Dad was in the umpires' room because he thought that now that he was an umpire, he didn't belong out there. But the fans thought otherwise, I guess, because Dad had been a Yankee from 1927 to 1933. They started yelling and clapping, 'We want Pipgras. We want Pipgras.' So Dad came out then and stood in the line with the Yankees honoring Lou."

The greatest honor, of course, was that which Lou cast upon himself. Weak, halting, and "shaken with emotion," he stood in front of 61,000 people and gave what writer John Drebinger termed "as amazing a vale-dictory as has come from a ball player." No greater display of courage, sportsmanship, and pure class has ever been seen on a ball field.

One week later, Yankee Stadium hosted another major event, the seventh annual All-Star game. The venue could not have been more appropriate, since six of the nine American League starters were Yankees, with Crosetti and, titularly, Gehrig as reserves. Johnny Murphy and Lefty were also named to the team but Lefty, the most successful pitcher in All-Star history, did not make it into the game.

When the regular season resumed, as the Yankees soared toward their fourth straight pennant, Lefty struggled. Some games he pitched wonderfully, giving up just a run or two, and then four days later he would get hit hard.

Despite his affection for Lefty, Joe McCarthy undoubtedly cost him perhaps years of his career by sending him to the mound, hurt or not, whenever he could throw a baseball. At the end of 1939, that same attitude cost DiMaggio a vital milestone and Joe never forgave McCarthy for it. On September 10, Joe was hitting .409. No one had hit .400 since Bill Terry of the Giants in 1930, and no American Leaguer had done it since Harry Heilmann in 1923. No Yankee had ever turned the trick. DiMaggio burned to get the mark, and the way he was hitting, no one doubted he would.

Then disaster struck. Joe got an infection that swelled his left eye almost shut and blurred his vision. He'd already had more than enough plate appearances to qualify for the batting title, and the Yankees were seventeen and a half games ahead in the standings, so Joe simply needed to sit out the last couple of weeks or until his eye improved.

But McCarthy wasn't going to have any "cheese champs." He insisted Joe play every day, bad eye and all. Joe did. He lost twenty-eight points on his batting average and finished the year at .381. He was the runaway winner of the Most Valuable Player award, but the sting of being denied a .400 batting average never lessened. "McCarthy had to know the agony I was going through," Joe was quoted as saying years later by George De Gregorio, "and I'll never understand why he didn't give me a couple of days off. I guess it was the rule of the day . . . you played with anything short of a broken leg."

Lefty finished the regular season with a 12–8 record, matching the least number of decisions he'd recorded since his rookie year. His ERA was a respectable 3.41 and his innings pitched second on the team at 198, but he had become a question mark, and both he and McCarthy knew it.

For the team, however, there were no such questions. The Yankees once again powered through the World Series against Cincinnati without losing a game. For the first time ever, a team had won four Series in a row.

For Lefty and Joe, however, the postseason was a disappointment, although for different reasons. The torn muscle in Lefty's right side was extremely painful and, worse for a pitcher, limited his range of motion. His condition became sufficiently serious that he checked into a hospital. Although reporters later insisted that Lefty "wanted to pitch," which he certainly did, and that Doc Painter had "confirmed that the injury had healed," what was not in the newspapers was that McCarthy had visited Lefty in the hospital and insisted that he travel with the team to Cincinnati and give it a try. Gomez then started game three, but throwing the ball was sufficiently excruciating that even Lefty's determination could not get him through the second inning.

As for DiMaggio, although Joe hit .313 in the four games, he had only one extra-base hit—a home run—which for him amounted to a bust.

JUST OVER A WEEK after the Series ended, Bridget Grady died. As Lefty put it, "Five foot two with eyes of blue, framed by wire spectacles. Oh, how we missed our Granny's laughter on the lanes of Lexington and watching her bustling around her kitchen in her cottage next door to our home at 83 Oak Street." Soon after her funeral, they flew to San Francisco for Joe and Dottie's wedding on November 18, at Saints Peter and Paul Church.

Many portraits of Dorothy DiMaggio have been unflattering, but June saw her differently. "Dottie became a terrific baseball fan and one of my best pals. We were young and full of fun and out for a good time together. She sparkled and could laugh when it rained. Dottie saw the bright side no matter how gloomy Joe might be. She got him to laugh and lightened his mood.

"When the Yankees were on the road, some mornings Dorothy and I dropped into the Carlos Dance Studios for conditioning classes. We did lunch and went shopping for fashionable outfits and perfumes on Fifth Avenue, looking for an unexpected bargain, and then browsed for unique hats and designer shoes in the specialty shops along Broadway. Dorothy and I loved to dress up and go out on the town. And we didn't have to be told that we were lucky that we could afford to do this when so many were counting their pennies.

"Other mornings, she and I dropped into Conte's restaurant, always a favorite eatery with the Yankees. Joe wanted Dorothy to cook Italian and she didn't know how, so she set up private lessons and wanted a chum along. Sounded like fun to me. 'Sign me up,' I said. I was already immersed in the Italian language and I knew Lefty would be thrilled if I could throw a dish of veal parmigiana together.

"I still smile when I remember Dottie whispering to me, 'Joe's mama says fresh oregano is the secret to cooking great Italian.' So the two of us were doing a Mama DiMaggio, with oregano plants growing in clay pots on the windowsills of our hotel apartments. Without doubt, Mama's oregano tasted better than our variety covered in city soot.

"When Joe and Lefty were in New York, if they were ringside at Madison Square Garden for a prizefight, Dottie and I were at a Broadway musical, and after the shows we ran backstage to say hello to our friends in the cast and go out for some night lunch with them. Other times, we'd get together for bridge, Lefty and Joe against Dottie and me.

"If there was an off day, Lefty rang up DiMaggio, who called the Fungs, who called another bunch, and the crowd of us drove off to Bear Mountain State Park for a day of hiking, swimming, and a picnic. And, come a free weekend, we all dashed over to Lexington for Ping-Pong, good eats, and laughter at our family home on Oak Street."

And there was Chinatown. "At least once a week, we met for dinner at Ting Yah-sik, a restaurant on 21 Mott Street," Paul Fung Jr. said. "June and Lefty, Joe and Dottie, Tommy Henrich, my parents, and others. When it was crowded the owners held a place for us. If it was really jammed, we'd sit in the pantry among the pots and pans and jars of ginger preserves, eating with chopsticks, laughing over spareribs and chop suey. We also twirled chopsticks uptown at Lum Fong's on West 52nd street and Su Chan's House of Chan, Lexington Avenue between 54th and 55th streets. When we arrived at Su's, the specialties of the house were waiting for us on a long banquet table. The décor of these uptown Chinese restaurants was elaborate because they catered to a more monied clientele than in Chinatown, but the fortune cookies were the same. The restaurateurs were all in competition with one another but they met socially, went to ball games at Yankee Stadium, and ate together. Everyone usually ended up at the Fungs' on Riverside Drive for a nightcap, no one leaving before 1:00 a.m."

But for Lefty and June, late-night stepping out was about to end.

29.

"YOU DON'T TELL JUNE
SHE CAN'T DO SOMETHING"

———

FOR THANKSGIVING DINNER 1939, SUNNY AND FRANK CONVILLE WERE in New York—unusual for the globe-trotting performers—and they, Lefty and June, Nellie, Pitzy Katz, and the Fungs all got together at Polly Klein's penthouse on Central Park West. Polly, of course, was the reason Pitzy had hitched a ride with Lefty to Nevada in order to divorce his wife in 1937. Sweeney, Polly's Sealyham terrier, fat and wealthy, was under the table, fast asleep on the mink coat thrown on the floor for his comfort. Nothing was too good for Sweeney. He even had his own box seat at Yankee Stadium.

"Dinner ended," Sunny recalled, "with cocktails and nuts, then we all got up to say our goodbyes. As we did, June fainted dead away on the floor."

Lefty picked June up and carried her to the sofa. The others hovered about, not sure whether to call a doctor or even if they could get one. Finding a doctor on Thanksgiving was no easier in 1939 than it would be today. Sunny said, "I bet she's pregnant. In the movies when the heroine faints, she's always pregnant."

Sunny was right. June went to her obstetrician the next day and the pregnancy was confirmed.

June and Lefty were overjoyed but the obstetrician was not, since just eight months before, June had been literally minutes from death. A few days later, the doctor called Lefty on the telephone and said, "June can't have this baby. Another pregnancy will kill her. Take her to Lexington for

Christmas, then bring her back to New York, and I'll tell her she has to abort before the first trimester is up."

Lefty called Sunny and told her what the doctor had said. "Knowing June as I did," Sunny said, "I knew her doctor was going to have a battle. You don't tell June she can't do something. I don't care what it is. If there's one basic ingredient to June's personality it is that she will not accept that she can't do what she intends to do. June will tell you quite pointedly, 'I certainly can do it. And, what's more, I will do it.'

"So, after the holidays, Lefty brought June to New York and the three of us went to see the obstetrician. After the examination, the doctor said, 'June, to safeguard your life, you have to abort.' June sat back in the chair, her hopes dashed, momentarily stunned by the news. But her shock soon turned to defiance, as I suspected it would. 'Oh, no you're not. Nobody is taking my baby.'

"The doctor tried to reason with her, to no avail. He finally said, 'June, we're all in agreement on this decision. You have to abort.'

"June began to cry. 'Nobody is telling me what to do,' she said. 'Not you, not anyone. I'll run away. I'll have this baby and you won't even know where I am.' "

After a few moments, June asked the doctor who had delivered his children. The doctor told her it had been Judson Smith at Massachusetts General Hospital. Then he asked why.

"Because I want another opinion."

Lefty, June, and Sunny left the obstetrician's office, made an immediate appointment with Judson Smith, then drove to Boston. "They're going to take my baby," June told Smith. He examined her and then said, "You can have the baby, June."

"I can? Do I have to lay in bed for months like before?"

"No."

"Can I swim? Play golf?"

"Sure, you can swim," Dr. Smith said. "And you can play golf as long as you can get the putter past your belly. By all means, play nine holes, even eighteen. But the minute there's trouble, I'm going to step in and restrict your activity."

"We were all elated with the news," remembered Sunny. "In fact, everyone we knew was ecstatic, and June kept saying over and over, 'We're going to have a baby. We're going to have a baby.'

"Still, the family was worried. But not June. My sister had determined that she would give birth to this baby and she would do it by leading the active life she loved. And so, with the blessing of Dr. Smith, June was out on the golf links in the morning and in the pool in the afternoon. Her craving for egg foo young and chop suey practically every night drove us crazy. Lefty christened the baby-to-be 'Lotus Blossom.' "

With the promise of a Gomez family finally reaching fruition, Lefty still had baseball to consider. He furiously tried to get in peak shape, but no amount of running, swimming, or racquetball can rehabilitate a sore shoulder. Lefty could pitch through pain, but he couldn't will a couple of extra miles per hour on his fastball.

Then, before contracts were mailed for the 1940 season, Joe McCarthy made an astounding statement. "There's nothing wrong with Gomez's arm," said the man who had dragged him from a hospital bed to pitch hurt. "Whether he has a good year or not seems to depend on whether he gets in good shape in training camp." Four days later, Lefty was the only member of the team asked to take a pay cut for the upcoming season.

As spring training began, McCarthy and Barrow both pronounced Gomez still a mainstay of the pitching staff, but whisperings that his career was over were heard both in the press and in Yankee offices. In early March, Lefty was feeling shoulder pain but team officials, speaking through Doc Painter, insisted they were not alarmed. Three days after reporting the discomfort, Gomez threw and was reported as having "plenty of stuff." But on March 21, the *New York Times* reported, "A mysterious pain in his left shoulder which, incidentally, Gomez has made light of all along, and a stiff neck he contracted when exposed to the high winds of early camp activity, have combined to keep the southpaw out of action. He has confined his activities to careful throwing and routine exercising in the drills at Huggins Field."

"Your whole profession, your whole life, is centered in your arm," Lefty said later, "and all of a sudden you can't get it to move like it used to.

It's frightening, because all you want is to be a baseball player. That's what you know how to do. You're in the pink of your career and you get hurt and you can't play anymore."

To reporters, Lefty was all good copy and buoyant optimism. A newspaper reported, "On the eve of his debut, Gomez expressed satisfaction with the condition of his arm. 'I have been troubled with a slight pain in the arm and another in the neck,' he said today. 'I have been taking things easy because I didn't want to aggravate the pain in the arm. It's all right now, though, I'm pitching tomorrow.' "

And whatever his private feelings, Lefty continued to keep the team loose, often with his new partner in crime, George "Twinkletoes" Selkirk. "I got really burned up at Gomez and Selkirk one day," McCarthy told the *Sporting News*. "Gomez was always slow leaving the mound at the end of the inning and Selkirk bet him a new hat that he would beat him to the dugout. There were two outs, two on, and a fly ball was hit to the field opposite from where Selkirk was playing. He started running the moment he was sure that the ball would be caught. He was only a few yards from the mound when Gomez saw him. So the pair of them staged a red-hot race, Lefty winning by a stride. Fortunately, the fly ball was caught, but I exploded. The Yankees would have been the laughingstock of the league if that ball had fallen safely."*

Lefty had inventive ways of needling the new Yankee right fielder. "Selkirk took his golf seriously—a bit too seriously, according to Lefty," Bing Russell recounted. "Sometimes we flew Buddy's plane over the golf course in St. Pete, watching for Selkirk getting ready to hit a tee shot. We'd swoop down to about fifty feet, cut the engine so it was quiet, and Lefty would holler something out the window. Broke Selkirk's concentration. He'd wave his club at the plane, trying to climb into the air to wring Gomez's neck. In those days you could bring your plane down low over people and no one would call the FAA and pick your license like they do today."

---

* McCarthy also said, "Selkirk was one of my favorite players, taking over Ruth's spot at bat and in right field. George was under heavy pressure that first year but he came through brilliantly. No player ever had a tougher assignment."

Despite continued shoulder soreness and a knee that he banged up in an exhibition game, Lefty was tapped to open the season against Washington on April 19. On a cold and rainy afternoon in front of only 15,299 fans, the Yankees staked him to a four-run lead in the first inning. He pitched well for five innings, giving up only one run, but had to come out when his shoulder stiffened.

He would not pitch again until July.

During those two and a half months, Lefty tried everything—chiropractors, workouts at Jack Dempsey's gym, and visits to doctors at leading medical centers. In May, McCarthy tried him against Class C minor leaguers and he was pasted. His curveball had plenty of break, but there was no fastball to set it up. From there, he left the team and returned to New York, then was sent by Ed Barrow to Johns Hopkins for X-rays. There he met another sore-armed star hoping for a miracle.

"I think I have a couple of ligaments crossed in my shoulder," Dizzy Dean told reporters. "I'm washed-up unless these docs can do me some good." Dean did not get good news and neither did Lefty. But neither did they get bad news. In fact, the sort of injury from which each suffered did not show up on X-rays. Diz was right about one thing, though—he was washed-up. Except for one inning in 1941 and another in 1947, 1940 would be his last year. He finished with a 3–3 record, appearing in just ten games. The great right-hander finished with a lifetime record of 150–83 and left behind an indelible imprint on the game.

As May drew to a close, it became apparent that Judson Smith had been correct. June would soon give birth to a healthy baby and Lotus Blossom was going to need an actual name. June, wishing to honor her husband's heritage, solicited the help of Richard Grozier, editor and publisher of the *Boston Post*, to suggest "personal names of Spanish origin." Grozier did his homework. For girls, he came up with such mellifluous suggestions as "Karabel" (beautiful face), "Ampara" (a protector or helper), "Chispa" (a spark), and "Paloma" (a pigeon). After apologizing for the brevity of the list ("many of the names given to the Spanish today are of Latin origin"), Grozier suggested "Juanita" ("the Spanish form of 'Jane,' which is of Hebrew origin signifying a gift of the Lord"). But, he concluded, if the baby was a girl, "we here at the *Boston Post* suggest that the baby's name be Vernona Lois, and since her father's name is Vernon Louis, naming her Vernona Lois would give the baby the same initials, VLG, as Lefty."

As the due date approached, the celebrations began. "Paul Fung and my teammates threw a surprise baby shower for the papa-to-be at Paul's apartment. They presented me with a shiny black English buggy autographed in white ink by my teammates. It sat on very high wheels and the ride was bouncy."

Then, at 6:00 a.m. on June 15, 1940, at Phillips House, the maternity wing of Massachusetts General Hospital, with Lefty on a road trip in St. Louis, June gave birth to a 7-pound-6-ounce baby girl, who, as Richard Grozier had suggested, was named Vernona Lois.

For Lefty, his daughter's birth was a glorious interlude in a year of struggle. "Vernona was the only good thing that happened to me in 1940. I was on the field in St. Louis when the news of the birth of our first child broke. Reporters and my teammates were shouting their congratulations when McCarthy walked up and acidly asked, 'What's this all about, Gomez? You haven't done a damn thing all year.' 'Joe, I must have done something,' I said. 'June gave birth to a baby girl today.' "

Lefty's initial experiences of fatherhood would be recognizable to many men. "When I arrived home at night after a ball game and swimming laps in the pool at the New York Athletic Club, my job was to put the baby to bed for the night. If she was fussing, it could take an hour. So I tied a string from my rocking chair to her cradle, and as I rocked back and forth reading the daily newspapers, her cradle rocked too, and soon Vernona was sleeping soundly."

THE 1940 AMERICAN LEAGUE race was the tightest in over a decade. On September 15, three teams, Detroit, Cleveland, and the Yanks, were within two games of one another. Over the next week, however, the Yankees fell four and a half games off the pace. With nine games to go, they would almost have to win out to capture an unprecedented fifth straight pennant. The schedule, however, smiled on them, as they were slated for two games against the seventh-place Senators and then three against the dreadful, last-place Philadelphia A's. The Tigers, on the other hand, had to go up against the second-place Indians.

The Yankees put on a charge, sweeping the Red Sox and winning the first two against Philadelphia. But the Tigers won as well and the New Yorkers found themselves two and a half games back with four to play.

On September 27, for the third game against the A's, the Yankees had to face a pitcher named Johnny Babich. Babich, who would finish his career with a record of 30–45 in five seasons with weak clubs, had unaccountably beaten the Yankees four times in the 1940 season. His presence on the mound that day, with the pennant on the line, was specifically due to his fellow Richmond High School alum, Vernon Gomez.

"I had played Sunday semipro ball around the East Bay area," Babich said later. "I'd go down to Rodeo to see Lefty when he was back from the Yankees, and he'd tell me, 'Johnny, keep pitching. You're going to be a big leaguer one of these days.' At the time, only a handful went to the majors from East Bay and I was getting discouraged. But I knew Lefty had made the Yankees in '30 so there was hope."

Hope indeed. Babich pitched shutout ball for eight innings, gave up two meaningless runs in the ninth for a 6–2 win, and knocked the Yankees out of the race.

Lefty, only thirty-one years old, finished the year 3–3, same as Dizzy Dean, having pitched only twenty-seven innings the entire season. And in Boston, Lefty Grove, forty, finished at 7–6, his ERA almost 4.00. Thus, as the new decade dawned, it appeared as if, of the five greatest pitchers of the 1930s, only Charlie Ruffing and Carl Hubbell (who had hung on, finishing 11–12) might survive into the 1940s.

After the season, Lefty returned to California and was the speaker at a CYO fund-raising dinner at Richmond High. Johnny Babich was there as well. "Lefty saw me sitting in the back of the room and said to the audience, 'There's a guy here tonight that I want to introduce because he owes me $5,000. Johnny Babich, stand up. John knocked the Yankees out of the World Series this year.'"

Later that fall, George Selkirk got his revenge for Lefty's golf course fly-bys. Gomez, raised in pioneer country, was of course an inveterate sportsman. He and June spent part of each off-season at Bud and Ooie Russell's cabin in Rangeley Lakes, Maine, where the men depleted the local deer population and the women tromped in the woods. But Selkirk was a *hunter*. A native of rural Ontario, Twinkletoes had spent his boyhood in the Canadian woods. Each off-season, he went north into the backcountry. This time Lefty decided to tag along. Selkirk warned him that the trip might be a bit more rugged than he was used to, but Lefty, as Selkirk put it, "would not be denied." Selkirk relented but told Gomez to bring warm clothes. Lefty thought what he wore in icy Maine would certainly be sufficient.

"I'll never forget that trip," Selkirk later told sportswriter Jim Ogle. "We took a train into some isolated area. The guide met us in a canoe and we went further into the woods. Gomez couldn't believe it. 'You have to go this far to hunt?' By now Gomez's teeth were chattering like castanets. Our cabin was heated only by a fireplace. When it was time for bed, I took off my thermal long johns and couldn't stop laughing at Gomez shivering in his silk underwear."

During the night, Selkirk was suddenly shaken awake. Lefty was standing by his bed, wide-eyed. "What the hell is that noise on the roof?" he asked.

"Oh, that's just a bear," Selkirk replied, and rolled over to go back to sleep.

Lefty never went hunting with Selkirk again.

But bears on the roof turned out to be the least of Lefty's problems. When he returned from the north woods, he began to hear rumblings that his career with the Yankees was over.

30

"THEY'LL HAVE TO CUT THE UNIFORM OFF ME"

—

IN DECEMBER 1940, A REPORT SURFACED THAT BARROW AND MCCARTHY were about to deal Lefty to the Brooklyn Dodgers. The Dodgers, a second-division team for almost two decades, had begun to improve rapidly and in 1940, under incendiary manager Leo Durocher, had won 88 games and actually finished in second place. There was no question that the Dodgers could hit, but their best pitcher had been a thirty-eight-year-old knuckleballer, "Fat Freddie" Fitzsimmons, whom Lefty had beaten to clinch the 1936 World Series. That Lefty had enough juice in his aching left arm to help on the mound was hardly a certainty, but his presence in Brooklyn would at least help cut into the Yankees' domination in the press.

By December 15, the deal was considered enough of a fait accompli that sportswriters were penning Lefty's Yankee obituary in a series of elegiac columns that recalled his pitching record, his vaunted wit, and his epic salary battles with Jake Ruppert.

Only, Lefty wasn't quite done.

He asked for a meeting with Ed Barrow to plead his case. Convincing the flinty, obdurate Yankee president that he was in shape, healthy, pain-free, and ready to pitch promised to be a tall order, even for Lefty. But the man who had retrieved a diamond ring from a sewer line was not about to quit without playing every card. So he showed up at the Yankee offices with reinforcements. Marching into the meeting with him were June, done up in her most dazzling array, and in her arms, "in all her six-month gurgling baby finery," was Vernona.

That Vernona could attend, even cradled by her mother, was fortunate. Just days before, she had barely escaped serious harm. So bouncy was the English buggy that Lefty had gotten as a shower gift that when her nanny—Elaine Klein, Polly's fourteen-year-old daughter—took her for a stroll in Central Park, the harness fastened loosely, "Vernona," as Lefty recalled, "bounced right out of it." Elaine was mortified, but Lefty took it with equanimity. "Things happen," he said, "but thank God, there were no broken bones in Vernona's noggin."

Both mother and daughter were in fine form for the meeting. Barrow, unaccustomed to being outnumbered by females, was taken aback. He listened as Lefty hurled his most important pitch, extolling his off-season conditioning program. Then June delivered the coup de grâce. "Please don't trade Lefty to Brooklyn," she implored. Then, glancing toward her daughter, she added, "I can't tell the baby her father's a Bum." Barrow laughed, an event newsworthy in itself, and then made an extremely un-Barrow-like announcement: "Okay, Lefty, you're on for 1941." Barrow then told the press, "There isn't a chance of any club getting Gomez from us now." What Ed Barrow could not have known was that, by giving in to sentiment, he had not only made a sound business decision but also likely enabled one of the greatest achievements in the history of sports.

Tenuous though his position with the team may have been, Lefty roared into spring training. He actually had gotten into superb shape. And, to help ease the anxiety of an uncertain year, the Yankees provided him with a new foil, a five-foot-six, 150-pound, sweet, shy, astoundingly naive kid from Brooklyn named Phil Rizzuto. Rizzuto had been called "Scooter" coming up, but Lefty immediately anointed him "The Flea."*

Rizzuto had been brought in to replace Frank Crosetti, who had hit only .194 in 1940 and was clearly worn-out after a decade of playing virtually every game. Cro would hang on as a backup until 1948, then become a Yankee coach for more than two decades. "I saw Crosetti start to

---

* Lefty's fastball might have lost some zip, but his clubhouse needle had lost none of its barb. Charlie Keller had been dubbed "King Kong" in the minors, an appellation of which he was none too fond. Bing Russell described him as "a wonderfully sweet guy with an apish face, bushy eyebrows, and thick body hair that covered his arms and legs, which were shaped like fireplugs." In the showers the first day after Keller was called up from Newark, Lefty looked over and asked, "Who scouted you? Frank Buck?" referring to the world-famous big-game hunter of Bring 'Em Back Alive fame.

work with Rizzuto," Bing recalled. "Cro, the veteran, talked to Rizzuto about the hitters and the pitchers, and here's Rizzuto, the rookie, who's taking Crosetti's job away. Winning games for the Yankees was more important to Crosetti than his own glory. I often thought Cro wore pinstripes for a lifetime as a player and third-base coach because he began to help Rizzuto right away."

Rizzuto recalled a different sort of help. "I'll never forget one day at Yankee Stadium when I was a rookie. The place was jammed, and I was nervous as I could be. My parents were in the stands, which made me even more nervous. Lefty was pitching, up by one run, and he loads the bases. He steps off the pitching mound, turns towards me in the infield, then motions for me to come in to see him. I point to myself and ask, 'Who, me?' He keeps waving me in. So I go up to the mound and see what he wants. Lefty says, 'Your mom and dad are in the ballpark, aren't they?' I told him yeah. 'Well, they should be pretty impressed that the great Gomez is asking you for advice in this crucial situation.' That was the end of the conversation. I go back to my position. Lefty strikes out the next guy, we get out of the inning, and win the game."

During Lefty's next start, Rizzuto returned the favor. Gomez was pitching against Charlie Wagner of the Red Sox and, giving up eleven hits and eight walks, he had to dodge trouble in almost every inning. Then, in the bottom of the eleventh, Rizzuto parked a home run in the left-field seats to win the contest 4–2. "It was his first major league home run," Wagner said later, after Rizzuto had spent years in the broadcast booth, "and he got such a big kick out of it that he kept announcing it on television. Whenever the Yankees were celebrating something, Rizzuto had one of the media guys ask him, 'And when did you hit your first home run, Phil?' and I thought, 'Not again.'"

Lefty and Rizzuto grew close enough that The Flea was named godfather to Lefty's son Gery in 1942.*

One thing Rizzuto could not master, however, at least not as well as his predecessor, was the hidden-ball trick. Bobby Doerr, Hall of Fame second

---

* After the baptismal ceremony, Rizzuto asked, "What am I supposed to do now, Lefty?" Lefty replied, "Start a trust fund for him, of course."

baseman with the Red Sox, was in awe of the dexterity with which Lefty and Crosetti had pulled it off. "Frank would go up to Gomez like he was flipping him the ball, but somehow he would take it in his other hand and kind of tuck it under his glove. A player looking at Cro would swear he had given the ball to Lefty, but he hadn't, and of course Lefty acted non-chalant. So Frank goes back to short, waits for a player to take a lead off second, and tags him out."

When the 1941 season began, fans had no idea that it was to be one of baseball's incredible years, featuring a milestone for a great pitcher, the setting of indelible records by two of the game's finest hitters, and a sad finale for a third.

On May 14, Joe DiMaggio failed to get a hit. No one thought much of it at the time, but the next box score that showed a similar result would not be published until July 17. But what was apparent in May was that the Yankees were in danger of repeating their third-place finish, perhaps even dropping in the standings. As the month entered its final week, their record was only 22–18, which left them five games behind the first-place Indians, a game behind the second-place White Sox, and only three games ahead of the sixth-place A's. The contending clubs continued to trade places. On June 1, the Yankees swept a doubleheader in Cleveland, Ruffing winning the first game and Lefty the nightcap. The sweep knocked the Indians out of first and left the Yankees a game and a half behind the White Sox. The next day, however, they lost to Bob Feller, and the Indians returned to first place.

All the while, DiMaggio continued to hit, nineteen straight by June 1, although he was strangely erratic in the field. In one game, he committed an unthinkable three errors. Joe refused to alibi, but Lefty finally told reporters that Joe had swollen glands and a painfully stiff neck.

On June 3, the Yankees arrived in Detroit with the top six teams in the league separated by only five and a half games. There they learned that the night before, Lou Gehrig had died.

Joe McCarthy and Bill Dickey flew to New York for the funeral. At Briggs Stadium before the game, the same field at which Lou had taken himself out of the lineup two years earlier, players and fans stood in silent tribute.

Lou's funeral was a simple affair on June 4 at a small church in Riverdale in the western Bronx. Mourners lined the ramp to the Henry Hudson Parkway, standing in the rain to witness the cortege. Ed Barrow was an usher, as was Pitzy Katz. June and Dottie DiMaggio attended and brought Paul Fung Jr., who had been one of Lou's favorites.

The service, as Mom and Pop Gehrig requested, was brief, less than eight minutes. Instead of a eulogy, the pastor simply said, "We need none because you all knew him."

Junior was by then a senior at the High School of Music & Art and had taken off from school to attend Lou's funeral. His mother, Mae, gave him a note to bring to school the next day: "Please excuse Paul junior from being absent yesterday. He attended the funeral of Lou Gehrig. Truly yours, Mrs. Paul Fung." The principal scribbled across the bottom in dark ink, "This is NOT an excused absence," and proceeded to suspend Junior from school.

The suspension was indefinite, and if it held, Paul would miss final exams and deadlines to hand in papers, thus threatening his scheduled graduation. Mae Fung was distraught and asked June for advice. June was in the principal's office like she had been shot out of a gun.

The principal, it seemed, thought the Fungs, both mother and son, had mocked him with an outrageous and false excuse for Paul's not being in school. When June walked into his office, eyes blazing, he first sat dumbfounded, then stammered that he recognized her from newspaper photos. In short order, they came to a meeting of the minds. The suspension was lifted and Junior graduated on time. "There's an exception to every rule," June said later.

In Detroit, the Yankees lost their next two games and fell to fourth place. Despite DiMaggio's continued hitting, a good deal of support from other powerful Yankee bats, and excellent pitching, especially by stalwarts Ruffing and Gomez, the team was only three games over .500 at 25–22.

For the remainder of June, however, the Yankees were nearly unbeatable. They won seventeen games against only four losses, and as July dawned, they led the league, one and a half games ahead of Cleveland. Philadelphia, Chicago, and Detroit were just about done, and Boston, behind the torrid hitting of twenty-two-year-old Ted Williams, was barely hanging on.

During that 17–4 run, Joe DiMaggio had hit safely in every game. As the month drew to a close, he edged closer and closer to the all-time record of 41 consecutive games, held by George Sisler. DiMaggio showed outsiders as little of his genuine feelings as did Lefty, but with each successful at-bat, the pressure increased. Day after day he had to get a hit, and night after night he had to think about the next game. At such times, it helps to have someone around to distract you and few were better suited to such a task than Vernon Gomez.

Lefty kidded, he prodded, he played pranks. When reporters hovered, he was at Joe's elbow. When they weren't, he shepherded Joe around.

Reder Claeys came to visit Lefty that summer, his first time in New York. "I stayed with Lefty, June, and baby Vernona in their penthouse in Manhattan. Joe and Dorothy lived in another penthouse a few blocks away. When it was time for Lefty to leave for the ballpark, he waved a white towel to tell DiMaggio he was picking him up, and Joe would respond with a wave of his towel. Then Lefty and I got into his black convertible and picked up Joe. One day, we stopped at a corner joint where two pitchers, Atley Donald and Red Branch, were playing pinball. Lefty banged the horn, they jumped into the car, and we were on our way to the Stadium. So we're driving up Broadway and I'm awed by all the famous skyscrapers. I pointed out the window and asked Gomez, 'Hey, Hayseed, what's that over there?' DiMaggio jumped up from the backseat and asked, 'What did you just call Lefty?' 'Hayseed,' I said. 'That's what we called him in Rodeo.' DiMaggio laughed so much he could hardly catch his breath. He was in the middle of his hitting streak, and Joe told me later that my comment helped him relax at the plate. The next day, he hit a home run against the Athletics."

When the Yankees played in Boston, Lefty, June, and an extended entourage, of which Joe was always part, repaired to Lexington. Sometimes the group grew even larger than anticipated.

"Lefty sent Paul senior a postcard from Lexington before an off day that said, 'Wish you were here,' " Paul junior recalled. "When it arrived, we jumped into our car, and at 3:00 a.m., Dad, Mom, and I were on Lefty's doorstep. He opened the front door in pajamas. 'What the hell are you doing here?' Paul held up the postcard. 'You wrote "Wish you were here," so here we are.' A few hours later, after June whipped up breakfast, a friend of Lefty's, Vince Bellizia, called. Vince owned an undertaking service and the Pine Meadow Country Club and he told us to meet him for some golf. We're on the eighteenth green yelling for him, but there's no Vince. So we went to his office in the pro shop and he scared the hell out of us. Vince was taking a nap in a casket."

Lefty performed other functions. According to sportscaster George Grande, Joe sometimes called him to come over somewhere in the city and move his car out of a parking space because Joe didn't know how to back up. "An outfielder's chauffeur," Lefty said. "Now I know I'm over the hill."

Joe himself later said, "Gomez kept me loose during the streak. He kept people away from me, but was always there to needle me if I was getting too serious off the field, or give me a jolt if I was staring into space in the dugout, wondering if I'd get another hit to keep the streak going. He had me laughing instead of worrying about the next game."

Just as Joe was poised to break Sisler's record, someone discovered that Wee Willie Keeler had hit safely in forty-four consecutive games in 1897, giving Sisler only the "modern record."

On June 29, Joe hit safely in both ends of a doubleheader in Washington to break Sisler's mark. On July 2, with Lefty on the mound, he erased Wee Willie Keeler from the record books.

The streak continued: fifty games, then fifty-five. DiMaggio himself admitted that "the pressure skyrocketed." Lefty worked overtime. He took Joe to hospitals to visit sick children, needled him incessantly, ran interference in public—anything to help keep his roommate focused.

Finally, on July 17, after Joe had hit in fifty-six straight games, the Yankees were to face the Indians in a night game. Lefty was once again scheduled to pitch. More than 67,000 fans showed up.

The story of the prescient Cleveland taxi driver is well-known but has never been related in correct detail. "I went out to the park in a taxi with DiMaggio," Lefty said. "The driver knew who DiMag was and offered his good wishes. As Joe was paying the fare, the cabbie said to him, 'Make sure you get your hit the first time up. If you don't, you'll be stopped.' DiMaggio laughed, but as we walked to the clubhouse he kept repeating what the driver had said. In his first at-bat, Joe almost knocked Ken Keltner down. DiMag put everything he had into that swing. Ken made a remarkable play and Joe was thrown out."

In his third at-bat, after a walk, Joe hit another sizzler that Keltner speared, just nipping him at first. A double play followed in the eighth and the streak was over.

"How much did Joe's failure in that game trace to what the cabbie said?" Lefty asked. "No one can tell. But that's what happened."

Something else no one can tell is what Joe's fate during that streak would have been if Lefty had not brought June and Vernona to Ed Barrow's office and talked himself out of being dealt to the Dodgers.

Even after the streak was in the books, Lefty was not quite done with Joe. "On August 30," Joe related, "my teammates, led by Lefty, gave me my biggest thrill in baseball. He and I were having dinner in the Shoreham Hotel in Washington. We finished dessert and Lefty said to me, 'Listen, Joe, I've got to pick up something in Selkirk's room. C'mon along.'

" 'No,' I said. 'I'll meet you in the lobby.'

"But Lefty insisted. 'C'mon. I'll only be a minute.'

"So I went. When we entered Selkirk's room, the entire Yankee team was there with glasses of champagne poured and raised. Coach Art Fletcher led the team in singing, 'For Joe's a jolly good fellow,' and Frank Crosetti gave a hip-hip-hooray. Lefty picked a package up from the table and handed it to me. It was a sterling silver humidor, engraved with the signatures of every member of the team. In the middle of the cover was a line drawing of me swinging a bat with the numerals 56 and 91 on either side: 56 for the consecutive games in which I made a hit and the 91 for the number of hits I made during the streak. It was so unexpected and I knew the Yankees didn't throw parties like this. I was at a loss for words but managed to say, 'This is swell. I don't deserve it.' I opened the lid and went around the room saying, 'Cigars? Cigarettes?'

"Then Joe Gordon ragged on Gomez, saying, 'I want to congratulate you, Lefty. This is the first time in history that you kept a secret.'

"Bill Dickey called for a team toast and Johnny Murphy made it. 'Joe,' he said, 'we just wanted to let you know how proud we are to be playing on a ball club with you.'

"It was just a little party in a hotel room. Yet it was the biggest one I'll ever go to."

THE YANKEES' TORRID play continued and they soon had opened a twelve-game lead on the Indians. The pennant race was effectively over.

Two other remarkable achievements graced the 1941 season. The first occurred on July 25, when, after two failed attempts, Lefty Grove defeated the Indians 10–6 to win his 300th game. He had not appeared in his first major league game until he was twenty-five; he had won an additional 111 games in the minors. Dripping sweat in the locker room, a huge grin plastered on his face, Grove was asked if he was now ready to leave the game.

"Quit now?" he asked, and reporters said Grove was almost screaming. "They'll have to cut the uniform off me. I'm going for another three hundred. They couldn't be any harder to get than the first three hundred." But Grove did not win another game for the remainder of the season. On December 9, the Red Sox gave him his unconditional release. Without fanfare, one of the greatest pitching careers in baseball had ended.

Bing Russell had a favorite Gomez-Grove story. "Near the end of Lefty's career, the Red Sox were coming to town and Gomez was scheduled to pitch against Grove. The Yankees got to Grove early and hammered him out of there, but Lefty continued on. The Red Sox finally got to him and knocked him out too. So Lefty comes down the player's chute, headed for the Yankee locker room, and he realizes something is different. At first he can't figure exactly what. Finally he realizes he couldn't hear Doc Painter's radio broadcast of the game on the field. Doc always stayed down in the clubhouse with his radio on. As Gomez comes through the door, there sat Grove astride the bench with a fifth of bourbon and two glasses. Grove looked up and smiled, handing him a glass, and said, 'I knew you'd be along.' "

The second great achievement was not finalized until the last day of the season. Ted Williams had kept up his amazing hitting and, going into a final doubleheader, held a batting average of .39955, which rounded up to an even .400. Boston manager Joe Cronin gave Williams the option of sitting out the final games. With DiMaggio having been denied two years earlier, The Kid would thus become the first man to reach .400 in a decade and the first American Leaguer in almost two.

But Ted was cut from McCarthy's mold. No rounding up records for him. He went four for five in the first game, putting him safely over the .400 plateau, and then insisted on playing in the second as well. He went two for three, finishing at .4057, which rounded up to .406. No major leaguer has hit .400 since.

The Yankees finished 101–53 to win the pennant by seventeen games over Boston. It was a team of remarkable balance. Only two players drove in more than 100 runs, DiMaggio with 125 and Charlie Keller 122, and only three hit over .300—and one of those was Red Ruffing. But five of the eight starters scored more than 100 runs.

Pitching honors were also widely distributed. Lefty went through the season on guts and guile and finished with a record of 15–5, tying Ruffing for the most victories and, with one less loss than Red, led the league in winning percentage. Only two other pitchers won ten or more games, but three others won nine and Johnnie Murphy won eight out of the bullpen.

But Lefty was no longer a nine-inning pitcher. He started twenty-three games but completed only eight. Murphy as often as not finished up. "It was always nice to see Murphy coming in to save me," Lefty noted. "He listed me as a dependent on his income tax."

Lefty had developed other special relationships. "June and I lived only a couple of doors away from the New York Athletic Club. When the Yankees played a home series during the season, or whenever I happened to be in New York, I worked out there, running, swimming, and playing racquetball. After pitching, swimming was the main way I relaxed and lengthened the muscles in my body.

"Sometimes a big, burly guy would lumber over and engage me in conversation. Invariably, he ended with the same question: 'You wanna box?' Taking in his size, I said, 'Hell, no. I'll run around the track. I don't want someone like you poking my ribs.'

"One day, he followed me around the club, hounding me about getting in the boxing ring. Every time I said no, he gave me a jab in the ribs. I was so pissed off that he wouldn't take no for an answer that I left the club in a huff. June was waiting in the car. 'A guy in there is a damn nuisance. Box, box, box. Wants to knock me flat with a quick punch to the chin.' June asked his name. 'I don't know. He wrote a war novel . . . something about a bell tolling.'

"June exclaims, 'That's Ernest Hemingway! Go get his autograph for me before he leaves the club.' I told her, 'No way. I just told him he was a goddamn pest and to leave me alone.'

"Hemingway and I went on to enjoy a long friendship together. Down through the years, whenever we met, as a way of greeting, he'd give me a jab in the ribs."

IN THE WORLD SERIES, the Yankees were to meet the team Lefty had talked himself out of being traded to. The Dodgers had won their first pennant since 1920, when they were still called the Robins. The two teams had never before met for the championship.

Fans and players alike expected that Ruffing and Gomez, or Gomez and Ruffing, the two most renowned big-game pitchers in baseball, would once again lead the October charge. After all, after Ed Barrow announced that Lefty would remain with the team, McCarthy was quoted as saying, "When Lefty had it, he'd give it to you. He'd pitch every day if you wanted him to. He never had an alibi or an ache or a pain that would stop him from going in there when you asked him to. That's why I gave Gomez another chance in 1941."

The Series went five games, the Dodgers winning only once. McCarthy used five different starting pitchers. Lefty was not one of them.

Joe McCarthy never explained why he'd kept the best pitcher in World Series history on the bench for five games and Lefty never publicly discussed it. But after the Yankees had won, he drove with Bing Russell to Bud and Ooie's cabin at Rangeley Lakes. June and Nellie were to follow with Vernona a few days later.

"We're in the car. Lefty's not saying anything and I'm not either. All of a sudden, Lefty pulls over to the side of the road, stops, and puts his head on the steering wheel. He turns, looks me dead in the eye, and he says, 'It's a terrible, terrible thing to be so close to the game and so far away.' Then he put the car in gear and away we went. And the subject of not pitching in the 1941 Series was never mentioned again, never over a lifetime.

"Not to be in the game. It was an excruciating pain for him, a feeling so empty. Lefty always wanted to compete, put himself on the line."

31

EIGHTY INNINGS

W AR HAD BEEN RAGING IN EUROPE AND ASIA, AND ON DECEMBER 7, 1941, it came to America. Across the nation, thousands of young men and women rushed to enlist. Although some baseball players were among the early throng, most remained with their teams, but it wasn't for lack of patriotism.

In January 1942, Commissioner Landis had sent a telegram to President Roosevelt asking whether baseball should continue while the nation was at war. Roosevelt replied with the famous "green light letter."

"I honestly feel," the president wrote, "that it would be best for the country to keep baseball going. There will be fewer people unemployed and everybody will work longer hours and harder than ever before. And that means that they ought to have a chance for recreation and for taking their minds off their work even more than before. Baseball provides a recreation which does not last over two hours or two hours and a half, and which can be got for very little cost."

So while Hank Greenberg and Bob Feller led a contingent that enlisted immediately, Ted Williams, Stan Musial, Joe DiMaggio, Phil Rizzuto, and Tommy Henrich, among others, all played in 1942 before entering the service.

THE 1941 WORLD SERIES had been Lefty's last chance. At spring training in 1942, although he made light of it, the end was coming fast. His fastball was only a memory, and as Dizzy Dean had learned, there was only so long a pitcher could survive on slow stuff and experience. Decades of pitching whenever he could get a baseball in his hand had done Lefty in. "In those last years," he said, "I could go maybe six innings. Then my arm would stiffen up, and I just couldn't go any more."

In no position to bargain, even after a fifteen-win season, Lefty was the first pitcher to sign a contract for the 1942 season. He pitched well in the spring, but it was clear from his limited innings that his spot in the rotation was tenuous.

Spring training 1942 also provided evidence of the hyperbole that would later surround Joe DiMaggio. Dottie had given birth to Joe junior the previous October, and although Joe hadn't signed a contract, he, Dottie, Lefty, and June had come south together, accompanied by their children. As was widely reported later, Joe was stunningly prudish about his wives, both Dottie and later Marilyn Monroe.

"Dottie was a beautiful girl," said Bing Russell. "Gorgeous figure and a fun person to be with. Joe was so in love with her but he was also insanely jealous."

Such a relationship was primed for overstatement. A biographer reported that Joe was so outraged when he first saw Dottie in a two-piece bathing suit during a Jones Beach outing with the Gomezes during the 1942 season that, after ordering her to put her blouse back on, he drove off in a huff, abandoning the rest of the group and forcing them to beg a ride back to the city from a stranger. Dottie had then supposedly taken refuge at June and Lefty's, and when Lefty drove Joe to the ballpark each day, DiMaggio refused to acknowledge her existence.

In February, however, five months before the alleged Jones Beach incident took place, a news photographer snapped a picture of the two couples smiling on a beach in St. Pete. June, pregnant with Gery, is wearing a dress, but Dottie, four months after giving birth to Joe junior, is sitting next to her husband, her knee resting casually against Joe's arm, wearing what is distinctly a two-piece bathing suit. In another photo, also from spring training, Joe and Dottie, once again in a two-piece, were caught bicycling together, and in yet another they were sitting on a veranda. It seems as if Dottie wore her two-piece all through spring training and Joe did not once stalk off.

WHEN THE SEASON BEGAN, Lefty had been reduced to an afterthought on the Yankee staff, going sometimes two weeks between mound appearances. Still, he didn't lose his sense of humor. To replace Johnny Sturm, who had been drafted, the Yankees had acquired a journeyman first baseman named Buddy Hassett who liked to sing. Some sportswriter nicknamed him "The Bronx Thrush." Fodder for Gomez, as The Bronx Thrush recounted.

"After a night game in Cleveland, Lefty, DiMaggio, and I drop into a joint for a beer. I go to the gents' room, and when I come back, Lefty asks me, 'How's your voice?' I ask him what he means. Just then, the owner of the club grabs the mike and announces to the crowd, 'We have a young fellow here who sings Irish songs. Would you folks like to hear him?' The audience applauds and calls out, 'Yes!' 'Okay, Hassett,' Lefty said, 'you're on.' DiMaggio is sitting there, laughing his head off. I'm thinking to myself, 'What the hell is going on here?' but I like to sing in the shower, so I get up and croon 'When Irish Eyes Are Smiling' and 'Galway Bay.' The people clap and I return to our table. The owner comes up and says to Lefty, 'Okay. I'll give you $200 a week for three weeks.' When the guy leaves, I find out from Joe that Lefty told the owner he was a theatrical agent. 'I'm managing a young Irish tenor trying to break into show business. If you like him, let me know.' All this while I took a pee."

Sometimes comic relief in a grim year was provided by others. "Jack Dempsey, two-year-old Vernona, and I were on our way to Boston," Lefty said. "We're driving out of Manhattan and Vernona wants to drop the ten-cent toll into the basket going across the bridge. I stop the car and she tosses the dime out the side window but she misses the basket and the dime rolls onto the ground. The toll clerk comes out of the booth. He's yelling at Vernona. 'Pick it up! Pick it up! You're holding up traffic!'

"Vernona's crying and Jack jumps out of the car. He's not taking any more lip from the bastard. He grabs the guy by the lapels and growls, 'What the hell are you yapping about? Making the little girl cry over a dime. Put your own goddamn dime in.' Jack bounces the guy's feet on the cement, jumps in the car, and we drive away."

The 1942 season was played in the cloud of escalating war. FDR's dictum notwithstanding, many fans seemed uncomfortable enjoying themselves at a ball game while American troops were being pushed across the Pacific by the Japanese and mobilizing to fight the Germans in North Africa. Major league attendance declined from 9.9 million fans in 1941 to only 8.55 million in 1942 and would decrease another 1.1 million in 1943.*

But patriotic fervor was stoked by other venues of the entertainment industry. "To rally the country on Memorial Day 1942, Warner Bros. sold war bonds as 'tickets' to the New York premiere of *Yankee Doodle Dandy*," Elaine Klein reported. "The publicity stunt raised over $5 million. It was the first time Cagney attended a premiere and he won an Oscar for his performance.

"Lefty was out of town with the Yankees, so June called me at Polly's penthouse and told me she had two war bond tickets. I was fourteen at the time . . . so thrilled. I dressed to the nines and June looked stunning in a sapphire blue evening gown that highlighted the fact that there was a baby on the way and she was proud of it. As we stepped out of a cab to enter the Hollywood theater on Broadway, the photographers were snapping her picture and I could hear the fans cordoned off to the side shouting, 'It's June O'Dea. She danced in *Billie*.' I was so proud to be with her.

"June visited with James Cagney and his wife at the premiere and congratulated him on his performance. She said Cohan couldn't have done Cohan any better. The Cagneys were old friends of the family. Sunny and Frankie Conville had worked with him on the RKO vaudeville circuits. Before Cagney became Hollywood's Public Enemy No. 1 in films, he, Conville, and George Raft were singing waiters at Brighton Beach eateries."

On the field, the 1942 pennant race in the American League was as predictable as ever. The Yankees, who had yet to lose anyone significant to the military, once again won more than a hundred games and finished

---

* It would rebound to 8.7 million in 1944, when the war was going better, increase to 10.8 million in 1945, and explode to 18.5 million fans in 1946.

nine games ahead of the Red Sox. Such was the surreal nature of wartime baseball that the St. Louis Browns finished third.

Lefty pitched only eighty innings, starting only thirteen games and finishing but two. He gave up 67 hits in those innings and walked 65 more, against only 41 strikeouts. His record was 6–4, but on a weaker-hitting team, it would have been much worse.

The Yankees were prohibitive favorites going into the World Series against the Cardinals. Before game one, Lefty pitched batting practice for twenty minutes. Newspapers reported that, "once the definite series opener in happier days, nobody has any idea that Lefty will start a game." He did not, nor did he pitch out of the bullpen.

After thirteen years with the team, in which he had pitched brilliantly and pitched hurt, had been both a steadying and diverting presence in the locker room, and had been universally valued as a teammate, Lefty had been relegated to tossing batting practice.

The Yankees took the first game in St. Louis, then proceeded to lose the next four. A stunned team dispersed for the off-season, traveling to their homes in the uncertainty of a nation at war. When the Yankees reassembled in St. Petersburg the following spring, many of the younger players would not be there, and some of the older ones as well.

On January 26, 1943, Lefty was given his unconditional release by the New York Yankees.

PART 3

"WHEN I MARRIED LEFTY, I MARRIED BASEBALL"

32

"YOU COULD SEE IT WAS GONE"

WITH THE HUMAN TOUCH FOR WHICH HE WAS FAMOUS, ED BARROW did not bother to inform "one of his favorite players" of the end of his Yankee career. Lefty and June were staying at the Pine Meadow Country Club when a local reporter knocked on the door to tell him the news.

What baseball was only slowly coming to understand, army doctors already knew. After the 1942 season, when he reported to his draft board for a physical, Lefty was immediately rejected, classified 4-F, with torn muscles in his shoulder, back, and side. Lefty was none too pleased at being declared unfit and told the army officer at the draft board, "If I can shoot bullets to home plate, I can handle a gun overseas." But the officer, unfortunately, was a baseball fan. He replied, "You're right, but I seem to recall that lately you've been missing the strike zone. You're 4-F, Lefty. That's final. Take a job at a defense plant."

Reluctantly, he did. "The army got me a job at General Electric over in Lynn for $40 a week, counting nuts and bolts for the government. I'm counting them one at a time and the GE foreman comes by and asks me what I'm doing. 'Well, you put me on this,' I told him, 'and I'm counting the nuts and bolts.' 'We don't count them, Lefty,' the foreman said. 'We weigh them.'" Soon afterward, Lefty was made a dispatcher in the Marine Turbine Department, where he spent the remainder of the off-season.

After his release, Lefty was claimed at the waiver price by the Boston Braves. He'd gone from a first-place team to the bottom, but he refused to whine. "I pitched myself into an unconditional release," he told the press, then pronounced himself "tickled to death for the chance to play ball somewhere." He later acknowledged, "Of course, it was a surprise. These things always are."

Arthur Daley wrote, "Life with the Yankees will not be the same anymore. Lefty Gomez has departed and the stadium will be a more quiet and somber place. Its sparkle has transferred to the Boston Braves. Before Boston has completed its first swing around the circuit, Lefty will have acquired hundreds of new friends, including, perhaps, a couple of umpires. . . . Everyone was his friend. He had no enemies." Daley also acknowledged that "the speed and cunning have gone from his arm and Lefty is near the end of the baseball trail. Maybe he has reached it." The column closed, "Good luck, Lefty, it's sad to see you go."

As Daley intimated and as with Babe eight years earlier, it seemed that the signing was as much for publicity as for on-field improvement. The notion of El Goofo pitching for the equally eccentric Braves manager, Casey Stengel, already known as "The Professor," would certainly bring fans into the park. And the Braves needed whatever assistance they could muster. One night during the previous season, the announced attendance at 40,000-seat Braves Field was 750.

That the Braves had decided to give Lefty his shot was as much due to family connections as to the opportunity to provide diversion to the Braves' stunted fan base. Bob Quinn, who had bought the Red Sox from Harry Frazee in 1923 at a fire-sale price and had then been forced to sell the team to the Yawkey family ten years later for a Depression-era price, had become president and general manager of the Braves after a short stint as general manager of the Dodgers. The Quinns were old friends of the Gradys, and June's cousin Mary had once dated Quinn's son Jack. Quinn had therefore known Lefty for years and if anyone would give Gomez one last shot, it was him.

Still, there was no denying the theatrical aspect of the signing. "What a nine we had," Lefty said. "Stengel as manager and all of us non-draftable because of dependency, injuries, or bad health. We couldn't see, couldn't walk. Casey had been hit by a taxi and, after the accident, he hobbled around the field. Every two weeks this team of lame ballplayers left Braves Park and marched in back of Stengel with his bad wheel next door to the

Commonwealth Armory to have an up-to-date army physical to see if we could make the list."

Publicly, Lefty was of course upbeat. "The arm feels better this spring than it did last season. I could have pitched more last year, but McCarthy never used me after that night game in Philadelphia. Maybe he was trying to save Murphy."

Although he neglected to mention it to the writers, Lefty counseled Boston's young pitchers, even though their improved performance would threaten his own tenure with the team. Many of them credited him with making them more effective on the mound. One said, "Gomez has done more to rid the Braves of their defeatist complex than a dozen victories over the Dodgers would."

But to stick, even with the Braves, Lefty was going to have to demonstrate he could still pitch on a major league level.

He couldn't.

On May 19, the Braves chose to keep the younger pitchers Lefty had helped and gave him his outright release. Lefty told the writers that he just needed the weather to warm to increase his effectiveness. The moribund Phillies were willing to give him a shot, but Lefty signed with the Senators, resigned to a relief role.

Oswald Bluege, the Senators' manager, had been a fine infielder in the 1920s and 1930s. "We were in need of a relief pitcher. Well, Vernon . . . I always called him Vernon . . . had been one hell of a pitcher for a long time. I was going over the lists with Mr. Griffith. 'Well, there's not too much available,' Mr. Griffith said. 'Let's take a chance with Gomez. He might help us win a few ball games here and there.' So we claimed him, hoping against hope. But when he went out to pitch you could see it was gone."

The ending, as for so many athletes, was poignant. The Senators started Lefty in the second game of a doubleheader against the White Sox. His opponent was Thornton Lee and the umpire was George Pipgras. In front of 22,000 fans, many of whom had come to see him, Lefty pitched four and two-thirds innings, gave up four hits, four runs, five walks, and did not strike out a batter. The Senators kept him on the roster for another five weeks, but he did not pitch again.

Finally, on July 6, with Washington scheduled to open against the Tigers in Detroit, Griffith called Ossie Bluege on the telephone. "He said to give Gomez his release. It was up to me to tell him. Well, one of the hardest things for a manager to do is release a veteran, to have to tell a man he can't cut it anymore. When I walked into his hotel room, I said, 'Vernon, I guess you know what this is all about.'

" 'Yeah, damn it, I know,' he said.

" 'I hate to do it.'

" 'It's part of the game, Oz,' he said.

" 'It hurts like hell, it really does,' I said.

" 'You've got to do it,' Lefty said. 'It goes with the job. I wasn't helping the club. I don't blame you at all. You're doing the right thing.'

"And he went on like that. The son of a gun. I went up there to break the bad news to him, he saw how unhappy I was about it, and he ended up consoling me instead of the other way around. But that's the kind of guy Vernon was. A real pro. A real man."

The Tigers, generally acknowledged as the team with the weakest pitching staff in the American League, made no move to sign him, and Vernon Gomez, now an unemployed former major leaguer, quietly left town.

Whitey Lewis, a columnist for the *Cleveland Press*, penned a long, appreciative farewell. "The guy's arm must be gone altogether . . . when amateurish citizens who couldn't in normal times carry the water pail into major league ballparks are drawing solid pay for masquerading as athletes. . . . Now it's the minors or some laboring job for El Goofo, and I suppose you should stir your coffee and be hard and harsh about the whole matter. After all, other big league baseball players have washed out. Others have looked forlornly at arms that once were of steel, later were of putty. Yet Gomez should be different. He had something . . . glamour.

" 'Good copy,' screamed editors from coast to coast. Gomez was aware of the value of a statement properly produced and placed. Yet he was definitely sincere in his ever-boyish attitude toward baseball. I have ridden many trains with Gomez and the other Yanks and we have talked baseball well into the night. . . . He would tell wide-eyed about long hits he had seen and he would talk about the great players, and Gomez, the great pitcher, was just a kid sparking.

"They say he needs a pitching job, or some kind of a job now, to keep eating. I wouldn't know about that. I'd rather not even think about it. I prefer to remember El Goofo as a handsome pitcher with fire in his eyes, his arm and his voice, with glamour and sheen, the spotlight picked out. Best of all, I like to think of him as a competitor. That, Gomez was always."

Such mournful sentiment might come from the press, but it wasn't going to come from Lefty. Although he privately referred to the Yankee president as "Scrooge McBarrow," Lefty told reporters later many years later, "Baseball doesn't owe me a penny. Everything I have, my life, my family, my friends, I owe to baseball. Missing the era of the big pay-checks doesn't bother me. I wouldn't change my era for today's game. I played with people like Babe Ruth, Lou Gehrig, and Joe DiMaggio. I played against Ted Williams, Carl Hubbell, and Rogers Hornsby. How can you put a price tag on something like that? Besides, our salaries in the thirties weren't bad because the cost of living was low. Overall, I was satisfied with what I got paid and I'm proud to be able to say that I played when I did."

Lefty, June, Vernona, and Gery moved to Kew Gardens in Queens. They rented a house next to a mortuary, and Lefty told the press, "I have a permanent order in for the first good left arm that comes along."

Lefty charmed his new neighbors in the quiet residential neighbor-hood in the boroughs every bit as much as he had in the glitter of Manhat-tan. Ann Angrason, whose husband, John, owned the funeral home, described the scene: "Lefty was in and out of the funeral parlor all the time, he and Johnny chatting up the day. One time, during a funeral, when it's always very quiet, the mourners sitting there, sad and gloomy, Lefty suddenly comes barging in the front door, running up the front stairs, yell-ing, 'Hey Johnnyyyyyy!' When the buzz went around the chapel that it was Lefty Gomez outside, the people ran out of the chapel and started talking with him and soon he's spinning stories. Next thing you know, the mourners are laughing and they can't stop. He could make people laugh at a funeral. That was Lefty."

The Gomez house had an immense yard. If Lefty was outside, the trolleys that ran along Metropolitan Avenue often made an unscheduled stop. "The bells clanged, the trolley doors swung open, and down the stairs came the conductor to talk to Lefty, leaving the passengers looking out the windows at the two of them laughing away."

One of the neighbors, an elderly gent named Mr. Mountain, lived in an apartment across the street. "Every time he and Lefty talked," Ann Angrason related, "Monty said he wished he had a vegetable garden. He loved to hoe and weed, and watch vegetables grow. One day, Lefty said, 'Put your garden in my front yard. Just give me some vegetables once in a while.' Monty was out there the next morning. As the summer went by, his garden took up a third of the land. With wartime rationing, Monty's vegetables were a welcome addition to dinner plates of the neighborhood. In the cabbage patch, there was one cabbage that Lefty's Sealyham, Colonel, claimed for his own. Every morning he peed on it. It grew and it grew. Gigantic. The day Lefty picked it, we had a party."

For the kids, it was all a party. "Everyone piling into Mom and Dad's bed on Sunday morning for a pillow fight, then Dad reading us the newspaper comics . . . Mom ending the day with a favorite fairy tale . . . a three-story house furnished in art deco . . . chrome tables and chairs, white walls, white carpeting, and a white upright piano . . . draperies and slip-covered sofas in a vivid green, leafy design. Wartime in the forties . . . before turning on the lights, running through all the rooms and pulling down the green window shades so no light beams can be detected by enemy aircraft flying overhead . . . Mom's homemade soups on the coal stove, and her handmade clothes for the children . . . measles, mumps, and itchy chicken-pox scabs covered with calamine lotion . . . ice-cream cones from Dad to ease the pain . . . pigtails and crew cuts . . . Holy Child Jesus elementary school, spelling bees . . . multiplication tables by rote . . . after the homework, outside on the sidewalk, and strapping metal roller skates onto our shoes and whizzing up and down the uneven pavements till we fall, scraping our knees . . . hopscotch and Simon Says . . . tricycles, then graduating to two-wheelers with Dad holding the handlebars until we can pedal and balance by ourselves . . . *Pinocchio*, the family's first Disney movie, and returning home to find that we're locked out because Dad forget the house key, and he has to climb the oak tree to the second-story bedroom and break a window to get us inside . . . and the winter holidays and the subway ride to Macy's windows at Broadway and 34th Street, hand in hand with Mom and Dad, jostled along by the crowds as we pass by the magical displays of Christmas elves making toys for good little boys and girls . . . that was us."

With the family settled, Lefty took a job as recreational director for the Carl E. Norden Company, which manufactured precision bombsights. The factory was in lower Manhattan and boasted a four-acre recreation field near the entrance to the Holland Tunnel. Lefty was responsible for the industrial league baseball team, but also, among other tasks, supervising the bowling league, and sports as diverse as archery and ice skating.

Lefty still wanted to pitch somewhere, to stay in the game, so he signed on with the Brooklyn Bushwicks at $200 per week. The Bushwicks, a storied semipro team that operated from 1917 to 1951, played their games at 15,500-seat Dexter Park, which was not in Brooklyn but Queens, less than a mile from Kew Gardens. The field had once been a racecourse, and rumor had it that it was named for a horse named Dexter who had dropped dead and was buried in right field.

The Bushwicks were almost the perfect polyglot. The players were mostly white, the owner was a Jew, and the opponents were often teams from the Negro Leagues. They had hit against Satchel Paige and pitched to Josh Gibson. Jackie Robinson had played against the Brooklyn Bushwicks before he played for the Brooklyn Dodgers. When the major league season ended, the Bushwicks often scheduled exhibitions against ad hoc teams whose members had included Babe Ruth, Dizzy Dean, Lou Gehrig, Hank Greenberg, Phil Rizzuto, and Joe DiMaggio.

Max Rosner, the Bushwicks' owner, signed major leaguers whenever he could. Sometimes active players moonlighted after the season, often using aliases, to pick up a few extra bucks a week, and sometimes retired players signed on just to keep playing. Lefty didn't join the Bushwicks as a way to get back to the majors; he knew his career was over. But here was an opportunity to spend a bit more time doing what he loved.

"I walked over to Dexter Park in some old clothes and slippers that had been retrieved from the refuse heap," he related with the usual hyperbole. "The clubhouse attendant was a veteran and, because I showed up early, he must have figured I was just a has-been looking for a workout. 'There's a nail over there, bub,' he said. 'Hang up your jacket.' I looked at the nail and spiders were playing leapfrog in the cobwebs. The dressing-room man roused me from my stupor by shouting, 'Come on! You haven't much time. The regulars will be here soon. Here's a uniform to put on.'

" 'I'll bet Lincoln wore that,' I told him."

In his first game, Lefty not only pitched four innings of one-hit ball against the Black Yankees but socked a 400-foot triple, which raised the question: If the Bushwicks played against such high-class competition, how could Gomez achieve three bases, a feat never before seen in his almost twenty years of organized baseball?

The answer was simple. Lefty had boasted to Max Rosner that he would hit a home run. Rosner scoffed and money was put on the table. Lefty then persuaded the Black Yankee pitcher to put one right down the middle and the outfielders to pursue any ball hit to them without enthusiasm. All went according to plan until Lefty more or less collapsed rounding third. Three hundred sixty feet was simply too far to run on one hit.

Even with the Bushwicks to keep him in the game, Lefty remained determined to go overseas. If the army wouldn't let him fight, he would entertain. In early fall, he signed on for a three-month USO tour of Africa and Italy, part of a three-man sports contingent that included Fred Corcoran, head of the Professional Golfers Association tour, and former heavyweight champ Jack Sharkey. In Italy, the trio would join a larger tour that included comedian Joe E. Brown and Humphrey Bogart. Their assignment was to visit hospitals near the front lines and do what they could to cheer up wounded soldiers.

Since he would be overseas at Christmas, Lefty decided to have a festive pre-holiday celebration. A special Christmas tree seemed just the ticket. Ann Angrason's daughter Julie, twelve at the time, later recalled just how special it was. "Lefty wanted the children's mouths to drop open when they saw the tree, so he drove upstate and chopped down a monster evergreen. He tied it to the top of his car and drove back to Kew Gardens in the snow. He loosened the ropes and tried to drag it up the stone steps into the front hallway, but the tree was so tall and so wide that, once he pulled it in, he couldn't make a right bend into the living room without cutting the tree in half. He tossed the top half down the steps, and now he had the tree in the room but the evergreen was so wide, everything was lost to sight except the tree. June brought in boxes of tiny ornaments and they began decorating a tree that stopped in the middle. The ornaments looked lost because they were decorating a forest. I will never, ever forget it. When the kids came in to experience the wonder of it all, they get smacked in the face with an evergreen branch."

Lefty had taken a leave of absence from both Norden and the Bushwicks, and on November 20 he boarded a ship in New York harbor to head for Africa. Journalist James Kearns of the *Chicago Sun* described the tour. "A 2,000 mile trek through the Mediterranean, Sicilian, and Italian areas, where American boys fight and rest and recuperate, under the auspices of the USO. Gomez, Corcoran, and Sharkey did a 9 a.m. to 11 a.m. daily show on stage, when there was a stage. Then the little shows; kidding, talking, visiting, bed to bed in Casablanca, North Africa, Port Lyautey, Algiers, Bizerte, Constantine, Tunis, and then two months in Italy and France, nearly all of it in hospitals close to the front lines.

"They had about 50 minutes of sports movies with them . . . golf shorts, the recent 1943 World Series, past Series, and knockout rounds of heavyweight championship fights since Dempsey-Firpo. After the movies, Corcoran would interview Gomez and Sharkey, and Gomez would kibitz on Sharkey's replies. . . . He would quiz Sharkey on every fight he ever lost, and there were quite a few. Then the boys in the wheelchairs or the beds, or wherever the show was on, would ask question after question."

Corcoran remembered the commitment of his mates. "Gomez and Sharkey worked long and diligently at their job on the tour. . . . Lefty was standing next to the bed of a wounded kid in from the battlefield who looked up at him and said, 'I know you could pitch, but you have to admit you had a couple of weaknesses with a bat in your hand.' Gomez grinned and nodded his head. 'Only one weakness, really. A pitched ball.' "

The story the GIs always wanted Lefty to recount had occurred during an at-bat in Cleveland. "I was pitching against Bob Feller," Lefty recounted. "Bobby was a young kid who could bring it in blazing fast. He was also on the wild side, which added to the intimidation the sluggers felt at the plate. Late in the afternoon, black clouds rolled in from Lake Erie. It got darker and darker and every inning McCarthy asked Bill Summers, the umpire, to call the game so the hitters in those pre-helmet days wouldn't get skulled. Summers refused. He said thousands of fans were in the stands to see the game. By the time I stepped into the batter's box it was drizzling rain. Feller's ball was a misty blur. I reached into my pocket, pulled out a book of matches, lit one, and held it up in front of my face. 'Feller can see the plate,' Summers growled. 'I'm not worried about the plate. I want to make damn sure Feller can see me.' Summers fined me $50 for that caper."

The trip also had its odd and scary moments. "In Italy one day," Francis J. Powers reported, "after a rumor that the Allied forces had to retreat, the trio was moving towards the front, and Lefty was strangely silent as he watched truck after truck filled with soldiers going the other way. Finally, he tapped the driver on the shoulder and said, 'Will you find out if those guys are coming or going. I don't believe in getting anywhere before the army.'"

Lefty was also skittish of booby traps. "We moved into Italy behind the Fifth Army," Fred Corcoran said. "The closer we got to the front, the more leery Lefty became. He wouldn't touch anything that looked like it might have a wire or a package of TNT hooked on at the other end. And he always gave a wide berth to anything he saw lying on the ground unless he thought it had been lying there for at least a couple of centuries. On one occasion, up near the front, I stopped to pick up a ring I had seen half buried in the mud. He nearly knocked me down with the lunge he made to head me off."*

After he returned home in February 1944, Lefty described the experience for himself. "I'm delighted to be back in the States. Anyone who says

---

* During the tour, Lefty had another odd encounter with Moe Berg. "We were on our way from Italy to France and I saw Moe standing on a bombed-out street. I called out, 'Hey, Moe, how are you?' Moe put his index finger over his lips and kept looking around, acting mysterious. I just kept on going towards the front where we were to entertain the troops. Humphrey Bogart and Joe E. Brown were ahead of us and waiting. The entire incident lasted just seconds."

he isn't frightened at the front lines or during an air raid is crazy. I was so scared running for a shelter that I thought I was standing in the same place until I noticed I wasn't losing any ground on those in front of me."

He summed up the trip typically: "It's a good thing I wasn't pitching overseas. With all those planes flying overhead, the opposition would have won a hundred to nothing."

But there were also incidents for which levity was inappropriate. "Visiting with our boys in the hospital wards . . . even though wounded, they loved to play pranks on us, and I shared many a laugh with them. But we also saw men brought in on stretchers who were badly maimed, their uniforms bullet-riddled, many without legs and arms, others with their feet and hands frozen, their eyes bandaged, their lips clenched in pain but still holding on to that fighting spirit . . . the one thing that can pull them through the horror of their wounds. God, it's an awful sight and one I will never forget.

"There were also many touching moments. Sharkey, Bogart, Joe E. Brown, and I had entertained in a ward, and, after the show, one of the boys called me over. One arm had been blown off and the other was in a cast. He said, 'Lefty, I loved the show. I didn't applaud, but it wasn't because I didn't want to.' I was so touched by his generous spirit. He made me so happy that I was there to bring a laugh to boys like him, but it also made me very, very sad that war exists."

33

FIELD GENERAL

F OR THE REMAINDER OF THE WAR LEFTY REMAINED IN NEW YORK, FIRST working for Norden, then switching to a similar position with Westside Iron Works. In the early fall of 1945, an odd opportunity surfaced. A wealthy Venezuelan industrialist named Martin Tovar Lange asked Lefty to come to Caracas to set up pitching clinics for Latin players and black Americans who had come to South America to avoid the segregation of American professional baseball. Lefty was always pleased for the opportunity to teach baseball; he was especially pleased to be asked to teach these particular players. He had never agreed with the major league ban on African Americans and knew full well his visit to South America would draw attention in the press. Nellie was thrilled with the chance to play grandmother to Vernona and Gery in Kew Gardens, so Lefty and June flew to Miami and then on to South America.

Lefty arrived in a sprawling metropolis very much unlike New York. "In the mid-forties," he said, "Caracas was a cosmopolitan city in an oil-rich country, where most of the people were poor. There was a country-club set of wealthy coffee and sugar plantation owners, an almost nonexistent middle class, and the barefoot poor who lived in homes of tin-roofed cinder blocks without water or electricity. It was common to see university students sitting on the curbs studying their books under the street lamps because they couldn't afford lightbulbs.

"The politics were as hot as the coffee. They changed presidents quicker than we changed pitchers on a bad day. Shortly before our plane landed in Caracas, there had been a coup, bringing about a change in political leadership and turmoil on the streets. A riot could erupt at any time and anywhere. Protesters waved placards and pistols, shouting that unfair government policies were directed against the poor. Adding to the unrest were rumors that local Communists backed by Moscow wanted to nationalize foreign oil companies. Robbers were everywhere and they carried guns. If your pocket was empty, he'd shoot you for 'wasting his time.' June and I carried a $100 bill at all times. We didn't want to upset the robbers. One morning, I was having my shoes polished at a corner street stand when the shoeshine boy was shot dead by a stray bullet. For the rest of my stay, I decided scuffed-up shoes were in fashion."

Through it all, life went on, even moved forward. Two days after Christmas 1945, Tovar and three other Venezuelans founded the Liga de Béisbol Profesional de Venezuela, South America's first professional baseball league. The four teams would begin play the following month. Managing Tovar's team, Cerveceria Caracas, the "Brewers," was none other than that famed pitcher "of Castilian descent," Vernon Gomez. As the Associated Press pointed out, however, lineage was deceiving. "1. The team is comprised of Venezuelans. 2. The players speak no English. 3. Gomez speaks no Spanish. 4. And Lefty has never managed before."

Lefty, of course, found humor in the appointment—he said he might be forced to communicate in sign language, as in baseball signs—but his acceptance of the manager's position made an even larger statement than simply running clinics. A cadre of highly talented black and Latino ballplayers played winter ball in Latin America. Roy Campanella, for example, who would go on to win three National League Most Valuable Player awards and be inducted into the Hall of Fame, was the catcher for Vargas, the eventual league champions. Sam Jethroe, who would win the National League Rookie of the Year award in 1950 at age thirty-three, was on the same club. And so Lefty became the first important American major leaguer to manage a mixed-race team; he was, as he described himself, "a pioneer."

Pressure against segregated baseball had begun to increase with the close of World War II, and in August 1945 Branch Rickey infuriated much of white America by signing Jackie Robinson to a minor league contract. In November, Robinson joined a group of black all-stars in Venezuela that played against clubs from Caribbean nations. For the 1946 season,

Robinson was to report to the Dodgers' top farm team in Montreal. Canada had no segregation laws, but Montreal's road games would be in American cities.

With this most inflammatory issue at hand, the fact that an acknowledged star such as Lefty Gomez would publicly proclaim he found race irrelevant helped undermine the racial intransigence of big league baseball. In fact, Pee Wee Reese, the Brooklyn Dodgers' Kentucky-born shortstop who was later credited with gaining acceptance for Robinson, said, "Lefty helped break the color line in baseball. Lefty never saw color. He only saw ability. That's why, in 1945, when black players were still banned in major league baseball, he went to Caracas. It was his way of telling the brass back home that 'Hey, there's talent here and it has nothing to do with skin color.' "

"On the roster," Lefty noted, "were Regino Otero, Oscar Rodriguez, and Rafael Noble from Cuba, now in the Cuban Baseball Hall of Fame, and Chico Carrasquel from Caracas. Noble went to the majors as a catcher for the New York Giants. Chico Carrasquel broke into the big leagues in 1950 with the Chicago White Sox, and Regino Otero played first base for the Chicago Cubs and later, as a scout for Branch Rickey, signed Mike Scioscia."

Talented though the players might have been, Venezuelan baseball had its oddities. "The fans and the officials at the game took every play on the field very seriously. So seriously, in fact, that if the fans didn't like what a hitter did at the plate, they hurled curses and bottles of beer at him. One day, after my pitcher walked four men in a row, the referee blew his whistle and a police wagon drove onto the diamond and my player was put into the wagon and driven to jail. The police booked him on the charge that he wasn't trying to strike the guys out. In another game, a fistfight broke out in the sixth inning, and soldiers ran out onto the field and took the feuding ballplayers off to the pokey."

June, whose passion for exotic travel would never wane, saw the experience more romantically. "Caracas sits high in a valley, the city separated from the Caribbean by Mount Avila. We lived on the slopes in the Hotel Avila, a white stucco colonial hotel built by Nelson Rockefeller in 1942. The hotel was fifteen minutes from the blaring taxi horns of downtown

Caracas, a quiet oasis for Lefty and me with its lush grounds of fountains and flowers.

"The days were spring-like, around 68 degrees. But sometimes the nights became cold and clammy, so the hotel staff burned mahogany logs in the fireplaces. Mahogany was native to Venezuela and used as a cheap source of heat. Thinking of how expensive mahogany furniture was back in the States, the burning logs never ceased to amaze me. When Lefty returned from the ballpark, many times we rode the cable car from our hotel at the base of the mountain to the 1,200-foot summit, where we enjoyed a beautiful view of the city. Other times, we hiked to the top. When we ventured downtown sightseeing, we traveled on a trolley called the BoBo Express. The back streets were so narrow that when the trolley went by the apartments, people hanging out the windows could shake our hands. Lefty always wanted to ring the trolley bell, so every time we boarded the BoBo, he gave the conductor two American cigarettes so he could go 'ding, ding.' "

As a celebrity, Lefty was asked to any number of prestigious events. On one occasion, a high government official invited them to the Plaza de Toros for what he described as a "once-in-a-lifetime opportunity" to watch the great classical bullfighter Manolete. The official was prescient: Manolete was killed in the ring two years later.

"Lefty and I would not be enraptured, nor would we become aficionados of the bloody spectacle," June reported, "but I could appreciate the fearlessness of Manolete's artistry and understand why to this day he is regarded as the greatest of Spain's matadors. My memories of the slim and unsmiling Manolete are still vivid . . . he executed his famous passes, the Spanish-style classic caped moves, his body in profile to the ferocious bull, his feet planted squarely on the sand, never moving an inch as the bull repeatedly charged by him."

LEFTY AND JUNE LEFT Caracas in early spring. His squad had finished second in that inaugural thirty-game season, but his mere presence had drawn sufficient attention to the league that the results were reported in American newspapers.

After the Gomezes returned to Kew Gardens, Lefty got a phone call from Larry MacPhail, by then president of the Yankees, and another from George Selkirk, who was managing the Newark Bears, the team's top farm club. They asked him to step in as pitching coach at the Bears' spring training camp in Sebring, Florida. He agreed, but Lefty's stay in the high minors would be brief. "In mid-June, I received another phone call from MacPhail. He told me Garland Braxton, pitcher-manager of the Binghamton Triplets, the Yankee's class A club, had quit because the team was so lousy. Binghamton was last in batting and fielding in the eight-team Eastern League, which stretched from Buffalo to Reading, Pennsylvania. Larry asked me if I was up to the challenge of managing the Triplets, and I said yes."

With the initiation of AAA ball that year, Class A was now three rungs down the ladder, and the roster therefore consisted of kids just breaking in, old-timers trying to hang on, and a number of woefully out-of-shape servicemen, some recently discharged, some still awaiting discharge papers and thus still officially on the military rolls. Even worse, anyone who showed promise would immediately be raided by George Weiss, the Yankees' minor league director, and sent up the ladder, which was one of the reasons Braxton quit.

One of the servicemen was Leo Righetti, who was still in the navy and the only Triplets serviceman who had not been an officer.* "Jerry Coleman was a lieutenant in the air force and Vic Raschi was a lieutenant in the navy. I was an ordinary sailor. So Lefty says, 'Righetti is the only guy here that I can holler at.' "

In addition to his official responsibilities, being a manager allowed Lefty to live out a fantasy hefting the lumber; he appointed himself hitting coach. The light-hitting Coleman was one of his pupils. Lefty nicknamed him "Long Ball." "If he'd been a better pitcher at the time, I'd have been a better hitter," Coleman observed.

Not entirely as a result of Lefty's dual role, Binghamton's season was not a success. "We finished last on opening day," he said. "Any hopes of

---

* Leo's son Dave would pitch for the Yankees in the 1980s as both a starter and reliever before moving on to San Francisco. Dave threw a no-hitter in 1983 and was pitching coach for the world-champion Giants in 2010.

pulling the Triplets out of the cellar went down the drain every time Weiss grabbed another one of my players. When a game was rained out, we had a victory dinner." The barbs, however, were directed only at management, never the team. "The players gave me all they had. They hustled and worked hard. I could ask no more."

Managing in the minors engendered challenges not found in the big leagues. "Binghamton was at home, playing a night game. I looked around from the coaching box to give a sign to the hitter and noticed a little boy climbing high up on the screen behind the catcher. I called time and called Joe Gennarelli, the batboy, over and told him to have the boy taken off the screen and to tell his parents to either watch him more closely or leave the park. Joe soon came back and said, 'Mr. Gomez, we can't send the kid out of the park.'

" 'And why not?' I barked.

" 'Because he's your son.' And, while watching Gery to see that he got down safely, my base runner was picked off second and we lost the game."

In January 1947, Lefty and June thought about sinking roots. They bought twenty-nine acres in Durham, Connecticut, about fifteen miles northeast of New Haven, with an announced intention of building a California-style ranch house on the property. But Lefty and June never did anything simply. The site they had chosen for the house was on top of a cliff, a two-mile trek through the woods from the nearest road. So before they could build the actual dwelling, they would need to hire someone to build a road for it.

Fortunately, they didn't have to look far. A contractor they knew named Dick Pirone also lived in Queens and had a terrific reputation for honesty and quality of workmanship. He also just happened to be married to Babe Ruth's eldest daughter, Dorothy.

"I met Lefty when Dottie and I were still living in Bayside," Pirone said. "He wanted to move his family to the country and decided to buy acreage on a mountain in Durham. An architect had drawn up some blueprints for their dream house. Lefty asked me how the plans looked and I told him the construction was okay but the costs were out of line. He asked what they should be and when I told him, he said, 'How about building it for me at that price?' Lefty and I never had a contract, just a handshake. That's the way he was."

However the deal was struck, Durham was going to be a long-term project, at least three years. Soon after the land purchase, Lefty was off to the Triplets' spring training in Edenton, North Carolina.

Lefty's second year at the Binghamton helm did not promise to be a good deal better than his first. At least he couldn't finish lower in the standings. When asked how his club fared, he remarked, "To tell the truth, we finished with nine guys."

One of his spring training charges was a raw, seventeen-year-old New York pitcher named Eddie Ford, whom Lefty dubbed "Whitey." Ford stuck around just long enough to lose $5.

"One night," Whitey recalled, "I went to the carnival with my room-mate, two or three blocks from the hotel. We had a ten o'clock curfew. At about a quarter to ten, we decided to go on the Ferris wheel, figuring it'd be over in five minutes and we'd walk back to the hotel. So we get on and it goes round and round and round. The guy running the wheel won't stop it. It's getting close to ten, so we start yelling at the guy. He pretends not to hear us and we keep going around. Finally he lets us off exactly at ten, and we start running like hell back to our hotel. Who should we run into in the lobby but Gomez? It's 10:05, which means we missed curfew by five minutes. It's my first spring training and I'm scared. Gomez gives us this look and asks us where we've been. We try to explain that the guy wouldn't let us off the Ferris wheel but Lefty doesn't believe us. 'You're fined $5 each,' he says. We had to give him the money the next day."

A few days after that, Lefty farmed Whitey out to Class C Butler.

"About ten years later," Ford went on, "I'm with the Yankees, and Joe DiMaggio has a television show between games of doubleheaders. One day he has Gomez as his guest. I'm watching the show in the players' lounge and Gomez starts telling Joe about the carnival and the Ferris wheel in Edenton, North Carolina. 'I saw Ford get on the Ferris wheel,' Lefty says, 'so I went to the guy running it and gave him a couple of bucks to keep the wheel going until ten o'clock. Then I walked back to the hotel and waited in the lobby for my two pigeons.'

"After the show, Lefty came into the clubhouse with DiMaggio. 'You son of a bitch,' I said. 'How could you keep that from me all these years? Give me back that ten bucks you fined me.' Lefty laughs, reaches into his wallet, takes out a ten, and hands it to me. 'We're even now,' I said. 'You only fined me $5.' "

But Whitey also said, "I think Lefty and I were a lot alike out on the mound. We worked hard and tried our best, but we could be pretty loose when we wanted to be. And we didn't berate players about errors on the field. Lefty and I pitched cool under pressure."

The nature of managing in Class A for the Yankees meant that sometimes Lefty wouldn't even know who would be on his roster. In 1945, the Yankees had signed a top prospect, a third baseman named Jim Greengrass. The contract stipulated that Greengrass would play at Binghamton in 1947. But he never showed up at camp. Given that Greengrass was supposedly a budding star, a commodity in short supply for the Triplets, Gomez repeatedly telegraphed George Weiss to report the absence, but received no answer.

Weiss, however, knew exactly where the young third baseman was: in the army. "I had been drafted and was in boot camp in Camp Lee, Virginia," Greengrass said. "In March, I read in the camp newsletter that Binghamton was coming to play an exhibition game against our team. I walked up and introduced myself to Lefty. He says, 'Goddamn, Greengrass, where the hell have you been? We've been looking all over for you. You're supposed to be with me. What are you doing here?' I said, 'Well, that's just the way it worked out.' "

Greengrass chuckled recalling the chance encounter. "Lefty had a hairless Chihuahua named Bambi that he called 'Skin.' He carried that little bugger in the pocket of his warm-up jacket. There he is, coaching first base, and the dog is poking its head out of his coat pocket." Greengrass sighed. "So I almost got to play for Lefty at Binghamton but by the time I got there in 1948 he had moved on."

After Binghamton's 1947 season ended—another last-place finish— Lefty was invited to manage Cienfuegos in the Cuban League. Unlike the Venezuela trip, when Vernona and Gery had stayed in Kew Gardens, this time Lefty and June brought them along.

The Gomezes lived at the Hotel Nacional in Havana, an elegant Andalusian-Moorish building facing out over the Gulf of Mexico. The Brooklyn Dodgers, who had trained in Cuba the previous spring, had stayed in the Nacional as well. Branch Rickey had brought the team offshore in part to ease Jackie Robinson into the major leagues.

"The Nacional was the center for English-based social gatherings," Lefty said. "It boasted a wealthy international clientele of diplomats, businessmen, and correspondents. A woman in a downstairs apartment from ours had seven daughters and a maid for each one.

"Vernona and Gery attended a nearby elementary school where the classes were taught in Spanish, of which they spoke not a word. Vernona was in third grade, Gery in first. They weathered the curriculum because June, who spoke Spanish, translated their homework assignments. In the holiday pageant, they opted for non-speaking roles. Vernona danced as Little Miss Muffet and Gery marched as a peppermint stick."

Inventiveness was a prerequisite at the holidays. "Vernona and Gery wanted a Christmas tree, but there were no pine trees in Havana," June said. "Lefty went on a walking tour of the neighborhood and returned to the hotel with an armload of branches cut from green hedges. He wired them onto a broomstick and stuck it into a pail of stones. We trimmed it with red ribbons, candy canes and put a gold paper star at the top. Santa must have liked it, because there were presents under the tree."

One of Lefty's pitchers was future Brooklyn Dodger star Carl Erskine. "When I got out of the navy, I played one season in the minors. Branch Rickey signed me in 1946 and wanted me to go to the winter league in Havana to get some experience. It was a fourteen-team league and we played all of our games in Havana. No travel."

Erskine was assigned to Cienfuegos. "Lefty kept his players loose and he knew the game. He didn't try to mastermind everybody. Lefty had a good style . . . a balance between hands-on and hands-off."

Lefty might not have been much of a batting coach, but he certainly could teach pitching. "He gave me a chance to work on my curve," Erskine said. "By the time I came back in the spring of '48, that's what caught the eye of Branch Rickey and the Dodger management. I talked to Lefty a lot about the mechanics of pitching.

"That reminds me of a classic Lefty one-liner. He was taking part in a debate on the curveball . . . whether the pitch actually curves. Lefty said, 'I dunno. I've heard the scientists say it's just an optical illusion. All I know is, when I lost my optical illusion, I had to quit.' "

Another of Lefty's pitchers was a six-foot-four African American named Max Manning, who acquired the sobriquet "Dr. Cyclops" for his Coke-bottle glasses. Like Ryne Duren, the Yankee relief pitcher of the 1960s, Manning was a flamethrower whose questionable eyesight kept hitters from digging in at the plate.

Manning was already thirty, too old to begin a march through the minor leagues. But others still had full careers in front of them. On his return to the States, Lefty told reporters, "I saw a lot of splendid Negro players in Venezuela and Cuba, and I believe that before the Negro player of the United States lies tremendous opportunities. Brooklyn has a fine prospect in outfielder Sam Jethroe and Larry Doby can't miss developing into a great player."

Cienfeugos, which Lefty claimed to have difficulty spelling, meant "one hundred fires." "And when we lost, they built half of them right under my seat."

Lefty was only barely kidding. "The Cubans were rabid baseball fans, screaming and betting on every play of the game at the Gran Estadio," recalled Monty Basgall, who played second base for the Pirates before becoming a coach for the Dodgers in the 1970s and 1980s. "Very excitable people out at the ballpark. Fistfights broke out in the stands. Many of the fans waved guns on every pitch, and we often heard the pistol shots ringing out in the grandstand."

"The Cuban fans were wild," Erskine chuckled. "They bet on every pitch, every inning . . . everything. We had an outfielder named Pages, pronounced Pa-ghes. One night, every inning he's cheerleading. 'Get some runs, get some runs.' Next night, if a ball got by him in the outfield, he hardly said a word. We figured out it was whichever way he'd bet that night."

Wild behavior was not confined to the ballpark, as Lefty and June seemed doomed to visit countries beset by political unrest. While managing Cienfuegos, Lefty was also a member of the faculty of the Universidad de La Habana, as pitching coach for the university team. He reported to Manolo Castro del Campo, director general of national sports in the Ministry of Education. He was also a leader of the Movimiento Socialista Revolucionario. Manolo was not related to Fidel, then a law student at the university and only a minor figure in the leadership of the Socialist movement that was turning ever more extreme.

"Violence on the streets was an everyday occurrence," June said, "and we could often be found ducking into cafés to avoid being shot. One day, Vernona and I were shopping for new sandals and a riot broke out in the square. A concerned pedestrian pushed us into a portable toilet to keep us from getting hit with a stray bullet fired by the university students running through the streets. 'Señora,' he insisted, 'no come out!' And there we stood, with the stench, for an hour, until the rioting stopped and we opened the door cautiously and ran home to the safety of our hotel apartment.

"A few nights later, on February 22, 1948," June recounted, "Manolo Castro asked Lefty to attend a faculty conference meeting at the Resumen movie theater. Manolo never tired of hearing stories about Ruth and Gehrig and the glamour of pinstripes, and he wanted Lefty to regale those in attendance with his days as a Yankee. Gomez, with his gift of gab, was happy to do it. As they were leaving the theater afterward, Manolo Castro was assassinated in a drive-by shooting and five people were wounded. Luckily, Lefty was not in the front line. He was directly behind Manolo and he escaped. When Lefty returned to the hotel, he said, 'June, you may be left with two fatherless children by the end of the baseball season.' "

Fidel Castro was suspected to have been involved in the killing, but he had an alibi and was never arrested. Rumors persisted, however, that he had been involved in the plot, and there were those—including Manolo's friend Ernest Hemingway—who would never be convinced that Fidel himself hadn't pulled the trigger.

The violence swirled but, as in Venezuela, baseball seemed to be granted neutral status by the warring factions and the season played out competitively and in relative safety. "Overall we did well," Monty Basgall said. "Cienfuegos was in first place until Christmas. After the holiday, the team dropped three games because the hitters went into a slump and we ended up finishing third. It was a crushing blow to Lefty to have the flag taken out of his hands."

"On the banquet circuit," Erskine added, "Lefty used to kid about his ability as a manager. But we had a pretty good team, in the thick of the pennant race, and that was a good league. A lot of major league players came out of that Cuban '47 winter league."

As their stay drew to a close, June discovered not all danger came from the streets. "At the end of the season, Señor Galey, the owner of the club, threw a banquet for Lefty, the ballplayers, and their families. An hour before the guests arrived, I went to check on the buffet. Everything looked delicious until I glanced at the 'Congratulations' cake and saw that it was moving. It was covered with cockroaches, chomping away on the vanilla frosting. When I screamed, the chef patted me reassuringly on the shoulder. 'Not to worry, Señora Gomez. I scrape off the bugs before I serve the dessert.' You can bet I didn't ask for a slice of cake."

Some of the Americans decided to restrict their diets. "Betty and I were newly married," Erskine recalled, "and we had a little apartment at the Hotel Nacional with a tiny balcony. Kind of romantic. We'd go shopping at the grocery store and there'd be these dead chickens hanging by their neck, strung up over the produce counter. The meat in the butcher case was dark and bloody. So we ate tuna fish. Betty learned to fix tuna forty different ways. And frozen peaches, because frozen food was just coming into vogue. That was our menu . . . tuna fish and peaches."

BACK IN THE STATES, instead of returning to the Triplets, Lefty accepted Larry MacPhail's offer to become a sort of roving pitching coach for Yankee farm teams east of the Mississippi. The Bronx Thrush replaced him at Binghamton. One week later, Lefty found himself ordered to minor league spring training in Boyes Springs, California, the same town in which the Seals had held their spring training when Lefty was trying so desperately to catch on two decades before. He wired the front office, "Someone has his geography all balled up."

Geography wasn't the problem. George Wolfman, later the baseball coach at the University of California, was coaching at Boyes Springs and had wired McPhail to get someone out there to help the young pitchers. So Lefty and June packed up the kids and Skin, the Chihuahua, and set out by car rather than train or airplane. "We wanted the children to have more than a bird's-eye view of America. To meet the people at the stops along the way. That's why we took the northern route west and the southern route coming back after spring training ended."

When Lefty arrived at camp, he saw that the best prospect wasn't a pitcher but rather a hitter. "Nobody ever had a batting stance quite like Gil McDougald's," Lefty said. "Gil's left front foot pointed to the mound; his other foot was at a right angle. His body was turned towards the infield, so the pitcher could read the letters on his shirt. He held his bat high and then let it droop towards the ground. It was so unorthodox that no one in the Yankee front office could remember his name."

But Lefty saw something the others had missed. "I noticed that Gil consistently connected with the ball, no matter what the pitch. So when McDougald was out of the lineup, I kept asking, 'Where's the kid with the funny stance? Get him up to the plate.' "

McDougald, who could play second, third, and short, went on to a sterling career with the Yankees, one of those players for whom statistics were meaningless. In 1957, for example, he hit only .289, with 62 RBIs and 87 runs scored, yet finished fifth in the voting for Most Valuable Player.

There was sadness in California as well. "In May 1948," Maye Lazzeri recalled, "Babe, Claire, and Julia were in Hollywood for the production of *The Babe Ruth Story*. Babe was on the set as a technical advisor to make sure that the star, William Bendix, looked like he could hit a home run and, of course, for the publicity. The three of them came to San Francisco. Lefty and I met them at the Fairmont Hotel and we had a belated birthday celebration for Babe. He was three months from dying. He had undergone radiation and drug therapy for throat cancer that had spread to his liver and lungs. We're sitting at the dinner table and he couldn't eat a thing, couldn't swallow a bite. He was gaunt and spoke with a raspy, painful voice. 'The only thing I can get down is liquid,' he said. 'A bottle of beer is my birthday dinner.' Lefty and I were heartsick. Babe was so weak and haggard-looking. No complaining. Just smiling sadly."

When Lefty returned to the East, he continued to conduct clinics for the Yankees. His combination of baseball savvy, infectious personality, and reputation for fierce integrity seemed to have secured him a solid future in the Yankee organization. But another opportunity would arise that fit even more perfectly than a career with the Yankees.

34

"NEVER MEASURE A PLAYER
WHEN HE'S GONE 0 FOR 4"

BOB QUINN'S BRAVES FINISHED SIXTH THE YEAR THEY LET LEFTY GO. The next year, 1944, they finished sixth again. The Braves' fans apparently didn't like the trend; attendance dropped from 271,000 in 1943 to 209,000 the following year, by far the lowest in either league. The last-place Phillies finished second-to-last in attendance, drawing 160,000 more paying customers than the Braves.

On St. Valentine's Day 1945, his seventy-fifth birthday, Bob Quinn tossed in the towel. He divested his ownership interest in the team and his son Jack, Mary Grady's old boyfriend, succeeded him as general manager. The elder Quinn would titularly remain on to help put the team's minor league system in order, but Kenesaw Mountain Landis had died the year before and Quinn let it be known that he would be happy to serve as Landis's successor. Quinn was personally beloved, but his record in Boston did not inspire the trust of his fellow owners. In April, they voted once again to go outside of baseball and unanimously chose Albert "Happy" Chandler as commissioner. Chandler resigned his seat as senator from Kentucky to accept the post.

The following month, Quinn severed his remaining connections with the Braves and took a job with Wilson Sporting Goods. He was to travel throughout the eastern United States, promoting Wilson baseball equipment and uniforms at colleges and major and minor league teams. It was an arduous assignment for a seventy-five-year-old, but Quinn wasn't even the senior member of the team. Cy Young, just shy of eighty, worked at the same job.

Cy was one of Wilson's most valuable employees. Everyone—players, managers, coaches, and executives—wanted to talk with the man who had won 511 major league games, and appeal translated into sales. How much longer an octogenarian could continue the grueling schedule was problematic, however, so Wilson president L. B. Icely was on the lookout for someone younger to do the job. Quinn was an addition, certainly, rather than Cy's eventual replacement.

But life on the road is not for everyone. After three years, Quinn left Wilson to accept an offer to be president of the Baseball Hall of Fame in Cooperstown—not as lofty a post as commissioner, perhaps, but prestigious nonetheless. Before he left, Quinn told Icely to go out and hire Lefty. When Icely ran the idea by Cy Young and Turk Reilly, an old catcher who often traveled with him, they immediately agreed that he would be ideal.

"Wilson had the contracts for many of the uniforms, gloves, baseball shoes, supporters, undershirts, and sliding pads," Lefty said. "My first job would be to drive to the Florida spring training camps. We would swing through the major league clubs, then Cy and I would continue on through the minor leagues and to colleges, visiting and making personal appearances."

A sales and goodwill position in which he would meet players and chat was a perfect match of requirements and skills. In October 1948, he took the job. "I was connected with baseball and I knew the equipment. Wilson knew I didn't need a training program. Of course, I had to learn how to measure the thighs, hips, inseams, knees, and chests of the players because they now wore custom-fitted uniforms. In my day, we were tossed pants and shirts large, medium, or small. Now they have water-cooled jockstraps. The custom fit doesn't make the player hit any better. He just looks better on television."

So Lefty piled Cy Young into his car, driving from camp to camp, the old man puffing on a pipe in the passenger seat, spinning tales of turn-of-the-century baseball. "I'm a storyteller myself and I was spellbound by Cy's experiences. He had a laconic wit and gave me a window on the game before I came on the scene."

Cy also became a close family friend. After Lefty finally moved to Durham, Cy would come by, sit out on the patio, and chuckle at the Gomez kids while he ate sandwiches and sweets.

Fred Post, a longtime columnist for the *Hartford Courant,* recounted his favorite Lefty anecdote. "Early one morning, the phone rang and the voice on the other end of the line said, 'Fred, I've got the world's greatest pitcher at my house. Come on down and meet him.' I told him, 'Lefty, go back to sleep. I know you're the world's greatest pitcher. I'll be over to see you at about eleven o'clock.'

"When I drove to his home, I walked in and was met by a wizened old man with all the fingers on his right hand busted. At the other end of the table sat another wizened old man. Lefty turned to me and said, 'Fred, I want you to meet Cy Young.' Lefty was right. He did have the world's greatest pitcher at his dinner table. The other old-timer was Turk Reilly."

Almost overnight, Lefty became the company's top sales representative. He was soon traveling more than 100,000 miles each year promoting the company and baseball at all levels, youth to professional. Within a few years, twenty-four out of the twenty-six major league clubs endorsed Wilson products. (Both Chicago clubs were holdouts.)

"My territory was the entire United States, including Hawaii and Alaska, and all the Canadian provinces. In addition, I covered the spring training camps of the Grapefruit League and the Cactus League. I've given speeches in every major city, every state, and in many, many small towns. No wonder I have good timing.

"Wherever the promotional work for Wilson needed a push, I went. I was not only representing Wilson . . . I was also a goodwill ambassador for baseball and as such I was representing kids who love the game. On the promotional level, I did the goodwill to the distributors because they are your company, your top salesmen. I showed them the new innovative lines of Wilson baseball equipment, the new models, answered questions about the technical advances, made speeches for everything and everyone. My job was to encourage the distributors to carry more of the Wilson line. Sales and promotion. The company calls you a consultant. They give you a fancy name but it boils down to sales and promotion. You know,

Wilson has been very good to me and at the same time I've been very good for Wilson."

Lefty applied to sales and promotion the same work ethic he had employed on the mound. Lefty Nelson, Wilson's East Coast regional sales manager, saw Gomez's work up close.

"First of all, he worked sunup to sundown. He really punished himself with work at Wilson and scheduling on the banquet circuit. Second, he had an innate ability to read people. He could size up a guy in five minutes, tell if the deal was going over or not. And the premium was Lefty had entrée to anyone anywhere based on his personality and past performance. He had played and broke bread with Ruth, Gehrig, DiMaggio, to mention only a few of the greats. In other words, before five or ten minutes had gone by, Lefty is telling amusing anecdotes while he's asking a young player how he's doing, helping him. Lefty's wit was fast. He broke the ice."

Integral to his success was his ability as a guest speaker, and Gomez developed into perhaps the most accomplished raconteur the game has ever known. He was sought after constantly, and wherever he spoke, Wilson went with him.

"The speeches that I give are almost always combined with a banquet," Lefty noted. "Guess after traveling to the place, they feel they have to feed you. And when I give a speech, I know who's sitting there . . . the makeup of the audience . . . and I tailor the talk to the room. That's number one for a performer. Can't talk in a closet. My style is that one story leads to another—an idea, a word and experience, even the similarity of names, can lead to another story. As a rule, my speeches are after the dinner, so the audience has finished chewing by then. When I arrive in town the day of the speech, I go down early to the hotel dining room and order a sandwich. Then at the banquet I only eat the salad. I do better on an empty stomach."

A wonderful example of his technique came at a benefit for Bill Cunningham, a highly respected sportswriter for the *Boston Globe*. Lefty was among a gaggle of luminaries from the sporting world. Everyone wanted to say a few words, including three heavyweight champions—Gene Tunney and Lefty's old pals Jack Sharkey and Jack Dempsey—but no one wanted to follow the featured speaker, Richard Cardinal Cushing. The cardinal was known to go on. And on. Even the heavyweights chickened out. But Lefty said, "Doesn't bother me. I'll follow the cardinal."

Lefty Nelson was in attendance. "The cardinal goes to the podium, blesses the crowd, and begins to talk . . . a long-winded speech about the trials and tribulations of St. Paul as a Roman soldier named Saul, who persecuted Christians until the day the Lord knocks him off his horse with a bolt of lightning, His voice calling out from the heavens, 'Saul, Saul. Why do you persecute Me?' Cushing has it all, in every biblical detail. He put the crowd into a stupor. Would he ever stop talking? He finally winds it up and walks down from the dais. Gomez goes to the mike. He turns to Cushing and says, 'Your Eminence, you stole my speech.'

"Only Lefty would dare to talk to a cardinal like that, but Lefty didn't stop there. 'And there's something else I can tell you about the trials and tribulations of St. Paul, because I pitched for them in 1930 when they were in eighth place.' That knocked down the house. Even the cardinal doubled over, losing his red hat and almost splitting his robes."

Lefty's ability to speak off the cuff and make people laugh emanated from an extraordinary level of empathy, not just for those he knew but also for those he met casually. Seymour Siwoff of the Elias Sports Bureau, baseball's preeminent statisticians, knew Lefty for forty years. "Vernon and I would be walking down the street, and people would stop and say something to him. You could see from their faces they felt uncomfortable, thinking, 'Oh my God, look who we're talking to. Lefty Gomez.' He'd laugh, make a joke, and right away these people felt comfortable talking with him. Instead of ignoring their feelings, Lefty was more than just pleasant. That's a remarkable quality. An art. Gomez never dealt with press clippings because he was genuine all the time. I never was with him that I didn't have a smile on my face. That's the truth."

It took someone of those sensibilities to maintain a friendship with DiMaggio. "Joe was a legend from his first at-bat, all the way up from the minors to the majors," Siwoff said. "That's a lot of pressure on a young kid. They'd go to a restaurant, and if the public was bothering Joe, he'd gripe at Lefty. And if they didn't pay attention to him, Joe wondered why they didn't. He sulked at the dinner table. He could sulk anywhere. Lefty laughed at Joe's antics and didn't take him seriously. Joe felt safe in his company. Over a lifetime, he recognized what Lefty did for him. When you saw them together you saw the bond between them. They understood one another. The friendship was written on their faces."

"Gomez had a common touch and he lived his values," Lefty Nelson added. "He could talk to the players of today because he kept up with the changes in the game. He wasn't an old fossil. And the young players looked up to Lefty. He was a money pitcher. The Yankees put the ball in his hand and sent him out to the mound when the pennant or the Series was on the line."

Lefty had his own take. "Anyone I work with in baseball is a friend of mine, and that's why I love my work. The territory I cover has kept me in front of the public and, like anything else, to be successful you move with the times. The work kicks my butt and prevents me from being an old fogy wandering around in the past."

And it all worked. "To be a success at Wilson," Lefty Nelson said, "Gomez had to be competitive. He had more baseball contracts for Wilson than any other person connected with the firm, ever before or since. It wasn't the price. It wasn't the quality. Or the Wilson name. It was Gomez, pure and simple. The ball clubs knew what he stood for. That's what they bought. It was Gomez asking for that order, whether it was the Red Sox, the Yankees, or the New York Penn League, whatever league it was."

Tom Mullaney, a Harvard Business School graduate and partner at McKinsey & Company before becoming president of Wilson Sporting Goods after the company was bought by PepsiCo in 1970, had a keen appreciation of Lefty's skill. "Lefty knew the Wilson merchandise. He knew baseball, and he had the introductions to the owners and players. Lefty's the only man I've ever seen who was welcomed in every single dugout that he ever went near. Unbelievable how the people crowded around him. He had a savvy business sense . . . how other people were feeling and thinking. And sometimes people missed this because Lefty was a soft sell. He was one of the great salesmen, as good a salesman as he was a pitcher. He had a most disarming approach but he knew how to get the job done. I always felt, in many ways, that Lefty looked at getting the job done at Wilson, making the sale, like being out on the mound. His thinking would be, 'I gotta get the guy out, retire the side. I'm out here with a job to do and I've got to do it.' But seeing Lefty's calm demeanor, you'd never guess. Lefty controlled the uniform business. The only thing I felt sorry about was anybody that had to sell against him. That guy was going to be very hungry. Against Lefty, he didn't have a chance."

And once the sale was made, Lefty felt an acute responsibility to the customer. "He made it very clear to people working with him that when a ball club placed an order, he wanted Wilson to meet the deadline. His name was on the line for good service. He was a perfectionist. Gomez was a professional at Wilson like he was a professional on the mound. But if you didn't observe him in this way, you might think he was a casual, happy-go-lucky fellow telling baseball stories. He was that but, more importantly, Lefty was professional in everything that he did."

In 1962, Wilson and the American Baseball Coaches Association initiated the Lefty Gomez Award, which is bestowed each year on "an individual who has distinguished himself amongst his peers and has contributed significantly to the game of baseball locally, nationally, and internationally." The award often goes to a college coach and past winners include legends Rod Dedeaux of USC, John Winkin of the University of Maine, and Ron Fraser of Miami.*

Bob Carpenter, owner of the Philadelphia Phillies, understood Lefty's commitment to excellence. "Gomez and Wilson gave the Phillies the best product. That's all I know. We had a contract with Gomez because the Wilson uniforms were tops. And that's why I said as long as I'm with the Phillies, Lefty will have the uniforms."

When Lefty was near Delaware, he stayed at Carpenter's home. There the tables were turned on the famed prankster. "Lefty and I had a lot of fun together, but we teased him a lot too. Lefty's room was next to mine

---

* Fraser, one of the most successful coaches in the history of any sport and credited with elevating college baseball to the prestigious level that it currently enjoys, won the award in 1989. At the ceremony, he spoke with June. "Lefty changed my career. He had an uncanny sense of ability, and he knew before most that the farm system was on its way out and that the colleges were going to take its place. I was accepting a position in professional ball and when I mentioned this to Lefty, he talked with me for three hours in my hotel room. 'Ron,' he said, 'get yourself into college baseball.' I did as Lefty suggested and here I am today."

and we'd get people to call him on the phone and ask him silly baseball questions. Lefty didn't know we handpicked the callers and all night long they'd wake him up, asking him really dumb questions about the game. How long could Lefty take it before his patience ran out?" Carpenter laughed. "We gave him a hard time."

Integral to selling the uniforms, of course, was making sure they fit right. That sometimes required a surprisingly sophisticated touch, both with chalk and with timing. "I learned real quick working for Wilson that, when it comes to uniforms, never measure a player or ask him how his uniform fits when he's gone 0 for 4. What you'll hear is . . . 'Armpits too tight, inseam sagging.' Go in when he's 5 for 5 and 'It's the greatest uniform I ever had.' First he's a prospect, then a star, then a tailor."

There were occasions, however, as Lefty Nelson described, when no degree of preparation was sufficient in the critical game of uniform fitting—it was spontaneity or bust.

"Wilson made both the Braves' and the Yankees' uniforms for the 1958 World Series. We made the Yankees' first . . . the traveling grays and the home whites . . . and shipped them to New York. After that, we had a three-day deadline to make the Braves' uniforms and get them to Milwaukee. When we finished the tailoring, there was no time to ship them out for game one, so Lefty and I packed the uniforms in a station wagon, drove all night, and arrived at County Stadium in Milwaukee at nine in the morning. But we couldn't get into the Braves' clubhouse because the equipment guy had the door chain-bolted from the inside and wouldn't open it for us. He'd locked himself in because his wife had caught him cheating on her and was after him with a gun. Lefty banged on the door. 'Let us in. We've got to fit the damn uniforms.' The guy yelled back, 'Is my wife out there?' And she was. With the gun. The guy said, 'If I open the door, she's going to shoot me.' Gomez shouted, 'I'm going to shoot you if you don't.' Finally the guy opened the door a crack and we squeezed in. The equipment manager locked and bolted the clubhouse door behind us.

"Each player had to knock on the door and it had to be unchained. All of a sudden, the wife appeared again, trying to sneak into the clubhouse behind one of the players. Just in time, the guy slammed the door in her face. As all this was going on, we're having the players trying on their uniforms. Warren Spahn, who was pitching that day, had a high kick, so when we made his uniform up, we gave him extra ball room. But today, Spahnnie tells Gomez the crotch is too loose. I'm with three players, Hank Aaron, Eddie Matthews, and Johnny Logan. Matthews and Logan like the fit, but Aaron says, 'It's too big and I'm not going to wear it.' So I ask Gomez what to do. If Aaron won't wear his uniform, the other two are sure to find something wrong too. Already Lefty and I can hear them starting to gripe. So Lefty says to me, 'Fit Aaron now. Tell him you're going to have his uniform dry-cleaned to take up some of the slack and the tailor will alter the rest. Tell him you called the tailor from the road for just such an emergency.'

"So I chalked up Aaron's uniform, then did the same for Matthews and Logan. As soon as the players took the field for the pregame workout, Lefty and I wiped the chalk marks off the uniforms and hung them back in their lockers. After infield practice, they come back into the clubhouse to change into their game uniforms. Aaron walks by. 'Fits pretty good now.' Matthews, Logan, and Spahnnie are happy too. We didn't do a thing except listen to their gripes and chalk them up. But that's how quick Lefty was. He knew the tension of a World Series, that the players would be uptight and find fault with anything."

Spahn beat the Yankees 4–3 in ten innings that day, although the Yanks won the series in seven games. The equipment man survived, although the fate of his marriage is unknown.

Life in the uniform business also required a sense of when less was more. Willie McCovey once asked Lefty to speak to Bob Lurie, the Giants owner. Lefty asked why. "We want blacker socks," McCovey said. "See? Black like my leg. But Lurie won't listen."

"Why don't you just forget the socks, Willie?" Lefty replied.

Occasionally, however, no amount of resourcefulness would help. One spring training, when Lefty asked Yogi Berra his hat size, Yogi replied, "How do I know? I'm not in shape yet."

"Billy Martin called Lefty 'Omar the Tent Maker,' " Nick Priore, a Yankee clubhouse man recalled. "You know how Billy got the 1 on his shirt?

They put 12 on, but the shirt was so big on him that all you see was the 1, so they made him number 1."

Lefty was not the only one who could find comic material in his skill with the chalk. "At spring training camp in 1950, Casey Stengel is in his second year managing the Yankees and I'm in my second year with Wilson, preaching the glories of their equipment to the major league clubs. Stengel was holding a press conference in the Yankee dugout as I walked in. Casey sees me and spins vintage Stengelese to the press. 'Now, here's my friend Lefty Gomez. Do you guys know that Wilson sent Lefty over to London for six months to teach him how to be a tailor?' That's Casey talking to the press, making up this bullshit. I broke out laughing. Casey was a great manager and great to me."

But how Casey thought of Lefty was a bit difficult to pin down. "After the season opened, I was gabbing in the Yankee Stadium clubhouse when Casey asked me to drop over to the Essex House, where he and his wife, Edna, a beautiful woman, were living. He wanted to talk about a publicity blurb I was doing for an article he was writing. So, early the next morning, I stopped by their hotel suite and rang the doorbell. Through the door, I heard Edna say, 'Don't open the door yet. I have to put a robe over my nightgown.' And Casey says, 'Never mind, honey. It's only Lefty.'"

35.

"I ONLY DO WHAT I LIKE TO DO"

"IN FEBRUARY OF 1950," JUNE REPORTED, "LEFTY BECAME A COUNTRY squire in Durham, an ex-Yankee among laconic Connecticut Yankees. Our dream house had been built, furnished, and the two-mile driveway had been carved out of the side of the mountain. Electrical and telephone poles had been sunk into the earth, linking us to a six-party line, and an artesian well brought up pure spring water.

"We moved into our home, perched on a cliff. Floor-to-ceiling windows gave us a panoramic view of treetops and sky. The view of the changing New England seasons was glorious. The locals called our house 'The Monastery.' They were curious why Lefty had come there, so far from the spotlight."

"I guess I settled on a mountain cliff," Lefty observed, "because, loving planes like I do, I wanted to be high. June liked the beauty and quiet of the Connecticut woods, yet she was close enough to take the train if she missed the noise of the city streets. We were welcomed by the townspeople as if we had lived in Durham all our lives. It was a great place for our children to grow up with an appreciation of nature."

Art McGinley, sports editor for the *Hartford Times,* later wrote, "Gaining entrance to the Gomez house is no small feat. It's almost a two day journey by pack mule from the main road. The men who climbed Mt. Everest wouldn't find this ascent easy."

"Along our winding, rocky road, Lefty nailed traffic signs on trees, here, there, and everywhere," June noted. "Things like 'Kings Highway,' and 'Keep Single Line,' and arrows to Knoxville, Paris, and the Golden Gate Bridge. He put 'No U-turn' where anything like that would be impossible. At the mountaintop, a visitor came to a clearing and found a Chrysler with a Connecticut license plate, GOOF, parked in front of our modern nine-room ranch-style home."

"Folks thought I ripped the traffic signs off the highway," Lefty added, "but I didn't. The first traffic markers were sent to me by fans who worked in the New York Police Department. When sportswriters wrote about my collection, other fans from all over the country sent me more. And such signs as '8,000 Miles to Tokyo' were gifts from GIs."

"Durham had eight hundred people and looked like everyone's idea of picture-postcard New England," June said. "Main Street was bordered by maple trees and houses had plaques flaunting circas, with designations like 'Capt. Adams House, 1793.' There was a white clapboard town hall, three Protestant churches, and Ackerman's General Store, where residents picked up their mail and bought pickles from the brine barrel. For the opening of the Durham Agricultural Fair, the last weekend in September, thousands of people poured into town, kicking up their heels and raising dust unstirred the rest of the year.

"Over the next eighteen years, our children lived in the wilderness of the Connecticut woods, but a forty-five-minute Jeep ride brought them to the New Haven railroad, where they could board a train for New York. They went to art galleries or Madison Square Garden or listened to Leonard Bernstein at the Philharmonic's Young People's Concerts. And a subway ride to the Bronx to see the Yankees was always on the calendar. The children had tickets to the all glamour events . . . All-Star games, World Series . . . and went with Lefty into the dugouts.

"I raised the children around the baseball season and shared Lefty with the game. He was on the road for six to seven weeks at a time, then would return for a day or two, only to be gone again. I saw more of him when he pitched. But when I married Lefty, I married baseball.

"Some of the players' wives didn't think living in New York was a big deal. Their hearts were in their small hometowns. That's okay, but in our marriage, baseball was primary. I became a fan. I grew up on the city streets. New York was my hometown, and to me, the Yankees represented New York."

A third child, Sharon, had been born in 1948 and, three years after the move to Durham, Lefty and June had their fourth, a boy they named Duane. Lefty was forty-four, which some thought rather advanced to be fathering children, as Carl Erskine related.

"Before the 1953 World Series opener, the Dodgers were working out at Yankee Stadium. I had just finished batting practice and went to the Yankee dugout to get a drink. Lefty was there and we were alone, except for Jack Lang, the sportswriter, at the other end of the bench. Lefty and I exchanged news. I told him how Betty and the children were doing, and Lefty talked about Gery and Sharon, and Vernona's upcoming piano concert. Then he said, 'And Duane, the baby, is six months old.' We didn't know that Lang had been ear-cropping. He yelled out, 'A baby? Lefty, you have a baby at your age?' And Lefty shot back, 'That was my arm that went dead.' Just broke me up."

Lefty's continuing association with baseball helped enrich the lives of his kids. Each spring, as Lefty moved up and down the Atlantic coastline for Wilson, June and the family went to St. Petersburg with the Yankees. "Our children brought their school assignments from up north. It was a fight to the finish to get the weekly work done and sent back to their teachers. But it wasn't all work and no play. Once, we went to the Keys to fish with Ted Williams, one of the world's great fishermen. Afterwards, Gery and Duane wanted Lefty to take them fishing off Municipal Pier, but Lefty turned green just walking across the bridge. So the boys and I dragged the fishing gear to the pier, cut the worms, and cast off. We didn't catch any fish, but we had a lot of fun."

When the Yankees came north, the family returned to Durham and the isolation of their mountaintop retreat. "Living without neighbors, our children had to find ways to fill their free time. Twenty-nine acres afforded them an outdoor stage where they could pretend to their hearts' delight. They ran through the woods, skirting brambles, tree trunks, and mountain laurel. Some days they were Robin Hood and his Merry Men, bows slung over their shoulders. Others they played cops and robbers; the good guys fired cap pistols as they scaled the rocks in hot pursuit of the bandits wearing red bandanas. They picked mushrooms or watercress or jumped into a rowboat at the pond and glided among the lily pads. When blizzards blew across the cliff, we were snowed in for days. No one complained about the 'No school' bulletins as they ran off to ice-skate on the pond.

"By necessity, our children came together for fun, or they found it alone. Vernona studied classical piano, traveled to New York for lessons, then gave concerts. Gery made intricate model airplanes or shot hoops. Sharon's horse was corralled in a barn, tucked in amongst the trees. She rode Chief around town and at the Durham Fair, jumping hurdles and winning ribbons. Duane was passionate about boxcar racing. He practiced maneuvers up and down our dirt road and raced competitively from age eight."

But Lefty was not one to be completely isolated. "Durham held New England–style town meetings," June continued, "and if Lefty was in town, he was there. One time, a discussion arose about the lack of funds to establish a Little League field. The burghers voted down the field, then moved on to the next piece of civic business . . . a fence around the town cemetery. Gomez jumped up from his chair. 'What kind of thinking is that?' he demanded. 'I veto that decision.' The citizens sat in shocked silence. 'Look at it this way,' Lefty continued. 'Nobody outside the cemetery wants to get in. And the people who are already in can't get out. What good is a fence? Use the money to build a baseball field.' As Lefty's goofy logic sank in, the townspeople began to laugh. They called for a revote on the field. Thanks to Gomez, it passed unanimously."

"Once we had a field," Lefty said, "my two sons played Little League. Gery was a right-handed pitcher and, when he wasn't pitching, played first base. He really gave the ball a ride. Duane played eleven years after his brother. Duane could also clobber the ball. My two sons racked up more hits in one season than I did in my entire career.

"At one game, the umpire didn't show up. I found myself behind the plate with Gery at bat. I thought umpires were blind when I pitched, so when Gery took a pretty good pitch with two strikes on him, I called him out. Can you imagine calling your son out on strikes? Well, I did, and boy, did I hear about it. On the way home, Gery was feeling badly because it was the first time he had struck out in several games. Sharon spoke for the rest of the family when she gave me the raspberries: 'Dad, you played for the Yankees and you don't know a strike from a ball?'

"When I was home, I tutored my boys in mechanics and conditioning, but I was never an advocate of 'like father, like son.' I wanted Gery and Duane to choose their own careers, so they'd love their work and their life. Our four right-handed children ran the gamut of public, parochial, and boarding schools. They all attended universities. And I'm proud to say Gery did a three-year hitch as a marine in Vietnam."

Lefty's connections could also bring a little excitement to a sleepy town. "In February 1960, Gery's varsity basketball team won the championship of the Shore Line Conference with an 18–0 record, and a victory party was scheduled at the Durham Lions Club.

"Gery idolized DiMaggio and I thought how thrilled my teenage son and his teammates would be to receive a varsity letter and a handshake from Joe. DiMag has always been a great guy . . . never a pop-off, always quiet and reserved, but I don't think I ever met an athlete who believed in his ability more. So I rang him up in Florida and asked him to come to Durham as a surprise guest. When Joe walked into the banquet hall, the crowd went wild. Joe was a sensation, shaking hands and signing autographs. At the podium he gave the guests a chuckle or two by spinning stories about our Yankee days together, and ended his remarks by saying, 'There was never a dull moment when Lefty and I were roomies. About the only things we had in common were our love of baseball and the closeness of our birth dates, November 25 and November 26. Otherwise, Lefty was always talking and I was silent and aloof. If I said hello, it made the newspapers.'

"I picked up the mike and said Joe's speech was uncharacteristically verbose. 'Generally, Joe doesn't complete a sentence in a day . . . just a word here, a word there.' I was recently playing in a celebrity golf tournament and so was DiMag. The first day, Joe is nowhere to be found, so I asked the club pro if he had seen him, and he said, 'No, but I've seen Howard Hughes four times while I was waiting.' "

Lefty's exceptional wit and timing were no secret to television and radio producers. He had been a frequent guest panelist on the radio show *Information Please,* hosted by Clifton Fadiman. From there, he was hired to cohost a pregame and postgame radio show on WINS-1010 in New

York City with Ethan Allen. Allen, by then a sportscaster, had been a big league outfielder for thirteen seasons with the Reds, Giants, and Phillies. After his career, he coached at Yale (where one of his players was future president George H. W. Bush), wrote how-to books on baseball, and invented a wildly popular board game, All-Star Baseball.

"Allen and I commented on anything pertaining to sports, and gave the scores of any game in progress in any sport. But we did more than read, replay, and rehash . . . we did stories with human appeal. Before the WINS broadcast, we talked to people on the street, fans in the stands, newsmen, and, of course, players in the locker rooms. A people-oriented script. Our spontaneous format was more of a risk but it made the show more creative."

Soon after the move to Durham, television came calling. Lefty was hired to host a show on WKNB-TV in New Britain. "It was a fifteen-minute slot on Saturday nights. I discussed the week's baseball activities, gave scores, and conducted interviews with national and local sports figures. Sandwiched in between the commentary were updates on tennis, football, basketball, and, if time permitted, one or two of my baseball stories to bring a chuckle to the viewers."

He also had a joint appearance with June on the hit quiz show *What's My Line?* in which a panel of four, using only yes-or-no questions, attempted to guess odd occupations of various contestants. One of the segments was a "mystery guest," for which the panel was blindfolded and tried to determine the identity of a celebrity, who answered questions in a disguised voice.

"Host John Daly told the panel to put on their blindfolds and asked the mystery challengers to please sign in on the chalkboard. June and I walked out as Minnie Mouse and Goofy. The audience went into gales of laughter. And no wonder. I certainly looked goofy with my long nose and big shoes, and June was very mousy with her round black ears and red-and-white polka-dotted dress.

"I scribbled Mr. and Mrs. Goofy Gomez on the chalkboard and then we sat down next to Daly. I answered questions with a bark and June with a squeak. We got through a couple of rounds until Bennett Cerf guessed who we were. That didn't surprise me. Cerf and I had traded many a quip when I was a Yankee."*

Lefty would be a guest on any number of quiz shows, panel shows, and interview shows, including twice on *The Tonight Show* with Johnny Carson, although he arrived without the nose and ears.

Still, he was never drawn to a television career. "I knew I had the talent to be a TV entertainer, but I didn't like the format. So much rehearsing and red tape. Canned laughter, canned applause. Politics on the set. I felt like the originality of the material, the delivery, and the audience's response to it was a result of the director and the producer. The end result was that it wasn't me. I like being Lefty Gomez. I know who he is. I didn't like being a TV entertainer and I only do what I like to do."

---

* Cerf, of course, asked Lefty for the autograph for James Michener that eventually provided the genesis for this book.

36

"THE BEST POSSIBLE SPORTS EXPERIENCE
FOR EVERY CHILD WHO HAS THE DESIRE TO PLAY"

———

I N 1951, A NEW JERSEY BUSINESSMAN NAMED MARIUS BONACCI BEGAN A
ten-team baseball league in Hamilton Township for players ages thirteen
to fifteen, boys who had grown too old for Little League. He called it the
Little Bigger League. After an article on Bonacci's idea appeared in the
Sporting News, towns across the nation began to initiate similar programs,
ninety-eight in that first year. In 1952, with continued expansion, some of
the groups got together and held a "World Series" in Trenton. In 1953,
the name was changed to the National Little Bigger League, and, in addition to the championship series, a number of tournaments were held re-
gionally or at the state level.

The following year, the league's national board approached Claire
Ruth and asked if they might use Babe's name to headline the program.
Claire was not one to lend attribution to an organization without due care,
but here seemed the perfect vehicle to keep Babe's name alive for coming
generations. "Babe was a man who loved children and baseball," Claire
said. "He could receive no greater tribute than to have a youth baseball
program named after him."

So, in 1954, the organization's name was changed to the Babe Ruth
League. And Claire was also not one for passive participation.

"Claire lived a beautiful life after Babe's death," observed Maye
Lazzeri. "If the Yankees wanted her at a baseball function, she was there.
And she did so much for youth baseball promoting the Babe Ruth League,
building Babe up, not herself, keeping his name and his love of the game

alive for children. And Lefty was at her side so many times at the Babe Ruth League functions."

"As long as she was alive, Claire went to every single tournament, all the age divisions, every year," June added. "She enjoyed having Lefty along because they could reminisce about Babe and relax together. Her work with the Babe Ruth League was amazing. She never was too tired or too busy to do another interview if it was for Babe and youth baseball. I've seen her give one interview after another; then, when it seemed finished, a reporter would ask for another. Claire would run a comb through her hair, pick up her purse, and say to Lefty, 'Okay, let's go.' "

The program spread across America and then spilled over the border. In 1966, a division was added for sixteen-to-eighteen-year-olds; in 1974 a division for thirteen-year-olds only; and in 1982 a division for five-to-twelve-year-olds. In 1984, a softball division for girls was begun. In 1989, Carl Yastrzemski became the first Babe Ruth graduate inducted into the Major League Baseball Hall of Fame, followed the next year by Joe Morgan and Jim Palmer. Nolan Ryan, Michael Jordan, and Peyton Manning all played Babe Ruth baseball. Currently, almost ten thousand leagues operate around the world and more than 1 million boys and girls take part. Babe Ruth baseball is arguably the most successful amateur volunteer sports program ever. And to honor those without whom the program could not function, in 1991 Babe Ruth International instituted a Volunteer of the Year Award. They named it after Lefty Gomez.

Certainly no one epitomized the spirit of the league more. "The Lefty Gomez Volunteer of the Year Award," the release read, "is the highest award bestowed in Babe Ruth Baseball. Its recipient must embody the spirit of the Babe Ruth League philosophy, which is to provide the best possible sports experience for every child who has the desire to play."

Lefty was elected to the Babe Ruth board of directors in 1964 and remained a board member for the rest of his life. He and Claire attended every Babe Ruth Baseball World Series and myriad other functions across the nation. Beginning in 1961, Lefty was the keynote speaker at the Tournament of Champions, the welcoming banquet for the parents, volunteers, and media at the Babe Ruth World Series. He also gave the Breakfast of Champions talk the following Monday morning. During the event and all through the year, Lefty was at ground level, working with the volunteers, the same role he played at the Little League World Series in Williamsport and for American Legion Ball

Lou Pavlovich, editor of *Collegiate Baseball,* noted, "My most vivid memory of Lefty is when he came down to help the Babe Ruth World Series in Nogales, Arizona, in 1979. I don't know what happened, but balls that were supposed to be signed by another ballplayer weren't signed and the tournament sponsors were extremely upset. Lefty took up the slack and started signing whole boxes of balls. Nor would the other player—one of baseball's immortals, by the way—wear the big black sombrero embroidered with metallic silk thread that had been presented by the tournament host. So Lefty put it on and waved to the crowds as he motored along in the parade. He saved the tournament."

Most times, Lefty's extraordinary bigheartedness was foisted on anonymous boys and girls on town fields across America. Occasionally, however, he helped a kid destined for bigger things. Jim Lonborg remembered Gomez as the first man ever to help him with pitching mechanics. "I was a senior in high school and Lefty had come down to participate in an open clinic at Cal Poly. You dropped by if you wanted to and they gave you instruction. Lefty was out on the mound working with the pitchers. At the time I really didn't have aspirations of playing major league ball. I was kind of late in developing and was playing for the exercise and the sheer joy of it. I was more interested in getting into premed.

"I threw a couple of pitches, and in two seconds Lefty said to me, 'No, son. That isn't the way your foot is supposed to be.' I had put my foot across the rubber instead of in front. I still chuckle at the memory. Little did he or I know that seven years later I'd be pitching for the Red Sox in the World Series and win the Cy Young Award."

Lefty touched thousands and thousands of youngsters in his thirty years in the Babe Ruth League, sometimes in far-flung corners of America. The 1980 Babe Ruth League World Series was held at Ardean Aafedt Stadium in Williston, North Dakota, sixty miles south of the Canadian border and eighteen miles east of Montana. At the banquet, after the team from Rotterdam, New York, had won the event, Lefty and Dick Case, the league president, were joined by the North Dakota governor, Williston's mayor, and other dignitaries. After ceremonial dances, Lefty and Case were asked to join the Sioux nation as blood brothers. "Chief Jerry White Cloud said it was a thank-you for bringing Babe Ruth youth baseball to the Sioux children, and after he performed the ceremony, he presented Dick and me with beaded warriors' headdresses of white eagle feathers. The workmanship is exquisite, and I was deeply touched."

37

"MY OWN DAMN FAULT"

———

BUT LIFE ON THE ROAD HAD ITS PRICE. LONELINESS WAS CERTAINLY A regular companion, and even though Lefty called every day to speak with June and the kids, a long-distance telephone conversation does not equate to being home. More and more frequently, he would have a few drinks here and a few there, and end up drunk in his hotel room. Lefty's eating habits didn't help. A salad for lunch, and then he spoke the way he pitched—on an empty stomach.

Publicly, Lefty exhibited no signs. For his speaking engagements, he remained well-groomed and well-spoken. But privately, the problem began to become more obvious and more acute. Bing Russell recalled an incident when Lefty was vacationing at Kennebago Lake in Maine. "He had every drink on the bar by noon . . . whiskey sours, straight, on the rocks, boilermakers. During his Yankee days, he took care of his body. He was always in condition. But later in life . . . in the fifties . . . I don't know how he lived through his horrendous traveling schedule . . . talking with the brass of the major and minor leagues, attending the winter meetings and baseball events as a goodwill ambassador. That schedule alone would kill the average guy. I don't know why he worked so hard. I don't think he knew why. He just wanted to be around baseball and people all the time."

Lefty Nelson agreed. "His insane traveling and appearance schedule for Wilson was the main cause of the drinking. Add to that the banquet circuit all across the U.S., Hawaii, and Mexico, with a trip to the Philippines, and you get the classic alcoholic meltdown."

"I was a functioning alcoholic," Lefty said. "I woke up with a hangover and worked the day with a blinding headache. It was my own damn fault.

Good Friday, 1957, I was in Chicago. I dropped into a church and, on my knees, I asked for help. I knew I was dying. June and the children were in Lexington with Nellie at the Grady house for Easter vacation, so I decided to go cold turkey and take a train to Boston and surprise them. After church, I saw Lefty Nelson at Wilson headquarters and told him I was in serious straits. He said he'd seen it coming for three years. Nelson tried to get me to go to a doctor, but I said no, that I was going home to my family. If I was going to die, I wanted to be with them."

Lefty arrived in Boston on Saturday, April 20, and called Lexington from the train station. Nellie answered.

"Lefty said he wanted to be with the family for Easter and asked if June would pick him up. June rode her Studebaker to South Station and found Lefty standing on the curb, suitcase in hand. He blew her a kiss and offered to drive the return trip. June moved over to the passenger seat and Lefty laid his overcoat between them. He put the car in gear, drove twenty miles an hour, and almost hit two pedestrians in a crosswalk. Then, all the while out to Lexington, he talked to his overcoat, which he called 'George,' telling it funny jokes and going off into fits of hysterical laughter.

"While Lefty parked the Studebaker, June came through the front door and said, 'Nellie, I have something terrible to tell you. Don't say anything to Lefty when he comes in. Be careful. I think he's off his trolley.' Lefty came into the house and said, 'Hello, Nellie. Hi, kids,' and then hung his overcoat on a hanger. He talked to 'George' and then pulled a sweater from his suitcase, put 'Harry' on the back of a chair, then introduced 'Harry' to 'George' and tried to strike up a conversation between the overcoat and the sweater. 'This is a great thing if it works,' he said, turning to us.

"June, the children, and I watched him, transfixed at the horror of a man we loved now gone crazy. He kept hearing voices and wondered why we couldn't hear them too. June and I finally got him to the upstairs bedroom, where he flung himself down on the bed, fully clothed. Sweat was pouring off him and his hands were shaking uncontrollably. He continued to talk to people who weren't there. By 9:00 p.m., everyone went to bed but didn't get a minute's sleep, except four-year-old Duane. Every two hours or so, Lefty was walking up and down the stairs, out onto the verandah, and then back into the parlor. He turned off the light and hollered at Vernona, Gery, and Sharon to lie on the carpet with him so the robbers shooting through the windows wouldn't harm them. June and I sat at the dining room table until 4:00 a.m., looking for a solution. In one of his more lucid moments, I went into the parlor and talked with him. 'Lefty, dear. Will you please go to a hospital? If you don't, your brain will snap and you'll be in a state asylum for the rest of your life.' 'I'll go, Nellie,' he said, 'but please don't send me to a state hospital.'

"So June rang up the family GP and he made arrangements at a hospital in Arlington, the next town over from Lexington. Five hours later, at 10:30 a.m., Easter Sunday, with June standing by his side, Lefty checked himself into Rings Sanitarium.

"The psychiatrists told June that Lefty had a nervous breakdown caused by exhaustion and alcoholism. The attempt to go cold turkey had thrown him into DTs, delirium tremens. For ten days Lefty was in a locked private room, attended by two male nurses. He went through hell. Crocodiles sprang at him from under his bed, snakes moved up the sides of the wall and down onto his pillow, and when he went to eat his food, he saw black beetles on the plates. There were days when he looked right through June, not knowing or seeing her at all."

But, even at the lowest depths, Lefty never completely lost himself. As Nellie also related, "The senior psychiatrist said, 'Generally, a patient in as bad a condition as Lefty smashed the walls and broke the furniture. But Lefty didn't. In my memory, he's the only one that sick who didn't have to be put in a straitjacket. Lefty must be a very kind man inside because if he had been filled with violence, it would have erupted.' And he kept his sense of humor through his darkest hours. He told the nurse not to step on the alligators and the snakes, and to stop putting ants in his orange juice, then said he wanted a sign, 'Gomez's Zoo,' on his locked door. And the nurse put it up. Another time, Lefty said to the nurse, 'You take my watch away and leave me my belt. I could hang myself with that.' "

On May 1, Lefty had recovered sufficiently to be moved to a less restrictive part of Rings, and was allowed to walk the grounds unsupervised. Although, because he had signed himself in, he could leave without a doctor's certificate or court order, Lefty was under no illusions as to the severity of his condition and was determined to see himself through the full course of treatment.

As soon as he could receive visitors, June brought Vernona, Gery, and Sharon for a visit with their father. "It was a beautiful day," Nellie recalled. "Lefty was sane, but he was so weak he could hardly walk. But, thank God, Gomez had his mind back. Wasn't God good to give Lefty the desire to seek help before he had to be taken away to a mental institution?"

Lefty Nelson also visited Gomez regularly. "After the worst of it, when he was on the road to recovery, the doctors let him take walks out on the lawn. I'd try to lighten things up, you know, give him a laugh by skipping around through the tulips, acting silly. He'd say, 'Don't do anything like *that*. They're watching us, Nelson. I'll never get out of here with the stuff you're doing.' "

When Lefty told June he needed slippers, she brought a pair that glowed in the dark so he could find them easily when he got out of bed after the nurses turned the lights out. She put them in the closet of his room.

"When I came in to visit him," Lefty Nelson said, "Gomez says he told the psychiatrist to go look at his slippers. That they light up in the closet. But the psychiatrist refused to look. Lefty said, 'The doc's afraid I'm going to shove him in the closet and skip out.' "

On May 5, Lefty was discharged from Rings. Although from there forward, he'd have a beer once in a while, he "smartened up and gave up drinking on the road."

38.

WINNING FRIENDS AND INFLUENCING PEOPLE
FOR THE UNITED STATES ON TEN DOLLARS A DAY

ONE YEAR LATER, ON MAY 13, 1958, DURING A LATIN AMERICAN TOUR, the motorcade carrying U.S. vice president Richard Nixon was set upon by hundreds of demonstrators on the streets of Caracas. Three windows of the vice president's limousine were smashed with "melon-size rocks," and Nixon was showered with shattered glass. The Venezuelan foreign minister, sitting next to him, was struck in the eye with a shard from the window. The planned wreath-laying ceremony was cancelled, as were all other scheduled events, and the vice president repaired to the heavily guarded American embassy to meet with what government officials he could. Communist insurgents protesting against the ruling right-wing junta were blamed for the attack. Just days before, Nixon had been spit at and assailed with eggs and oranges in Lima, Peru.

Communist anti-American instigation was rife throughout Latin America, but nowhere was the threat of actual overthrow greater than in Cuba. Fidel Castro, no longer a student agitator, had become leader of a full-fledged revolutionary movement on the eastern end of the island. Castro's rebels were beginning to gain traction against the American-backed troops of the dictator, Fulgencio Batista.

After the vice president's return to the safety of Washington, D.C., United States government officials set about finding ways to improve America's image with its southern neighbors. Someone at the State Department thought it might be a good idea to send a couple of goodwill ambassadors to Latin America, people who were so universally popular that they could reshape public opinion without exposing themselves to excessive risk. And so Secretary of State John Foster Dulles personally summoned that famed diplomat, Vernon Gomez, to the nation's capital and asked if he would accept the assignment.

"When I met with Dulles in Washington," Lefty recalled, "I asked him to describe the trip. Dulles laughed and said, 'How to win friends and influence people for the United States on ten dollars a day.' In other words, hold youth baseball clinics, meet government dignitaries and pro ball officials, and then pay for your hotel room on ten bucks."

Lefty had returned from Cuba just months before. At the behest of a local sugar magnate, Roberto Maduro, who also owned the Havana Sugar Kings baseball club, Gomez had spent some weeks tutoring Cuban Little Leaguers, "Los Cubanitos." In fact, Lefty had been conducting clinics on and off for a decade. For the 1958 trip, Lefty, as he often did, brought along June and Vernona, and the family stayed at the famed Miramar Yacht Club. In addition to running the clinics, Lefty was guest of honor at the Los Cubanitos World Series. So, in asking Gomez to return to Latin America, Dulles was hardly pulling a name from a hat.

Lefty agreed and with umpire Jocko Conlan he set off in late autumn on a three-month tour that would take them to Venezuela, Colombia, Ecuador, Argentina, Peru, virtually every country in Central America, Haiti, the Dominican Republic, and finally Cuba. At each stop, the two would teach local children the rudiments of the game, perhaps coach some of the older players—Jocko must have handled the hitting instruction—and chat with government representatives about the friendly intentions of the United States.

The secretary of state had been correct. American baseball was clearly far more popular than American politics, and the tour went remarkably well. Lefty and Jocko were greeted warmly at every stop and the local officials were ecstatic at having a great American pitcher, one whose name happened to be Gomez, tutoring their youngsters. As the trip wound down, just after New Year's 1959, Lefty returned to Cuba, where he looked up his old boxing buddy, Ernest Hemingway.

"The night Hemingway invited me over for dinner to Finca Vigia, his villa near Havana, he was having a private showing of *The Old Man and the Sea.* The book had been published in 1952 to great acclaim, then filmed the year before with Spencer Tracy in the lead role.

"During the course of conversation at dinner, the murder of Manolo Castro del Campo came up, which I had seen, of course, when I was managing Cienfuegos. Manolo had been a friend of Hemingway's and had let him referee boxing matches at the Universidad de La Habana, where I was running pitching clinics for the university students.

"Hemingway never got over Manolo's murder and had written a short story about it, called 'The Shot.' Later that night, while we were watching the movie, Hemingway said to me, 'Lefty, my driver will take you back to the Hotel Nacional. Stay in the hotel and don't come out for any reason. Do as I say and don't ask any questions.' We parted, and off I went back to Havana. That night, Castro and the revolutionary forces came out of the hills to usurp control of the government."

Hemingway was widely believed to be both a supporter and a friend of Fidel's, so much so that he was investigated by the FBI. But in "The Shot," the assassin of the barely disguised Manolo Castro was the equally barely disguised Fidel. Though he never openly showed animosity toward the famed American, Fidel was said to have been none too pleased to be accused of murder by a gringo writer. The following year, the government seized Finca Vigia, as well as thousands of books and manuscripts that Hemingway left behind when he moved to Idaho—where, in 1961, he took his own life.

Lefty, on the other hand, was known solely as the manager of Cienfuegos and a tutor to Los Cubanitos, and thus was well-thought-of across the Cuban political spectrum. He did have one problem, however: His passport was not valid.

When Lefty had traveled to Washington to meet Dulles, he was told to bring his passport, which was due to expire. He gave it to one of Dulles's aides and it was returned before he and Jocko departed. But a bureaucrat had slipped up; the passport was never renewed. For much of the trip, no one noticed, including Lefty. Lefty and Conlon were, after all, traveling under the auspices of the U.S. government. But after Batista's overthrow, Castro's men began reading the fine print. Lefty was informed his passport was invalid and that he could not leave Havana.

Lefty went to the American embassy, which was in as much postrevolutionary disarray as the government. There he was again told he would indeed need the permission of the Cuban authorities in order to leave. The embassy officials said they would go through channels but could make no promises in the current chaos; Lefty might be stranded in Cuba indefinitely. To the shock of the local diplomats, however, within days permission for Lefty to leave was granted, invalid passport and all. When Lefty returned to the embassy, he was told that the authorization had been issued by Fidel Castro himself.

39

"YOU DON'T HAVE TO SHOVEL RAIN"

———

"WHEN WE MOVED TO CONNECTICUT," JUNE SAID, "I TOLD MYSELF that I'd been on a road trip since early childhood and I never wanted to move again. But the West beckoned to Lefty. When I asked why, he quipped, 'You don't have to shovel rain.' But it was more than the weather. Lefty wanted to return to where his family had lived since the gold rush. So we sold our house to a New York writer looking for solitude. He and Lefty stood on the cliff, with no neighbors visible anywhere, and Lefty said, 'If solitude is your game, you'll find it here.' "

In 1968, Lefty and June rented a house in Fairfax, in Marin County, a ten-minute drive from San Francisco. Duane, by then a teenager, attended Sir Francis Drake High School. After some years, the family moved farther north, to a three-bedroom house in Novato, the town in which Bill Gnoss, later the mayor, had brought in the ringer to pitch against Lefty and Point Reyes in 1927.

June described the purchase. "I'll give you an inkling of how Lefty is about family matters. I picked out a house in Novato that had a swimming pool because I swim eighty-four laps a day. Getting Gomez to look at the house was tough because he was always on a Wilson trip or the banquet circuit for youth baseball. Finally, a day came when he was available.

"The agent met us at the front door and told us the house had just gone into escrow. 'But,' she said, 'the house across the street is for sale. It doesn't have a pool but the owners are anxious to sell.'

"When I went inside, Lefty was outside talking to the owner. Entertaining him, no doubt, with baseball stories. 'Oh, well,' I thought, 'he'll be in shortly.' The house tour ended, and Lefty and I went to the real estate office and signed the sales contract with the understanding that the closing would be in a few months. The next day we left for spring training. As we're driving to Arizona, Lefty turned to me and said, 'By the way, June, that house we bought. What does it look like on the inside?' I couldn't believe it. Lefty had never gone inside the house. He just bought it."

"We were wondering who was moving in next door," Paul Davis recalled, "because Lefty's son, Gery, had his Mercedes parked in the driveway. Then he had borrowed George Foreman's Rolls-Royce to move Lefty's baseball memorabilia from Fairfax to Novato. I called my wife, Karen, to the window and said, 'Will you look at the cars? *Who* is moving in next door?' "

The Novato house was ideal for the Gomezes. It was set among gardens that held flowers and fruit trees. Lefty's specialty was roses—salmon pink, and yellow tinged with red, varieties he had learned to love as a boy watching his mother grow them in Rodeo. Lilacs dotted the grounds and pink geraniums spilled over the sides of Mexican terra-cotta pots. June's herb plantings—marjoram, basil, chives, dill, and spearmint—filled in the gaps.

"June bought the wrong variety of lemon tree," Lefty noted. "The lemons were as hard as marbles. Just try and squeeze one. You'd have to be a blacksmith."

Other fruit was more malleable. When the pears were ripe, they were picked, put in bags, then brought to the Davises next door and the Pardinis across the street. "Share the pear wealth!" was Lefty's motto.

The location was also ideal. The Rolling Hills Athletic Club was less than ten minutes from their house. June played bridge and tennis and swam her daily laps. Even closer were the ball fields of San Ramon Elementary School and San Marin High. Lefty often dropped by to watch the neighbors' children play Little League and varsity baseball.

"Our young son Tommy was a con artist," Paul Davis said. "He rang June's doorbell and said, 'You're my favorite neighbor,' so she would invite him in for chocolate chip cookies."

"Tommy loved when Lefty walked over to the Little League games and sat in a lawn chair behind the third-base line to watch the kids screw themselves into the ground trying to hit the long ball," added Karen Davis.

"Tommy would wave and call out from the bench, 'Hi, Lefty,' and Lefty would turn to me and say, 'Aha. The politician sends his regards.' Then Tommy's teammates would look over at this Hall of Famer and say to Tommy, 'Lefty Gomez is here? Why is Lefty Gomez at our game?' and Tommy would smugly answer, 'Oh, Lefty's here because I'm here.' "

Tommy Davis wasn't the only one who rang the Gomez doorbell. The news was out that the Gomez house was a veritable baseball museum. The walls were papered with pictures of past and present greats, and niches were stacked with gloves, bats, and autographed balls. Lefty delighted in holding court, answering questions and sharing anecdotes.

"After classes, grammar-school and high-school kids were at the door," Lefty said. "Sometimes fifteen to twenty at a time . . . we talked baseball. On the weekends, their parents and grandparents stopped by to talk about the game. Some of the kids have been here a zillion times and they laugh when I show them the old flat baseball gloves. One kid asked me, 'Did you wear this glove inside your other one, Lefty?'

"Another boy picked up a 1934 picture of the American All-Stars in Japan. The ballplayers and their wives were standing around an indoor pool at a private home and he asked me why Babe was in his underwear. 'Because,' I said, 'as we walked into the house for the swimming party, the owner handed us bathing suits. But not to Babe. He didn't have any trunks big enough for Ruth, so Babe swam in his BVDs.' "

Larry and Terry Williams were identical twins who became particular favorites. They began coming by the house to talk baseball when they were in elementary school. As high-school seniors they were still coming.

"Lefty was so easy to talk to even though he was a Hall of Famer," Larry Williams said. "We were there for hours looking at his stuff. So many hours that when we returned home our mom said, 'How do you know you're not bugging the man? Don't stay over there so long. Give him a break.' We'd laugh and go see Lefty whenever he came back from a road trip."

Even as kids, Larry and Terry understood that friendship comes with responsibility. "As soon as the kids found out there was a Hall of Famer in Novato, everyone was on Lefty's doorstep asking for an autograph. He showed them baseball stuff, signed autographs, and gave them Topps bubble gum. One day, my brother and I stopped by to say hello and we noticed the kids were tossing the gum wrappers on his lawn. We didn't think that was polite at all. So we stuck around and picked them up.

"Terry and I decided to take charge of the lawn situation. When the autograph seekers arrived, we told them, 'Okay, get in a single line. Go in the door, get an autograph, look at the pictures, talk to Lefty, pick up the gum, and don't throw the wrappers on the lawn. *Lefty don't like that.*' Sometimes the autograph seekers saw a sign tacked on Lefty's front door, 'Sorry, ran out of gum. Come back tomorrow,' and the kids knew they had depleted his supply."

"When I first bordered our front gardens with red rocks," Lefty added, "the kids came up to the door hopping from rock to rock. One day, I said to a bunch of them, 'Next kid I see on those rocks, no bubble gum.' Shortly afterward, Lieutenant Gary Barner of the Novato Police Department dropped by my house for a chat. When he backed his car out of the driveway, he drove over the rocks. Some kids were coming up to the door for autographs and one of them yelled out, 'You won't get any bubble gum from Lefty. You ran over the rocks.' "

Lefty's celebrity had spread through Novato and fans downtown were on the alert for a Hall of Famer strolling by. At the Roger Wilco grocery store, Lefty was walking down the cereal aisle with a grocery cart one day, when an elderly woman accosted him and asked, "Are you the legend that lives in Novato?"

Lefty was startled, drawn from his reverie over the relative merits of Wheaties and Grape-Nuts Flakes.

"The Yankee legend," the woman went on. "My grandchildren have been to his home. The autographed picture of the legend looks like you. You *are* the legend."

Lefty protested that he was not a legend, but simply Lefty Gomez.

"You're the legend. I *knew* it." The woman then scurried away.

Another day, Lefty was on his way to Petrini's for frozen yogurt, and as he crossed in front of a parked Brink's truck that held Petrini's profits for the day, the guard behind the wheel jumped out of the truck and ran after him.

"Hey, Lefty. Can you sign these pictures for me?"

"Who's watching the money?" Lefty rejoined.

Of course, not everyone got their signals precisely correct. At one point, Lefty brought a pair of slacks to the dry cleaner, but didn't bother keeping track of the ticket. When he returned to pick up the slacks, the owner claimed not to have them. Lefty insisted the cleaner definitely did have them. Finally, after months of haggling, Lefty asked to go through the cleaning receipts. Lefty was right and there they were—but not under Gomez. The owner had listed the slacks under Lefty Grove.

Being back in California meant Lefty could be close to some old friends. "I just loved seeing Lefty come into our house," said Bing Russell's wife, Lou. "For years, when our children were growing up, Bing didn't allow them to watch a lot of television. He didn't believe in it. But of course, like most children, they liked TV. If the set was on and Bing drove up, the four of them would run over to shut it off. Well, one time, when Lefty happened to be there, the television was on and the kids were sprawled on the floor watching a baseball game.

"As they ran to shut it off, Lefty said, 'What's going on? Right in the middle of the game?' The kids said, 'Daddy doesn't allow TV watching.' Lefty didn't say anything. Bing came into the house and we all sat down for supper. When we were finishing dessert, Lefty says, 'Hey, Kurt, how about turning on the television?' knowing full well that Bing was not going to be fond of the suggestion. The kids loved it. They watched their favorite programs and Bing said nothing. So from that day on, every time Lefty stopped by our home, the kids were doubly thrilled because they got to watch TV."

Lefty took over in other areas, as Bing noted. "I was a working actor with a threadbare collection of clothes. Lefty would come into L.A., look in my bedroom closet, and say, 'You're going shopping.' I was thirty, forty years old.

"Lefty always had connections. If you wanted a suit, he knew a guy who made them. Before I knew it, I had twenty pairs of pants, ten shirts, jackets, and shoes. Then he'd give me some sport jackets and raincoats he wasn't using, and I'd have a wardrobe for practically nothing."

Still, Bing would never comport to the high Gomez sartorial standard. "I wear what I have on with no interest in what it looks like. One of the reasons I went into show business was because actors weren't wearing neckties. Lefty was just the opposite. His shoes had such a high polish you could see your reflection in them. So I'd be doing a Western and he'd ring me up on the set and tell me he was in town. I'd leave and pick him up for lunch. Of course, I'd walk off the set unshaven, in a dusty old cavalry outfit and muddy boots. He'd take in my appearance and as we walked to the restaurant he'd say, 'Walk twenty feet in front of me or twenty feet behind me, but not with me.' All the time we're walking, I'd be yelling out to him, 'Is this far enough behind you, Lefty?' "

The year after Lefty and June moved west, on January 9, 1969, one of their strongest ties to the East was cut when Nellie Grady died at the age of eighty-four. She was at Grandma Grady's house at 77 Oak Street in Lexington, sitting at the breakfast table set with orange juice, coffee, and a bowl of oatmeal. Nellie had just returned from morning Mass when she suffered a sudden heart attack. She was buried at Westview Cemetery in Lexington four days later.

40

SOMETHING YOU CAN ONLY HOPE FOR

LIKE THE ALL-STAR GAME, THE HALL OF FAME BEGAN AS A DEPRESSION-era novelty and grew into a venerated institution. In theory, it was created to celebrate the centennial of the game's founding. But it got the wrong date, commemorated the wrong man, and was placed in the wrong location. And, to complete the picture, the Hall was begun not by a baseball man but by an art collector.

Stephen Carlton Clark was the youngest of four brothers whose grandfather, Edward Clark, had been cofounder of the Singer Sewing Machine Company in Cooperstown, New York, a town named for the father of the man who wrote *The Last of the Mohicans.* Stephen Clark was born in 1882 and, upon the death of his father in 1896, was bequeathed one-quarter of the vast family fortune. Stephen went to Yale, was elected to the New York state legislature as a Republican in 1910, won a Distinguished Service Medal in World War I as a lieutenant colonel, became a newspaper publisher in 1925, and, beginning in early adulthood, amassed one of the finest private art collections in the world. His brothers shared his passion for European and then American painting and planned to jointly endow a museum in their hometown. Had that plan been brought to fruition, Cooperstown, New York, would have become home to one of the most important art museums in the world. However, one brother, Robert Sterling Clark, balked. After he withdrew from the plan and, along with his wife, Francine, endowed his own museum in Williamstown, Massachusetts, he and Stephen virtually never spoke again.

With the art museum idea dead, in 1935 Stephen Clark gazed out over a Cooperstown not famed throughout the world as a cultural hub but instead ravaged by the Depression. Cooperstown, however, had another potential claim to fame, although one far removed from Degas and Renoir. According to an utterly preposterous legend perpetuated by a man of questionable sanity, Abner Doubleday had invented the game of baseball in 1839 in a cow pasture right there off Main Street. That Doubleday was a cadet at West Point at the time and almost certainly nowhere near Cooperstown, and who besides claimed to despise outdoor sports, was not the least of the evidence against the tale.

Nonetheless, just after the turn of the century, Cooperstown was proclaimed the birthplace of baseball by a commission created by sporting goods magnate Albert G. Spalding. In the early 1920s, town fathers had erected Doubleday Field in the anointed cow pasture, but no one outside Cooperstown took the story very seriously and the field languished. With the future of his hometown at stake, however, Stephen Clark would not be deterred by history nor by sibling rivalry. In 1934, when his assistant Alexander Cleland came across some artifacts in an attic, one of which was an antiquated baseball, Clark exhibited the treasures in a local club and set about creating a very different sort of museum than he had originally planned.

Clark and Cleland tried to persuade baseball's leadership to support the idea, but despite the desperate straits in which the game found itself, Commissioner Landis was unenthusiastic. But Ford Frick, Babe Ruth's former ghostwriter and president of the National League, saw in the idea an enormous promotional opportunity. From there it is unclear whose impetus was most crucial but in August 1935 plans were announced to induct ten of the game's immortals during baseball's centennial, four years hence. In December, a ballot with thirty-three potential inductees was submitted to a selection of sportswriters; a 75 percent majority was required for admission. When the votes were counted, only five men had cleared the three-quarters hurdle: Ty Cobb, Babe Ruth, Christy Mathewson, Honus Wagner, and Walter Johnson. By December 1936, plaques for each of the inductees were presented to Alexander Cleland for installation. The National Baseball Hall of Fame and Museum was born.

In 1937, eight more men were voted in, including Cy Young, Tris Speaker, Ban Johnson, Connie Mack, John McGraw, and Napoleon Lajoie. Three more immortals were named in 1938, and another ten in 1939, including Lou Gehrig and, fittingly, Albert Spalding, without whom Cooperstown would have remained a city of sewing machines and Hawkeye. By the day of the official opening, June 12, 1939, twenty-six men had been enshrined, only eleven of whom were still alive. Ten of those eleven appeared for a commemorative photograph. Ty Cobb arrived late—ostensibly delayed in transit, although strong suspicion existed that the vitriolic Georgian refused to have his picture taken with Landis, one of an army of men he loathed.

The ceremonies themselves and the accompanying press coverage were as if for a coronation. Postmaster General James Farley was even on hand to issue a commemorative postage stamp. It seemed that a national baseball museum, Clark and Cleland's desperate throw, had, like the All-Star game, been an idea waiting to happen. Cooperstown almost instantaneously became baseball's shrine.

But shrines engender controversy. While choosing Babe Ruth or Walter Johnson or Lefty Grove was a relatively straightforward affair, other potential inductees engendered passionate debate, either because of their inclusion in or omission from the Hall. One of these turned out to be Vernon Gomez.

Lefty's dominance on the mound was not in question, nor was his greatness under pressure. Yet, year after year, he failed to garner the requisite votes from the sportswriters to gain admission. Finally, in 1972, Lefty was voted in unanimously by the ten-man Veterans Committee, which had been established to ensure that managers, executives, umpires, and players unjustly passed over by the writers would not be denied admission. He was part of a class that included, among others, Yogi Berra, Sandy Koufax, Josh Gibson, and Early Wynn.

Lefty had watched for decades as others were recognized while he was passed over, though he had never complained, never even mentioned it. But after his election he said, "Every boy who loves baseball dreams of being a major leaguer. I know I did as a boy of six. My dream came true as a New York Yankee, and I was lucky to pitch in World Series and All-Star games. But the Hall of Fame is something you can only hope for."

When the Veterans Committee announced its selections on January

30—outfielder Ross Youngs and Will Harridge, the guiding force behind the All-Star game, were chosen as well—Lefty and June were headed to Honolulu, where Lefty was to emcee the Hawaii Pro Sports Banquet at the Waikiki Sheraton, an event to raise money for the Muscular Dystrophy Association and the Sultan School for Handicapped Children. Sharon, who was dog-sitting the current family Chihuahua, Mr. Magoo, got the news from Cooperstown. She called the airport but her parents had already boarded the plane, so she phoned Western Airlines and a message was relayed to the pilot of Flight 579.

A flight attendant handed Lefty a note telling him of his induction. Then the captain came on the intercom and said, "The crew joins me in congratulating Lefty Gomez and his wife, June, on Lefty's induction into the Baseball Hall of Fame."

"We were 30,000 feet in the air on a flight from San Francisco to Honolulu when the flight attendant handed me the note," Lefty recalled. "It was a thrilling moment. It's unusual for me to be at a loss for words. As a rule, I can talk underwater. All I can say is that I'm thankful to everyone who cast a vote for my induction."

At home in Novato, Sharon continued to field telephone calls. "The phone rang all day and all night long with congratulatory wishes for Dad. It was a great moment for the family."[*]

After they returned to California, Lefty and June visited Bing and Lou Russell. Before his arrival, Kurt and his sisters had strung a huge white

---

[*] For the induction ceremony at Cooperstown, Lefty invited his family, among them his grandson John Banas. "When Grandpa was inducted, Roy Campanella, who had been inducted three years earlier, was there as well. Of course, Campanella had been in that horrible automobile accident that left him a quadriplegic. I was a starstruck ten-year-old kid surrounded by legends. Lefty asked me, 'Johnny, would you like to meet the players?' I nodded energetically, then Lefty, aware that a boy of my age might not realize the extent of Campanella's handicap, looked down at me and whispered, 'Whatever you do, knucklehead, don't ask Mr. Campanella for his autograph. That would be awkward for the both of you.' People are gathered around Campy, so we waited our turn. All I could think of was, 'Don't ask him for his autograph.' When we finally get to the head of the line, Lefty introduced me. I was so determined not to slip that I stuck out my hand and said, 'Glad to meet you, Mr. Campanella.' Fortunately, Campy had regained enough movement in his arms to actually shake hands with me. He was so gracious. What a nice man. As we walked away, Grandpa had his arm around me, but I heard him sigh and mutter, 'What a knucklehead.' "

banner with red lettering across the front of their house, which read, "It's great to live with a star! Welcome Mr. Magoo!"

Not everyone was as pleased with Lefty's selection, however. Dick Young of the New York *Daily News* remarked, "The next selection will be Joe Garagiola, because he's as funny as Gomez." In a column on February 1, Arthur Daley of the *New York Times* expressed similar reservations. "The writers have grown increasingly irked in recent years at the repeated election by the veterans' group of former players previously rejected by the writers," Daley wrote, in surprisingly awkward prose. "The one who turned on new heat in this growing dispute between the writers and the Cooperstown directors is Lefty Gomez." Daley went on to suggest that since Lefty's total wins fell short of the unofficial 200 criterion, his selection was based more on personal charm than achievements on the mound. Daley described Lefty as "the long-time pet of everyone who ever pounded a typewriter in a ballpark." But if those writers did not see fit to elect him, therefore, who were the committee members to allow him in?

But Young had demonstrated remarkable ignorance of a game he wrote about for decades, and Daley had things backward. Lefty didn't get into the Hall of Fame because of his gregariousness; rather, it almost kept him out. For if longevity and lifetime statistics were preeminent measurements of enshrinement, how to explain Dizzy Dean? In a career shorter than Lefty's—500 innings shorter—Diz won 39 fewer games than Lefty, while losing 18 fewer. That gave Gomez a better winning percentage, .649 to .644. Diz had Lefty in ERA, 3.02 to 3.34, but was 2–2 in the World Series to Lefty's 6–0. Diz only had three years in which he dominated, from 1934 to 1936, while Lefty's dominance stretched over a decade. Lefty had more career strikeouts and more shutouts. One can argue which one of them was marginally superior, but for either man the margin would not be large. Yet Dean was voted into the Hall by the writers in 1953, while Gomez had difficulty reaching 50 percent of the vote.

Lefty's problem was that, unlike Diz, he didn't call attention to his own achievements. Instead, he minimized them. Lefty made himself the butt of his one-liners, even as to his performance on the field, as his many Johnny Murphy and Jimmie Foxx lines would attest. Diz, on the other hand, might send up his rural roots, or even his cranial capacity, but never his pitching. The other issue was the spectacular nature of Dean's career-ending injury: one line drive off his toe. Lefty's injuries were less obvious but equally debilitating.

And then, of course, there was Koufax. Sandy had a lifetime record of 165–87 in twelve seasons, for a winning percentage of .655. While from 1963 to 1966 Koufax was dominant as any pitcher in history, his retirement at age thirty should have worked against him every bit as much as Lefty's at thirty-three. Yet Sandy was voted in the first year he was eligible.

The simple fact is that the Hall of Fame is a measure of greatness. What all three pitchers had, in addition to skill and talent, and what should have gotten each of them in as soon as they were eligible, was guts. They were the men their teams called on to get the tough win, and each would pitch and try to help his team until his arm fell off. All three nearly did.

When told of the adverse comments, Veterans Committee member Joe Cronin, onetime Yankee opponent and, in 1972, president of the American League, noted, "If they'd had to stand at the plate with a bat in their hands when Gomez was pitching, they wouldn't have thought he was so damn funny."

DUANE

———

UANE GOMEZ HAD GROWN UP TALL, POPULAR, AND ALMOST UNIVERSALLY admired.

"We started out together in high school," said his longtime girlfriend, Karin Moffat. "There were a lot of lawns near the school, so we would eat lunch together or sit out on the grass. Duane was an overachiever, always working . . . for money, for grades. He paid for things that he needed on his own. He drove June's car and he paid for the insurance.

"Duane excelled in math and when I was struggling with geometry he was breezing through calculus. He played baseball, but his real love was basketball. He was a star on the team. I was a majorette and on the cheerleader squad, so I saw him at games and practices."

Duane's friend Philip Harrison recalled, "Duane and I worked at the Shell station. I'm five-ten and I prided myself that I was sort of a good-looking guy, but when I stood next to Duane, blond and lanky, all six feet three inches of him, the girls all went for him."

Helen Kealey, another close friend, added, "He was extremely loyal. Quick to laugh. He didn't make snap judgments, or if he had, he kept it to himself."

Duane also had rare compassion. John Banas related, "We lived on different coasts and saw each other only a handful of times, but to this day I remember Uncle Duane as one of the most thoughtful people I've ever known. He was like Lefty in that you immediately felt at ease with him. My father is a renowned cardiologist, devoted to medicine. In 1966, I was four and Dad was just starting out as a doctor. He was a good-looking, fit, classic work-ethic kind of guy, who always wore button-down shirts and ties under his lab coat. He wanted well-mannered children and decked us out in bow ties, kneesocks, and knickers. Well, that Christmas, I went to Woolworth's and saw the one thing that I had to have. It wasn't a baseball mitt or a train set. It was a Betsy Wetsy doll. Now, maybe I was in touch with my paternal instincts at a young age, but that's what I wanted. Needless to say, that caused quite a ruckus with Dad, and the scratching of Betsy Wetsy off my wish list became such a family scandal that it reached Uncle Duane's ears thousands of miles away. Duane was only thirteen, and without telling anyone, he saved up all the S&H green stamps he had earned and, instead of picking something out of the catalog for himself, he ordered the doll and had it shipped to our apartment. I was one happy four-year-old when I pulled Betsy Wetsy out of the package. What could my dad say in the face of such sheer selfless generosity by a teenager? But that was Duane."*

In high school, Duane became interested in motorcycle racing. He approached it with an intense sense of responsibility that couldn't have been further from the outlaw image that many associated with bikes. When he was seventeen, he wrote in an essay: "The iron machine, as we call a motorcycle, is the same as the horse who helped the cowboy pursue his destiny in the West. . . . In the wind, you know you're alive, in a way a car driver could never feel. When you think of how you can cross streams and deserts in quest of your freedom, I feel sorry for the car driver, insulated from the world by two tons of steel, glass, and gimmicks. If you have ever had the wistful yearning to be a cowboy, free with your trusty steed, to follow the sun across the big country, climb aboard tomorrow. If you are a dreamer, the big country is where you can stretch your mind beyond the horizon. And a motorcycle will take you there, but, go there in the right form. Let's work together."

At nineteen, he was a freshman at the College of Marin and was racing in competitive events throughout California. He often asked June to come, but she said she couldn't. June knew Duane was a talented and disciplined rider but the speed of the motorcycles darting in and out of the pack was

---

* Getting a doll for Christmas did not seem to hurt John's development. He is now an attorney, father of two, and CEO of a software company.

simply too frightening. She told Duane she had to stay at home, where she wasn't visibly confronted with the danger. He didn't press, but on August 5, 1973, he was to race at Sears Point, a key race at the highest level of competition. He told June, "Mom, Sears Point is really important to me. I want you there. Please, just this once." June put aside her fear and replied, "Yes, I'll be there." Since she was going anyway, she decided to film the race as a surprise for Duane and for Lefty, who was in Pennsylvania, giving a speech at a fund-raiser for handicapped children.

At the race, June settled into a seat in the grandstand and stuck her eye to the viewfinder. Duane was easy to see in his distinctive red jacket and helmet. Never taking her eye from the camera, she followed her son around the track, lap after lap of the two-and-a-half-mile course.

"WHEN THE PLANE TAKING me home from Pennsylvania landed in Chicago," Lefty said, "a United agent came aboard and said, 'Mr. Gomez, your son Duane is in critical condition. United is holding a plane for you to return you to San Francisco.' I knew it was bad when I landed in California, because Gery and Sharon were standing at the gate and wouldn't give me a direct answer to 'How's Duane?'

"Duane was dead. In the heat of the race at Sears Point, a kid lost control of his motorcycle and fell onto the ground directly in front of Duane's bike. In that instant, Duane chose to risk his own life and save the boy who had fallen in front of him. He swerved out of the narrow lane, towards the embankment. The surgeon told me later that a helmet can only protect just so much. Racing at such high speed, the impact of the motorcycle against the embankment broke Duane's neck and he bled into his brain. He never regained consciousness except for a flickering of his eyelid. June never told me the details. She couldn't talk about it. The boy who fell on the ground walked away from the race. He rang our doorbell the next day and said he was sorry he lost control of his motorcycle.

"They had called Bing Russell and he was flying up from L.A. to be with me. Bing was at Duane's wake and the funeral. Bing kept me going, walked me through the saddest day of my life. All I know is, I went away and Duane was alive. I returned home and he was dead. June couldn't say his name for two years. She walked around in a trance, staring straight ahead, looking right through me. It was the first time June had seen Duane race because she couldn't bear the tension, but Duane said it was the most important race of his life. He wanted to win it and he wanted his mother there. So June went. She filmed the race and, of course, she filmed his death."

"When I married Lefty and the children came along," June said, "I told myself my marriage and raising our children will be my career, and I'll do my best, every day of my life. I did it, through thick and thin. I stuck to my promise. I stuck to Lefty and to my children. And I will never, ever understand why Duane had to die so young. Why? What more could I have done for this marriage and our children?

"Losing a young son in a tragic accident leaves an unquenchable sadness. When Duane died, I took all his pictures off the walls. I packed away his guitar, his records, and his sound system. Then I stopped listening to music on the car radio. Pictures of Duane and hearing the popular songs he loved come over the radio put a knife into my heart. I couldn't stand it."

Karin Moffat added, "Duane was all about winning, but a win at Sears Point was especially important to him. When you think about it, Duane did win the race because he did what he had to do. He could have driven right over that guy and killed him or maimed him for life. But Duane didn't. He chose another way. There are different ways to win."

"He had a very strong, sweet personality that no one who met him could forget," June said. "I think of him often and I always wonder what Duane would have done with his life. Lefty does well under pressure and I fall apart. When Duane died, I was shattered, broken into a million pieces. I needed someone like Lefty to be cool about it, to think levelly. I couldn't think straight, couldn't see straight. I was numb. Our son was dead. It couldn't be worse. The worst tragedy of our lives. I was out of my mind. I didn't know where to turn for help. I went to the parish priest and told him I couldn't stop grieving. I thought he'd be compassionate and show me a way out of my despair. But the priest was very curt. 'What's the matter with you? You don't have a problem. You are the problem.' I left the rectory in tears. I didn't return. A few years later, over a cup of coffee, I read in the *Chronicle* that the priest had jumped off the Golden Gate

Bridge. When I had talked with him, he made me feel like such a loser. I wish I had known at the time that he was the problem."

After a time, June began to cope. "I began yoga and Transcendental Meditation. And I decided to get more mileage out of my hours in the pool by swimming for needy children. Over time, I found that I had the will and the strength to move on. I was stronger than the tragedy of Duane's death."

June also began driving cancer patients to area hospitals for radiation or chemotherapy sessions, then picking them up and returning them home after the treatments were completed. Their relatives often wrote letters thanking her not only for the taxi service but for the inspiration. One letter read, "My mom says June's energy and encouragement was the best medicine she'd ever had. June told her, 'You're going to make it. I know you will. Hang in there.' "

Perhaps the most remarkable occurrence in that horrible tragedy came as Duane lay in state in a funeral home. John Winkin, who would go on to become one of the most revered and respected collegiate baseball coaches in the nation, recalled, "The day of Duane's wake, Lefty was scheduled to give the Breakfast of Champions speech at the Babe Ruth World Series in Manchester, New Hampshire. With his son lying in a coffin, Lefty phoned the banquet from the funeral parlor. He gave that speech by telephone over the loudspeaker to the young ballplayers in the national tournament. Lefty told the boys, 'Go out and do your best for the team. Go out and win. Never accept defeat.'

"Lefty Gomez was an inspiration to me personally," Winkin went on. "My daughter had run away from home and there were rocky years trying to straighten things out. She'd come home, then run away again. I'd get discouraged, discouraged enough to give up. Then I'd think of Lefty and say to myself, 'Wait a minute, Winkin. Lefty gave that speech to those Babe Ruth ballplayers while his son lay dead in a coffin in the next room. Your daughter is still alive.' "

SIXTEEN YEARS LATER, soon after Lefty died, June opened his brown leather wallet and found among the family snapshots and business cards a picture of Duane and his girlfriend smiling in tux and gown just before they went off to the senior prom. Underneath the photo Lefty had tucked the $10 bill he had given Duane before the Sears Point race, "in case of an emergency." A doctor had found the bill in Duane's pants pocket and Lefty had carried it for the rest of his life.

43.

"WE'RE GOING TO MISS LEFTY"

IN THE FALL OF 1973, LEFTY WAS APPROACHING THE MANDATORY RETIRE-ment age at Wilson and assumed he would be "put out to pasture." But instead Tom Mullaney approached him and asked, "How would you like to keep working for Wilson, Lefty?" June later said, "Tom Mullaney gave Lefty his life back because he didn't retire him at sixty-five."

Lefty thus continued on his furious schedule, still logging 100,000 miles annually. For almost three years he encountered no difficulties, but then, on October 26, 1976, he experienced chest pains while playing in a golf tournament. They continued to bother him the following day. Lefty brushed off the episode, but June called her cardiologist son-in-law, who said, "Get him to a hospital, even if a cop has to arrest him and take him in handcuffs." Lefty muttered, "I don't know what all the fuss is about," but at Stanford Medical Center, after a series of diagnostic tests, he was told he needed bypass surgery.

The doctor was heart transplant pioneer Norman Shumway, who revealed during Lefty's first visit that he was a rabid Detroit fan. He recalled a number of games where Lefty had bested his Tigers when he was a kid. "How many times did you beat us?" Shumway asked. Lefty said he didn't remember, but he'd look it up.

Back home, he checked the record books and found he'd beaten Detroit twenty-four times while losing seventeen. The next day, Lefty returned to Shumway's office with a printed sign: "Detroit Tigers 24, Gomez 17." Afterward, Lefty admitted to inverting the record. "I love you as a surgeon," he told Shumway, "but I'm never sure about a fan. I wanted to keep my doctor happy."

Shumway wanted to operate in mid-December, but Lefty persuaded him to wait three weeks so he could spend Christmas with his grandchildren, including John and Andrew, who were flying in from the East Coast. Presents for all of them were, of course, under the tree on Christmas morning. Andrew was eight at the time.

"John and I got Pong, the original classic videogame, and we hooked it up to Grandma and Grandpa's television. But more importantly, Duane's Gibson guitar was under the tree with my name on the holiday tag. I loved guitar and Grandpa Lefty said they were giving it to me because Duane's music should go on and I was the one to do it on his Gibson. I was thrilled with the gift, but being only a kid, I don't think I could possibly have realized how difficult it was for them to part with something that Duane loved.

"Grandpa Lefty rarely mentioned Duane's death. The only time I ever saw him really distressed was the time he temporarily lost the old ragged miniature camel that hung from the rearview mirror of his car, a long-ago Father's Day gift from Duane when he was five years old. When I found it under the front seat, Grandpa's face broke into a smile and he said, 'Good work, Andy,' and he gave me a hug."

On January 14, Lefty had successful heart surgery. In the intensive care recovery unit, Dr. Shumway asked, "Lefty, do you know you had a triple bypass?"

"No, Doc," Lefty replied, "but if I did, it's the only triple I ever got in my life."

Within weeks, he was again traveling for Wilson and promoting youth baseball and soon afterward had fully resumed his grueling schedule. In July, he told a sportswriter at Candlestick Park, "It's been about six months since the operation and I feel great. When I went on the operating table, I prayed, 'Let me finish this game, God,' and here I am. Dr. Shumway's orders are to walk a lot. That's easy for me. I walked a lot of guys when I was pitching."

The Hall of Fame induction six years earlier was the beginning of a seemingly endless series of honors that were bestowed on Lefty in his seventies. In November 1978, a thousand people attended his seventieth-birthday party at the St. Francis Hotel in San Francisco. Gery and Bing Russell helped coordinate. Friends came from across the nation. Among the guests were Joe DiMaggio, Joe Cronin, Billy Martin, Giants owner Bob Lurie, Padres owner and McDonald's founder Ray Kroc, Gene Autry, Johnny Mize, Frank Crosetti, Maye Lazzeri, Elaine Klein, Eleanor Gehrig, Reder Claeys, Buddy Hassett, Tommy Henrich, Dorothy Ruth Pirone, Satchel Paige, and Ted Williams. Norman Shumway, ignoring Lefty's true record against his beloved Tigers, came to wish his former patient well. Only Paul Fung, in Germany, could not make it, but sent a telegram, which he signed "Mascot, little Paul Fung Jr." Other telegrams of congratulations and friendship poured in.

The affair was formal, of course, and at one point Vernona, in a long red gown with a spray of flowers in her hair, descended the spiral staircase to use the ladies' room. As she was walking across the hall to return to the ballroom, a man fell into step with her. "Hey, listen," he said eagerly, "I'm going to a sensational party for a Hall of Famer, Lefty Gomez. How about going with me? You can crash the party and I'll introduce you to Lefty. He's a legend."

"That sounds like fun," Vernona replied. The two went back to the party and the would-be lothario fetched her a drink. After a few minutes, the man escorted her to the guest of honor and said, "Lefty there's someone here who would love to meet you."

"Hi, Dad," Vernona said.

The deflated suitor sighed. "You got me," he said.

THE FOLLOWING YEAR, 1979, Lou Spadia, former owner of the San Francisco 49ers, teamed with the San Francisco Chamber of Commerce to create the Bay Area Sports Hall of Fame. Rather than a museum, like at Cooperstown, the BASHOF would operate largely as a vehicle to promote youth sports. So, instead of spending money on a building, plaques of those in the Hall were to be hung in the United Airlines pavilion at the San Francisco airport, allowing funds normally used for upkeep to go instead to the kids.

The first group of honorees included Joe DiMaggio, Willie Mays, Hank Luisetti, Ernie Nevers, and Bill Russell. The following year, the inductees were Lefty O'Doul, Frankie Albert, Bob Mathias, Helen Wills, and Lefty Gomez.

To introduce him at the induction ceremonies, Lefty turned to Jack McDonald, the man who had scooped his sale to the Yankees from the Seals in 1929. "I was very pleased when Lefty asked if I would introduce him," McDonald said, "but I think he chose me because he knew I wouldn't make the intro too damn long."

The plaques at the airport attracted any number of those who would not make a special trip to a museum. It also attracted some other viewers.

"It was one of those last-minute plane commutes to Las Vegas," Gery said. "I rushed to the San Francisco airport, figuring I'd probably have to fly standby. I checked in at the United counter and asked the agent if there was a seat available. The guy looked and said, 'Yes, there is. It's funny, we have another Gomez on board. I think it would be amusing if I put you side by side.'

" 'Sure,' I said. 'What's his name?'

" 'He's a ballplayer. Hall of Famer. Lefty Gomez. Matter of fact, before you get on the plane, go over and look at his plaque from the Bay Area Hall of Fame that's in the United pavilion.'

"Knowing that Dad only flew first-class and I always flew coach, if the agent was going to give me an upgrade, I'd humor him. When I boarded, Dad was sitting in a first-class aisle seat with an open briefcase balanced on his knees. I said, 'Excuse me, sir,' and made a move to the window. He looked up and said, 'Gery? Where are you going?'

" 'Las Vegas and I'm sitting with you.'

" 'Since when do you fly first-class?'

" 'Since right now.'

"Just then, the United agent ran on the plane to see if we had introduced ourselves. He said to Lefty, 'This fellow here has the same name as you do, Mr. Gomez.' 'It's even funnier,' Lefty replied. 'This is my son, Gery, and he belongs in coach.'

"At the Las Vegas banquet that night Dad sat on the dais while the master of ceremonies gave him a twenty-minute introduction. When he finally got to the podium, he began his speech by saying, 'I thought my clothes would go out of style before he handed me the mike.' "

IN 1982, TSUNEO IKEDA, owner of the Nippon Sports Publishing Company, invited Lefty and June back to Japan to celebrate the fiftieth anniversary of the 1934 tour. Ikeda moved up the commemoration by two years because few participants were still alive. Babe was long gone, as was Lou. Even the old spy Moe Berg had passed from the scene. In fact, only four members of the American team remained, Lefty, Charley Gehringer, Earl Averill, and Joe Cascarella, but only Lefty made the trip. There he would meet the three surviving members of the Japanese team.

Where Lefty and June had taken weeks to arrive by boat in 1934, this time they arrived in hours. "We flew directly from San Francisco to Tokyo on a Japanese airline and with the time zones, we lost one whole day," June said. "We arrived at three in the morning, our time. We were exhausted. Tsuneo's son Ike greeted us with newspaper reporters who wanted interviews and photographs. We went with Ike to the Keio Plaza Hotel, where Lefty did a press conference. When we went to rest, the reporters informed us that they would be back early the next morning. No sleep, nothing to eat, but we expected that with the changing time zone, so we dealt with it."

The schedule was daunting, as many as fifteen interviews and appearances in a day, shooting television documentaries, followed by banquets in the evening. The schedule was choreographed to the minute. The most important events were the public appearances. Lefty, for example, threw out the first ball at the Japanese World Series in Tokyo. "They asked me to wear my old Yankee uniform. I'm fit and I'm trim but I still think they clocked me at twenty-one miles an hour."

The Japan of 1982 bore little resemblance to the country Lefty and June had visited as newlyweds. Skyscrapers dominated skylines, automobiles had replaced bicycles as the main mode of travel, and women wore Western dress in place of kimonos. Lefty and June traveled by bullet train instead of rickshaw.

And substantial changes had taken place at the games themselves. As June reported, "Reserved seats at the ballpark reminded me of my old grammar school chairs, with a little shelf next to the seat. During the games, girls ran up and down the aisles taking orders for full-course dinners. What a luxury to have the Japanese delicacies brought to you as you watch the game. A far cry from fighting your way for a greasy hot dog with mustard.

"In the States, there are pregame and postgame interviews, but in Japan after each inning a TV commentator talked with the players in the dugout. A bench roundup. In the heat of battle, it must be a challenge for a hitter to keep his cool when an aggressive reporter says, 'I see you've fanned in your last two at-bats. You're not helping the team. What's the problem?' On the other hand, if a player hit a home run, a young girl ran out with a bouquet of roses. He held up the bouquet, the fans cheered, and the player ran off.

"If a pitcher was knocked out of the box, he couldn't run into the dugout and sit on the bench like an American player. He had to go to the sidelines and throw the ball back and forth to a catcher to show the crowd he still had his stuff. Just not the right stuff for that day. I doubt it's good for the pitcher, because his arm is already tired and he's discouraged at having been pulled out of the game. But he went out there, throwing the extra pitches.

"The Japanese fans are passionate. It was comparable to what baseball was to the fans of the thirties in the U.S. In many ballparks, there's a sign with a gauge on the side that looks like a giant thermometer. As the fans scream, it records the volume. In addition, the fans wave all sorts of flags. Home runs, double plays, the last out of an inning . . . all the plays are marked by flag waving and screaming."

The tour had originally been scheduled for two weeks, but Lefty and June were such a hit that their hosts extended their stay by a week to allow the Gomezes to travel around the country and sightsee free of obligations.

After Lefty and June returned home, he was invited to throw out the first pitch at the fiftieth anniversary of the first All-Star game, also to be played in Comiskey Park, July 6, 1983.

"In 1983, June and I celebrated our fiftieth wedding anniversary and the fiftieth anniversary of the All-Star game. On July 5, I pitched in the Old-Timers' Game, then the following day threw out the ceremonial first pitch. In the inaugural game, I worked three innings, gave up no runs, and allowed two singles. Fifty years later, I worked a third of an inning and gave up one run and two hits. They talk about pitchers losing three inches off their fastball. Me? I've lost sixty feet."

But the fiftieth anniversary of the All-Star game wasn't the fiftieth All-Star game. Because baseball had initiated an ill-fated two–All-Star game schedule in 1959—which lasted only four years—there had been a previous fiftieth anniversary game celebration in Seattle in 1979. For that one, Lefty and Carl Hubbell had been honorary captains. King Carl, who by then was living in Phoenix, had also by then become one of Lefty's closest friends.

IN OCTOBER 1984, another invitation arrived.

Charles M. Conlon is widely considered the greatest baseball photographer in history. Working from 1908 until 1942, Conlon captured thousands of images of virtually every star player for three decades. His photograph of Ty Cobb stealing third base in 1909 has long been considered one of the game's iconic images.

In October 1984, the Smithsonian's National Portrait Gallery in Washington, D.C., held an exhibition of Conlon's work. As Lefty remembered, "Ballplayers who had been captured on Conlon's glass negatives were invited to attend the opening of the exhibition but many had to decline due to prior commitments or illness. For example, Hubb had suffered a stroke, so of course couldn't attend. The three who did attend the festivities were Leo Durocher, Bill Terry, and me.

"Security at the Smithsonian was tight and everyone spoke in hushed tones. We're three brash ballplayers and that whispering to one another took some getting used to. But, that aside, from the very first moment we arrived, Leo, Bill, and I were filled with a sense of history. On display were so many things that I had read about as a kid. To think how many times I traveled to Washington, D.C., over my baseball career and never went into the Smithsonian until the Charles Conlon exhibition in '84.

"Seeing all the photographs in the exhibition pulled me right back to the thirties and to the ballplayers of that era. Charlie Conlon was an artist and a fun guy to have around the dugout.

"After Durocher, Terry, and I toured around the exhibit for hours, we were starving. We returned to the area where, upon entering the Smithsonian, the guide had rather pompously said to us, 'Do you three gentlemen realize that right where you're standing is the exact spot where Lincoln stood when he became president of the United States?' Durocher started stomping on the floor with his shoe. 'Hey, Abe, send up some hamburgers, will you, please? We're dying of hunger.' All the students milling around us who were so serious a minute ago are now laughing their heads off. The Smithsonian staff didn't ask the three of us to leave but I think they were glad when Leo, Bill, and I walked out the door."

Three years later, Lefty met Bill Terry again, at the 1987 Hall of Fame ceremonies. Ted Williams was there as well. "Bill was closing in on ninety but he still had the no-nonsense attitude of the first baseman who played for John McGraw. And he was still gutsy enough to tell Williams how to hit the ball. Teddy Ballgame loved it." The afternoon waned and the last two men to hit .400 continued to swap stories on the verandah of the Otesaga Hotel. Lefty and Bill Dickey came by just as Williams was explaining how he had figured out what pitchers were going to throw him. "How the hell could Ted know what we were doin' out there?" Dickey asked Lefty. "*We* didn't even know."

At the Cooperstown autograph session, June asked Williams for his. Ted looked up at her and said, "June, you're married to the greatest son of a bitch I know." When she told Lefty, he said, "Coming from Teddy Ballgame, that's the best compliment I ever got in my life."

Robert Obojski, a sportswriter who covered Hall of Fame weekends, wrote, "All Hall of Famers are invited to attend the annual induction ceremonies. Some never trouble to attend after their own election, but Lefty Gomez was always on hand to welcome the new inductees and their families and to take part in the various ceremonies. He loved to sit in an easy chair, talking baseball by the hour with his fellow Hall of Famers, reporters, and fans. And I never saw him turn down a request for an autograph."

Lefty had his own take on autographs. "How do you know your career is over? The fans don't give you a clean ball to autograph. Instead they offer you one filled with other autographs and say, 'See if you can squeeze your name on it somewhere.' "

LEFTY'S UNFAILING GRACE and generosity with his time made him an obvious draw at memorabilia shows. But those very qualities were initially a problem for promoters. The shows work on a signature-per-hour basis, where the ex-player is paid strictly for volume. First he signs a certain number of flats and balls in his hotel room, then an additional number at autograph sessions. There can be some chatting as the line of fans moves, but to make their contracted quota, many players restrict conversation to "Hello" and a perfunctory grunt or two. Some players were notoriously surly.

Lefty simply refused to operate that way. "I like the fans and I'm going to talk to them. I'm too old to change. To hell with the quota." When the promoters were told, they decided to forget his quota and "book Gomez as a nice guy. We need that at the shows."

It was a wise decision. Lefty was a hit and created just the atmosphere that enticed fans to pay their way in.

Once, a teenager in a Yankee jacket, glasses, and a baseball cap came up to Lefty's table and handed him a picture to autograph. The young man began asking questions about being a Yankee and playing with Ruth, Gehrig, and DiMaggio. He had a painful stutter and it took a good deal of time for the sentences to come out. Lefty smiled and listened, answering every question in detail. The other fans in the long line grew impatient, but Lefty didn't care. Lefty had had a speech impediment when he was a kid in Rodeo, and he knew firsthand how embarrassing it was to stutter. When the young man was done, Lefty handed back the autographed picture. The teenager walked away with a huge smile.

On another occasion, as Lefty was walking to the parking lot, a van pulled up and a man jumped out with two kids holding pictures. The father said he had gone to the wrong location for the show. Now his kids were upset because they had photos of Lefty Gomez and wanted to meet him and get his autograph, but it was evident as they pulled into the parking lot that the show was over. Lefty spoke to the two boys about baseball and then asked for the pictures. He signed them, and as he did so, the father pulled out some cash and handed it to him. Lefty laughed and said,

"Thank you, but I don't want your money. Buy your kids an ice-cream cone."

Dave Sigler, a friend with whom Lefty sometimes traveled, witnessed Lefty's technique. "If Lefty was at a weekend show, we'd all go out Friday night and have dinner and then return to the hotel room and talk baseball till we were ready to fall asleep, then see each other the next morning. One Friday, a fan gave Lefty a Goofy the Dog baseball cap, with long earflaps. Lefty laughed and put it on. After the session, we planned breakfast for seven-thirty, but at six in the morning Lefty was ready to go. He called and asked, 'You ready?' I told him to come on over. Well, in two minutes he was knocking on the door, and when I opened it, Goofy's wearing the Goofy cap. Six in the morning and Lefty's out to make you laugh."

Not all requests came at shows, as June related. "Lefty and I were at Sunday Mass in Scottsdale, Arizona, during spring training. The parishioners joined together in saying the Our Father, then turned to the person next to them, shaking hands and saying, 'Peace be with you.' Lefty turned to the stranger next to him, said, 'Peace be with you,' and the guy said, 'Lefty, would you sign this ball for me?' "

In 1986, Lefty, as he always did, attended the winter baseball meetings in Hollywood, Florida. Lou Pavlovich, editor and publisher of *College Baseball*, was there as well. "At the pros' annual banquet each year, someone is selected as King of Baseball for outstanding contributions to the game. Lefty was sitting at a table with other members of the Wilson team when it was announced that the King of Baseball would be crowned. The ritual is for a spotlight to circle around the darkened room and settle on the winner.

"So lo and behold, the spotlight stopped on Lefty. It came as a complete surprise—Lefty had received no advance warning. The huge banquet hall was as silent as a tomb as everyone tried to see who the new King of Baseball was. Lefty, who likes to know in advance about things like this, had an immediate reaction. 'Oh, shit,' he growled, and most of the room heard him."

The crowd took Lefty off the hook with a standing ovation while he was given a cape and crown to wear. "You'd think they would let you know about this so you can be prepared," he said during his acceptance speech. Then he added the sort of remark that almost kept him out of the Hall of Fame: "A standing ovation is a strange sight for me. I was never around in the seventh inning." Privately, he said, "This was really one of the nicest awards I've ever received. It's really a great honor."

As Lefty aged, he became even more of a fixture in Yankee lore. In 1987, he was given the Lou Gehrig Pride of the Yankees award and a plaque in Monument Park on the same day as his old pigeon, Whitey Ford. He was also a regular at Old-Timers' Days, as was his old roommate.

"DiMaggio always wants to be introduced last. And rightfully so. He's a great ballplayer, if not the greatest. But we're going to have a little fun with that and make Joe wait a long, long time in the dugout, until he's fuming. Standing out there in front of the crowds, I'd call down the line to Whitey, Billy, and Mickey, 'Keep waving those baseball caps to the fans, boys. Keep them clapping and cheering. Let DiMag wait.' "

Lefty and June began their 1988 spring training Cactus League tour as always. Lefty soon found he couldn't stop gaining weight. By late March, he had ballooned to 195 pounds.

"It wasn't my diet, because I eat like a sparrow. So I didn't think anything about it until I noticed that I had a hard time getting an old pair of shoes off my feet. I'd been spraying the shoes with Armor All, but it didn't help. I told June, 'I'm not going to use that stuff anymore. It's shrinking my shoes.' "

June convinced Lefty to see a cardiologist. His shrinking shoes were actually swollen feet caused by fluid retention from congestive heart failure and he was once again hospitalized. In the ICU, his heart went into atrial fibrillation and he underwent cardioversion, application of DC current to restore a normal heartbeat. Afterward he seemed fine. He spun his yarns for the staff and signed autographs for the many kids who popped into his room.

Before Lefty was discharged, the doctor had a talk with him. "You have to exercise, stay on your medication, and no smoking," the doctor said sternly. "It's a question of life or death."

Lefty was uncharacteristically silent.

"Well?" the physician prompted.

"Doc," Lefty replied, "I haven't decided yet."

Once out, Lefty resumed his regular grueling schedule. He did make some minor modifications, however. "In January of '89," June recalled,

"Lefty and I were in Nashville for the American Baseball Coaches Association. The lobbies and the ballrooms of the Opryland Hotel seem endless. Lefty and a group of baseball executives were walking toward a scheduled event in a room that seemed miles away. Suddenly the men noticed that Lefty wasn't with them. They thought nothing of it until they finally reached the other end of the complex and there was Lefty laughing with a bunch of people.

"The guys couldn't figure out how he'd done it. When they asked, Lefty replied, 'Hailed a cab, what else?' Lefty had left the group, gone outside and thumbed down a taxi, and taken it to the last exit door of the Opryland Hotel. 'I don't waste energy on the small stuff,' he said."

On February, 1, 1989, Lefty gave a speech to five hundred people, then afterward he experienced chest pains. Two days later, when the pain didn't subside, Lefty headed for Marin General with June and Gery. To get to the entrance, he had to climb a steep set of stairs dubbed "Cardiac Hill." "Great way to admit a heart patient," he said. After he checked in, Lefty was immediately put in intensive care. The hospital was extremely crowded and he was moved three times from a private room to a semiprivate one. He told the nurses he wanted Mileage Plus credit for the room changes.

Initially, June was told that Lefty could go home within a week. But as his stay in the hospital lengthened, his condition became more ominous. Doctors heard rattling in his lungs and suspected pneumonia.

"I think Lefty knew he was dying when the pneumonia set in," June said, "but we gave him hope. His will to live was so strong. That last year, I didn't realize how sick Lefty really was. No one did. He kept to his traveling schedule and all his speaking engagements without complaint. Lefty pushed himself relentlessly. As a kid, he saw Lizzie and Coyote work morning to night, fighting the elements to survive. He took their work ethic to heart. 'People shouldn't be afraid to work,' he said, 'There's a lot of work to be done.' "

Phone calls came from everywhere, old friends like Bill Dickey and Frank Crosetti. At one point, the ICU receptionist came running down the hallway to tell Lefty that George Steinbrenner had called. "The nurses at the station are laughing at me," she said. "I asked him twice to spell his name. I don't follow baseball. I'm an opera buff. If his name had been Mozart I would have known how to spell it."

The family was told to emphasize the positive, to talk of happier moments to keep Lefty's spirits high. "Dad, those were good times in 1936," Vernona said, "when you were pitching in St. Louis and Mom sang at the municipal opera."

Lefty's voice suddenly got stronger. "June was dazzling on the stage. She lit up the set of *Kid Boots*. Every night, my teammates and I ran over after the game to catch the operetta."

June sat up, surprised. "Gosh, Vernon. I'd forgotten about *Kid Boots*. What a memory."

"Yes, *Kid Boots* and another one," Lefty went on. "I can't recall it . . . wait, it was *No, No, Nanette*. June was the star. Everyone cheered. I was a damn fool to ask her to give up the stage."

June came over to him and said softly, "Vernon, I loved being Mrs. Lefty Gomez. Every minute of it."

Late the next afternoon, as she sat by Lefty's bedside holding his hand, June turned to her children. "I always loved to hold Dad's hand. His fingers are so long and his palm so wide. My short little fingers felt so safe there."

At noon on Valentine's Day, Bing Russell walked into Lefty's room. He was wearing gray pants, scuffed boots, and a threadbare, stained ruby-red blazer.

"Now listen, Lefty," Bing said, "your stories always made me laugh like hell and now it's my turn to do the same for you. So don't give me a hard time about my ratty blazer."

"I gave it to Bing a hundred years ago," Lefty said softly.

"Yes, you did. In my starving-actor days."

"He's showing me his star wardrobe . . . how far he's come," chuckled Lefty.

"Damn right I am," laughed Bing. "I've come full circle. Buddy's son, Lefty Gomez's kid brother, and now Kurt Russell's father."

As weak as Lefty was, doctors told the family he could go home if he could beat the pneumonia. But that was too tall an order, even for the ferocious competitor.

Vernon Louis Gomez died on February 17, 1989. Within minutes of the announcement, the phone in Novato began to ring continuously.

"February 26 would have made fifty-six years that we were married," June told reporters. "We had such a good time, all that laughter. Even up to the end his last words were a joke about baseball. The doctor leaned over his bed and said, 'Lefty, picture yourself on the mound, getting ready to throw a fastball. On a scale of one to ten, how severe are the chest pains?' And Lefty said, 'Who's hitting, Doc?'"

WHEN BILLY MARTIN heard the news, he hopped a plane from New York to San Francisco. "I wanted to be the first to pay my respects at Lefty's wake. I loved the guy. But when I entered the Redwood Chapel in Novato and looked at the register, I saw DiMaggio had beaten me to it. Joe's name was on the first line."

The outpouring of sentiment came from across the nation and from as far away as Canada, Europe, and Japan. One of the most apt remembrances came from Fred Post, sports editor for the *Middletown Press,* Lefty's local paper in Connecticut. "He was the funniest man I ever met in and out of the world of sports. Just thinking about Lefty Gomez brings a smile. He was also one of the greatest of all left-handed pitchers in the history of major league baseball. Hailed as the next Lefty Grove when he first went to the bigs, he became the first Lefty Gomez and that ain't chopped liver."

Lefty was buried in Mount Tamalpais Cemetery in San Rafael. At the service at Our Lady of Loreto, a guitarist played "Take Me Out to the Ball Game" at Lefty's request. The congregation joined in, smiling as they sang.

"Fung found out I was giving the eulogy at Lefty's funeral," said Bing Russell. "Paul couldn't attend because he was in Germany. His daughter Lori, a sergeant in the army, had given birth to his first grandchild. He called and asked me to put two roses on Lefty's casket, one for him and one for me. I couldn't find a florist that was open that early, so at the church I yanked two roses out of the Yankee floral bouquet that George Steinbrenner had sent and put the roses on Lefty's casket. Two white roses for two kids lucky enough to have known Lefty Gomez for a lifetime."

Perhaps nothing better epitomizes Lefty's place in American lore than two contrasting condolences. The first came from the White House:

> *Dear June,*
>
> *Barbara and I were saddened to learn of Lefty's death and we share in your sorrow. He will be greatly missed, but his memory will live on in the hearts and minds of his many friends and admirers. Our thoughts and prayers are with you for strength and peace during this difficult time. God bless you and your family,*
>
> *Sincerely,*
> *George Bush*

The second occurred the day after Lefty died. Five very young boys rode up on bicycles to the Gomez home in Novato. They tossed their bikes on the lawn and rang the doorbell to present June with a handwritten note. It read simply:

> *We appreciate the time he took for us. We're going to miss Lefty.*

EPILOGUE

———

OF ALL THE ACCOLADES THAT WERE BESTOWED ON LEFTY THE ONE that would have pleased him the most was having three baseball fields named after him, places where kids could play the game he loved.

The first, in Fairfax, had been dedicated in 1972, when Lefty was inducted into the Hall of Fame. The other two were dedicated in 1990, the year after he died. One of those was in Rodeo, on the very spot where young Vernon played sandlot ball; the other was in Novato, about two blocks from where neighborhood kids lined up for autographs and bubble gum. June threw out the first pitch at both ceremonies and fired them in the strike zone.

The months after Lefty's death had been difficult for her. "Reading the cards and letters coming in from friends and fans, it made me happy to know that Lefty had touched so many lives. But I cried over their words of appreciation because they underscored my loss. I found I could write only one or two thank-you notes at a time because my stationery became tearstained and I had to crumple up the paper and begin again."

Then, six months later, her sister died. "Sunny lost her yearlong battle with cancer. When she had been confronted with the diagnosis, she had taken the news with courage, as I knew she would. Sunny had brushed up against death on a daily basis as a USO entertainer in Europe and the Pacific during World War II. With the outbreak of the Korean War, Sunny and Frank Conville worked the foxhole circuit again. On USO stages set up a few yards from the firing line, they brought a much-needed laugh to the war-weary soldiers."

As always, June pushed on. " 'Time mends a broken heart' is a refrain

I sang on Broadway. I found it to be true for me. Over time, as the fun of each new day beckoned to me, I began to run with it."

And June ran at her usual furious pace. She continued her volunteer work for the American Cancer Society, played in bridge tournaments, and swam her eighty-four laps every day at the local health club. She got a medal when she reached 150 miles in the pool and for each one the club made a donation to charity in her name. She hiked and did aerobic dance and yoga to round out her fitness routine. "Spectator fun comes at basketball and baseball games cheering my grandkids," she said.

But from that first trip to Japan in 1934, June's passion had been travel. Since then, she had trekked through virtually every country in the world and sailed down rivers from the Amazon to the Yangtze. "I love history and sharing present-day experiences with people in faraway places. To talk with them in person. Even as a young actress, I didn't call up agents or producers. I went to their offices. I wanted to see the glint in their eyes."

On the road, she was, as always, prepared for anything. Once, camping out in the Sahara, the guide called the tour group together to tell them he had to make repairs to the jeep. "I don't suppose anyone has a Phillips screwdriver handy?" he asked. "Oh yes," June piped up. "I have one in my cosmetic bag."

After Lefty's death, she began to spend three months a year in Mexico. She had become fluent in French and Italian studying opera in the thirties, and now she studied conversational Spanish at the university in San Miguel de Allende. "For my first oral exam, I waxed on about American *beisbol.* The professor gave me a thumbs-up.

"But flying home from Mexico in April 1992, I experienced gut-wrenching pain. I hailed a taxi at the airport and went to the emergency room at Marin General Hospital. An exploratory operation revealed that I had cancer, aggressive and life-threatening. The tumor was removed and the surgeon said chemotherapy would return me to good health. Another physician disagreed. He said, 'Get your papers in order, Mrs. Gomez. You won't live out the year.'"

Her family and friends were stunned. June seemed the healthiest person they knew. She didn't talk about the disease; she focused on healing. "I don't want to die," she said. "I'll miss all the fun." And after four months of chemotherapy, the cancer went into remission. "Most days I was able to keep up my activities. My one complaint about cancer is that the cure takes up all your spare time."

But when she had a checkup at the end of November, the cancer had returned. Three weeks before her eightieth birthday, June was hospitalized at Marin General.

As she lay in the hospital bed, hooked up to a multitude of IVs, she asked Vernona to help her address her five hundred Christmas cards. Vernona had designed cards for Lefty and June since 1972; they always coupled a family photograph with a funny inscription. For example, the 1973 version had a photograph of an eight-year-old Lefty, with a mop of blond hair, standing with his arms crossed next to Jack, his collie. "I'm a free agent, but my dog won't let me sign. Seasons Greetings. June and Lefty Gomez." The 1992 card featured "Triple Exposure," a black-and-white photograph of Lefty on the mound taken by Vincent Lopez taken in 1936. The first exposure has Lefty rearing back, the second in mid-delivery, and the last following through. Each exposure was made separately on glass plates against the same background to achieve the illusion of motion. The finished photograph had hung in the International Salon of the American Museum of Natural History at the 1939 World's Fair. Inside, the inscription read, "In Florida, a troubled rookie who'd just been touched for a home run by Ted Williams went up to Lefty and asked, 'How would YOU have thrown that ball, Mr. Gomez?' Lefty advised, 'Under an assumed name.' " At the bottom, the card read, "Season's Greetings. June O'Dea Gomez."

June dictated the inscriptions from bed as Vernona filled them in. June wanted the cards to be in the mail by Friday, December 4, so that everyone at the baseball winter meetings could receive them. They finished with no time to spare. The cards were put in the mail at 5:00 p.m.

The next morning, Saturday, December 5, June turned to Vernona and said, "Hand me my lipstick, dear. I'm going out in style."

June's funeral Mass was celebrated at Our Lady of Loretto in Novato and burial followed, as it had for Lefty, at Mount Tamalpais Cemetery in San Rafael. The Gomez monument has a laser-engraved photo of Lefty and June laughing at the 1938 World Series after Lefty's win against Dizzy

Dean and the Chicago Cubs. June chose it for the fans and friends visiting the gravesite because, as she said, "Seeing the photo, they'll smile. They'll join in the laughter that once was Lefty's and mine."

LEFTY AND JUNE WERE born at the beginning of the twentieth century and died at its close. The century framed their lives and they were travelers through it. Both Lefty in dusty California and June on the pavements of New York were steeped in an ethos that demanded hard work, honesty, and iron determination. Be it on the diamond, on the stage, or in their personal lives, both were indefatigable competitors and potent individual presences, yet both understood the importance of subordinating personal ambition to the needs of the team. Both went from inauspicious child-hoods to celebrity, yet never lost their association with and respect for the ordinary American. And with respect came exceptional generosity, both of person and spirit, which infected all who came in contact with them.

Through it all, neither Lefty nor June ever really changed. On the last day of her life, June was still the same girl who had tap-danced noisily in the aisle to get a part in *Honeymoon Cruise;* on the last day of his, Lefty was still the same Vernon Gomez who had loosed skunks under the Rodeo schoolhouse to get a day off from class.

It has become a cliché to say of someone who has died that we may never see their like again. In Lefty's case—and in June's—it happens to be true.

Vernona and Lefty at a Yankee Old-Timers' Game

ACKNOWLEDGMENTS

WOULD LIKE TO EXPRESS MY APPRECIATION TO THE MANY PEOPLE WHO shared their memories of June and Lefty with me and who gave so willingly of their time to answer my many questions.

Many of the conversations took place over a lifetime as a tag-along with my parents at All-Star and Old-Timers' Games, World Series, spring trainings, and Cooperstown induction weekends. Other conversations were friendly chats at home or by telephone. In all of these discussions, I found that everyone had a favorite story that shone brightly on their unique relationship with my mother and dad. Each of their memories added a personal brushstroke of color to the lives and personalities of June and Lefty.

With special thanks to:

BASEBALL

George Steinbrenner, Paul Fung Jr., Mrs. Babe (Claire) Ruth, Joe DiMaggio, Ted Williams, Carl Hubbell, Satchel Paige, Hal Schumacher, Bill Dickey, Charlie Gehringer, Eleanor Gehrig, Julia Ruth Stevens, Dorothy Ruth Pirone, Casey Stengel, John Mize, Marjorie Mize, James Cobb, Bill Terry, Joe Cronin, Robert Carpenter, Billy Martin, Mickey Mantle, President George H. W. Bush, Jimmy Piersall, Babe Dahlgren, Maye Lazzeri, Mrs. John (Betty) Murphy, Jimmie DeShong, Cy Young, Ben Chapman, Ola Chapman, Mary Jess Dickey, Allie Reynolds, Charlie Devens, George Selkirk, Albert "Happy" Chandler, Mario de la Fuente, Al Lopez, Buddy Hassett, Lou Boudreau, Marius Russo, Phil

Rizzuto, Mark Koenig, Robert Doerr, Charlie Wagner, Mrs. Joe (Mildred) Cronin, Robert Quinn, Roy Campanella, Yogi Berra, Eddie Collins Jr., Jane Pennock Collins, Jimmie Reese, Robert Brown, M.D., Atley Donald, Charlie Keller, Jim Lonberg, Joe Sewell, Lefty Grove, Tommy Henrich, Ethan Allen, Rick Ferrell, Luke Appling, Cool Papa Bell, Lou Boudreau, Enos Slaughter, Willie McCovey, Jim "Catfish" Hunter, Robert Feller, Ralph Kiner, Red Rolfe, Myril Hoag, Dario Lodigiani, Frank Crosetti, Jerry Donovan, Bill Posedel, Leo Durocher, John Babich, Ernie Lombardi, Thornton Lee, Leo "Doc" Hughes, Ray Pinelli, Mike Murphy, Harold "Pee Wee" Reese, Monty Basgall, Regino Otero, Rafael Noble, Jocko Conlan, Carl Erskine, Dino Restelli, Dee Fondy, Nick Priori, Gary Hughes, Robert Maduro, Joe Cascarella, Mrs. Earl (Lotte) Averill, LeMorn Pipgras, Rose Hillerich, Leo Righetti, Whitey Ford, Jerry Coleman, Lt. Jim Greengrass, Vic Rashi, Gil McDougald, Ossie Bluege, Ray Kroc, Buzzie Bavasi, Mrs. Jean Yawkey, Gene Autry, Pat Olsen, Del Webb, Al DePalma, Jerry Peplis, Mike Murphy, John "Paddy" Cottrell, Rose Hillerich, Chief Sheldon Bender, Tony Freitas, Seymour Siwouff, Ralph Nelles, Rex Bradley, Lou Spadia, Robert and Marion Merrill, Fay Vincent, Sy and Gloria Berger, Cappy Harada, Geri Vaskas, Joe Gennarelli Jr., Ken Browne, Jim Hubbell, Joseph McDole

JUNE O'DEA & SUNNY DALE'S STAGE CAREERS

Sunny Dale, Senator George Murphy, Nellie Grady Schwarz, William Frawley, Martha Raye, Edie Brown, James Rasmussen, Dan Dwyer, Nancy McLaughlin, Mary Louise McLaughlin, Peter McCauley, Sr. Ann Bartholomew, SND, Ann Grady Fleming, Mary Fleming, Dorothy Jane Keyser Youtz, Betty Keyser Means, William Means, Susan Garst, Valerie Vincent, Msgr. Vincent Mackay, Valerie Wood, Sr. Irene Marie Hace, RCE, Raymond Werchen

THE GOMEZ FAMILY GENEALOGY

Eugenia Ohman, Harold Lapham, Brother John F. O. Brien, CFX, diocesan archivist

LEFTY'S RODEO DAYS

Harry, Jim, and George Lakeman, Reder Clayes, Taft Prairo, Ditty Sher, Marye and Vernon Fereria, Stephen Plesh, Dr. Arthur Gomez-Lumsden,

Frank Wilson, Louise Kennett Wilson, Stan LaFontaine, Mrs. Emil Bellman, Bernard Cummins, Lorne Chenoweth, Hinton Keeler, Lilith Gomez, Milfred Gomez Sr., Earl Gomez, Vivien Sadler Pearsal, Milfred Gomez Jr., Gladys Gomez, George Gilliam, Frank and Emma Orr, Richard and Teresa Trigilia, Elberte Harte, Harold Narron, Stewart Sweet, Lawrence Sweet, Betty Maffei and June Whiteside of the Costa County Historical Society

RICHMOND HIGH

Bill Millevich, George Gordon, Philip Hempler, Lou Leverone, Joe Valenzuela

POINT REYES

Lawrence Tresch, Jim Albergi, Selma Farley, Bill Gnoss, Owen and Olive Musico, Joanne Muscio Domer, Jake Jorgensen, Tom Keena, Evelyn Muscio Koenig, Evelyn Muscio Molseed, Fred Perry, Judy Muscio Riccioli, Fred Rodoni, Andrew Schmidt, Ed Stohlman, Ray Malgrade, Martha Borge, Roger O'Donnell

FLORIDA SPRING TRAINING AND NEW YORK LIFE

Jack Dempsey, Postmaster General Jim Farley, Bing Russell, Louise Russell, Bud Russell, Ooie Russell, Mae Fung, Carol Fung, John Altieri, Olga Staff, Harry Kellogg, Viola Chan, Elaine Klein Carter, Maurice Tydor, Frank Cuccia, Susie Hoyt Niccum, Craig Williams, Ann and Julie Angrason, Elizabeth Murphy Marvos

THE 1933 ALL-STAR TRIP TO JAPAN AND THE 1982 RETURN TRIP TO JAPAN

Ikuo Ikeda

THE USO, AT HOME AND ABROAD

Paul Marr, POW Bill Greene, Jack Sharkey, Fred Corcoran, Frankie Conville, Carolyn McNeil, Sunny Dale

LEFTY'S SEVENTIETH-BIRTHDAY CELEBRATION

John Ascuaga, Reno Barsocchini

DURHAM, CONNECTICUT

Gery Gomez, Sharon Gomez, Dick Pirone, Linda Ruth Tosetti, Angelo Rusconi, Mary Rusconi, Billy Arrigoni, Bill Stannard, Cele Stannard, Wally Camp, Karl Koss

WILSON SPORTING GOODS

Thomas Mullaney, John Mullaney Sr., John Mullaney Jr., Patty Berg, Leonard Nelson, Gene DaCosse, Angelo Palozzi, Ray Kolas, Jack Fette, Harry Brown, Debbie Giannosa

FAIRFAX, CALIFORNIA

Karin Moffat, Philip Harrison, Patricia Grubbs Davey, Helen Kealey Segale

NOVATO, CALIFORNIA

Sgt. Gary Barner, Paul Davis, Karen Davis, Chrissy Davis, Tom Davis, Linda Gomez, Norma Pardini, Larry and Terry Williams, Billy Paganelli, Mrs. Cynthia Close and the sixth, seventh, and eighth grades of Ramon Grammar School, Gus Bertoli, Msgr. James Keene, Chuck Bruscatore

LEFTY AND JUNE AS GRANDPARENTS

Andrew Banas, John Banas, Scott Carstensen, Vernona Elizabeth Gomez, Jennifer Gomez, Serena Gomez, Tiffany Gomez

ARIZONA SPRING TRAINING

Patricia Comiskey Ryan, Joe Archuleta

LEFTY'S TRIPLE BYPASS

Norman Shumway, MD, John Banas Jr., MD

MEMORABILIA

Dave Sigler Sr., Dave Sigler Jr., Barry Halper

BABE RUTH INTERNATIONAL LEAGUE

Ron Tellefsen

LEFTY, AMERICAN BASEBALL COACHES ASSOCIATION

Dr. Robert Smith, Dr. John Winkin, Ron Fraser, Duane Banks, Jay Hicks, Joe Hicks

LEFTY AND THE MEDIA

George Grande, Mel Allen, Willie Weinbaum, Bob Steele, Bill Moen, Rob Roth

WRITERS

James Michener, Joseph Durso, Jim Ogle, Jack Hand, Jerome Holtzman, John Steadman, Herb Caen, Jack McDonald, Oscar Fraley, Lou Pavlovich, Art McGinley, John Fox, Fred Post, Al Stump, Red Smith, Bill Lee, Dave Albee, Al Corona, Louis Kaufman, Art Rosenbaum, Harry Jupiter, Bill Sobranes

PHOTOGRAPHERS

Vincent Lopez, Bill Fox, Willie Kee, Dick Collins, Bernie Esser

VIDEO AND SOUND ENGINEER

James Twomey

BASEBALL HALL OF FAME MUSEUM AND LIBRARY, COOPERSTOWN

Howard C. Talbot Jr., Edward Stack, Richard Sliter, William Guilfoile, Bill Deane, Pat Kelly, James Gates Jr.

OTESAGA HOTEL, COOPERSTOWN

Bill and Corky Holiday, Hal Evans, Rose Bridger

LEFTY GOMEZ WEBSITE: LEFTYGOMEZ.COM

Rhonda Hostetler

LEFTY GOMEZ BASEBALL FIELD, FAIRFAX, CALIFORNIA

Dedication spearheaded by Tom Reed

LEFTY GOMEZ SAN MARIN BASEBALL FIELD, NOVATO, CALIFORNIA

Dedication spearheaded by Richard Kruppa

LEFTY GOMEZ BASEBALL FIELD, RODEO, CALIFORNIA

On May 8, 1991, the California Office of Historic Preservation designated as a point of historical interest the Rodeo Baseball Field where Lefty as a boy played thousands of innings of sandlot ball. Dedication spearheaded by Jerry Johnson

LEFTY: AN AMERICAN ODYSSEY

In my quest to bring a true portrait of Lefty and June to press, I'd like to thank my coauthor, Lawrence Goldstone, an ardent Brooklyn Dodgers fan who periodically checked my unbridled exuberance for Yankee pinstripes. One example among many was the day I alluded to Bill Dickey, Lefty's battery mate, as "the greatest catcher in the game." Larry's rejoinder came in high and inside: "The greatest? What about Roy Campanella?"

I am indebted to my son, John Banas III, for his legal counsel, which guided my every step in bringing a manuscript from a book proposal presentation to the printed page.

For their enthusiasm for this project and their publishing expertise, I thank Gina Centrello, president and publisher of the Random House Publishing Group; Libby McGuire, publisher of Ballantine Bantam Dell; Mark Tavani, editor; and the entire staff of Ballantine Bantam Dell.

And finally, thanks to Michael Carlisle of Inkwell Management, for his unwavering belief in the story of Lefty and June, and for the care he has taken in guiding this book from idea to reality.

INDEX

abbreviations: VLG is Vernon "Lefty" Gomez

VERNONA GOMEZ is the daughter of June O'Dea and Vernon "Lefty" Gomez. As a child, she bounced on Babe Ruth's knee, made sand castles on the beach with Joe DiMaggio at spring training, and won at cards with the legendary 511-game winner Cy Young who pulled the Old-Maid from her hand, much to her delight.

Growing up in a baseball family, Vernona was a tagalong with her parents at All-Star and Old-Timers' Games, World Series, spring trainings, and Cooperstown Induction weekends. An eyewitness to many of the adventures chronicled in the book, Vernona has maintained lifelong friendships with many of its contributors.

She is an avid Yankees fan and has done extensive research on American history of the nineteenth and twentieth centuries, with a special focus on baseball and musical-comedy theater. Vernona is also a concert pianist who made her debut in Carnegie Recital Hall at the age of eight years old. She is the owner and director of the Creative Coaching Music Studio in Southport, Connecticut.

LAWRENCE GOLDSTONE is the author or coauthor of thirteen previous books and a recipient of the New American Writing Award. His writing has appeared in the *Boston Globe, Los Angeles Times, Chicago Tribune, Miami Herald,* and other periodicals. He has also been a teacher, lecturer, senior member of a Wall Street trading firm, taxi driver, actor, quiz show contestant, and policy analyst at the Hudson Institute. He lives in Connecticut with his wife and daughter, and has never forgiven the Dodgers for leaving Brooklyn.